ALSO BY ELINOR LANGER

Josephine Herbst

A HUNDRED LITTLE HITLERS

A HUNDRED LITTLE

HITLERS

THE DEATH OF A BLACK MAN,
THE TRIAL OF A WHITE RACIST, AND THE RISE
OF THE NEO-NAZI MOVEMENT IN AMERICA

Elinor Langer

METROPOLITAN BOOKS
Henry Holt and Company   New York

Metropolitan Books
Henry Holt and Company, LLC
Publishers since 1866
115 West 18th Street
New York, New York 10011

Metropolitan Books™ is a registered
trademark of Henry Holt and Company, LLC.

The passage from George Lincoln Rockwell's *This Time the World* is reprinted
by permission of Bob DeMarais of National Vanguard Books.

Misspellings and grammatical errors that occur in the words of the characters in this book
have been left as written or spoken, and have been neither corrected nor indicated.

Library of Congress Cataloging-in-Publication Data

Langer, Elinor, [date]
    A hundred little Hitlers : the death of a black man, the trial of a white racist, and
the rise of the neo-Nazi movement in America / Elinor Langer.
        p.   cm.
    Includes bibliographical references.
    ISBN 0-8050-5098-1
    1. White supremacy movements—United States.   2. White supremacy
movements—Oregon—Portland.   3. United States—Race relations.   4. Portland
(Or.)—Race relations.   5. Racism—United States.   6. Racism—Oregon—Portland.
7. Hate crimes—Oregon—Portland.   8. Murder—Oregon—Portland.   9. Seraw,
Mulugeta, 1960–1988.   10. Ethiopian Americans—Crimes against—Oregon—
Portland—Case studies.   I. Title.

E184.A1L2575 2003
305.8'034073—dc21   2003042167

First Edition 2003

Designed by Kelly S. Too

Printed in the United States of America

1   3   5   7   9   10   8   6   4   2

To my husband and son

At a trial, events are often seen in a distorted perspective. A violent event has taken place, and we work backwards from it, considering primarily the evidence bearing on that event. If we work forwards, in a natural sequence, from a natural starting point, this evidence may wear a very different appearance.

—Julian Symons
A Reasonable Doubt

CONTENTS

EPILOGUE

A HUNDRED LITTLE HITLERS

PROLOGUE

1

Later, as he sat in the Oregon State Correctional Institution serving a thirty-year sentence for the death of Mulugeta Seraw, Kenneth Mieske was haunted by the "ifs" that, had any one been different, would have changed his life. First there were the "ifs" that would have deflected the moment from ever coming into being. If only he had gone to work as he was supposed to. If he hadn't had to wait for Julie. If only Desiree had come back earlier or later. If the Ethiopians had found a parking space. Then there were the "ifs" that would have changed what happened afterward. If we had only called the ambulance ourselves. If we had waited for the police. If we had taken the case all the way to trial. But there was a deeper "if" that ran beneath his reflections like a riverbed under water and determined not only why Kenneth Mieske and I were talking in the first place but what our conversations had to do with the existence of this book: If only those Sand Niggers had never come here.

2

If the reader is wondering "Why should I care?" about the self-serving musings of a racist killer, the answer is that they are part of a larger story. The killing of Mulugeta Seraw grew out of a violent confrontation between skinheads and Ethiopians on a dark street corner in the small hours of Sunday, November 13, 1988, in Portland, Oregon, so it is first of all a criminal story; but more than any other single event till that time, the killing also revealed the emergence of a new strain of American racism that openly associates itself with Nazism, so it is a political story as well. In fact, the criminal and the political are intertwined. Without the documentation arising from the criminal, and later civil, proceedings, the story could not be as fully told, but at the same time, the judicial processes themselves shaped the ways it could be understood. Law and history do not make good companions. The law is a formal system through which each side makes its way to a previously stated conclusion. History is an open-ended inquiry full of surprises in which nothing ever fits exactly right. When the history of a political movement is seen through the calculus of the law: when the law, which should itself be subject to history, is instead its source: when the transcript of a political trial becomes the principal historical record, which is what happened in this killing: too much is omitted. On a bleak Sunday morning a black man who only moments earlier was laughing and talking with his friends was beaten to death with a bat, but with the brutal collision of white and black seen as a lynching from the start, how it occurred seemed beside the point. Seeking to soothe a troubled city, a public prosecutor dropped a plumb line

through the depths of the Seraw killing and came up with an interpretation the people of Portland wanted to believe, and later the
Southern Poverty Law Center did the same; but where a line falls
depends on the position it is dropped from in the first place, and in
a case where what is at stake is not only the moral responsibility for
an individual death but the social responsibility for an upsurge of
American racism, the relationship between the legal truth and the
historical truth should not be taken for granted.

My own plumb line starts from a different position. Portland is my
home. Mulugeta Seraw lived a few miles from my present house,
but much closer to where my husband and I lived when we first
moved to the city years before. The street on which he lay dying
was near a park where we had often walked our dog. Of the three
members of the skinhead gang East Side White Pride who were soon
arrested for the killing, one—Kenneth Mieske—was a rock musician
involved with a circle of Portland's more bohemian writers and artists that included a number of people I knew; the second—Kyle
Brewster—was the recent homecoming king of a large public high
school and the son of a well-known civic activist whose good works
also overlapped with that of friends and acquaintances of my own;
and the third—Steven Strasser—was a neighbor, living with other
skinheads only blocks away in a building in which I had recently
considered renting an office. When Strasser was arrested, the checkout line in my local supermarket was all abuzz. As I listened to
gossip and read in the paper the first depictions of Nazi tattoos,
Nazi literature, Nazi flags, I felt uneasy. I know my friends and
neighbors were also dismayed, but the word *Nazi* tolls for a Jew
differently than it does for others, and I heard it tolling for me.
Initially it appeared that the arrested skinheads were heading for a
joint trial and I made arrangements to write about it for the *Nation*.
If the intimations of the press and the authorities were right, covering the skinhead trial could be like covering the Munich trial of
Adolf Hitler.

In the months after the killing, accounts of the skinhead move-ment continued to flood the Portland media. Evidence from the skinheads' apartments released by the district attorney suggested that the "Nazi" identification of the members of East Side White Pride was real and deep, while reports from around the country suggested that something similar was happening elsewhere as well. At the same time that the importance of this newest incarnation of American racism was becoming clearer, however, the scope of the court proceedings through which it might begin to be exposed was being diminished. In March 1989, four months after the killing, the cases were severed, meaning there would be no joint trial, and two months after that, starting in May, they were individually plea-bargained, meaning there would be no criminal trials at all. With the support of the *Nation*, I put aside the idea of trial coverage and began work instead on an investigative article that would start to answer at least some of my own questions, but as a citizen I was disappointed. The more I learned about the death of Mulugeta Seraw and the skinhead movement that lay behind it, the more I believed there was a mountain of fact and feeling out there that the people of Portland—and not only Portland—needed to know.

The day after the third plea bargain, in October 1989, the Southern Poverty Law Center of Montgomery, Alabama, and the national Anti-Defamation League filed a multimillion-dollar lawsuit in fed-eral court in Portland charging California neo-Nazi leader Tom Metzger, his son, John Metzger, and the White Aryan Resistance (WAR), their organization, along with Kenneth Mieske and Kyle Brewster, for civil liability in the death of Mulugeta Seraw. As some-one who had been following the case from its beginning, I found the lawsuit puzzling. Through my research I already knew that Tom Metzger was one of the most ambitious racists in the country, but the Portland skinheads I had talked to had not mentioned him and he had been fifteen hundred miles away from Portland, in Fallbrook, California, when Mulugeta Seraw was killed. The emphasis in the

complaint on the Metzgers' "agents" was particularly puzzling. The
charge that the Metzgers had "sent their agents" to Portland to incite
skinhead violence suggested that the chief witness against them was
likely to be a much-touted California skinhead WAR follower
named Dave Mazzella, who had indeed been in Portland at the time
of the killing, but from what I had gathered, Mazzella's role in Portland was ambiguous. He had been in town less than six weeks when
Seraw was killed, the members of East Side White Pride seemed
not to have liked him very much, and now he was gone. Whether
he had been a police or FBI plant in the Portland skinhead movement all along or had "turned" after the killing I had no idea, but
when someone goes from being a conspicuous skinhead to testifying
against a conspicuous racist, it is an obvious question. A second
California WAR follower, Michael Barrett, was also a candidate for
the "agent" role, but he had been in Portland only a week. The heart
of my difficulty with the SPLC complaint, however, was not so
much factual as political: specifically its interpretation of the relationship between "leader" and "led." It seemed to me that like the
radical movements of the 1930s or the 1960s, the Portland skinhead
movement was an authentic grassroots phenomenon and that the
skinheads had created it on their own. Like certain noxious sulphurs
bubbling up at times from beneath our Northwest volcanoes, like
the volcanoes themselves, it was a spontaneous eruption. The death
of Mulugeta Seraw did not need an "outside agitator" to explain it.
Responsibility for the killing belonged chiefly to Mieske, who had
wielded the bat, and then to Brewster and Strasser, who had participated in the fight, but Strasser was not even named in the suit.
The logic of Metzger's responsibility implied in the lawsuit seemed
to be, on the contrary, the "Great Man" theory of history. It took
me back to college debates about Napoleon or Stalin, albeit on a
petty scale. Far from being of purely intellectual interest, however,
the "leader" versus "led" issue here was of considerable importance
for understanding the sources of violent racism in our society. If the
Portland skinheads out of their own experience had stumbled
toward Nazism themselves and found it attractive, that would mean

one thing. If they were indoctrinated by a nefarious adult propagandist, that would mean something else.

3

A Hundred Little Hitlers is my own version of events that have been described in other ways both in the press and in court. Based on my own readings of thousands of pages of official documents, as well as on my own interviews and research, it is an attempt to take the reader step by step into the territories I entered myself as I tried to understand what really happened, how history differed from the way it was represented in a civil trial, and why it matters. More a narrative than an argument, the book is a detailed reconstruction of the death of an Ethiopian man and the birth of a political movement told from the bottom up, through characters and incidents, rather than from the top down, through the issues they collectively represent. In both "History" (part one) and "Law" (part two), my intention has been the same: to try to show the elements I have come to believe determined important moments and, where history and law diverge, to let the divergence speak for itself. The story in these pages is a story that is not yet over. Set in a particular city, it is a tale repeated, in its essentials, in many other cities both in the United States and around the world. Set in the 1980s, it is about the roots of social forces that loom larger and more powerful now. *A Hundred Little Hitlers* is about abstractions such as history and law, right and wrong, truth and lies, racism and justice, but it is told in its particulars. If it is as disturbing to read as it has been to write, I will have done what I set out to do.

PART ONE

HISTORY

All history is local history.

—WILLIAM HESSELTINE

THE DEATH OF MULUGETA SERAW

What happened matters because truth matters.

—THOMAS POWERS

4

Fall closes in on Portland. All through October, the air is clear and dry and the trees put forth such brilliant leaves you might think, for a moment, you are in New England; but at the beginning of November, as the time shifts back, trees shed, the rains start, and soon the streets are so filled with sodden leaves waiting to be collected that, after steering their cars through the evening traffic, most people want to stay home. In the East, the smell of fall is the smell of leaf smoke. In Portland, it is the smell of leaf rot.

About three o'clock in the afternoon of November 12, 1988,

when the light was already darkening in the sky, a group of skin-heads known as East Side White Pride made their separate ways to the apartment of a skinhead art student named Nick Heise for a political meeting. Of the dozen or so skinheads who were present, the only ones important enough to this story to require identifica-tion are the ones we have already met—Kenneth Mieske, lead singer in a metal band called Machine and stage manager for a local rock concert production company; Kyle Brewster, the high school home-coming king, who had moved out of his parents' house after grad-uation and was working as a bicycle messenger downtown; Steve Strasser, a street kid who had been one of the earliest skinheads in the city; Dave Mazzella, not strictly a member of East Side White Pride but a prominent California skinhead with a knack for publicity who had been in Portland since early October; and Mike Barrett, another well-known California skinhead, in town only a week, who often traveled with Mazzella. For the rest, their particulars do not matter. Some were teenagers, some in their twenties, some were shaven, some even had hair, but who was who is of little conse-quence. They were a skinhead chorus, acting, in their capacities as skinheads, as every other skinhead in every other city at the same time might have done. For the most part even they called one another only by nicknames—tags such as "Popeye," "Pewee," "Heckle," "Jeckle," "Drug Doug," "Pogo,"* and "Prick."

The meeting was something of an effort. They usually met at the pad Kyle shared with Prick in the low-income Hawthorne district, where they drank beer, watched TV, and helped raise one another's consciousness with such jokes as "What are the three best years of a nigger's life? Second grade," "Why do niggers smell? So blind people can hate them too," "What do you call a nigger with half a brain? Gifted," which had them rolling on the floor, but the elec-tricity had been turned off at that apartment so they had to switch to Nick's. There were other obstacles too. It was hard to get going on Saturdays. The skinheads thought of themselves as members of

*This name has been changed.

the white working class and they liked to follow its rhythms. Monday through Friday they worked; Friday evenings, if not earlier, they drank; and on Saturday they had to sleep it off. Many of them had girlfriends who also worked and Saturday afternoon was often their first chance to get together. Once they did haul themselves out of their couches to get to a meeting, they were glad of it but the comforts of home and the comforts of belonging were at odds. At the end of the day came the parties. By then they were ready for the fighting that had brought them together in the first place and through which they had each won the right to wear the membership patch of East Side White Pride. But especially with the change of weather, afternoons were slow.

The purpose of the meeting was to discuss a question that had been bothering some of the members: whether lately their violence had been going too far. The skinheads liked violence, they planned for it and instigated it, and for several of them a weekend without violence was like a weekend without beer, but a number of recent fights outside their usual circles where the rules were mutually understood had brought in the police and the skins had started to be hassled on the streets. Then, too, there was another problem. A few months before, a girl-run skinhead group called POWAR— Preservation of the White American Race—had gone on television talking about white power as a political force and, of all things, repudiating violence, and though their reputation had fallen on the street, they had gotten a lot of attention. Elsewhere in the country, the skinhead movement was taking a more political direction and ESWP wanted to be part of it. They had a post office box, through which they corresponded with a number of skinhead and neo-Nazi bands and political groups in the United States and elsewhere. They had a couple of address stamps, one for envelopes, one for fliers, so they could list themselves as the contact on fliers such as "White Power, Death to Race-Mixing," put out by the SS Action Group of Michigan, or "White Revolution Is the Only Solution," put out by California's WAR. And they had begun to sketch out fliers of their own. Most of this material was simply passed around at meetings and landed on their own walls, but lately they had been moving out with it a bit, flying around town on skateboards, plastering telephone poles, stickering windshields, littering malls. The other business up for discussion besides mellowing out a little was the idea of getting out a publication of their own. Such a project was so much more organized than anything they had done before it was strange even to admit being interested in it, but skinhead papers or zines were popping up everywhere in the country—they all read them—and if others could get it together why couldn't they? Sprawling around the apartment with their inertia and their ambitions neck and neck, they tried to marshal their talents. Ken, the unofficial secretary, could be in contact with groups elsewhere. Kyle, who had written for his school newspaper, could write a column. Nick, the art student, could draw.

Chief among the participants at the meeting was America's most famous skinhead, Dave Mazzella. Unlike the Portland "homeboys," many of whom had known one another for years, Mazzella was practically a stranger. He had arrived from California several weeks earlier with a skinhead named Mike Gagnon, who had since left, and he had been in their midst ever since. Mazzella was one of a small group of California skinheads who had made a number of national television appearances with Tom Metzger, and the Portlanders had greeted him warmly, but his welcome was wearing thin. A ready fighter, he had demonstrated his mettle by getting into a fight in the parking lot of the Safeway across from Kyle's within hours of his arrival and they had already shared some heart-pumping action at nearby Laurelhurst Park and at outlying Rocky Butte, but on other types of sharing such as expenses he was nowhere and the ESWPers were starting to resent it. What's more, he was relentless. In their own way, in their own time, the members of East Side White Pride were moving from their gut racism to a greater awareness of the dangers facing the white race in general, but Mazzella was in such a hurry. Just now when they had mustered all the concentration they could for the discussion so far, he had a new scheme—that that very night they should take to the streets of downtown Portland and hand out some newspapers put out by the Aryan Youth Movement, the youth branch of Tom Metzger's WAR. It was typical of Mazzella's indifference to the real lives of the Portland skinheads that he could even mention such an idea. Saturday night might be "Boys' Night Out" among the original skinheads of London, England, but it was "Couples' Night Out" among the skinheads of Portland, Oregon, and the girls were not going to like this. Thanks in part to some of the doings of Mazzella himself since he had been there, the tension over the exclusion of women from the afternoon meetings of ESWP was already rising and their exclusion from anything after nightfall would make it worse. Then, too, some of the girls looked forward to the Saturday night action as much as the guys did and, given the looseness of some of their relationships, if they didn't start out the evening together there was no telling where they might end up. For the guys who were girl-less it was one thing, but for the ones who were attached it was something else. On the other hand, once the idea was out there it was hard to resist because it flowed so naturally out of what they were discussing. Talk about skinhead "image." Imagine the surprise of the people of Portland when, staring in fear at a troop of skinheads bearing down on them on the street, they found themselves facing not boots and taunts but—ideas. The *Oregonian* might even cover it. Besides, it was practically a favor. The newspapers in question had been stacked in Dave's van since he got there, being used for seats, and, beer-stained and tattered, that was all they would be able to be used for if he didn't get rid of them soon. Surely the Word was more important than that. POWAR had leafleted recently, passing out an "Application for Employment" at a Jesse Jackson campaign rally in Pioneer Courthouse Square ("Place of birth: Free clinic_____, Alley_____, Zoo_____, Colonel Sanders_____, Unknown _____ . . ." "How many words can you jive a minute?" "How fast can you steal and strip a car?" and so on) and had had a great time. The final answer to the question "Why do it?" was the question

"Why not?" It was a leap of sorts from what they had so far undertaken only casually into purposeful political activity, but in the
end no one wanted to say no. They chose a time and a place for
their later gathering point, then went home to break the news to
the girls.

5

The farms of Debre Tabor in Gondar province in the highlands of
Ethiopia are far away—far from the city of Debre Tabor, where
people go for trade and conversation, far from the provincial capital,
also called Gondar, far from Addis Ababa, and far from Portland,
Oregon, where the events of this story mainly take place, but it is
necessary to pause there for a moment not simply to acknowledge
a dead man's beginnings but to note—again—how in our era people
wash up everywhere and how the fates of the people of one region
of the earth and those of another are intertwined.

In the year in which this part of our story could be said to start,
Ethiopia was still a great kingdom. It was ruled from the capital city
by the perennial Emperor Haile Selassie, 225th descendant of the
union of King Solomon and the Queen of Sheba, who had so far
outlasted all his foes, and the constancy that seemed to mark the
life of the dynasty marked the lives of the people too. On October
21, 1960, in a tiny little collection of mud-thatched houses so small
it was barely even a hamlet, a son, their second child, was born to
Fetenech Berhanu and Seraw Tekuneh. In the Ethiopian way that
makes the father's first and the son's last name the same, he was
called Mulugeta Seraw.

Mulugeta's father was a farmer, as was his father's father and his
mother's father, as were all the fathers in their families' histories,
limb upon limb of an old Amharic family tree with roots in the land
at least as deep as those of the monarch himself. They lived as families in their region had always lived, waking early, toiling hard,
working mainly for enough food to sustain their own households

but with something usually left over in the way of grains or spices to take to the market at Debre Tabor. It was a life scarcely touched by the outside world. There were no telephones in the countryside and no mail except what was carried by an occasional traveler from Addis visiting home. If, passing by, you called out to the father, "Good day, sir. How far is it to Debre Tabor?" he would answer in the hours that it took to walk there—"Four"—and when he was asked the size of his farm in the Portland courtroom to which he was transported like an ancient coin burnished for the occasion, he replied in cadamas—"Six"—the number of turns of an ox it took to plow the land.

The family lived peacefully with its neighbors, farming side by side with them in a centuries-old system by which, beyond the separate plots necessary to maintain each household's self-sufficiency, the lands of the surrounding high plateau were held in common, but in one respect they were different from the others for they were neither Coptic Christians nor Muslims but Protestants. Around the turn of the century, Mulugeta's mother's great-uncle, an official of the Coptic Church, had set out on foot along with two others on a journey to Asmara, three or four months away, to seek the truth about religion and, after encounters with numerous European missionaries, returned home a baptized Adventist and one of the first leaders of the Ethiopian Seventh-Day Adventist Church. Mulugeta's father's family were also Adventists, an affiliation central to the marriage, for the Adventists were firm believers in education who had founded schools at nearly every level of Ethiopian life, and it was at a boarding school at Debre Tabor that Seraw Tekuneh's uncle, a church elder, had noticed Fetenech, while scouting for a bride for his brother's son. That Fetenech had been sent away to school was remarkable for a girl, a tribute to the authority of her great-uncle, who had persuaded her father, and though she was interrupted before she had scarcely begun, first by the death of her mother and then by her marriage, her belief in the importance of education remained devout. Seraw Tekuneh had himself at one time studied to become a missionary and he shared her view. The chores came first, as they have for struggling family farmers everywhere since the beginning of time, but when the chores were done, the commands of God in that distant highland household included "Study and Learn."

According to the stories told by his father and uncle, which are all we have, Mulugeta was a beautiful, graceful, and sensitive child, slow to anger, quick to learn. By five he was herding cattle single-handed. By twelve he could handle all the other chores around the farm. He loved the animals, loved the sweet smell of spices that everywhere scented the land, loved his brothers and sisters and all the other relatives who were nearly as often around, but most of all he loved his mother, Fetenech, so much younger and sweeter than his stern, exacting father; when she died giving birth to her sixth child when Mulugeta was barely ten, it was the greatest sorrow of his young life. For him, from then on, the center was gone from the farm.

Of the many relatives who filled his childhood, none was more important to Mulugeta than his mother's brother Engedaw Berhanu, who came to live with them when Engedaw was twelve and Mulugeta was one. Fetenech and her brother had always been close. In raising her brothers and sisters after their mother died, Fetenech had been both mother and sister to Engedaw, and now Engedaw became both uncle and brother to her son. The story of Engedaw Berhanu is the story of every poor child the world over who has ever wanted to learn. He had come to his sister's household to go to school. A bright child who had taught himself to read and write, he passionately wanted an education but there was no school in his village and his father needed him at home and it took the combination of Fetenech's insistence that her brother should have the chance she had lost and his own determination to persuade their father to let him go. When he not only placed first in his class but returned home his first summer having already mastered the English alphabet, his father understood at last and never opposed him again, even selling a cow a year or two later to support him more comfortably in the school at Debre Tabor. From the time he entered the elementary school in his sister's village, Engedaw never stopped in his search for learning. Now here, now there, now teaching, now on scholarship, he scraped his way through the patchwork of church-run schools throughout northern Ethiopia, and as he did so no one was prouder of him than Mulugeta. From the boarding school at Debre Tabor where he himself began to study when he was about ten, Mulugeta sent his report cards off to his uncle wherever he happened to be at the moment and Engedaw responded with praise and encouragement. After Fetenech died, they became even closer than before.

In 1970, having exhausted the educational offerings of the church, Engedaw moved to Addis Ababa to attend Haile Selassie University. Although outwardly his life was moving smoothly, inwardly he was troubled because over the years he had become a protégé of the Ethiopian Seventh-Day Adventist Church and he was working in its publishing house by day and going to school at night when he suddenly discovered that somewhere during the course of his education doubts had taken hold and not only did he no longer agree with the elders who had nurtured and trained him for most of his life, he wasn't even sure he liked them very much. He wanted to stay in the capital, where he lived with a number of younger relatives whose educations, like Mulugeta's, he was helping to support, but as his relations with the Adventists grew strained it started to become uncomfortable. Haile Selassie University was the only university, religious or secular, in Ethiopia. There was no place outside Addis to go. When he told his family he was thinking of leaving the country, they were not too concerned. Foreign study was not unheard-of, it was not forever, and with more and more members of the family interested in education themselves, maybe others would follow. In 1972 Engedaw contacted an Ethiopian high school friend who was attending a community college in Walla Walla, Washington. The next year he left Ethiopia to continue his studies in the United States.

. . .

In 1973, when Engedaw Berhanu left Addis, Haile Selassie was still
on the throne, but in 1974 he was overthrown and the life of Ethiopia that had long seemed so changeless was revealed to have been
in motion all the while. At first the revolution was nearly unanimous
because resentment of the imperial regime, in its final years, had
become widespread, but soon the unity between the military and
the civilian elements dissolved and the country was engulfed in a
multifactional civil war that ranks with the bloodiest in modern
times. Having finished eighth grade in Debre Tabor, Mulugeta had
been invited by an aunt to live with her in Addis Ababa so he could
go to high school and he was there during the Red Terror of 1977
and 1978, when the blood began flowing in the streets. What he
saw, what he felt, there is no way to know, but what he probably
saw were the bodies of a lot of dead children his own age because
according to many observers the streets were filled with them and
to not see, one would have had to be blind. "It was hard. You don't
want to come from work to home. You rather stay at work. Because
when you come to home they will arrest you or you will see people,
your friend maybe, maybe your sister, on the street," said Hirut
Abebe-Jiri—born, like Mulugeta, in 1960—in the course of a lawsuit she brought with two other Ethiopian women in an American
court against a former Ethiopian official they said had tortured them
there, and her words will have to speak for Mulugeta. Another
plaintiff, Elizabeth Demissie, asked to describe the effects on her
present life of the detention and torture she endured at home,
replied, "For a long time I cannot be focused what I want to do in
life because I don't know what life means really. This is just an
escape for me from Ethiopia." "Professor," their attorney asked an
American political scientist testifying on their behalf, "the complaint
filed in this case alleges that three young women were forced out
of their homes, detained, imprisoned with no legal process, and tortured. Based on your expert knowledge of Ethiopia during 1977 and
1978, did human rights abuses of that kind occur?" Answer: "In the

thousands." Q.: "And the complaint also alleges that one person, a relative of one of the plaintiffs, was pulled out of his home, shot, his body left on the street. Is that something that in your opinion occurred in Ethiopia?" A.: "Many, many, many times." Q.: "Finally the complaint alleges that another relative of one of the plaintiffs was in prison, removed from the prison, and never heard from again. Nobody ever found—no word ever given to her family about her fate; is that something—?" A.: "Widespread." With the number of people who perished in the Terror commonly estimated at about twenty thousand, and about another thirty thousand detained, if anything other than sheer luck saved Mulugeta and his family it appears to have been their obscurity. Toward the end of the decade, there began a great exodus, people of every sort leaving the country by any means possible, walking out through neighboring countries, obtaining tourist visas without intending to return, or departing officially as students—about a million in all. About another million died of famine. As the country fell apart it was hard for even close relatives to know what was going on with one another for letters were circumspect and traveling perilous, but eventually, in 1979, Engedaw heard from Mulugeta that he had finished high school in Addis and wanted to come to the United States. An American family with whom Engedaw had become friendly in Walla Walla agreed to sponsor him. In November 1980, he arrived.

By the time of Mulugeta's arrival, Engedaw had finished college in Washington and was studying for a master's degree in social work at Portland State University in Oregon. It was there that Mulugeta now joined him. He moved with Engedaw into a small apartment in suburban Beaverton, got a job at a fast-food restaurant and within a short time a better one as a custodian at a Beaverton Catholic elementary school, and enrolled at Portland Community College, where he took courses in business and engineering. Whatever were the trials of exile, he seems to have worn them lightly. To the people who came to know him at the elementary school he seemed an "extraordinary human being." In a letter written to the *Oregonian* after he died, a first-grade teacher described him as a "pure spirit" who performed his services with great gentleness and consideration, a man whose religious nature expressed itself in the way he behaved every day. A picture taken on the school playground of Mulugeta and another man clasping hands as if they are captains of opposing teams about to compete suggests a young man very comfortable with himself for Mulugeta is small and the other man is large and Mulugeta is black and the other man is white yet they are standing there smiling into each other's eyes in such a way that you know that whatever is going on at this moment has nothing to do with size or race or even winning the game, only with sharing the joy of life.

When Mulugeta had been in Portland about a year and a half, Engedaw moved to California, where he got a job as a psychiatric social worker, married, and started a family. Mulugeta stayed on alone, first in the janitor's room on the grounds of the Beaverton elementary school, later in Portland, where he lived with an assortment of other Ethiopians all trying to reproduce in friendship the family ties that had sustained them at home. He and Engedaw saw each other often, Mulugeta visiting the Bay Area, where he became very attached to Engedaw's baby daughter, Engedaw returning to Portland when he could. It was on one such occasion, the last time they were together, when they set out from Portland for the wedding of a friend in Walla Walla, that Mulugeta confessed to Engedaw what he had not told his own father—that he, too, was a father, that a girl in the household of his aunt in Addis was the mother of his son, Henok, whom he wished he could see. In 1986 he took a job as a bus driver for Avis at the Portland airport, initially part-time, so he could continue his studies, then full-time, so he could send more money home. He made $5.00 an hour, advancing, after several raises, to the grand sum of $5.80. He worked cheerfully and faithfully, took his turn as Employee of the Month, and as usual made many friends, but with his two-week paycheck generally averaging only $400, financially it did not add up. On the other hand, it really didn't seem to matter so much. Somewhere between the Terror in Ethiopia and an intestinal illness requiring a long hospi-

talization in Portland, the drive that had always characterized Engedaw was softened in Mulugeta. When Engedaw came, he was in a
hurry, acquiring his first degree in three years and expecting to go
back, but to Mulugeta and his contemporaries, time meant little.
Things being as they were, whether people's relatives still in Ethiopia would ever get out to join them was very uncertain, and
whether anyone in America would ever see home again, no one
knew. As the Ethiopians in Portland became less a number of random refugees and more of a community, Mulugeta became a popular figure. Some people settled in and found a foothold in business
or the professions and these were his friends, but others could not
settle down and they could not get or hold jobs and in the great
chasm of meaning that was now their lives they drifted or drank or
became enraged or dispirited, and these were also his friends. Young
in age but universally felt to be old in wisdom, he moved freely
back and forth between the groups as a kind of counselor without
portfolio, talking and listening to all. As the exiles' ties to Ethiopia
ebbed, those in Portland strengthened. Eventually they established
an official Ethiopian Community Organization to provide the foundation for a formal communal life. A shadow within the larger
shadow of Portland's blacks, relatively unnoticed by their neighbors
white or black except as another of the exotic dark-skinned foreign-
ers lately appearing on the streets, among themselves the Ethiopians
were gradually beginning to feel more secure here, and as they did
so no one was more at home than Mulugeta.

On the day that was to be his last, Mulugeta seems to have done
nothing in particular. It was a misty Saturday, November 12, 1988,
a good day to stay in and catch up. Perhaps he did his laundry or
cleaned his apartment—we will never know. He lived with a roommate in a small, neat apartment complex at 212 Southeast Thirty-
first Avenue known as the Parklane, one of many such complexes
in a mixed-income residential area immediately west of one of Portland's loveliest public gardens, Laurelhurst Park. He seems to have

liked trees, for his second-story apartment was something of a nest, looking out at a tall, solitary silver pine that rose from the courtyard to the sky only inches from his door, a tree uprooted since then by elements beyond its control and now, like the man who was comforted by it, no longer there. Perhaps he went for a walk that morning, enjoying the November mud, the eternal green. It was on just such a day that he had arrived in Portland eight years before. Perhaps he wrote a letter to his family. Sometime during the afternoon he was joined by a friend and former roommate, Solomon Zerewerk, also known as Tilahun Antneh, a volatile thirty-one-year-old political refugee who had recently escaped deportation from the States for a few low-level run-ins with the law. They sat together in the living room for a while watching a football game on television and talking; then Mulugeta got dressed for the evening. He wore a pink shirt, gray slacks, gray socks, and gray loafers. The Parklane apartments were so close to the Pine Terrace apartments at 3101 Southeast Pine around the corner, where the skinheads were meeting that, had they wanted to, Mulugeta Seraw and Nick Heise could have rigged up an old-fashioned tin-can telephone on a wire between their two units or thrown pebbles at each other's windows to signal that they were ready to come out and toss a ball. Just around the time that the members of East Side White Pride were leaving the Pine Terrace to go home and tell their girlfriends the plans for the evening, Mulugeta and Tilahun Antneh were leaving the Parklane to go out for dinner.

6

There is something about a swarm of skinheads greater than the sum of its parts and as they gather at the Hawthorne Safeway at 9 P.M. they all feel it, not just the muscle strength multiplied by their identical uniforms of ESWP bomber jackets and Doc Marten boots but the moral strength that comes from knowing that on this night they are going out to serve an ideal. For the skinheads this is all happening for the first time. As far as they know, no one else in the history of the world has ever dressed for a political demonstration; no one has ever stored up the necessities, if only cigarettes and beer; no one has ever said farewell to his girl to face who knows what unexpected enemies in the hours that lie ahead. The combination of the seriousness of the act of taking their racial convictions into the community and the faint atmosphere of heroics surrounding their departure is strangely exhilarating. As they look at one another around the parking lot, they see themselves momentarily not as others see them—losers—but as advance soldiers in a racial war that is just getting under way.

They cross over the Willamette River into downtown in two cars, ten in a van—Mazzella's—and three in a car belonging to someone who is not a member of East Side White Pride but close enough to the others to be welcome. In the van especially it is hard for them to sustain the mood for with the seats gone most of them sprawl in the back amid the stacks of yellowing Aryan Youth Movement newspapers, it has already been a long day, and between their bodies rolling around on the floor and the beer rolling around in their bellies, these particular racial soldiers are practically AWOL right from the beginning. The newspaper they are to distribute is a four-page, single-space historical-futurist fantasy of white rebellion that not one single person I talk to later remembers having read, which is easily explainable by its unreadability alone, but that may not be the whole story for no one remembers much else about that part of the evening either, whether because it is overshadowed by what happened afterward or because of the beer is not clear. They park in the vicinity of the downtown Safeway at Southwest Tenth and Jefferson, a familiar spot, then set off on foot with the papers to the Park Blocks, Pioneer Courthouse Square, and the Metro Cafe, where they thrust a few into the hands of passersby and stick them under windshields, then on down to an underage nightclub on Fourth, Skoochies, where they hand out more of them to kids waiting in line. Some of the skinheads—Steve Strasser is one—have a conversation or two with the people taking the handouts, but since they are far from knowing how to organize anyone, practically including themselves, the conversations are pretty much limited to "Hey, man, got a light?" or "Shit, it's cold out here" and the only one whom anyone later recalls talking about the necessity of white power is Dave Mazzella. At Skoochies, a man presumably grasping the only immediately intelligible part of the paper's message—an oversize cartoon in the center of the front page of a muscular Aryan flexing his arm, hand outspread, demanding to know "WHITE PEOPLE, What Are You Waiting For? NOW Is The Time"—says, "Right on!" and offers them a half case of beer, and the skinheads are suddenly beside themselves with victory, for not only have they carried out their mission of conducting a well-mannered foray into downtown—they have made a recruit!

The free beer is the signal that the political phase of the evening is over. Not that beer has ever been really absent. In fact, it has been flowing in and out of them so steadily since the day began that if you had wanted to know who was where when as they made their way through downtown all you would have needed was a dog. But they are now at the level where the beer itself generates the need for more beer, they are thinking about the girls, and, after polishing off the half case in the vicinity of the van, they decide to move on. No sooner are they back in their cars than the common purpose that has been binding them together dissolves, their separate long-ings return, and they begin a series of random maneuvers for the sake of this one or that as they head toward a rocker party in the vicinity of Southeast Fifty-third and Woodstock, where they have planned to meet the girls. Along with many other seemingly small details, these movements and moods will matter later.

Dave Mazzella is the first to switch subjects. The girl he is hot for is in Vancouver, Washington, across the Columbia River, and if the guys would only put out the money for him to get his gas hog over there he'd go. The guys refuse. Next, Ken Mieske urges Dave to stop and pick up two musicians from his band, Machine, Dave agrees, and the two longhairs pile in with the skinheads and come along. Kyle Brewster passes out in the van. He never makes it to the party. At the party there is bad news on two fronts. The keg is dry, and the girls with whom they are hoping to reunite have already been there and gone. At this report the group dissipates still further. There is lots of milling around. The time is a little after midnight. Not yet ready to end the night, the two groups of skinheads return to their cars and drive off without Ken, who has met two more of his longhaired friends, one with a car, and has cast his lot with the other part of his life for the rest of the evening. In the van they are starting to get thirsty. They stop at a convenience store, where Steve Strasser and Nick Heise steal beer by sauntering from the cooler toward the exit as if they intend to pay but dashing past the cash register at the last minute, then fall to panic when the skinhead who has taken the wheel balks at driving what is now an escape vehicle down a rutted dead-end street and turns it over to another skinhead, who does not know where he is going, then on to two more parties, where they again fail to find the girls, and from this point they are not operating on a plan at all, they are cruising, until Nick says, "What the hell. Let's go back to my place," and they do, clomping up the stairs in their heavy boots, laughing and shouting, waking up a lot of the neighbors along the way. The second car, with the rest of the members of East Side White Pride, is nowhere in sight. That group has given up and gone home. The car with Ken and the longhairs is also cruising. They also stop at the two parties, with the same luck, and also, by chance, at the same convenience store, where a shaken cashier, not connecting the longhairs with the skinheads who have just pulled away, rails about the theft and whines to them, "Why does it always have to be me?" Now the longhairs know where the skinheads are, or just were, and can guess where they might be going. The musicians, fading, ask to be dropped off at home. Ken is not about to give up. He is really starting to worry about his girl. At about one o'clock in the morning Ken and the two others stop by Nick's still searching for the girls.

7

The girlfriends are doing their best. East Side White Pride is noto-
rious for chauvinism even among local skinheads, but this is going
too far. The girls are strong, they are proud, they are racists, and if
this "Boys' Night Out" bullshit had been the rule over the last several months they would have missed some of the best scenes of the
year. Besides, it is rough on their relationships. All week long they
are separated from their sweethearts by their ordinary identities as
student, waitress, countergirl, clerk, and they count on Saturdays as
a time of public showing of the private feeling that exists between
themselves and their guys. On the other hand, the plan is already
decided, there is nothing they can do about it, and to make a stink
could well be more humiliating than going along. In the parking lot
of the Hawthorne Safeway, where most of them gather for the send-
off, there is great excitement. The guys dash in and out of the store
for last-minute supplies of beer and cigarettes and the girls do the
same. Surrounding Dave's van, the girls hover near their prospective
heroes for as long as possible, each delaying the moment when her
man ceases to belong to her and belongs to the group. Then they
say their farewells. As the East Side White Pride literature-
distribution brigade takes off, the girls make a tentative plan.

They connect at an apartment not far away, five girls who have
never been alone together before, united only by their relationship
to East Side White Pride. Apart from their bomber jackets and
British-imported high-laced Doc Marten boots, the girls have little
in common. There is Patty Copp, a nineteen-year-old community
college student who hopes to become a veterinarian (it is her apartment); Heidi Martinson, eighteen, who works for a credit company
and lives at home with her family in one of Portland's wealthiest
suburbs; Julie Belec, an almost-but-not-quite street kid, a sixteen-
year-old dropout who does a lot of drinking and drugs; Carol
Shawver, who calls herself "Desiree Marquis," eighteen, a black-
garbed, white-faced "gothic" punk who works in a downtown deli;

and Deanna Johnson, nineteen, another punk rocker—but all this is already more than they know, for to one another they are mainly stand-ins for their mates (Kyle Brewster, Steve Strasser, Ken Mieske, Nick Heise, and Pogo, respectively) and when it comes down to it, not one of them can name more than one or two of the others' last names. To cover over the gaps in the moment they begin to drink—a bottle apiece of Boone's Farm wine in some cases, a forty-ounce Coors in another. Patty and Heidi slip off to Patty's bedroom and smoke some dope. Soon they are all feeling more at ease. As the alcohol level rises, so does the level of confidences, particularly about tonight. Whatever their individual attitudes toward East Side White Pride, collectively they know a put-down when they see one. This particular demonstration of male superiority is especially galling because the other major skinhead gang in town, POWAR, includes many girls, some of whom are their friends, and for the ESWP girlfriends to be left out of a simple expedition of the kind the POWAR girls have already undertaken on their own is too much. Dave Mazzella himself has been teaching them since he got here that they ought to be shouldering more responsibility for the race—and now this! The more they talk the more restless they get. A minute feels like an hour. It is time they got out of this stuffy room. Close enough already to assist one another with makeup, they adjust their faces in the bathroom, then pile into Patty's car and set off.

They swing by the rocker party at Fifty-third and Woodstock to check for the guys, then head for the Pine Street Theatre, better known simply as "Pine Street," one of Portland's principal rock venues, where the thrash metal band Nuclear Assault is entertaining for the apocalypse with songs such as "Live, Suffer, Die," "After the Holocaust," "Stranded in Hell," and "Nuclear War." There has been growing tension beween Nazis and anti-Nazis in the Portland punk scene lately—in San Francisco, where it is also increasing, the Dead Kennedys have even written a song about it, "Nazi Punks Fuck Off"—and the girls' appearance creates a stir. In the parking lot they are confronted by a twenty-something man in a cowboy outfit who tells them he is a Jew and proud of it and suddenly they are in a fight, Heidi in the lead, pushing him in the chest with her fist, screaming "JEW! JEW! JEW!," Julie taunting "So, you're a Jew!," the others circling round, kicking him, until a longhaired friend of theirs, joining the act, gets too close to the cowboy and receives a bloody nose and another longhair joins in to defend the first and soon all is mayhem and the Jewish cowboy is taken by security guards back into the building and out the rear as the girls give chase, whereupon, high from the first charge, they begin badgering a foreigner, who, along with his girl and another couple, dashes to his car, followed by Patty, kicking at his door, after which they head for their own car and take off, exhilarated, two rockers across the street yelling after them, "Nazi punks," and as they shoot out into the night their only regret is the one they all share: "The Jew got away!" Otherwise it has been a great evening. From strangers they have become a platoon. Proud of their showing, they stop again at Patty's to look for Kyle and to use the bathroom, then leave to drop off Desiree, who is woozy and wants to go home.

8

Lyon's Restaurant is a warm, bustling commercial establishment right on the border between the white and black parts of town, one of the few places in the city of Portland where any hour of the day or night you might find an equal number of whites and blacks eating side by side, and it is here that Mulugeta Seraw and his friend Tilahun Antneh stop for dinner. The party to which they are headed is not far away, at an apartment in the vicinity of Northeast Twenty-seventh and Clackamas, a neighborhood much like Mulugeta's but with perhaps a greater number of blacks. After the clearance of the Portland ghetto to make way for the Convention Center—and Lyon's—Portland's blacks moved north and east, and in inner Northeast, unlike in the rest of the city, Portland's whites can occasionally find themselves the minority. The food is dependable at

Lyon's, the service unhurried. They eat slowly, have a beer or two, and still reach the party early in the evening. Tilahun Antneh is driving. The official occasion for the gathering is the departure of the host's brother, who has been visiting from Philadelphia, but the real occasion is the emptiness of exile. Like most of the events of the Ethiopian diaspora, like the diaspora itself, the Ethiopians' farewell party is largely male. About twenty men and one woman drink, talk, and laugh. Those who later describe it to the police think Mulugeta was having a good time. Sometime past midnight, a community college student who has had a little too much beer and gin begins interrupting the other guests, who are telling stories and jokes, and the other guests become annoyed, in particular another student, named Wondwosen Tesfaye, who tells the first one to cut it out, whereupon he himself is told to cut it out, et cetera, and a fight seems about to begin until Tilahun Antneh, who is getting ready to drive Mulugeta home, invites Wondwosen Tesfaye to come along. Mulugeta has to be at work at Avis early Sunday morning and he needs to get to bed. The other two are planning to drop him off at his apartment and then return. Tilahun Antneh and Wondwosen Tesfaye do not know each other very well, but Wondwosen is another friend of Mulugeta's. Wondwosen's sister has a boyfriend named Umar who lived with Mulugeta at his aunt's house in Addis Ababa and whom Engedaw Berhanu also helped bring to this country. Umar and Mulugeta had in fact come at the same time. Mulugeta Seraw and Wondwosen Tesfaye know many people in common and they like to talk. "Where is Umar now?" either one of them might have asked the other. "In Los Angeles." "How is he doing?" "Fine." Portland is a small city and they arrive too soon. When they reach Mulugeta's apartment there are no parking spaces and they sit in the car in the middle of the street for a while chatting on. Tilahun Antneh is behind the wheel smoking, Wondwosen Tesfaye is in the passenger seat with a cup of gin, Mulugeta is in the backseat with a beer. It is a comfort to be together in the darkened car like that in spite of the hour. It is hard to turn the handle to depart.

9

The Pine Terrace Apartments is a flimsy, two-story motel-style building where when the toilet flushes in one unit you can hear it in another, and if the neighbors had wondered "What's the rush?" as the skinheads raced up the outside stairway back to Nick and Desiree's shortly before one in the morning, they would not have wondered long. After a day of drinking that for some of them started as much as twelve hours earlier, their stomachs have caught up with their kidneys. In the scene that follows someone is always in the john. They put on some music and try to party but all that male bonding is exhausting even to skinheads and their energies are rapidly slipping away. Nick, skinhead by night, is a student at the local museum school by day, and a few of his friends browse with him through his work of several years—beautiful, delicately drawn, death-haunted fantasy illustrations of stories by H. P. Lovecraft and Michael Moorcock, as well as stories of his own. Others play "quarters," a low-budget drinking game on the order of spin the bottle. Around the edges of the smoky room the rest sprawl aimlessly in clumps of two or three, their moods as volatile as their intestines. Steve Strasser, charged up both by the trip downtown and by the great beer robbery, is busy bullying one of his friends. Kyle Brewster, so drunk that every time he has sat down over the last several hours he has fallen asleep, awakens and begins longing for his girl. Mike Barrett is vomiting in the bathroom. About the only one on whom the beer and hours have not left their mark is Dave Mazzella, who is trying to reverse time and turn the party back into a meeting, once again urging Nick to send some of his drawings down to Metzger's newspaper in California, while Nick, intent on nothing so much as how to explain this drinking party to Desiree, who will be thinking about the terms of his probation, is scarcely nodding along. It is a hopeless effort. This meeting is simply adjourned. Everybody is waiting, but nobody knows what for. The one member of East Side White Pride who can always be counted on to make things happen no matter where or when—Ken Mieske—is not even in the room.

Suddenly there is a loud car on the street, more loud steps on the stairs, a loud pounding at the door, and there he is on the threshold, the missing member, Ken Mieske. Ken has not yet found his girlfriend, but at least he has found his party. He is just bounding down the stairs calling out to the others to come up when a second car pulls up to the intersection and out pile the girls—Julie, Ken's; Patty, Kyle's; Heidi, Steve's; Deanna, Pogo's; and Desiree, Nick's— and just as Nick has feared, Desiree is raging because Nick has been in jail for a burglary and Desiree, who has waited for him through his imprisonment, is not eager to wait again. Slamming the car door, running up the stairs, shouting "I want those assholes out of my apartment!" she commands the high ground of her doorway like an MP busting a bar and issues her order, which is "GET THE FUCK OUT!" Not far behind her are the other girls, searching amid the sluggish ruins of a skinhead evening for their respective mates. Ken signals his driver friend "Forget it, there's no party," and the long-hair, mistakenly thinking he has been snubbed, guns the motor of his loud, mufflerless car and takes off, disturbing the sleepers in every house and apartment in sight. Desiree yells again and the skinheads obey her. Jarred by their sudden eviction, they swarm drunkenly back down the stairway, the couples reunited, the others alone. They stand around for a moment at the bottom, trying to regroup.

10

Now many of them are together again but the fizz has gone out of the evening and no one really knows what to do. Though there is some disagreement over whether to try for another party, by this time the nos have it and they straggle across the intersection toward their cars to head for home. They sort themselves out into two groups more or less according to where they are going. Dave Maz-

zella, Mike Barrett, and Pogo and Deanna, who all share an apartment a few miles south of Nick's, leave in the van along with several
of the girlfriendless members of the East Side White Pride skinhead
chorus they plan to drop off along the way. Three couples—Ken
and Julie, Steve and Heidi, and Kyle and Patty—remain. Steve lives
with Mazzella, Barrett, Pogo, and Deanna, and by rights he and
Heidi should be in the van, but Heidi's car has been at Patty's since
the girls went out together earlier in the evening and she wants to
get it back. The idea is for Patty to swing by her own place a few
blocks from Nick's to drop Heidi and Steve, then drop off Ken and
Julie, who live together in the basement of Julie's parents' house in
the same part of town, and then go home. There is a small delay.
Whatever else you might think of the values of Patty Copp, she
does not allow anyone, ever, to enter her car with an open con-
tainer of alcohol, period, and since Kyle and Steve are still drinking cans from the beer heist they all stand around for a moment
bullshitting about Mazzella and Barrett, how it looks like Barrett,
too, is starting to put the make on their girls, how they don't trust
him, and watering a bush or two on the corner in the process. Then
they get in the car. Kyle is in the front passenger seat beside Patty.
Ken, Julie, Steve, and Heidi are all squeezed into the rear.

On Saturday night both sides of the 200 block of Southeast Thirty-
first Avenue are lined with cars and as you enter it heading either
south from Ankeny or north from Pine you have to drive in the
middle because the lanes have been obliterated by the cars parked
on either side and the middle is all there is. Facing south toward
the corner, only half a block away, the Ethiopians in the car outside
the Parklane could perhaps have seen the skinheads as they trooped
across the intersection to their cars or at least heard them as many
of the neighbors did but in their hearts they are in another country
far from Portland, Oregon, and it seems that they did not see them
down the street, nor do they either see them or hear them when
Patty pulls her car up directly in front of their car in the middle of

Southeast Thirty-first Avenue and honks her horn. Tilahun Antneh
and Wondwosen Tesfaye are bending down in the front seat, perhaps over a light, and they do not respond, so she honks again and
Kyle rolls down his window and shouts, politely the first time,
"Would you move? Would you please move?" and Tilahun Antneh
looks up and blinks his lights, which have been off, on and off, and
he tries to start his engine but it fails, so he tries again, and it is at
this point, when they are already staring into each other's windshields, that everyone realizes that some of them are black and some
are white and it is understood that a new ingredient has been added
to the Saturday night brew. So swiftly that it is practically simul-
tantaneous the civil "Move your car!" becomes "Move your fuckin'
car!" and there is an answering "Bitch!" hurled at Patty and now the
windows of both cars are down and there are "Fuck you, niggers!"
and "Fuck you, assholes!" back and forth and when Mulugeta Seraw,
who has always been a peacemaker, gets out of the car so his friends
can leave he turns to the occupants of both cars, gesturing to them
to settle down as he does so because something ugly is already in
the air. In order for the cars to be on their way, they first have to
back up to reposition themselves, which they do, but as they pass
each other in the narrow roadway, Wondwosen Tesfaye, in the passenger seat, leans across Tilahun Antneh toward Patty Copp and
gives her the finger and Kyle Brewster, who, having snapped himself
out of his earlier stupor, has more or less assumed the captaincy of
the whites, leans across Patty and gives it back and, sliding back
toward his own side, grabs a gun that he himself placed between
the bucket seats earlier and waves it around until Patty wrestles it
away from him, shouting, "Asshole! That's MY gun!" and now there
are birds being flipped by everyone and more and more racial shouting and now that they are close enough for the skinheads to hear
the accents and know that it is not the local Crips or Bloods, of
whom they are afraid, they are shouting, "Sand Nigger!" and "Hod-
gie!" and even the war cry of the skinheads of the British National
Front, "Paki!," and Kyle, who has recently written a poem against
immigrants titled "STAY OUT," shouts, "Go back to your own

country!" and Tilahun Antneh, who is descibed in immigration papers as a freedom fighter against Mengistu, shouts, "I fought to get here and I'll fight to stay here!" and as the cars, traveling in opposite directions, move apart, both stop, and although the timing is so close here it would need a cosmic replay to guarantee it, it is probable that the Ethiopians stop first and Tilahun Antneh and Wondwosen Tesfaye get out of the car, fists clenched, and run back up the street, and Kyle yanks up the brake on Patty's car and flies out of the front seat and Steve Strasser flies out of the back and they run down, and as the four men meet in the middle of Southeast Thirty-first Avenue between the corner and the Parklane suddenly no one is tired anymore, they all are exhilarated, because if you are a skinhead this is what you have been slouching toward all week, violence, and if you are an Ethiopian exile you have been humiliated once too often already and you need a release, and for a few moments it is like every other street brawl going on across America at that hour, they agree on the ground rules, they expect no real harm.

But there is something about a street fight that cannot stop until it has played itself out and this one is not stopping, it is growing, for as Steve Strasser is fighting with Wondwosen Tesfaye and Kyle Brewster is fighting with Tilahun Antneh, Mulugeta Seraw turns back from where he has started to enter his apartment and races down toward Brewster and Tilahun Antneh, and Patty Capp turns to Kenneth Mieske, who is still in the car, and says, "WELL, aren't you going to do something about it, Ken?" and Ken Mieske grabs a bat he finds on the floor of the backseat by his feet and races down in the same direction, and Nick Heise and Desiree Marquis, who have not yet gone to bed, recognize their friends' voices from the shouting and run down the stairs of the Pine Terrace to the street, and Heidi Martinson, dislodged from the car by the exit of Steve Strasser, also runs over, and Strasser has Wondwosen Tesfaye on the ground on the east side, where he is crawling under a car, and Brewster and Tilahun Antneh are fighting face-to-face on the west, and someone is yelling, "Kill him! Kill him! Kill him!" and someone else is shouting, "You're a dead man!"; but of everyone who is present at this point and of everything that is happening the only thing that really matters is that as he runs down the street toward the action something in Kenneth Mieske explodes and he takes that bat and he smashes out the taillights of Tilahun Antneh's car and he next smashes out the right rear window and goes after Antneh himself while Steve Strasser crosses over from the other side and smashes out the left window with his boot, and as a horrified Tilahun Antneh leaps back into his car to escape the bat and drives away, Ken looks up and when he does he sees his white friend, his skinhead comrade, Kyle Brewster, struggling with the black Mulugeta Seraw, and he races down the few more steps to where they are fighting and with all the force of his burly body he brings the bat down between them, hitting Mulugeta Seraw on the side of the head from behind, and when Mulugeta crumples to the ground Ken stands over him with the bat for a moment more, bringing it down once, twice, maybe more, and Steve Strasser is in there too, kicking, and when they are finished a little pool of blood is already forming and Mulugeta Seraw, who only two minutes earlier was urging all of them to stay calm, is nearly dead. The only one who understands what has really happened before they see it on televison later is Kenneth Mieske. With those swings of the bat he has lifted himself out of obscurity into history, not, as he has dreamed, as a rock star, but as a racial murderer. "Ken Death," a name originally given to him by a friend in the Portland music world for his attraction to the heavy metal subgenre "death metal," is the name he will now be known by forever.

11

At five o'clock in the morning of November 13, 1988, Engedaw Berhanu was asleep in his Oakland, California, apartment when the phone rang and an Ethiopian friend from Portland told him Mulugeta had been hurt in a fight and was in the hospital. Knowing without knowing how that Mulugeta was already lost, he made his way to the Oakland airport, his wife and three-year-old daughter by his side. When he arrived at Emanuel Hospital in Portland at 9:30, the doctors thought he had already been informed. Years before, when he was still a boy in Ethiopia, one of his brothers had fallen ill and was taken to a hospital in Addis Ababa and he and his father had set out from their village to see him. The brother died, but members of the family who lived there had arranged a traditional Ethiopian mourning, setting out the food and the chairs and gathering together all their other relatives and friends so they would be ready even before the immediate family was told. A few days later, as they were leaving Addis to go home, Engedaw reminded his father that he should say a few words to the people who had been so kind and his father had said that there are two kinds of mourning, a good grief and a bad grief. A good grief is when someone dies in the family and everyone is there and comforts and consoles you. A bad grief is when you mourn alone. There had been bad griefs of many kinds in Ethiopia in the years since Engedaw had left it. Now he understood that there would be bad griefs in America too.

UNDERGROUND

I have tried to expose to the view of the public more distinctly than is commonly done one of the characters of the recent past. He is one of the representatives of a generation still living. In this fragment . . . this person introduces himself and his views and . . . tries to explain the causes owing to which he has made his appearance and was bound to make his appearance in our midst.

—Dostoyevsky's footnote to the title of
Notes from Underground

12

The home to which Kenneth Mieske returned when the night was done was a low-ceilinged, pine-veneered finished room he shared with Julie Belec in the basement of her mother and stepfather's rented house in a blue-collar neighborhood in Southeast Portland, not too far from the fatal corner. In another part of the basement, separated by a curtain, lived Julie's younger brother with his skateboards and bottle caps, but in Ken and Julie's section the decor was all their own and they had assembled it together. Posters from the local shows of assorted bands—ranging from the Accused, on which

a weird Mohawk-sprouting character someplace between a canni-
bal and an Amazon holds a dripping dagger in one hand and a skull
in the other, to Portland's own Poison Idea, on which a muscular
skinhead with large teeth and a menacing grimace holds another
dripping dagger against the neck of a gay male victim who will be
lucky to lose his beard rather than his head—slide into an undif-
ferentiated collection of antiblack and antisemitic posters, leaflets,
and fliers that nearly covers one wall. Some, like the drawing of a
microwave—"Jew Dwarfs! There is an oven in YOUR future"—or
the "Official RUNNIN' NIGGER Target" are more or less standard
issue in Ken and Julie's circles and are easy enough to come by, but
others reflect an individual search. There are a number of newspaper
clippings about Rudolf Hess, a picture evidently Xeroxed from a
history book of Hitler and Mussolini reviewing troops, another text-
book photo, labeled "Communists rounded up and held at bay by
stormtroopers, 1933," to which Ken has added the note "Poor little
Jew boys lining up to die," and a Xeroxed photo of the crammed
Jewish cemetery in Prague with the caption "Huddled in death as
in life, Jews from Prague's Old Town ghetto rest in the Old Jewish
Cemetery," which I suspect with its stones leaning crookedly this
way and that and its information that in some places the graves are
a dozen bodies deep must have tickled their sense of the macabre
as well as their sense of humor. Elsewhere around the room the
theme continues. Their videos are Leni Riefenstahl's celebration of
the 1934 Nazi Party rally at Nuremberg, *Triumph of the Will*; a
number of recent TV talk shows featuring the White Aryan Resistance's camera-ready skinhead contingent, including Dave Mazzella;
some segments of *Race and Reason*, a white-point-of-view television
show made for cable access by Tom Metzger. Their records, apart
from such American classics as the album of the Dead Kennedys
whose jacket features the dead Jack Kennedy and an album called
DayGlo Abortions, featuring Nancy and Ronald Reagan feasting on
a fetus, are mainly British skinhead music—*White Rider* by Skrewdriver, *Oi! Oi! Music!* by the Oppressed, *Face the Aggression* by the
Condemned 84. On a coffee table by the bed, at least on the day

of the police photographs, are some well-thumbed books about each of their favorite Nazis—Mengele, his, and Speer, hers. More Speer, along with William Shirer's *Rise and Fall of the Third Reich* as a kind of primer, sits on the shelf. There is a swastika made of gum wrappers. A sheaf of gory posters for Ken's own band, Machine, the lyrics to a work in progress, "Senseless Violence," and the well-framed group photographs of East Side White Pride taken by Julie herself in a place of honor on the wall confirm that Ken and Julie are not outsiders to this world, like children plastering their bedrooms with posters of stars they will never meet: they are members of it, they are in it, it is their world.

Ken Mieske was practically a legend. Of the waves of street kids and semi–street kids who made up the Portland underground music scene in the 1980s, some had identities and some did not yet and never would have identities no matter how many safety pins or earrings they wore, or where, or what they did with their hair, and it was plain to everyone who met him as soon as they met him that Ken was one of the ones who did. He had arrived in Portland from Seattle in 1981, at sixteen, been taken up by an older acquaintance, Jim Cartland,* and when Cartland joined with Mark Wells* to form the booking company CartWellShows* two years later, Ken came along with the territory, a link between the two promoters and their younger audiences. Stage crew, bouncer, discoverer of the hardest, farthest-out, "cutting edge" rock bands that he found in Seattle and elsewhere and persuaded Cartland and Wells to bring to Portland, he was visible to everyone in the rock scene, known by the stage name "Ken Death" for his love of the loud, fast, violent, not-for-the-squeamish death-metal music that drove away all but the most intense listeners. With Machine his reputation was becoming solidified, and there had been a previous band, Sudden Infant Death, but it was not so much either as stage crew or as musician that Ken

*These names have been changed.

Mieske stood out, it was by force of personality, energy, for there was an aura about him, a presence, that made those who knew him feel that he might have what it takes to be a star. Loud, funny, wild, and reckless, pound for pound there was more of him somehow than of most of the people in town. Filmmaker Gus Van Sant, then part of a loose Portland underculture, even starred him in a film personifying street life on the occasion of his release from prison on a burglary charge in 1987. A two-minute rumination on women and prison written by Van Sant and spoken by Ken from the middle of a highway, it was called *Ken Death Gets Out of Jail.*

The year between the fall of 1987, when he got out of jail for the burglary, and the fall of 1988, when he went back in for killing Mulugeta Seraw, was probably the happiest year of Ken Mieske's life. He had Machine, which was developing a new sound and which in the novelty-driven, ever-evolving world of American rock music might possibly, just possibly, have been going somewhere. He had East Side White Pride, a haven for the racist theories and feelings, unspeakable elsewhere, he had sharpened in prison, as well as a band of brothers he could trust on the streets. And he had Julie. Julie and Kenny were a natural match. They had met in 1984, when she was twelve and he was nineteen, at a smoky, drug-filled apartment known as "Homicide House" for the ambience favored by their mutual friend Tray Tanas, aka Tray Bundy (after Ted), to whom it belonged, and when they met again, same place, after Ken got out of jail they knew that they wanted to be together. Not only did they have a common history—they were dropouts, they drank, they sniffed, swallowed, or injected any drug in sight—they had a common vision, for Julie's racism was independent of Ken's, she had come to it on her own through study and investigation during the time he was pursuing it in prison, and unlike many of the girls who hung around East Side White Pride she was not a follower but a comrade. She could easily have been in POWAR, the girl-dominated skinhead crew started about then, but both in her own right and through Ken she was accorded a status in ESWP granted to no other girl, and she liked being associated with the boys. Delicate, feminine, with the kind of sharp, fine-boned beauty that with a change of dress could have placed her on the arm of an executive or in the pages of *Vogue*, she was strong, bold, and scrappy as well, sometimes she even carried a gun, and if necessary in a street fight she could get out there with the best of them and do her part.

Life in the cluttered little apartment was not quite all swastikas and music. A photo album now part of the police files includes some unusual items, such as portraits of some of their friends' penises and a shot of another friend shoving a large dildo between the legs of a small skeleton, but there are a lot of ordinary snapshots as well— friends, grandparents, an East Side White Pride basketball game, a visit of Ken and Julie's to the zoo. Their letters, too, written during various separations, have a certain conventionality of the "I love you" "Do you love me?" "I have to go to the store" "Bye for now" "Hi, I'm back" "I'm going to sleep" "Goodnight" "ZZZZZ" "Here I am again" variety that seems to lurk in the heart of every American teenager, but there are also real intimacies in there, fantasies and confessions of the kind exchanged only by true lovers in the night. Like other couples, Ken and Julie had their problems. He strayed. She clung. They fought, sometimes violently, over things as trivial and later embarrassing as whose turn it was for the Nintendo. But their love supported their politics and their politics supported their love. Among the photos detached from the album at some point for use as evidence are a number of pictures of Ken giving the Nazi salute, once even in a hot tub, partly clowning, as he often did, but partly not. Interspersed in the letters are the salutation, from him, "To my dear Julie, my White Patriot forever" or, from her, a reference to the Reverend Richard Butler of the neo-Nazi Aryan Nations compound in Idaho, whom she invokes almost as an arbiter in one of their fights. It was the future as well as the present that held them together. Once Ken told me that one of the things that interested him about Hitler was how he had been a nobody, a transient, "like a bum on the streets of Portland," and how he had risen up out of that nothingness to rule the world and I understood for a moment how that might well attract them for they were all bums on the streets of Portland—Ken, Julie, their friends—and without a vision they had nowhere to go but down. Julie was even studying German. Ken and Julie planned to have a family and to be married, in that order, and they were beginning to put their vision into practice. November 13, 1988, was their anniversary. They had a cat, Heinrich, after Himmler. They wanted a dog, who would have been called Rudolf, after Hess. And when Julie was pregnant with the baby they both wanted but later lost they decided to call him Joseph, after Mengele. They had no plans for the contingency that the baby might have been a girl, but Eva is the name that comes to mind.

13

Sealed into the sidewalk of a fashionable Northwest Portland neighborhood, directly across the street from a fine French restaurant, is a graffito from about 1984 signaling a new presence in the youth scene—PUSH, for Portland United Skinheads. The PUSH graffito is the single most public marker we have that the Portland youth underworld that spawned East Side White Pride was not simply the product of a theatrical imagination, a street cabaret staged by the city fathers along with the summertime Shakespeare in the park, but a living community of flesh-and-blood people, other people's children, invisible to most of the citizens of Portland most of the time but known to one another very well. To explore the history of this secret community is not a simple matter since the materials for its reconstruction are so thin. Such traces of it as remain owe their existence largely to police investigations, and the police are not in the business of creating systematic archives; they are solving crimes. Since neither for the scene itself nor for the individuals who were part of it are the available sources thorough and deep enough to tell us all we should want to know, it would be tempting to skip the effort of reconstruction altogether and proceed immediately to judgment, as many do—but that would be a mistake. For elusive as it is, the evolution of the Portland youth scene in the 1980s contains an important story: the story of the end of the World War II epoch, with its widespread refusal of Nazism, and the start of a new era. The transition begins with grafitti. In the word "PUSH" itself, the S is still soft and round, but above it is an "SWP" for Supreme White Pride, in which the S resembles the backward Z of the SS lightning bolts; in another "SWP" nearby, the Z is more rectangular, a partial swastika, and a whole swastika appears in the sidewalk just beyond. In "PUSH"s elsewhere in the city, the swastika-like Z is the norm.

Five years after the first swastikas and a few months after the death of Mulugeta Seraw I was standing in line with some friends at the Pine Street Theatre when there emerged from the parking lot a platoon of ten Nazi skinheads. Black-jacketed, black-booted, with shining heads and faces, they stood by in formation, a strange contrast with the disheveled punks also waiting in line, as their leader conferred with the club bouncer, who held his ground firmly: No Entry. I do not know who those particular skinheads were, nor does it matter to this story. What I do know is how frightening they were, and all the more so because they were young and drunk. Their leader was a round-faced, rosy-cheeked all-American teenager who looked as if he had just stepped out of a Hitler Youth recruiting poster. The followers looked all too eager to be led. Standing only a few feet away from them in a loose crowd, I felt my sense of myself as a particular individual with a particular history seep away into something that I can only describe as a universal vulnerability: a fear that I would arbitarily be singled out. What if, rebuffed by the bouncer, the little storm trooper would cast about for a way to retrieve his wounded honor and, scanning the crowd, alight on me, shouting out the words shouted by the skinheads' girlfriends in this very parking lot the night Seraw was killed: "So, you're a Jew!" It could have happened. It often has happened. And what would have happened next? And if this fear affected me, a middle-aged woman with some experience in holding on to a sense of self under shifting circumstances, how much more must it have affected the young punk rockers, flotsam to begin with, who, caught in what might well have become a standoff between the ten of them and the hundred or so of us, seemed to be doing exactly what I was: staring out past the drunken skinheads across the space between us, hoping not to be noticed. The ability of a small group to control the behavior of a larger one can be described by only one word: Power. In the years that followed the first grafitti, starting around 1985, the skinheads had it.

To account for the infiltration of political violence into the Portland youth scene, one must look to several sources. First would be the skinhead movement in Britain, and particularly the metamorphosis from its interracial origins in the mixed white and Jamaican working-class neighborhoods of London's depressed East End in the late 1960s to its gradual almost complete identification with the fascist British National Front beginning in the late 1970s. Second would be the San Francisco punk rock scene, originating at roughly the same time, a scene so rich with such fine distinctions as those between "thug rockers" and "skate rockers" that when the first skinheads appeared with their Nazi regalia they seemed to be, and indeed were, just another cultural tendency. Not all San Francisco's kids became "punks," not all "punks" became "skinheads," and not all "skinheads" became "Nazis," of course, but that trajectory soon became an established one. With the San Francisco scene receiving so much national attention, how much the emergence of skinhead movements in other cities owes to imitation and how much to parallel courses is hard to say, but here is what happened in Portland.*

---

*A segment of skinheads and former skinheads in Portland and elsewhere is emphatic that the nonracist skinhead tradition continued as well, and it is true that after some of the events described below, consciously antiracist skinheads did begin to appear in the city, most notably a group known as SHARPs, for Skinheads against Racial Prejudice, but the thrust of the movement in England, in the United States, and in Portland was always toward racism. This account is concerned only with racist skinheads.

In the early 1980s there arrived in the city from California two young brothers, Hank and Eugene Mulligan, who in spite of sounding Irish were reportedly Scottish and, whatever their British isle, brought with them the seeds of the original skinhead movement, which they were the first to scatter about in Portland. Eugene Mulligan was the founder of PUSH, Portland United Skinheads, the first skinheads who, as we have seen, literally left a mark. In addition to the Mulligans there were other transients, some from cities where skinheads had also already begun to define themselves in opposition to the punk communities and some from cities where they had not. At one point or another there was "L.A. Dan," said to have been a member of a Southern California skinhead group named after a white supremacist group known as the Order, "Bash Dave" Stout— for Bay Area Skinhead—out of San Francisco, and a host of other first-name-onlys such as "Weejoe," "Tex," and "Harvey" of whom there are few traces but who loom as large in the memories of those whose school was the streets as football heroes and student body presidents do in the memories of those whose schools were schools. They lived on the fringes of the punk scene in assorted communal apartments and squats shared with a number of local street kids, including a few whose induction into the skinhead movement via PUSH proved only the beginning of a long skinhead association. Nick Heise, the skinhead outside whose apartment Mulugeta Seraw was later killed, was one early member. Steve Strasser, one of the skinheads involved in the killing, was another. To the disgust of Eugene Mulligan, some of the early skinheads were girls, including two who would later found the girl-heavy POWAR, doubtless in part because of that very disgust. The spirit of PUSH seems to have been as much criminal as political, something of an *American Clockwork Orange*. "We never worked. No one in PUSH worked. We just went out and committed petty crimes and drank beer and did drugs all the time," one of the members told me; and since the drugs included heroin, the number of crimes, for remarkably few of which they ever seem to have gotten caught, was great. They must have carved their graffiti almost in passing.

The political consciousness of these 1985 Portland skinheads is not fully captured by any existing historical label. A new coinage—something like *anarcho-proto-fascist*—is required to get it right. Bravado was central. There was a violence test for membership called a "lineup" that consisted of an official one-on-one fight to prove the applicant would not back down on the street, though a few people joined just by hanging around or slipped past Eugene in a variety of other ways, as had the girls. Members had tattoos that said PUSH, but unlike later East Side White Pride patches, which were all the same and were earned, the PUSH tattoos were all different, self-styled, and almost anyone could get one or more. As for the designs, some unequivocally Nazi symbols like the swastika and the ZZ lightning bolts were already present, but the preponderance was not so much Nazi as German nationalist—an Iron Cross, a World War I helmet with a German flag—as if, mysteriously, a particular stage in the history of Germany and a particular stage in the iconography of the skinhead movement went hand in hand. Little remains of this group except its mug shots, but there is one document by Eugene Mulligan himself, an illustrated envelope from a February 2, 1988, letter to a former follower written as the Mulligans were finally being deported to Scotland, and here is how it goes. On the front there is a large "SKINHEADS UNITE," a larger "PUSH," and, in addition to the lightning bolts and a few caricatures, "Paky Bashing Soon" and "Boot Party by Dr. Martin" (*sic*) drawn around the stamp as if to say that the return to Glasgow would have its good points. On the back are "Bald is Beutiful" (*sic*); more lightning bolts; a skull with a sword stuck through it and the words "Shove the Dove," which has to do with the scorn of skinheads for "peace punks"; a drawing of a hand bearing the tattoos "Oi," a swastika, and "SWP," and gripping a dagger; and finally and most significantly, across the back flap in bold writing, a direct expression of classic racism: "They come into this land from the jungles and from trees." In spite of the childishness of the renderings, you can practically see the progression. Although most of the people who can speak about PUSH at all say that it was not primarily either racist or Nazi, there was a direction. PUSH was loose, chaotic—it came together and fell apart more than once even before the Mulligans left town—but for the Nazi skinheads who followed, the "PUSH days," the "PUSH time," the "PUSH era," all things I heard it called, are a hallowed memory. If the Portland skinheads were ever to write their own history, the story of PUSH would be chapter 1, "The Pioneers."

Another source of the political violence in the youth scene was some of its musicians. Lest the reader be misled as to scale: in the mid-1980s the "Portland music scene" consisted essentially of three clubs—Starry Night, a large, Fillmore-type ballroom, which promoted relatively mainstream music; the Pine Street Theatre, a converted church with countercultural roots going back to the 1970s, which booked mainly punk shows; and Satyricon, a dark, much-beloved hole in the wall of Portland's Skid Row, which gave over its stage to a lot of local talent—peripheral venues all in the annals of American rock music, but places to which young people came from every corner of the city and every suburb to glimpse the world. Compared to the sizes of audiences in San Francisco or Seattle, the numbers of these young people cannot have been very great—with a metropolitan-area teenage population well under a hundred thousand, it seems a fair guess that at most twenty-five thousand would have ever attended concerts even once in any year, with perhaps a few thousand becoming regulars—but their experience was intense. What came together at the weekend concerts, wherever they were held, were not only the individual children of the Portland area whose tangible sociological characteristics such as rich or poor, student or dropout, dopester or drunk are so often thought to carry more of the weight of explanation than they actually do, but a host of invisible forces of change and decay that were manifesting themselves through young people all over the globe at the same time. The violence of the skinhead movement and the violence of the rock scene are usually treated separately, but in Portland, at least, they arrived simultaneously and they have to be taken together. In an epigraph to his film of the white-power band Skrewdriver's 1987 *White Noise* music festival in England, the neo-Nazi intellectual Michael Hoffman II quotes Céline, who, evidently anticipating "hardcore," wrote: "The only defense and the only resource of the white man against robotism . . . is to return to his emotive rhythm." But the stories of violence in the "pits" of Portland make the skinheads at the *White Noise* concert look almost genteel.

Of the many bands that formed locally in these years, two were particularly associated with violence: Poison Idea, which began in 1980 as the self-designated "Kings of Punk" and disbanded in 1993 with much of the local punk world acknowledging its royalty, and Lockjaw, a hardcore band lasting from 1982 to 1986 that, according to Ken Mieske, whose band, Machine, was its direct descendant, had the ambition of being "the most hated band in Portland" (Machine's was to be "the most hated anywhere") and that, judging by its reputation, may well have achieved its goal. The role of Poison Idea is hard to recapture not only because it changed over time but because the political vocabulary of the rock community is so hermetic. The band itself is described as being "Nazi" and "anti-Nazi" both, depending in part on when the particular observer checked in or out, and its lead singer, a sometime member of a short-lived underground club of sorts known as East Side Fist that preceded East Side White Pride, is remembered both as having encouraged "fag bashing" by, for instance, publicly supporting an antigay ballot measure on the November 1988 ballot and as having threatened to stop playing in Portland if violence continued. About the spirit of the band throughout its career, however, there is little dispute. It was angry, contemptuous, venomous—"poison"—and its members, who between them weighed enough to be eligible for the scales at a roadside truck stop, were always drunk. If "Punk Rock was a desperate scream of life in a mostly dead world," as one local obituarist put it, "Poison Idea grabs the rotting corpse of that world by its decaying shoulders, kisses it full on the lips, sticks their tongue down its throat, then throws their head back and laughs." Imagining the band's final appearance before it happened, he predicted that it would be, "as always, a raucous and dangerous party—a combination high school dance and street brawl, vision quest and riot. The band stands perched on the edge of the abyss," he wrote. "What lies beyond they neither know nor care."

Lockjaw was a different matter, an openly right-wing hardcore band whose lead guitarist shaved his head in 1985 and whose loud, hard, fast explorations of hatred and violence validated the gut feelings of many skinheads. Unlike Poison Idea, whose members left East Side Fist when its racist direction became clearer, members of Lockjaw remained, taking refuge when it became convenient in what I have come to think of as the "Punk Defense": It was a joke. It wasn't serious. We didn't mean it. A 1985 Lockjaw LP titled *Shock Value*, whose cover featured the command "Fuck off left-wing scum!," a picture of serial killer Ted Bundy, and a tribute to the white supremacist Order, whose leader, Robert Mathews, had been killed by the FBI in a siege near Seattle the year before, was particularly controversial, raising heated argument over this very point— Do they mean it or not?—a debate that calls to mind Freud's famous thesis on negation that things present themselves negatively first, as in "I don't know who I was bashing over the head in my dream last night but it certainly wasn't my mother." It is the same with *Shock Value*. Just because I thank a neo-Nazi on my record album does not necessarily mean I admire him. Does it? Or does it? With Portland now on the circuit of assorted groups whose spirit may be best summarized by the San Francisco punk band that finally stopped trying to outdo all the others and called itself merely Something Really Offensive, Poison Idea and Lockjaw were by no means the only bands at whose shows violence took place, but for a period of at least a few years wherever Poison Idea and Lockjaw were—and they were often together—there was violence.

The best account of what happened when the skinhead movement and the music scene came together is an anonymous letter written in May 1988, six months before the killing of Mulugeta Seraw, to the alternative newspaper *Willamette Week*, which had just published the first major discussion of neo-Nazi skinheads to appear in the local press, an article titled "Young Nazis," by a groundbreaking investigative reporter, Jim Redden. According to the letter writer, who was describing the years 1985–88, during which he had held three different jobs in the clubs,

> Skins do a lot of their gathering at concerts and shows where they intimidate everyone from the door person to the kids watching the performance. They travel and fight in packs. It's hard for even the largest door person or bouncer to repel twenty skins who descend on the door at once, demanding to be let in for lower prices, or ignoring the fact that they have been "86ed" from a venue for causing violence in the past. In the dancing "pit" at "hardcore" shows, male skins gang up on individuals who "looked at them funny" and slash innocent people with their spiked rings. Female skins beat up girls in the bathroom at Pine Street Theatre, with no provocation whatsoever. The skinheads drink outside the venues where there are shows, increasing the need for paid security outside, as well as inside the hall or club. They carry baseball bats with swastikas on them, knives, brass knuckles, etc. . . .
>
> For those of us who work at establishments frequented by skinheads, the intimidation factor inherent in gang-type activity is all too real. How can a club owner or employee ever criticize one skinhead without the fear of having all the establishment's windows broken by the gang? You can't throw out one violent skinhead without incurring the wrath and retribution of all of the skinheads. Before almost every hardcore show, rumors run rampant about who or what the skins are ganging up against on this particular night. I have heard them threatening people who dared to stand up to them, that they would kill them next time they encountered them on the street. No matter how hollow these threats may turn out to be, it's terrifying to the lone individual who actually does see skins on the street every day. . . .
>
> The escalation of the number of skinheads in Portland in the last two years is absolutely staggering. Perhaps not very many of them are organized in groups like POWAR [the subject of the Redden article], but it's amazing how cool it has become to dress in a

bomber jacket and boots and braces, purchase a Skrewdriver t-shirt, and a few albums. I've lost count of how many kids I've seen shave their heads and adopt the uniform in just the past few months. I cannot believe that they are all ignorant of the political beliefs that go along with the outfit, and it seems likely that at least some of them will be joining their look alikes in gang-type intimidation in the future. . . .

Please do not print my name or address. If you publish this letter, just sign me

Intimidated

The amount of violence in the music clubs in these years seems truly astounding. Not only were there brutal scenes of the kind referred to in the letter, but in March 1986 there was even a murder at Satyricon when four skinheads, including Bash Dave and Michelle Colmus, later of POWAR, lured a white man outside on the pretense of a drug buy in order to rob him and one of the men knifed him instead. At least as astounding as the amount of violence is its ideological character. Much as the original skinheads in Britain were reacting in part against what they saw as effete "mods," so their descendants in Portland were reacting against what they saw in part as effete punks. As odd as it may seem to adults to whom the whole scene is little more than a decadent blur, when the skinheads entered a club en masse on a particular night, they were not merely blindly asserting power: they were acting out a political agenda involving who was playing and who was coming that, at least in their own opinion, was a matter of right against left. An illustration of the intensity of this right-left struggle is an August 21, 1986, show at Pine Street to benefit an antinuclear coalition called Citizens' Action for a Safe Environment. The bands were to have been MDC, a leftist hardcore punk group from San Francisco, BGK, from Holland; and Cheetah Chrome Motherfuckers, from Italy. Already angered by MDC's last-minute cancellation, the crowd became even angrier at the appearance of fifty or so skinheads armed with bats, pipes, and knives. The Dutch group played, but when Cheetah Chrome Motherfucker was confronted with fifty skinheads giving the stiff-armed salute and shouting, "Sieg Heil!" and "White Power!" they refused to perform, saying their fathers, presumably members of the Italian resistance in World War II, had fought the Nazis then and they were not going to play for them now, whereupon the audience degenerated into small warring clusters, each on the verge of violence, yelling and screaming at the top of their lungs about, of all things, National Socialism. Eventually the two bands were escorted out and a riot was averted but a group of skinheads, including Ken Mieske, later showed up at the Southeast Portland house where BGK was staying. Until 3 A.M., when the skinheads jumped the fence to avoid the police finally summoned on a noise complaint, the arguments continued.

As the late arrival of the police for "noise" suggests, the only policing of the scene was self-policing. Club owners, gradually seeing the implications of the violence, particularly its threat to their staying in business, began to enforce policies on the order of "No Bats!" and tried to persuade the skins, whom they usually knew personally, that if they wanted to continue to attend shows they would have to obey the rules. Musicians and other members of the community began to attempt to speak out. It was after the Cheetah Chrome Motherfucker show that Poison Idea threatened to stop playing. In the letters column of a zine called *Two Louies*, local band member and rock critic Rick Mitchell, later with the *Houston Chronicle*, opened an attack on Lockjaw's "lunatic right . . . glorification of violence" that elicited a number of pro-Lockjaw replies, including one written "with the consent" of its bass player, later of Machine, affirming that, indeed, "every member of Lockjaw is an extreme patriot and very right wing." The last word in the debate was a brick thrown through the window of Mitchell's car as it sat parked in the street outside Satyricon. To a generation whose images of right-left political violence are shaped by the historic confrontations in Germany in the 1920s and 1930s, it may be hard to see the youthful fighting in the clubs of Portland as anything other than "the second time as farce," if that, but it is important to grant the truth of their experience to those who lived it. "There was a time when, if you were a punk, you had to watch your back," one of them told me. "I knew the Nazis, and so was safe." In the words of a punk follower who was only twelve in 1986 and who seemed to me to be mourning the utter ignorance of adults of all that was real in his life at the time: "That was a very violent year."

Nor was the political violence only in the music clubs. It was also in the streets. Near midnight on October 9, 1986, two years before the killing of Seraw, police encountered Steve Strasser at the head of a crowd of twenty to thirty skinheads armed with sticks, pipes, and an ax en route from a downtown park to a nearby club, where they were allegedly going to attack black pimps for soliciting their girls. "Strasser was observed to be giving the rest of the 'Skinheads' orders. He would march them around and [they] appeared to be receptive to his commands. He was clearly the leader in charge," according to a police report. Portlanders whose lives placed them on the street at night recall other mass appearances of armed skinheads about that time, sometimes around Portland's official gathering spot, Pioneer Courthouse Square, sometimes near the clubs and downtown. There were also numerous individual incidents—a synagogue trashing, beatings of blacks, an eruption of writing on walls. "It breaks my heart to see a white woman fuck a nigger, or vice versa," one grafitto proclaimed. The owner of Starry Night, who was Jewish, had swastikas painted on his door. With the skinheads already such a presence, no account of the years through the death of Mulugeta Seraw would be complete that did not ask why there was no response to these occurrences. When the skinheads swaggered through the city's parks and streets at will: when they commandeered bus stops: when they went to movies, shopped for groceries, or showed up on their parents' or landlords' doorsteps in their Nazi-style bomber jackets and boots: were the citizens of a city just beginning to overcome its long-standing reputation among blacks as "the most prejudiced [city] in the west" so inured to that prejudice that the existence of a new movement shrieking with

every semiotic instrument at its command that racism and antisemitism were again on the rise did not stand out? Or, like the signer
of the *Willamette Week* letter, like the punk rockers outside Pine
Street and the author of this book standing with them, were they
simply "Intimidated"?

14

The first time Ken Mieske flew into a rage, at least the first time anyone noticed, he was two and a half years old, and he had come to
live again with the woman who would later become his adoptive
mother, Sharon Schaub. Sharon loved Ken, and she had since the
day he was born, but he was wild, undisciplined, something was
always happening when he was around, and one day after a minor
incident she swatted him gently on his little diapered behind and
sent him to his room. "Now I want you to picture this tiny two-and-
a-half-year-old person," she told me during a long afternoon's conversation. "I closed the door and I went out into the living room and
I heard this noise, this crash, and I went back into that room and in
that space of time that little boy had taken a chest of drawers and
on-ended it, he had pulled the curtains down from his window, he
had undone the bedding that was on his bed. The room was like—I
was shocked. And he was just—he was shaking and he was just—I
have never seen anything like it in my life. And I thank God I had an
instinct and I grabbed him and held him and I can't tell you the
strength that was in this kid. And I held him as tight and as lov-
ingly—it wasn't a cruel thing, it was—you have an instinct to grab
and I did. And I held him as tight as I could. And then he just went
limp after a minute and he slept almost the rest of the afternoon." A
picture still in a position of honor on her wall shows the child she is
describing, a bright-eyed, curly-headed, sunny-looking little toddler
with an enormous smile. But with all that had happened to Kenny in
the years before he came there, it is a miracle that he could sleep or
smile at all.

· · ·

If Ken Mieske were ever to try to locate himself on an Aryan family tree, he could not begin with the "Mieske," for it was not a name to which he had any natural connection. He was born on August 12, 1965, in Seattle to a nineteen-year-old woman named Carlene Brooks and her boyfriend, Kenneth Hastings. It was her third pregnancy—the others had ended in abortion or adoption—and when the two decided to keep this baby, the couple married. Carlene Brooks and Sharon Schaub lived in the same housing project and during several years of Carlene's baby-sitting for Sharon's son, Michael, who was then about six, the two women had become friends. It was Sharon who brought Carlene to the hospital to deliver the baby, Sharon who brought her home, and Sharon to whom she turned when Ken was ten days old to say that the baby would not stop crying and his father was slapping and shaking him and she was frightened and did not know what to do. Sharon came over and took the infant home for a few days and she took him again when he was about a year and his mother had run off and his father had brought him to her asking her to keep him overnight and had disappeared for two weeks, and she took him again, for a year, from age two and a half to age three and a half, when Carlene wanted him back, and again not long afterward when Carlene's second husband was also, as Carlene put it, "not being nice" and told her he could never love a child who was not his own. It was the last time that eventually became a permanent adoption, though not without the complication that there were periods that Carlene herself and a son from the second husband lived with Sharon, Michael, and Kenny in a menage à cinq, with Sharon responsible for them all. Only once did Sharon not take Kenny when Carlene asked, because she was leaving for California with her own second husband, hoping to preserve the marriage, and she still regrets saying no, feeling that if she had only taken Kenny permanently earlier, perhaps things would not have turned out as they did. When Kenny was not with Sharon in his early years he was more or less nowhere, shoved around to any indifferent relative, friend, or neighbor his mother, father, or grand-mother could press into service. Sharon did not always know what was happening to him in any particular household, but what was happening to him in the ones she did know about was terrible enough. He had no love and no security. Nothing ever belonged to him, not his body, not even his name. At the time of his adoption by Sharon when he was seven he was offered a plausible choice of five last names, those of his two biological parents, those of Sharon's two ex-husbands, and the maiden name Schaub, actually belonging to her stepfather, she had gone back to using herself. He chose "Mieske" because it was the name of his new older brother, Mike, who often looked after him, but there never was a "Mieske" father in his life.

The change of mothers did not change Kenny's life all that much. Sharon's connection to Ken is so deep and natural that when she told me she had always felt she was meant to be his mother I felt it too, but she was not exactly a pillar of stability. The truth is that Kenny was not the only needy member of the family. Sharon was generous, but she was demoralized. Her life was not working out very well. A "fifties person"—her words—she had grown up with all sorts of romantic ideas about love and marriage at which she thought she was failing, and her opinion of herself was low. The addition of Kenny to an already troubled life seems a kind of surrogate romance, a step out of ordinary reality into a mythical territory where the tasks are so great that only the greatest heroine could ever succeed at them and failure would have to be correspondingly grand. And failure was probably inevitable. Even under the imaginary conditions of the fifties, with a husband, a house, two children, and all the time to enjoy them, had one of those children been Kenneth Mieske life would have been trying enough, but under her real conditions of single parenthood, a small apartment, a squalid housing project, and a full-time job it was overwhelming. At two and a half Kenny was not yet able to hold a spoon. He could not sit still, he did not like to be touched or held, and he could not cry. He was so funny, good-natured, and plainly innocent of wrong intentions that people liked him because it was impossible not to like him, but he was always a difficult child to be with. At five he was put on Ritalin. That same year, 1970, when she was thirty-one, Sharon developed uterine cancer. She had a complete hysterectomy, followed by a sudden menopause, and that was followed by several months of cobalt and radiation treatments, during which she was extremely ill. The next year, still dreaming her fifties dream, she obtained a mortgage and with a federal subsidy bought a small house on a quiet street in the rural suburb of Federal Way that she moved into with Michael and Kenny. Carlene and her second son, who had lived with them in the apartment during the months of Sharon's illness, came along.

It was in the new house that everything Sharon had been struggling with got to her and she had a nervous breakdown highlighted by a suicide attempt in which six-year-old Kenny was the one who found her. She spent some time in a psychiatric ward and the next three years on welfare. "I was home," she says, "but I don't know what the boys were doing. I really don't. I don't remember." Kenny was starting the local elementary school, which was actually called Camelot, Michael was graduating from high school and leaving home, Carlene and her child were in and out. With the welfare system weighted toward legal adoption, Sharon's maternal relationship to Ken was now officially ratified, with Ken learning in the process for the first time that Carlene, not Sharon, was his biological mother. But from then on it seems that nothing was ever really all right. To Sharon it seemed that the older Ken got the more unmanageable he became. To Ken it seemed that his mother's rules were impossible to follow. As Sharon felt better there were times when she and Ken were able to put aside their problems and simply enjoy each other's company, but more often, it seems, there were fights. What happened during their fighting is hard to know because the subject is painful for both of them and they do not like to remember, but it is plain from what they do say that the threat of violence was not one-sided but two- and that it was never far from the surface. "Most of the abuse was verbal [but sometimes] I slapped him on the bottom or shoulders and . . . even his face and it wasn't very nice," Sharon wrote the sentencing judge in a 1989 letter. "I wish to God I could undo all of it." By the time Kenny was eleven or twelve the family romance was over. Except for visits, he never lived with Sharon again. On Sharon's side there is a great guilt over what has happened to Ken. On Ken's side there is a sense of absence, of loss, that may include not only Sharon but Carlene. A song of Ken's the Portland police found particularly revolting when they discovered it in his apartment is about an aborted fetus who wants to crawl back into its mother. It is called "Homesick Abortion."

One day when Ken was about twelve and living in a group home in Vancouver, Washington, Sharon came down to get him for a weekend visit. Driving along the freeway back toward Seattle in the dark, she suddenly heard his voice piping up beside her, "Does God think I'm the devil because I do all these bad things?" It was not mere theological curiosity. Although he had not yet done anything "bad," he must have already sensed in himself the power to do so. He had a fascination with evil, with the Devil, that proceeded outward from his inner self toward his music and toward Nazism, in both of which it found a congenial home. There was a light side to Ken, which was what made him so popular—it was the same kind of funny, high-energy, happy-go-lucky quality that had entertained people when he was a baby—but there was also a dark side that was never very far away. Almost everyone I talked with about him remembers seeing him commit some violent act. He once beat a girl he was living with so badly that she had to go to the hospital. In a fight with Julie he bit her on the stomach so hard he left teeth marks and a bloody bruise. One friend describes fighting with him as "like playing with a Doberman. Scary. Too intense." He fought with his fists, with his boots, with beer bottles, sticks, a shard of bat, alone, in groups, with people he knew, and with people he didn't know. The only fight I heard about he didn't win was with Johnny Rotten of the Sex Pistols at Pine Street when Rotten supposedly slashed him with a razor across the chest, and that one may very well be apocryphal. But violence is more than a physical matter. It is a state of mind in which the fighter is in the position of a God, with the power of life and death in his hands. It is not that far a step from blood on your hands to blood on an altar, from the cracking of heads to a celebration of skulls, from the smashing of bones to an infatuation with skeletons, from the random viciousness of the street fight to the ritual evil of the occult. Ken did not go that far, but he did not have to. The occult came to him in the form of the horror movies that he rented with his friends, in the horror posters that decorated the places where he lived, in the horror music that he lived by and tried to emulate. The band that meant the most to him was Venom, a British death-metal band known for its demonic themes. It "tuned its guitars way down and made it sound really evil," which "would just bring out the evil in me, you know? In everybody," Ken told me. His favorite album, *Welcome to Hell*, included "One Thousand Days in Sodom," "In League with Satan," "Mayhem with Mercy," and "The Witching Hour." He recited the poem on the jacket to me, a four-line tribute to Satan the police also found written on a small scrap of paper in his apartment. From the imagery of death metal it was hardly any leap at all to the Nazis and specifically to the SS, the mystical brotherhood whose black uniforms, boots, and death's head insignia are so familiar to Ken that he uses the vocabulary of the music world to describe them: "hardcore." The love of darkness was not the only source of Ken's attraction to the Nazis but it was the beginning. The rest came later.

Portland's Union Station is a handsome red brick and stone building set apart from the bustle of the city on a broad plaza, with a red-tiled roof, a tall, brick-trimmed clock tower with a working clock still cranked by hand once a week, and a long, curving entrance so old-fashioned in its appearance that, even though the cobblestones are gone, when you drive around it to drop off or pick up passengers you can practically hear the horses clop. Inside, too, the station belongs to a different era: plain marble walls, marble floors, benches like church pews, and a simple but decorative handmade wooden ceiling so wondrously high that merely to enter the world it encloses makes you feel you have more time and space than you had the moment before. It is a calm, reassuring structure, full of freedom and possibility, and it must have seemed so to Ken as he stepped off the train from Seattle in the late spring of 1981 to meet the man who, next to Sharon, would become the most important person in his life, Jim Cartland. The relationship between the thirty-year-old Jim and the fifteen-year-old Ken has so much the form of scandal—"Man Seduces Boy!"—that it is important to say at the outset that in spite of occasional intimacies it was not fundamentally sexual but a warm, complicated, changing, lasting human connection probably best conveyed by the word that Ken chose for it in its early period: *uncle*. Indeed, if there was any seduction to begin with it is as likely to have been the other way around—"Boy Seduces Man!"—because when they met Ken had been struggling for survival on the streets of Seattle for several years and had seen and done a lot while Jim was a sheltered Roman Catholic former policeman who was still in the closet. However it was, the interest was mutual. What made that fifteen-year-old boy pick up the phone and announce to a thirty-year-old man he had met only once that he was going to be on such-and-such a train and what made that thirty-year-old stop what he was doing and pick him up they alone know, but that is what happened. Ken called in the morning, three months after a conversation at a party. By afternoon he was in Portland.

At the time of Ken's arrival Jim was living with a roommate in a small wooden house in a leafy glade just off lower Taylor's Ferry Road and he gave Ken a room. Jim had recently bought a restaurant he was remodeling, the Hillside Cafe,* and he was also able to give Ken a job. The Hillside Cafe is one of Portland's authentic landmarks. First a whorehouse, then the Fish Hole,* an eatery as famous for its long lines as for its food, it is a narrow, angled, two-story

---

*These names have been changed.

frame building set so casually into a cliff it is practically waiting for an earthquake to bring it down. With its crowded, beat-up, dark wooden tables and its small, crooked rooms, it is the incarnation of funk, the kind of place where, like it or not, everyone is in contact with everyone else, workers and customers hang their coats on the same hooks, the cook smiles out from the window of the tiny kitchen, and in a way the waiters are superfluous because everything is so close at hand it would be easy enough to simply get up and serve or, for that matter, cook your dinner yourself. In the opening days of his stay in Portland it must have seemed to Ken as if a curse that had been laid on him at birth had finally been lifted. The renovation was hard work but the crew included Jim's brother and sister-in-law, assorted friends, and students from a nearby college, and it felt communal. When the cafe was ready, Ken stayed on, first as a dishwasher, later as an apprentice cook. With the help of one of Jim's friends, a musician, he also began learning how to play the guitar, something he had always longed to be able to do. The life they shared during the early period is recalled by Jim as "harmonious." It was not particularly intense. There were always other people around. There was a dog. There were day trips to the Columbia River's pastoral Sauvie Island and elsewhere. Ken spent a holiday or two with Jim's family in Portland. Jim met Sharon in Seattle. For a short while, Ken even went back to school.

Then, gradually, things started to change. At some point Ken began using hard drugs—mostly cocaine—and as he did, his emotional demands and his violent outbursts increased. At the same time, Jim's personal life was changing. Although their closeness was more familial than sexual, there was a line between them that had to do with the fact that "basically Ken was straight and basically I was gay," Jim says, and at a certain stage in his coming out he began finding his young companion a burden. Knowing that the separation would be hard on Ken, Jim gave him six months' notice, telling Ken that he wanted more space and privacy, that at the end of that time he would move into an apartment alone, and that Ken, too, should start preparing to be on his own. "I was nineteen when I was kicked out. You're almost nineteen. I'll be here for you as support, but I'm not going to keep on operating like this," Jim says he told him. From then on, things became even stormier. Ken did his part in helping ready Jim's house for rental, and he was still working at the cafe, but as the deadline drew nearer, there were frequent emotional scenes. Jim was determined. He no longer wanted his parental role. Toward the end of 1983, he moved into a conspicuously one-person studio apartment in a picturesque old mansion overlooking downtown. After a couple of years of what was undoubtedly the safest, most protected life he had ever known, or would ever know, Ken was alone.

When musician "Greg McMetal" rechristened Ken Mieske "Ken Death" in 1984, he was not only giving Ken a stage name: he was also giving him an identity. The birth of Ken Death was not the first time Ken tried on a different face. According to Sharon, all his life, whenever he passed a mirror, he would rearrange his expression, and he would do the same in conversation if another person happened to come along or someone left. But "Ken Death," sometimes simply "Death," was more than a fleeting image: it was a whole new configuration. Ken Mieske was just another skinny teenager with straggly hair, a long, thin, sad face, haunted eyes, and a broken heart. Ken Death was a prophet, turning the world inside out and warning his audiences, "I will embrace something that you think is bad, I, Death, and declare it good." His appearance changed, too, and it kept on changing. His hair could be long or short, beautiful or shaved, and he became thicker somehow, stronger, a muscular showman with a fierce visage, an aggressive presence, a violent message, and no heart at all. Of all his friends, his audiences, only Jim really understood that the other Ken was still very much present: a lost, lonely, scared, rejected boy who would periodically return to Jim and plead to be taken back, once even staging a suicide attempt—his second—to persuade him. But Jim no longer trusted Ken enough. Others in Portland's creative underculture were drawn by the stance itself, by an intensity of spirit in which Ken, no matter what he was doing, always seemed to be running at full throttle. Walt Curtis, Portland's unofficial street poet laureate and author of the underground classic *Mala Noche*, a novel of the relationship between a straight Mexican teenager and a gay Skid Row shopkeeper that became the film that launched Gus Van Sant, was one friend. Van Sant, whose continued interest in such characters would be reflected in both *Drugstore Cowboy* and *My Own Private Idaho*, was another. When local film-maker Jim Blashfield inquired around town for a young actor game enough to shave his head and sport a Mohawk in the music video of "Boy in a Bubble" he was making for Paul Simon, he was referred to Ken Death.

But "Ken Death" was not the only new manifestation of Ken Mieske to emerge in the years after he left Jim's. It was also now that he became a racist, something that he had never particularly been before. The process was gradual. Before gangs, black or white, there was a good deal of tension between young blacks and young whites on the streets of Portland, and one summer night a group of blacks had come after Ken when he was alone at a bus stop, called him "cracker" and "honky," and beaten him badly enough that his pride was shaken. He had seen other whites feel the sharp sting of racial hostility, but now it was him. Around the same time a friend had loaned Jim *The Rise and Fall of the Third Reich*, by William Shirer, which Jim had read and found interesting but which Ken had also read and found fascinating, straining his limited education to take it in, asking Jim, "What does this word mean?" "What does that mean?" until he had devoured the entire sixteen hundred pages. Soon he was asking Jim other questions, which all came down to one—"How can black people talk about black pride and be separatists and that's okay but when white people just want to hang out together they're called racists?"—a question to which Jim says he never found a good answer. Another source of Ken's growing awareness of race was his contact with musicians from foreign bands. As stage crew for CartWellShows, which was formed about the time Jim moved downtown, Ken met people from many countries where the meeting of rock music and racial politics was already taking place. A member of Celtic Frost told him, "You should go over to England for a couple of weeks and see how really bad it is over there. They're letting all these Pakistanis in our country and they're taking our jobs and throwing us out on the streets." A roadie for the West German band Running Wild complained that Helmut Kohl was letting in too many Turks. "When you go to Berlin you see nothing but ragheads," is what he said. Still another influence was the local music scene with its growing numbers of increasingly violent skinheads for whom political substance was rapidly beginning to follow style, as we have already seen. Whether "Ken Death," a more or less honorary member of Portland's left-leaning, gay-leaning artistic underground was more fundamental an identity than "Ken D. Mengele," as he was sometimes known in the rock world, is a moot point, for they were both interrupted by a third Ken, the driven, desperate, drug-hungry personality observed by Jim Cartland in 1983 who would have been perfectly at home on the set of *Drugstore Cowboy* had he only shown up for auditions as Van Sant had hoped. That Ken needed drugs to keep him going—amphetamines, cocaine, LSD—and he stole to get the money to buy them. In 1985 he and a friend stole $72 worth of meat and about $100 cash from a sandwich shop not far away from the Hillside Cafe. For a while he got by with a brief sentence, probation, and occasional further brief periods of jail time for minor probation violations, but in 1986 a burglary at a private apartment committed on the very day he was released from one of the shorter sentences caught up with him. From late 1986 on he was in the hands of the Oregon correctional system, awaiting disposition. In January 1987, he was sent to the remote Eastern Oregon Correctional Institution, between the Cascades and the Wallowas, in Pendleton, to begin serving a longer term.

A man in prison tends to be all things to all people, and from the mail Ken received in EOCI it is possible to see the array of images of himself he inspired in the worlds he left behind. From his gay friends came worldly, sophisticated, and at times explicitly sexual chronicles that take for granted that he is either one of them or at least very close: "Let me cum in your mouth." From skinheads came letters already decorated with swastikas and "In Pride We Stride," as well as sermons on Aryan etiquette: "First I'll speak of your being a white man and a skinhead. Then of your treachery," the treachery being both his failure to write when he said he would ("Does this mean your word is *nothing?*") and his epistolary romance with a skinhead chick also admired by skinhead X ("You knew how I felt and you still tried to make her your old lady. Say, man, you need to *get right*"). "Uncle" Jim drew a swastika with a slash through it, meaning "No Nazis," and he and his partner, Mark Wells, both told Ken to go straight and get his GED and they would have a job for him when he got out. Sharon implored him to stop using drugs. Friends from the music world wrote with plans and projections for a future band. Whatever letters may have been coming in to Prisoner #708-9-4-17, however, and for that matter, whatever letters he may have been writing back, it is clear from his records that during the period he was in Eastern Oregon his conception of himself as a "Nazi" was secretly deepening. His journal entries typically end with "Sieg Heil!" He is reading *Inside the Third Reich*, by Albert Speer. When the inmate serving the shortcake at lunch one day gives him a smallish piece he calls it "a Jewish portion," yells "You Jewish dick!" and almost gets into a fight even though the inmate is twice his size. Nor is his commitment really so secret—at least in prison. He is one of a group of seven inmates with shaved heads. "Inmate Mieske's difficulties come from his own continual discussion of being a Nazi and being somewhat abrasive to other inmates," an official report concludes. One factor in his growing commitment appears to have been his friendship with another skinhead inmate, a relative of the Reverend Richard Butler of Idaho's Aryan Nations, for whom the inmate seems to have been acting as an underground scout. Ken's petition to the authorities for a "Pork Free Diet" reflects an infusion of Butler's Christian Identity theology into his beliefs. "I am a firm believer in Gods word and also instructed by my church elders that it is not profitable for a child of God to eat the swine as written in the ancient scriptures of my faith which govern my religious beliefs. See leviticus 11:1:8. I claim this right according to the 1st ammendment to our Constitution," Ken wrote. Prison itself, with its fostering of a need for any identity, Christian or otherwise, to assert against all the others, probably also played a part. Ken was not a deep thinker and the inconsistency between his attraction to Nazism and his affection for the many friends who for one reason or another the original Nazis would have put in camps seems at first to have passed him by, but it was quite a feat of blindness all the same. The officials reading his contradictory correspondence as it poured into Pendleton could well have wondered which way he would turn.

When Ken left prison in the fall of 1987 it must have seemed that he was coming home. Jim picked him up, helped him settle into a halfway house, and gave him back his job with CartWell. He worked with Van Sant on *Ken Death Gets Out of Jail*. Friends from the recently defunct band Lockjaw invited him to become the vocalist of a new band, which became Machine. But there was one way in which the city to which he returned was different from the one he had left: it was during that year that Portland's loose, free-floating skinhead population had begun to form itself into gangs. "Gangs" is a word all skinheads despise. "What shall I call them then?" I asked Ken. "A bunch of drunken skinheads," was his reply. Nonetheless, "gangs" will do. After considering POWAR, whose roster included Michelle Colmus, the skinhead girl involved in the 1986 Satyricon murder, with whom he had corresponded while they were both in prison, he cast his lot with East Side White Pride. Gradually, it seems, in spite of his lack of thought, his simultaneous commitments to a bohemian community best personified by Jim and Gus and a political community best personified by East Side White Pride began taking a toll. In prison whatever conflicts he may have felt would have been remote, theoretical, abstract. At home they were achingly concrete. By the fall of 1988, a year after Ken's release, Oregon was engulfed in the first of many divisive debates over the civil rights of homosexuals. A grassroots campaign had resulted in an intricately worded initiative to repeal an executive order promulgated by Governor Neil Goldschmidt against discrimination on the basis of sexual preference in state government, a proposal known as Ballot Measure 8. On Saturday, November 5, 1988, in front of a large crowd at the Pine Street Theatre, where Machine was opening for two other bands—a performance to which he had explicitly urged Jim to come—Ken entertained the audience between sets with a loud, angry, mean-spirited defense of Measure 8, which was, in the local dialect, an attack on gays. Jim was hurt and appalled. When Jim confronted him about it, Ken apologized, but he continued wearing a "Yes on 8" button until the election. With no more access to Ken's inner life than what the facts suggest, we do not know what symbolic overthrows that Declaration of Independence on November 5 may have contained or what previously controlled forces it may have unleashed. But on the following Saturday, November 12, after a week in which he celebrated his Pine Street debut mainly by violating his probation and staying drunk, Ken Death Mieske called in sick to CartWell, which needed him at Pine Street. Later that evening he killed Mulugeta Seraw.

15

In the spring of 1989, when Ken Mieske, Kyle Brewster, and Steve Strasser were still anticipating a joint trial and I was still planning to write about it for the *Nation*, Dana Anderson, the mother of Kyle Brewster, agreed to have lunch with me. Kyle Brewster's mother is a well-known civic figure. I had seen her often in pretrial hearings, an impressive combination of tenderness and competence, leaning over to button Kyle's shirt higher one moment, making notes the next. She had also taken the stand one day in support of a motion to move the trial out of Portland. Between the night of Seraw's death and the hearing several months later she had clipped nearly two hundred articles about the killing. In person she was just as she appeared at a distance: involved and objective, emotional and articulate, vulnerable and brave. Throughout our meetings she never once tried to exonerate Kyle. Her personal suffering was in the private sphere, the killing of Seraw was in the public sphere, and she never confused the one with the other. Whatever Kyle had done was between Kyle and God as well as between Kyle and the law, and he would have to pay for it. She accepted that. The discomforts that arose from her dual position as the mother of a child reviled by the entire liberal community and a member in good standing of the community doing the reviling she accepted too, seeming to keep both her maternal and her political allegiances intact. She was critical both of the press, in which the defendants had been convicted virtually before they had been arrested, and of the judicial proceedings, in which they had failed to carry a single point, but she kept her moral balance, never allowing her dismay at the public uproar over the death of Seraw to undermine her fundamental abhorrence that it had occurred. It was hard to imagine a better citizen than Dana Anderson. A daughter of her times, she had marched for civil rights and against the war in Vietnam, and she kept her commitments. She worked on behalf of the public schools and library, the community colleges, and other democratic institutions, and she lived in an integrated neighborhood, something which, in Portland, one has to make an effort to do. Then, too, she was a practicing Christian. It was easy to picture her, in another setting, a righteous Gentile. When Engedaw Berhanu told me later that of the many people who were in a position to do so, Dana Anderson was the only one who ever took his hand and said, "I am sorry for what happened to your nephew," I was not surprised. I liked Kyle's mother and I sensed she liked me. We seemed to have much in common. Inadvertently, over the barriers created by our very different connections to the death of Mulugeta Seraw, we became almost friends, a relationship that has both deepened and complicated these words. For her part, although she eventually felt free to discuss her thoughts and feelings with me, she would not speak for Kyle. At her request, people talked with me who would not otherwise have done so, yet she never betrayed a confidence of her son's, never showed me a document from her legal files, never said or did a single thing that might undermine Kyle's belief that his mother was a person he could trust. For my part, there were questions I might have asked the subject of a formal interview that I was reluctant to ask her, for I could guess at the pain they would unloose. I never taped our meetings and rarely even made notes, for to have done so would have violated the spirit of the conversations. Slowly, however, as I began to piece together this portrait of Kyle, I realized that the qualities that I admired in his mother were beside the point. Mother and son were two different people whose biographies would never read the same. In the world, the idealism that was in the very atmosphere of his mother's generation was gone by the time Kyle came of age. In the home, there had been a marriage to a college lover that ended in divorce when Kyle was about three, a development that plainly had different implications for mother and son. Suddenly there were a new stepfather and new siblings. Kyle began using drugs when he was very young. The more I learned the more I saw that Kyle's history was littered with a succession of futile crisis interventions that must have left fundamental problems unresolved. When a friend is sitting in your office crying about a son in prison today you do not push too hard about the things that happened yesterday. We sometimes chatted about the ordinary issues of child rearing—How dirty can a room be? When is hair too long? How much pizza is enough?—rather than graver matters. If she said, "Kyle left home one day," I might smile with her about the fact that he had also packed his lunch, instead of asking, "Why?" If the detectives said, "The neighbors said, 'She was always gone,'" whether that was the neighbors' jealousy, the officers' prejudice, or a fact, I might not probe. What I remember best is the day when, overcome by the darkness that had entered Kyle's life and her own, she pronounced her own judgment on their common family history: "I wasn't a perfect parent—but I wasn't that bad."

. . .

In 1981, when Kyle Brewster was about twelve, a group of white officers from a Portland police precinct dumped four fresh-killed possums at the door of a black-owned restaurant in the heart of the black community. What was unusual about what became known as the "possum incident" was not the slaughter of possums. For some time officers from that precinct had been shooting, clubbing, and running over possums with their patrol cars in a killing game whose rules and tallies were openly posted in the station house. Nor was it the identification of possums with black people that was unusual. For years even liberal Portlanders had believed that the animals were brought to the city by blacks who had come to work in the shipyards during World War II, and the association between the two was so much taken for granted it was part of the language. "Possum" could equal "nigger" or "nigger food" interchangeably. "They" are "stupid," "always breeding," they "take over your neigborhood," "eat garbage," "you have to watch out for them at night"—this was all common usage. The racist metaphor was hardly confined to Portland—"Why does God make armadilloes?" asks the "Nigger Joke Sheet" enjoyed by members of East Side White Pride. "So that niggers can have possums on the half shell" is the answer—but it was entrenched. What was unusual about this particular official insult to the black community in 1981 is that for the first time since blacks had settled in Portland, there was an outcry. Both when it happened, and a few months later when the officers, who had been fired by their commander, were reinstated by an arbitrator, the possum incident brought demonstrators into the streets.

It was already a period of racial turmoil. By 1980 the first phase of liberal compliance with the post–*Brown v. Board of Education* school desegregation guidelines was over and a more militant phase was under way. In Portland, desegregation had consisted in large part of the transfer of black children out of neighborhood schools in which they had formed a majority to innumerable other schools in which there would often be only one black child in a room.

Now, under the leadership of a new coalition called the Black United Front, blacks were seeking a return to neighborhood schools regardless of their racial composition, a demand that not only threatened a number of magnet programs designed to attract whites to the emptied black schoolrooms but clearly elevated self-development over desegregration in the black hierarchy of values. Nor were the struggles limited to the existing K–8 elementary schools, for partly in an effort to enlarge the catchment areas of particular schools to promote integration, middle schools consisting of grades 6–8 were now being carved out of the old K–8 schools, and the location of the new middle schools was intensely controversial. At one point there was a brief but successful boycott in which most of the five thousand black students in the Portland school system stayed home.

While racial policies were ultimately decided at the city's highest political and educational levels, it was at the neighborhood level that they had to be lived out, and it was mainly in the mixed Northeast Portland neighborhoods known as Irvington and Alameda, where Kyle lived with his mother and stepfather, that there was the most living out to be done. The school crisis did not necessarily destroy the interracial friendships that existed in the area—Kyle had black friends from kindergarten on, at least one of whom remained close enough to visit him in jail after Seraw's death—but it did change them. For the first time in the history of Portland the relationship of white to black was not purely noblesse oblige. With the moral force of the civil rights movement as yet unspent, blacks now had a modicum of power. As the militant phase of the civil rights movement came to Portland, the ideals of the white liberals who had supported it and the experiences of their children began to diverge. The progressive parents of the integrated Irvington-Alameda area might diligently explain the historical reasons for the anger the blacks were expressing so freely, but if you were a white child ostracized in the halls of the newly created, largely black Harriet S. Tubman Middle School you might well not care. Kyle himself went to a white-dominated middle school where racial incidents were less likely to occur, but the tensions from the changing school situation still spilled over onto the sidewalks. What seems curious in hindsight about a period when the city was involved in a major reconstruction of the entire public school system on account of race is that the children were not supposed to mention it. The children of that generation were carrying the weight of the massive moral and political transformation of Portland, Oregon, from a segregated to an integrated city, and when their large historical duty encountered small daily obstacles they had no one in the school system to turn to. There was no new curriculum, there were no special counselors, there was no structure of support. Every classmate of Kyle's I talked to has painful memories of experiences from that period having to do with race and school—experiences that the authorities did not address. For a powerful combination of ideological, bureaucratic, and political reasons it seems to have been the position of the school system that its latest policies were so self-evidently Right and Good that the children would just automatically go along. In this atmosphere of discomfort and denial it is not surprising that of all the acts of officialdom as the decade began the one that probably left the clearest impression on the children was the dumping of possums. It said what could no longer be said. When some of the boys in Kyle's class at Grant High School were looking for an outlet for their buried feelings years later, as we will see, the possums came naturally to mind.

Integration was not the only novelty that presented itself to Kyle and his classmates when they were still in elementary school. There were also drugs. As early as the fifth grade Kyle was smoking marijuana and drinking beer and wine, and these were followed in middle school by LSD, heroin, and just about everything else. A history of alcoholism in his family suggests that he may have had a biological predisposition to addiction, if that exists, but, whatever the reasons, between Kyle and drugs there was a natural affinity. As soon as he began "using," he seems to have wanted to "use" more and in the process some of the other pleasures of his childhood, including sports and good grades, were left behind. A 1986 interview with Kyle in his high school newspaper at a time when he was publicly trying to quit quotes him as boasting, "I could get it any time, any day. During the eight years [from 1979 to 1986] I put hundreds of thousands of dollars into drugs. In eighth grade I spent $800 in nine weeks." He got the money by dealing drugs and using stocks and bonds given to him by his grandparents, the article reports. "None of it is left." Since according to his mother those familial stocks and bonds did not exist, his figures are doubtless exaggerated, but it is clear that whatever he did have he spent. From both the 1986 high school interview and a portrait of the family that appeared in 1987 in the bulletin of an adolescent drug treatment program to which his mother and stepfather had turned, it seems that they had sensed something was wrong for some time, though only in a subliminal way. "My mother knew about my problem for five years but every- one told her she was overreacting," Kyle explained. It was not until the summer of 1983, between Kyle's middle school and high school, that the situation came into the open. From the drug treatment bulletin: "Kyle had been out mowing the lawn and a friend kept calling on the phone over and over. Finally, [his mother] said, 'Kyle came in and said to his friend on the phone "I don't have it yet man, but I'll get it and be right down," this moment I knew that he wanted the money for alcohol or drugs and I confronted Kyle about it. It was right then . . . that the bottom fell out of my world.' " Older incidents—a breaking and entering a few years before, missing money, an atmosphere so full of suspicion that, asked to describe their relationship with Kyle before the confrontation, his mother and stepfather called it a "War Zone"—fell into place. But rather than getting better, things got worse. Whatever the world of support groups and counseling into which the family now plunged may have done for the parents, it did little for Kyle. Nothing reached him. In ninth grade, he attended an outpatient drug program, but he also kept doing drugs. In tenth grade, he went to live with his father in a small town on the Oregon coast where "I was continually drinking and was high practically every day. Sometimes I even drank with my dad." That summer his father moved to Alaska and Kyle returned to his mother's house on the condition that he seek treatment for his problem. In August 1985 he started another outpatient program. "Feeling that Kyle was receiving help, the Andersons embarked on a long planned trip and Kyle was left at home with adult supervision. [He] continued to use . . . and did not keep scheduled appointments." When his mother and stepfather returned and realized what was happening they decreed that Kyle must either follow the treatment or live elsewhere, and he left. His father was also now in Portland and Kyle moved in with him to an apartment in which parental guidance was loose enough for at least one of his friends to have gotten the impression Kyle was living in a boarding-house. A poem he wrote called "Smack Sux" suggests that he wanted to stop but couldn't. A longhaired "rocker," he strode through his high school corridors in a heavy leather jacket and chains, the very picture of alienation that year. "Think Brando," advises a classmate. Finally, several months into his junior year, the school authorities acted. Pressed by his mother for an official intervention, they staged a meeting of his mother, stepfather, and father at which all agreed that something must be done. Shortly afterward, Kyle entered a live-in treatment center not far from his house, where gradually the chemistry of the group overcame the chemistry of the body and he decided to quit. In the late spring of 1986, free of drugs for the first time since elementary school, he returned to finish the eleventh grade at Grant.

The high school to which Kyle came back was a difficult place in which to get a foothold. With about a 70-30 white-black ratio it was by far the most integrated high school in the city, and a visitor to the crowded stadiums where Grant's mixed teams battled with the black Jefferson High in football or the white Wilson High in basketball to the cheers of its united supporters could be forgiven the impression that here, at least, all was well. But the reality was much more complicated. The often-quoted conclusion of the 1968 National Advisory Commission on Civil Disorders that "our nation is moving toward two societies, one black, one white—separate and unequal" well described Grant. As far as the academic program was concerned, blacks and whites might almost have been attending separate schools. There were few blacks in the honors classes to which whites could gain admission practically by asking and there were no blacks in the National Honor Society in Kyle's year. In extracurricular affairs, not only were the newspaper, yearbook, dance committees, and all the institutions other than sports that gave the school its identity run by whites, but among the whites who were doing the running were some of the most decadent colonial administrators ever to inherit their posts. Stoned, sloppy, and rude, they seem to have lived their high school years at the intellectual level of a record jacket—and it made very little difference to their futures. Middle-class to begin with, a significant number of Kyle's white classmates made their ways out of their drug-filled haze to good colleges east and west, and careers beyond. The working-class blacks, on the other hand, were going nowhere and everyone knew it. Yet no one was permitted to acknowledge it. A pious editorial titled "Racism Minor" in the usually facetious *Grantonian* in late 1986 proclaimed that "having attended public, racially well-mixed schools since kindergarten . . . Grant students are able to work with each other and blend into a spirited student body," but the truth was otherwise. Those kindergarten friendships were wearing thin. Instead of an open discussion of race and class that might at least have turned the focus beyond Grant toward the long histories with which everyone in the present was having to live, there was only mush. The black students were voiceless, but the whites had—possums. "Speaking of oppossums. Golly there sure has been a big hullaballo concerning these demonic beasts as of late," read a column by the *Grantonian*'s two featured columnists, "Mike" and "Bo," in 1987. "Not a Monday goes by without talk among the Studs of Grant High about weekend road kills. Hot oppossum pizza. Grantonians speak with pride about murdering the wicked creatures. [A popular senior] boasts that he had already killed two opposums in 1987, with nothing more than a modidified baseball bat. Mike and Bo say hunting season is open. Let's rid city of the evil opposums that roam the streets and sewers." The column was accompanied by a ratlike caricature captioned, "The possum is the Anti-Christ" that, however hilarious it may have seemed to white students, could only have given black students a chill.

The relative contributions of drugs, race, and sheer American adolescence to the culture of Grant in the late 1980s are impossible to disentangle. Society in general also played a role. For an age group instinctively sensitive to adult hollowness, the Reagan era was not exactly an inspiration. Blame it on fear of nuclear war, blame it on creeping economic stagnation, blame it on MTV, but whoever or whatever is to blame, the world of the students of Grant High School during Kyle's years was a profoundly cynical one that took the measure of the parent society and flaunted back its unacknowledged corruption. "We are evil, but evil is good," read the epigraph of the opening "Mike and Bo" column their senior year. When Kyle was voted Homecoming King that fall, it was in the same spirit. "The system," not Kyle, was being mocked. Kyle was genuinely popular. That a recovering stoner with bad grades, a newly shaved head, and a drinking problem should be their sovereign just happened to be what the students wanted to say. How Kyle felt about this ironic homage we will never know. On the surface, at least, he was comfortable. A member of the football team, a record reviewer for the *Grantonian*, a vocalist in a band called Da Junk, he was very much at the center of things. If anything, he seems to have been more grounded than most. His remarks to the student interviewing him about drugs, his record column, a comment to the yearbook photographer about playing varsity—"I grew up in this neighborhood and always knew that I'd go to Grant. It is something I took pride in. It feels good to know that I went out there and made a commitment to represent Grant High"—all have a sincerity that is not the school's characteristic tone. His record column in particular has an independent authority that is the voice not of someone playing to fashion but of someone trying to be his own man. The obstacle to Kyle's efforts to take himself seriously his senior year was that he was not taken seriously by others. Nicknamed "the mighty Kyle Brewster," he was looked on by the college-bound boys with whom he worked on the paper as a plaything and by the girls as a stud. "What is the most ridiculous assignment you've ever had?" asks a squib in the 1987 yearbook. "Getting married to Kyle Brewster" was one girl's response. "He was 'buff,' " another girl remembered. "My girlfriends used to talk about his ass." When racism was added to his personae during the course of the year: when he mentioned Skrewdriver in his columns: when he was heard muttering racial epithets in the corridors: that was not taken seriously either. Once he was thrown out of a party at the home of a liberal classmate for insulting blacks who were present—but only once. But "culture" can only explain so much. When an open racist in an integrated school is also the class mascot, a political interpretation is called for, and it seems to me that the celebration of Kyle Brewster that took place at Grant that year was not only a reflection of its general in-your-face cynicism but an expression of something more. In a way, he was like the opossums. Speaking at the 1987 Commencement, Governor Neil Goldschmidt, whose son was in Kyle's class, praised the Homecoming King's much-publicized victory over drugs as a symbol that "America permits many false starts, but where there is talent and desire there will be success." What the students knew that the governor did not know was that he was already a symbol of something else.

The summer after graduation Kyle moved out and it was in the space once filled by drugs and school that his new identity was hardened. Several people commented to me that Kyle seemed suddenly to change in this period. First came the hair. He had shaved his head for the first time in high school when his father ordered him to "get a haircut" and again the fall of his senior year when many members of the football team did the same, but now it carried an unmistakable meaning. Next, the tattoos: "WHITE POWER" across his chest, not just any "White Power" but an Aryan one, with the SS lightning bolts and a large swastika with a menacing skull in the center; "SKINS," in large letters across the back of his neck; "RIGHT WING," signified by an elaborate dragon, on his right upper arm; and "THE SOUTH WILL RISE AGAIN," together with a skinhead in Doc Martens and braces brandishing a Confederate flag, on his left. He got a job delivering blueprints for a small firm that also employed Ken Mieske, shared an apartment with another skinhead—"Prick"—and settled into a new routine in which race would play a leading role. It was 1987 and he was eighteen years old. This was the time that the skinheads who would become East Side White Pride were just beginning to come together. Kyle kept many of his older friends, both from Grant and from the music scene. He had the same girlfriend, Patty Copp, whom he had had off and on for several years. He played basketball, rode bikes, went to movies. He even went home for dinner from time to time. But he was not simply drifting, he had a direction. His old world had ended, but a new one was taking its place.

16

When Steven Strasser was arrested for heading a gang of armed skinheads in an attempted attack on alleged black pimps at a downtown Portland nightclub in October 1986, he had a singular experience of leadership. According to the police report, as he was charged with riot and placed in a patrol car, "his comrades attempted to free him from custody and 23 police officers, [a] Mounted Patrol Unit, and 3 dogs were used to quell the disturbance." Cries of "Free the Prisoner!" and "Free Steve Strasser!" rang briefly in the air. Unlike Ken Mieske and Kyle Brewster, famous in their own circles long before Portland ever heard the name Mulugeta Seraw, Steve Strasser, the third member of East Side White Pride involved in the killing, was generally inconspicuous. He had

left home in a Denver suburb in 1983 at fifteen and come to Portland to live with an uncle on a small farm in the northwest hills
where you could gaze out at three great Cascade peaks—Mount St.
Helens, Mount Adams, and Mount Hood—but such bucolic pleasures were not that compelling to a young punk rocker and he seems
to have spent more of his time in town. His relatives were part of
a mellow rural subculture in which those on the way up, those on
the way down, and those on the way nowhere found common
ground in their mutual desire to live as they pleased, and the school
he entered in Portland was much the same—a loose, democratic,
citywide K–12 magnet known as the Metropolitan Learning Center,
which overrode distinctions of wealth and class to offer an array of
children united mainly by their common resistance to "structure"
and "authority" the freedom to be themselves. It was a school where
you could do as much or as little as you chose, and its graduates
went off both to first-rate colleges on the one hand and to peniten-
tiaries on the other; but what was doubtless even more attractive to
Steve Strasser about the MLC than its educational theories was its
location, for it was right in the middle of the Northwest Portland
neighborhood where the early members of Portland United Skinheads (PUSH) did their hanging out, and it was among just that
collection of nocturnal phantoms that he found his place.

The newcomer was eager to please. He was "ingratiating,"
remarked one of his teachers at the MLC. "I had the feeling that if
you asked him to go to the window and jump out he would do it."
His new comrades noticed that too. He was a follower, "a *real* follower," one of his ESWP friends emphasized. "He's the kind of guy
you would say, you know, you'd be sitting around like, 'God, I need
a pack of cigarettes. Hey, go up to the store for me and get a pack
of cigarettes.' And he'd go." He was always doing people favors.
When he had money he gave it away and when he didn't he made
no demands. The friend: "I'd say, 'Steve, you hungry?' 'No, just
having a cup of coffee.' 'Come on, order something to eat, man.
You got to eat.' 'No, no, no.' And then he'd get his paycheck and
he'd buy beer for everyone. I remember walking to a tattoo parlor

and him seeing some scraggly old bum and going, 'Joe! Hey! I haven't seen you in months!'—and he went into his pocket and 'This is all I got, man,' and I'm like, 'Steve, Steve, it's your last two dollars, don't do that.' 'Oh, I know him, we used to hang out together' "—and his money would be gone. Steve's loyalty extended to the street. He did not go out of his way to find trouble, but if it found him, he stood his ground. "If I said, 'Look, Steve, this is so-and-so, my friend,' he'd be, 'Okay, great.' And if I left and was gone and fifteen people came and started pushing my friend around, Steve would do what he could because I told him this was my friend. He literally jumped in front of a guy wielding a knife at me one night, which [was] the most incredible thing I ever saw because I've never been so scared in my life." He was kind to animals and to the younger students at the MLC who sometimes tagged along after the older ones and got in their way, and when one of his earlier girlfriends had become pregnant and had the baby, he loved his infant daughter with his whole heart.

The setting for this sweetness of character was the underground music scene beginning around 1984, the year of the first swastikas in the Portland sidewalks. As the PUSH skinheads turned from punk rock to British Oi music, Steve Strasser was swept along. He was what he heard, and whether it was punk, which called for one style, or Oi, for another, he always looked the part. In a photo in the MLC yearbook published in spring 1986, he is still a punk wearing a Mohawk, but sometime later that year he shaved his head. With the look came the politics. In spite of the egalitarian atmosphere both of his uncle's farm, a loose, sixties-style communal place where the door was literally always open, and of the Metropolitan Learning Center, where he had black, Mexican, and Asian friends, he began developing racist ideas, and if they never reached great depths they seem to have reached farther than anything in Steven Strasser had previously reached and they were not lightly held. A friend he had known since he moved to Portland recalls getting a phone call around the time Steve became a skinhead demanding an answer to the question "Are you a Jew?" A one-page paper among his effects

entitled "Encounter with Niggers" appears to be a deliberate chart-
ing of his efforts to raise his own consciousness. "SHIT, STUPID
FUCKING NIGGER! Shine my boots. Monkey Face" is scrawled
across the bottom of the page. As sincere in his beliefs as in other
things, even when it was in plainly in his interest to deny them, he
never did. In the police interviews that followed the killing, and in
talking to the psychologist conducting the presentence investigation
that was his only hope of influencing the judge, he stuck to his
position on "separatization." "Everybody should be racially conscious. . . . People should have the choice to be separate," he maintained. Norman Mailer once wrote that evil is to know what is good
and do one's best to tamper with it, whereas wickedness is merely
one's readiness to raise the stakes when one doesn't know what one
is doing, and by that standard, Steve Strasser was merely wicked.
He understood very little. As the criminal and then the civil case
moved along he realized that by things that he did or didn't say or
do he had a chance to affect his own standing and he began to
protect himself, but he never grasped the moral picture. From jail
he wrote his family about "the biggest mistake I probably made" in
the whole situation. The "mistake" was not becoming a racist, which
led to his involvement in East Side White Pride. It was not being
part of the fight that killed Mulugeta Seraw. It was the moment
after the fight when he gave his housemates a graphic picture of
what happened and cast himself in a central role. The "mistake" was
"telling the people I lived with what happened."

17

The winter of 1987–88 was a fine time to be a skinhead in Portland,
Oregon. Not only were there more all the time, but among those
who had been skinheads for a little longer, a greater sense of historical mission began to take hold. Beneath the humdrum details of
daily existence—the humiliating jobs, the crummy apartments, the
endless consumption of beer and burritos—a movement was swell-

ing worldwide that linked their narrow provincial existence to one of the boldest visions in human history and they were part of it. Indeed, they were in the vanguard. The first issue of the Skrewdriver publication *Blood and Honour,* "The Independent Voice of Rock against Communism," with its invocation of "National Socialism and its great martyr, Adolf Hitler," which appeared around that time, reached Portland almost at once and was passed around pad to pad, hand to hand. As word came in about skinheads in Chicago or Detroit who were standing ready to carry the white man's burden into the streets and actually doing it, so too did the skinheads elsewhere hear of Portland. Everywhere one turned, there were brothers. When a Portland skinhead was beaten up by blacks on a city bus and an account appeared in the news, he was consoled by a skinhead from clear on the other side of the state. "Sorry about your beating you got from them fucken ape nigger baboons I wish I would of been on that bus it would of been one on one. I bet all them white people that didn't help you on the bus are either scared of there own shadow or nigger loven faggit one of the two," the note began. There was also the thrill of intellectual discovery. Books and articles on fascism, catalogs of Nazi memorabilia and militaria, biographies of Himmler and Göring began to fill their shelves. "I follow my course with the precision and security of a sleepwalker." "I cannot be mistaken. What I do & say is historical." "HEIL HITLER, Our Savior," read the notes made by one skinhead from his study of *Mein Kampf.* "In the first period of our movement's development, we suffered from nothing so much as from the insignificance, the unknownness of our names, which in themselves made our success questionable. The hardest thing in this first period, when often only six, seven, or eight heads met together . . . was to arouse and preserve in this tiny circle faith in the mighty future of the movement," Hitler also wrote. The skinhead reader also noted that.

The new sense of solidarity was immediately reflected on the street. "Skinheads are violent and if they're not, they're not skinheads," is how one of them put it. Violence was the heart of their

identities. High on beer and on the sheer physical joy of being skinheads, they made their Saturday night rounds, marking their territory with stickers and swastikas, insulting interracial couples, baiting
individual blacks and gays. Wildest were their own fights, those
sacred, unpredictable moments when a party would be brought to
a sudden standstill by the eruption of a white-on-white boot party
whose outcome, sometimes involving the eyesight, kidneys, or even
lives of the losers, could remain in doubt for days. Less often, bands
of cruising skins would jump out of their cars to confront a group
of blacks, at least once even challenging a gang of Bloods in Pioneer
Courthouse Square. At the same time as the skinheads were exult-
ing in their private, existential experiences of power and domination, they were starting to try to find ways to work together.
Skinheads have enemies, therefore skinheads need friends: it was a
natural progression. It was now that both East Side White Pride and
POWAR came together out of the same underground community
and were joined by a third group, known as Youth of Hitler. East
Side White Pride chose an informal, leaderless structure in which
no one had more authority than anyone else and there were no
written rules, while POWAR struggled to write its bylaws. "The
organization stands for the preservation, purity and safety of the
white race. We are warriors for this cause and we must uphold these
beliefs for future generations," began the POWAR preamble. "To
preserve the white Race by keeping faith in our ancestors and not
polluting our blood by race-mixing. To guard the white race by
helping other whites and keeping mud races and trash from polluting and destroying our people. To this cause and these beliefs we
will forever stay faithful, loyal and dedicated." There followed a set
of rules governing the admission of new members, standards both
for the conduct of meetings and for conduct in general, and a hierarchy of officers from a president "to enforce all business . . . and
head all judicial settings" to a sergeant at arms "to keep charge of
the colors" next to which ESWP's looser, more brotherly style looks
practically anarchic.

. . .

Of all the Nazis living or dead who might be said to have encouraged the Portland skinheads to see themselves as part of a larger political movement, none was closer at hand than an obscure medical transcriptionist at Emanuel Hospital, Rick Cooper, who was also publisher of a quarterly newsletter called the National Socialist Vanguard *Report*. Cooper, who graduated from high school in the Northeast in 1964, became interested in National Socialism during a turn in the service from 1964 to 1968, when he came to feel that everything he had been taught about the interchangeability of whites and blacks was a lie and that the blacks were not equal after all. "Why the lie? In whose interest is this lie?" he pondered to himself, until one day in his questionings he came upon *Mein Kampf* and the veils fell from his eyes: It was the Jews! The Jews are afraid that people will recognize that they themselves are a race rather than a religion and that is why they have loosed such nonracial ideals as communism and integration upon the world! The Jews are behind the blacks! He saw it now! Over the next years he educated himself further about other truths the latter-day Elders of Zion did not want the public to know, and in 1969 he found his way to the Virginia headquarters of the National Socialist White People's Party (NSWPP), successor to the American Nazi Party founded by George Lincoln Rockwell in 1958, and became its business manager.

All the while that Rick Cooper was entering the small, Hitler-worshiping underworld that was still the American Nazi movement in the 1970s, however, he was careful to maintain another life. During his initial ideological conversion he was attending Boston University and the University of New Hampshire; he later got a degree in mathematics in California. When he was working with the NSWPP in Arlington, Virginia, he took time out to run the Baltimore Marathon: "Time: 3:32:45 over hilly course placing in top 45% of finishers," says a photo postcard he still occasionally sends out of a lean, well-muscled, dark-haired young man in red running shorts and blue shoes. Morally offended by the financial dependence of the party leadership on a far-flung membership with whom its only connection was to collect dues, he refused to make his living from what he always calls "the White Nationalist Movement" and he believed other people should do the same. In 1983, he moved to Salinas, California, where with two comrades he formed the National Socialist Vanguard, a nonmembership, non-dues-paying organization consisting of the three of them, whose educational bulletin, the NSV *Report*, would be distributed free. They also founded a carpet-cleaning business known as ST—for Storm Trooper—Enterprises, partly to stay afloat but partly because of their deeper belief that if they did their jobs right, the day would come when they could throw away their Clark Kent glasses, strip off their ST uniforms, and their customers would realize that the prompt, courteous, reliable service people with the most powerful cleaning equipment in the area were—Aryans! The ultimate dream of the NSV triumvirate was to establish a racialist compound, to be known as Wolfstadt, somewhere in the "White Territorial Imperative" of the western United States, where the alien hordes their map showed entering the country from all directions had not yet taken hold. In 1985, they moved to Goldendale, Washington, a town of about thirty-five hundred people 115 miles east of Portland, where they hoped "to open a National Socialist headquarters on Interstate 84 and raise the swastika banner high above the Columbia River." Although for a while things went well because the area had never had a commercial vacuum service before, soon all the rural carpets that were going to be cleaned had been cleaned, and one of the Vanguard took their powerful, expensive equipment to another location. At around the same time Rick Cooper had an encounter with the local police over an allegedly stolen credit card that led to his exposure in the press and resulted in his large idea of an Aryan haven where committed racialists from around the country could safely await the Hitlerian resurrection dwindling into the small reality of a handful of Goldendale teenagers ambiguously "Sieg Heiling" him on the street. In late 1987, Cooper moved to Portland to work as he had earlier as a medical transcriptionist, commuting to Goldendale on weekends to continue to publish the *Report*. He started to meet the Portland skins. At the same time he was becoming known to the Portland media as a resource. Immersed in the history and personalities of the white supremacist movement, he could lead them through the characters in the Order story or the Aryan Nations as the occasion arose and he could put them in closer touch with the local out-croppings they were beginning to sense all around. What's more, he was always on time. Straightforward. Unthreatening. Cooperative. Here was a Nazi you could trust. No one had ever fired Rick Cooper for incivility or incompetence. He did his job. When the ABC-TV affiliate KATU began looking for another point of view to include in a planned public affairs show on racism in early 1988, it asked him to put out the word.

On March 20, 1988, less than two weeks after a violent assault by three skinheads on a man from Singapore named Hock-Seng Chin and his white wife as they were leaving a downtown Chinese res-taurant with their small daughter, ten Portland skinheads dressed in ordinary street clothes appeared with Rick Cooper on the widely watched Sunday evening talk show *Town Hall* to explain their posi-tions on racism. This move from the propaganda of the deed to the propaganda of the word was extremely well timed, and the skin-heads knew it. The Chin assault had left the press and the public at last unable to ignore what was happening in the streets and it was obvious that the Portland police would soon be more on their tails. At the time of the program these representative skinheads were at exactly that point in their political development where the idea of a strategy was no longer entirely foreign, and they took their responsibility seriously. Outreach was the order of the day. They even prepared in advance for their appearance, assembling a list of "Points to Stress"—such as "We have good reason for anti-social attitudes. A) It's difficult to find work because of all the non-whites infiltrating our country. B) They are just as prejudiced as we are &

hate us just as much as we hate them. C) We are sick of seeing white girls mongrelizing the race by latching onto pimps & pushers to stay alive"—some of which they actually managed to voice on the program. To the relief both of the management and of Rick, the show went smoothly. Weapons stowed, they passed through the metal detectors without incident, followed the orders of the nervous KATU security force, stayed calm and expressionless even in the face of the ridicule greeting Rick's comment that "the only total solution to racial problems is total geographical separation," and, in spite of the fact that the liberal speeches they were forced to listen to would at other times have made them gag, avoided throwing up. A POWAR skin had an actual exchange with a black state senator on the relative proportions of black-on-white crime to white-on-black crime. ESWP's Kyle Brewster contributed seriously to a discussion of racial stereotyping: "stuffy," "not culturally active," "locked up in their houses all the time," "just worried about money" were some of the things he said other people believed about whites. Off as well as on camera, the skinheads were polite to the other guests. Immediately following the program, the hosts indicated they would like to do another one, this time featuring skinheads alone, and the alternative newspaper *Willamette Week* began planning a major article. Another TV station also began developing a story. "Almost overnight, the Portland skins have emerged from the status of relatively ignored, loosely associated White racial youth to that of a more visible part of Portland's society and, more importantly, an integral part of the U.S. White Nationalist Movement," crowed Rick jubilantly in the next NSV *Report*. Considering all that was flowing from the successful *Town Hall* appearance, it was a reasonable claim.

The association between Rick Cooper and the Portland skinheads was not a one-way matter. Isolated after his move to the city, Cooper probably needed the skinheads more than they needed him, not only for companionship but for political reassurance. They gave him a sense of purpose. With the matter-of-factness that was so much part of his nature, he had no illusion that the skinheads would see him as anything other than the uncharismatic character he knew himself to be, but he could still offer them something. What he lacked in charm he made up for in usefulness. When the first issue of *Blood and Honour* arrived from England with the note "Rick: Use this with your skinheads," he knew just who would want to see it. When a flier arrived from the Chicago Area Skinheads' band, Romantic Violence, and Tom Metzger's WAR seeking support for a Skrewdriver tour of the country, he knew just where to pass it along. Through his own long-standing friendships with such key white supremacists as Tom Metzger in California and the Aryan Nations's Reverend Richard Butler in Idaho, he changed the skinheads' perceptions of them from glamorous but unapproachable strangers to ordinary human beings on whose support they could really call. There were many tensions in this relationship. As far as some of the skinheads were concerned, Rick Cooper was such a geek he gave the entire movement a bad name. He was a social embarrassment. Making one's living as a secretary was bad enough, but with his long, thin neck and thick glasses and a colorlessness bordering on servility, he looked like a bank teller in an old western about to hand over all the money to the robbers. As for Rick, he was continually worried that the skinheads could not be controlled. Talk about bad names. Rick himself was so upright he was puritanical, while many skins were involved in drugs, theft, and other criminal activity of which he roundly disapproved. Some of them did not even have jobs. It was great for the Vanguard to have a movement to be the vanguard of at last, but the skinheads were so wild and unorganized it was hard to know what they would do. When a skinhead follower of Tom Metzger's had called Oprah Winfrey a "monkey" to her face right on national television not long before, Cooper feared it had done more harm than good. As radical as were Rick Cooper's ideas, he was temperamentally conservative, while the skinheads were radical on the street. While Cooper generally took the long view, for the skinheads everything was of the moment. When KATU asked him to help organize skinheads for a second *Town Hall* program featuring POWAR, he urged POWAR's members to think of the future. "Our goal is to gain sympathy and eventual support from people watching *Town Hall* in the comfort of their homes," he reminded them.

The May 15, 1988, appearance of the POWAR skinheads and their supporters on *Town Hall* marked both the high point of POWAR's influence in Portland and the beginning of its downfall. Having agreed in advance that the moment was ripe for an appeal over the obstacle of the media directly to the hearts and minds of the people, the skinheads were so soft and reasonable they were practically mushy—a performance that more or less fooled the host and guests but did not fool other skinheads, who knew a sellout when they saw one. Sitting with their jackets off and their tattoos showing as the studio lights got warmer and warmer, the *Town Hall* skinheads denied their connection to Hitler and Nazism, denied that they were white supremacists rather than separatists, denied violence—they even apologized to Chin, who was in the audience, for the behavior of their fellow skinheads. According to legend, they had their asses kicked on the street immediately afterward by other skinheads who were watching the show at bars near the studio—and their reputations never recovered. Kelly McNeice, a relative newcomer to Portland who had been hanging out with POWAR and was one of the more outspoken skinheads on the show, confessed in a POWAR newsletter, "I am sorry I bowed down so quickly to ZOG's* power." Michelle Colmus, the skinhead girl involved in the 1986 Satyricon murder who was one of Ken Mieske's prison correspondents, explained in an editorial signed "Bargaining for Time" that the skinheads had known exactly what they were doing in cultivating the audience and that the end would eventually justify the means. Still, it was a delicate position. The word was out. "In the last 6 months here we have been witness to total communist exploitation in the media," Kyle Brewster wrote to a group of skins in Grand Rapids, Michigan, known as the Pit Bull Boys.

*"ZOG": Zionist Occupation Government, a shorthand for Jewish power commonly used on the racist right.

The skinhead name in Portland has been dragged through the mud for higher TV ratings and more newspaper sales. A group of "skins" in town went on a local show called Town Hall, much like a small scale Donahue. They called themselves sepratists not supremicists. They denounced skinheads as being violent. I don't know about you, but I don't look for trouble, but when it comes I'll face it with every last ounce of pride in my body. These sissyish faggots that call themselves skinheads even went as far as to applaud a black woman because they agreed with what she said. These same fools did a newspaper article for a local paper and got slandered themselves by the paper. . . . These two incidents have caused much unneeded attention. We cant even go to most places in town because we get ousted. The skins that were a part of that mess have since been excommunicated from us. We only want strong minded, intelligent young men and women to be a part of this world movement.

With his name more battered than his boots, POWAR's Kelly McNeice left town for a sudden visit to the Confederate Hammer Skins of Dallas, Texas, where he could bask briefly in their reflected militance and also write another newsletter report. Originally from Oklahoma, where California WAR leader Tom Metzger was planning to hold an "Aryan Woodstock" featuring, among others, a Tulsa skinhead band known as the Boot Boys, Kelly seems to have also taken this opportunity to visit home. His fellow POWAR skinhead Michelle Colmus went along. The purpose of the trip was vague, but the politics of the Portland skinhead movement had suddenly gotten so complicated that any perspective they could get on it was bound to give them a hand.

18

Summer 1988. POWAR down. ESWP up. Very up. Of the couple of hundred racist skinheads around town, only fifteen to twenty are actually associated with East Side White Pride, but many want to be. ESWP is what's happening. A movement is also what's happening. With their new post office box and new stamp they are beginning to buy stickers and fliers from racist organizations all over the country and give them an ESWP return address. It is just what the racist organizations want them to do. "Xerox these to make more to pass out. Double your effectiveness," a note enclosed in one of the batches of fliers urges. They also sketch some fliers of their own. Charged by a heightened sense of connection not only with one another but with the world, they roam the streets with a little more purpose than before. They sense power. Separately, too, things are going well for them. Of the three members of East Side White Pride who are central to this story, Steve Strasser has stopped pining for the mother of his baby daughter and found a well-off suburban girlfriend, Heidi Martinson. Kyle Brewster has moved in with the skinhead known as Prick to the apartment on Hawthorne that is the unofficial headquarters of ESWP and has gone back to his on-again, off-again high school girlfriend, Patty Copp, who is showing her commitment to his interests by beginning to take up white pride. Julie Belec is pregnant with the baby of Ken Mieske's they intend to name Joseph, after Mengele. It is to Ken that the most important things are happening. Through his stage work for CartWellShows he has gotten to know many bands and he is asked to go on tour with the Monsters of Rock concert that summer. Even more important, Lockjaw has packed up its equipment for the last time and two of its members invite Ken to become the singer for a new band. Another member of his short-lived band, Sudden Infant Death, is also joining, there is a fifth, from Dead Conspiracy, and here at last is the band Ken has been hearing in his head since he first got into music, Machine, a group whose sound is so hard, fast, loud, and violent that it is different from any band around. Even its poster is different, a collage of violent headlines, "The Violent Brain . . . addicted to violence . . . savage rapist of a 5-year-old girl . . . A gun is a great equalizer . . . If Hitler Asked You to Electrocute a Stranger Would You? . . . Cop kills baby . . . Warning: Material May be too INTENSE for those easily offended," and more. In July Machine plays at a small club in North Portland. Next is Satyricon. In August, while Ken is on the road, there is good news. Larry Hurwitz, impresario, is staging a huge twenty-band MetalFest at his club Starry Night the week after Labor Day. He wants Machine to open.

September 10, 1988. Dusk. The hall is only starting to fill. Up to the mike steps Larry Hurwitz, "ARE [significant pause] YOU [significant pause] READY [significant pause] FOR [very significant pause] MACHINE?" Ken takes the mike and withdraws to the side and the others find their places and then he is back, running back and forth across the stage, arms huge beneath his Holy Terror T-shirt, a hairy beast, a wrestler, a creature for which the observer instinctively imagines the protective barriers of cage or ring. For the rest of the act he never stops moving. Stalking, hulking, squeezing, leaping, shaking his head up and down so fiercely it looks like the force that drives it begins below the waist and ends past the brain. And the voice. This is not "singing." This is screaming, growling, shouting, grunting, the words a series of guttural undecipherable sounds. The numbers are "Bloodbath," "I Need a Gun," "Guns and Liquor": "Drunk and obnoxious, and I've got a gun, I am going to go out and kill someone": brutal images brutally delivered: and while he is delivering them Ken Mieske is truly their messenger not only because he knows the feelings but because he is an actor who understands becoming and he knows how to let his whole being be flooded by whatever is happening now: what he doesn't know is how not to. Somehow, he is not ridiculous. In the other bands the players leap, kick, twist, and growl and look merely childish or silly or sometimes even accidentally joyful, but Ken is convincing. Commanding the space, he is the incarnation of aggression and rage, there is no separation between Mieske and Death, the moment is elemental and professional at the same time, and Ken knows it, and the band knows it, and the audience knows it: this is part of what the rock scene has always been about: this is real: in the transmutation of his life's horrors into what is called music Ken Death has found his calling. Scouts in the audience? Listen! High from the set, the band members head downstairs for phase 2 of the evening, a continuation of their intensity by other means, an interview for a concert video modeled after Penelope Seferis's *The Decline of Western Civilization* being made by a local filmmaker. Here too they are explosive. Packed into a space so small it is a testimony to the guts of their female interviewer, they are wild and outrageous, somewhere on the line between "infantile" and "adolescent," outdoing one another with jokes about sex education and maggots in diapers, Ken and the drummer shamelessly competitive, unable to stay still, Ken mugging, burping, coughing into the drummer's face, flinging himself backward onto someone else's lap, the drummer repeatedly opening his mouth, pulling back his cheeks, and lewdly wiggling his tongue, the object of all this obscenity being—the camera. To the question "How do you guys want people to feel when they hear your music?" answered by the band that followed them as, "Good. Having fun," the drummer replies, "I want them to hate it," and Ken, "We want everybody to run around and start knocking each other in the face and throwing people on the ground," and they mean it: it is how they see Machine. Question: "Do you guys do serious amounts of drugs?" Ken: "We're drug-free. We drink, we get drunk, we get fucked up, we kill, we party, we drink, and we kill again." Question: "Where do you work?" Ken: "I work for Cart-WellShows, production manager." Interviewer: "That's cool." Ken: "Yeah. Fun beating people up for free." "What do you guys do during the day?" Drummer: "We sit around in closets and we—" Ken: "We sit around, we drink, we kill people, we have . . ." "What influenced you?" "Alcohol." "Ted Bundy." "Girlfriends who beat us up." "What kind of women appeal to you?" "Sluts." "Where do you want to be in five years?" Drummer: "Dead." They are joking, but they are not joking: it is the punk defense again. Ken alone is political, slipping in a number of references to Mengele, Richard Butler, ZOG, and the Zionists, but always for the laugh ("On our white skin we don't do drugs"), leaving room both for himself and for the others to take them back if they have to, just as Machine can evade

its songs by maintaining they are only about "reality," plausible deni-
ability being a useful commodity not only in politics but in rock.
Out of these gestures, these attitudes, a star is born. On the walls
of Starry Night after the killing someone will scrawl, "Ken Death
Lives!!!"

But for the moment Ken Death is offstage, he is through incarnating
reality, and he is thirsty. With the kegs not to be opened till the
last band has played, Ken and Julie make their way over to Kyle
and Prick's, where a number of East Side White Pride members and
other skinheads are hanging out. Whatever the skinheads have been
doing earlier in the evening, they are drinking now, and there is
plenty of beer. They load beer and themselves into three cars, cross
into downtown, and head toward Portland's showcase Washington
Park, driving fast, noisily, up through a series of elegant curves till
they arrive at the Rose Garden parking lot with its classic view of
Mount Hood visible sometimes even at night, framed by firs. It is
just such a night, clear and fine. The moon lights the sky. Racing
down the broad steps toward the gracious amphitheater where they
can loll with their beer, past the prize roses, "Sunflare," "Marina,"
and, yes, "Marian Anderson," they are approached by four large
white Portland State University football players who are also drinking, and for a moment the skinheads are afraid that the Vikings
dislike skinheads and will start something, but it is not so: "Right
on!" and "Let's go get some niggers and fags!" is what they hear. For
the next half hour they party together, one big racist family, but
suddenly they are out of beer. Heading up the stairs en masse the
skinheads collide with two more white men heading down, a skinhead demands a cigarette and is refused—the man has none—and
the skinhead knocks him down, kicks him in the head with his boots
until the man is practically unconscious, and throws him down the
stairs. Now the Vikings do balk—"Picking on one of your own?"
they challenge—and a white fight is just about to begin when in the
parking lot under the firs there appears a better target: a black and

white couple holding hands. The skins dance around, needling—
"Don't you know to stick to your own kind?"—and the girlfriend
pulls the boyfriend back—"Come! Don't get into it!"—and with half
the skins down below still beating the cigaretteless white man and
his friend and the other half up above terrorizing the couple in the
parking lot, the evening is finally coming into its own. Piling into
their cars once more, they leave Washington Park, speeding down
the curving drive, from the sublime to the seedy, right into the
parking lot of the downtown Safeway. They have never been more
together. Ken is in the lead—he has the ID. As they march into the
store fifteen or twenty strong straight toward the beer cooler singing
Skrewdriver's "Jewel in the Sea," the pride of the British Empire is
in their hearts. At the cooler they meet an opposing force, a black
security guard named Carl Carlyle, who does indeed dislike skinheads, and as his attempts to get them to shut up and stop intimidating the other shoppers are met with "Nigger," he dislikes them
even more. As the skinheads swarm past the checkout stand, one of
them spits at the cashier who refuses to sell him the beer, there is
one loud "Nigger!" too many, Carlyle takes his club and brings it
down on the face of one of the skinheads, smashing his nose, the
skinheads are out the door, Kyle Brewster turning back to taunt
Carlyle, "Come on out, nigger boy! Come out!" and, in spite of
being held back by the other employees, Carlyle is out too, it does
not take much taunting, he wants to come, it is not so much his
job, it is his honor he has to defend, and the fight is on. Instantly
he is surrounded. With so many against one it is hard to see what
he might do, but he is not a guard for nothing and he is holding his
own when someone not in the circle of which he is the center breaks
into it from behind and stabs him in the back, puncturing his lung.
He collapses. The skinheads scatter, signaling each other to keep
their mouths shut. And they do. This is what they want to be known
for: brotherhood. Kyle is picked up and let off the same night, Ken
is in jail for a week, others are interrogated, but though all the
members of East Side White Pride know who did it and discuss it
freely among themselves, their solidarity holds. Nor are the other

witnesses forthcoming. They are frightened. There is little evidence. There is only one person in Portland besides the skinheads who thinks he knows what happened, a police intelligence officer named Larry Siewert, who has been watching them since before the 1986 murder at Satyricon. He hears that the skinhead who did the stabbing also cut his own hand with the knife, and at the building where Kyle and Prick live he hears from the manager that the night of the stabbing there was a trail of blood from the parking lot right to their apartment door. Larry Siewert is a sharp observer, he is good man, he knows exactly where the skinhead movement has been and where it is going, and he is worried. He tells his bosses that with all that drinking and violence it is only a matter of time before someone dies. He hopes for prosecution but Carl Carlyle is just a security guard from Flint, Michigan, he recovers, and no one else seems to care very much. Later, charges from the Safeway incident will be folded into the charges against Ken and Kyle for the Seraw killing, but for the moment nothing happens. Jim Cartland also issues a warning. Talking to Ken on the phone during the week Ken spends in jail, Jim tells him, "You keep hanging out with those people, someone's going to get killed." Says Ken Death: "I should have took his advice."

ARYAN UPDATE

I spend a lot of time talking with reporters. The one question they always ask is if some black or some Jewish kid years ago beat me up. That is not how I became the way I am today.

—TOM METZGER, 1996

19

JANUARY 30, 1989

ATTENTION OPERATOR! THIS NUMBER TAKES NO COLLECT CALLS!

YOU HAVE REACHED ARYAN UPDATE, A PRODUCTION OF WAR, WHITE ARYAN RESISTANCE, PO BOX 65, FALLBROOK, CA. 92028. FOR A SAMPLE COPY OF THE WAR 16-PAGE NEWSPAPER SEND $1, OR $20 FOR ONE YEAR'S SUBSCRIPTION WHICH INCLUDES A COMPLETE LIST OF OUR VIDEOTAPE LIBRARY.

DATELINE—NEW YORK CITY: BRUCE, THE "JEW ANTI-SKIN" SKINHEAD WHO APPEARED ON THE GERALDO SHOW FREE-FOR-ALL, HAS TOLD US YOU CAN REACH THE LEADER OF THE JEWISH DEFENSE ORGA-NIZATION, MORDECHAI "THE MOUSE" LEVY AT TELEPHONE NUMBER 212-477-6243. IF A FAGGOT ANSWERS THE PHONE, HANG UP!

DATELINE—PENNSYLVANIA: THE JERK THAT SET UP THE BLACK ATTACK ON ROY FRANKHAUSER IN JAIL TURNS OUT TO BE A JEW PRISONER BY THE NAME OF HAROLD EMBER. THE JEWS ARE SETTING UP HITS INSIDE THE WALLS.

DATELINE—SUPERBOWL: AT LEAST ON SUPERBOWL . . . ONE SUPER-BOWL TRANSMISSION IN ONE REGION WAS INTERRUPTED BY A HACKER WHO PLAYED MUSIC FROM THE JETSONS AND STATED "THERE ARE TOO MANY JEWS ON TV." CAN ANYBODY VERIFY THIS STORY?

DATELINE—CHICAGO: TWO WHITE ACTIVISTS ARE RUNNING FOR OFFICE IN CHICAGO. ONE FOR MAYOR, MAYBE TWO FOR MAYOR. ONE IS ART JONES, ANOTHER IS WILLIAM GRUNSBACHER. YOU PEOPLE IN CHICAGO, GET OFF YOUR ASS AND GET TO WORK!

DATELINE—CBS-TV AND THE ADL: CBS IS DEVOTING AN ENTIRE YEAR TO ANTI-WHITE PROPAGANDA. GET READY FOR A TOTAL ANTI-WHITE BARRAGE FOR MONTHS. GREAT!

DATELINE—PORTLAND, OREGON: NOW THAT THE INITIAL BS IS WANING IN THE SKINHEAD-ETHIOPIAN CONFRONTATION, WE FIND THAT THESE BEAUTIFUL PEOPLE WERE HIGH ON CRACK AND MANY OF THESE BEAUTIFUL NEGROES HAD LONG ARREST RECORDS. SOUNDS LIKE THE SKINHEADS DID A CIVIC DUTY AND THEY DIDN'T EVEN REALIZE IT!

DATELINE—HATE CRIMES: WHAT A JOKE, AND ALL ANTI-WHITE! THE JEW-INSPIRED HATE LAWS WILL INSURE A NEW ARYAN ARMY BOTH ON THE STREETS AND INSIDE THE PRISONS. WAR THANKS THEIR ENE-

MIES FOR MAKING IT MUCH EASIER TO RECRUIT. '89 WILL BE A BAN-
NER YEAR IN THE DENIGRATION OF WHITE AND THE BIRTH OF
BACKLASH!

DATELINE—ARYAN WOODSTOCK: DON'T FORGET MARCH 4TH FOR
THE BIGGEST WHITE BASH IN YEARS IN CALIFORNIA. THREE SKIN-
HEAD BANDS SO FAR AND MORE EXPECTED!

AT THE TONE, FOR FURTHER INFORMATION ON WAR, THIRD POSI-
TION, LEAVE YOUR NAME, ADDRESS, AND PHONE NUMBER AND
SPEAK SLOWLY!

WHITE WORKER POWER!

Sometimes they were short, sometimes long, sometimes newsy,
sometimes philosophical, but the bulletins on Tom Metzger's Fallbrook, California, hot line usually took the form not so much of a
telephone message as of a radio transmission. "WHITE ARYAN
RESISTANCE   CALLING . . . WHITE   ARYAN   RESISTANCE
CALLING," he would begin, his voice echoing urgently through the
night, and he would be off reading from a teletype that existed only
in his mind, zooming in on places and events of interest to the
movement, an Aryan Walter Winchell uniting his far-flung listeners
in a common cause. Sometimes he would throw in chunks of anything that happened to be at hand: transcripts of a TV or radio show
on which he had been the guest, a phone conversation with a friend
such as the one he had recorded with Rick Cooper on October 24,
1988, only a few weeks before the death of Mulugeta Seraw, when
Rick had told him about all the skinheads moving into Portland "to
take advantage of the job situation and also to work in a relatively
fertile area in that white people in this area are basically sympathetic
to white racial causes." "It all sounds great, Rick," Tom had replied,
"sounds like a lot of action, and, unofficially, the fights and attacks
against the race-mixers and some of the race-traitors and the racial
scum has been picking up because of the new warriors moving into
the area, but I am sure there will be more on that later. When it

comes out it will be all at once." The January 30, 1989, message was no different from any other. With its observation on Portland randomly stuck between the other "Datelines" geographical and otherwise, that happened to be on his mind, to Tom Metzger it was just another broadcast. Without the Southern Poverty Law Center, which had long been taping and transcribing the message line and would use the Portland "Datelines" in court as evidence of Tom Metzger's connection with the death of Mulugeta Seraw, the words would no longer even exist, because WAR itself was neither well heeled nor well organized enough to preserve them. But there they were: a convenient record of the longtime racist's latest strategy of attempting to combine elements of the old-style white supremacist movement and the new skinhead movement into a single force. Of all the bulletins he delivered in the years his "Aryan Updates" had been on the air, Tom Metzger's references to Portland were the ones he would have most reason to regret.

20

In the late Depression winter of 1938, an eighteen-year-old girl with a bulging waistline stepped off the train from Chicago right out of the pages of Theodore Dreiser back into the life of her hometown of Warsaw, Indiana, where Dreiser himself had lived and observed the human condition fifty years before. Willodean Rickel Linton was neither the first unfortunate woman of Warsaw nor the last. "Aphrodite had many devotees in this simple Christian village," wrote Dreiser on revisiting the place where he himself had first known the pleasure and the shame of sexual release as a young boy. "The soil of the town, its lakes and groves, seemed to generate a kind of madness in us all." But after the madness came the reckonings. "During the short time I was there, there was scandal after scandal, and seemingly innocent sex attractions, which sprang up between boys and girls whom I knew, ended disastrously after I left," he continued. Deaths, suicides, and exiles of both parties to the breathless couplings that had left the girl "enceinte" are what Dreiser remembered next. As with bodies, so with souls. Sin and repentance were as closely united as cheek and jowl. Right next door to Warsaw lay the small community of Winona Lake, famous throughout the world as the headquarters of evangelist Billy Sunday, where the violation of the Sabbath by smoking, noisemaking, or general carousing was punishable by arrest and where there was no sale of alcohol on any day—which did not prevent a Warsaw cab driver from delivering bottles to the back door of the Sunday Tabernacle evenings and collecting the empties in the morning. According to Mrs. J. N. Rodeheaver, a member of the Christian-music publishing family associated with the Tabernacle, when Sunday was asked why so many of his conversions seemed short-lived, he would reply that the result of a bath is not permanent either but that was no reason for not taking one and repeating it as often as necessary. To judge from the number of lapses recorded in the annals of Warsaw, he must have been seeing some of his neighbors fairly often.

Willodean was not exactly unmarried, but her husband had left her, which was close enough. In South Bend, she had fallen in love with a draftsman named Thomas Linton who worked in an engineering firm and was a customer in the Chinese restaurant where she was a waitress. They were married in Chicago, but after a brief attempt to set up housekeeping in a Chicago suburb, Linton had gone off to California with his mother and Willodean returned to Warsaw pregnant and alone. It cannot have been a very pleasant homecoming. Her father, a farmer whose illness had propelled her to leave home and find work in the first place, died of cancer soon after she came back. Her son, called Thomas Byron Linton, after his father, was born only a few days later. With her family tending not so much to sympathize with Willodean as to scorn her for the big one she had let get away and with even the local sheriff conniving to let Linton out of jail, where Willodean had had him thrown for failure of child support on one of his surreptitious visits to Warsaw to see his son, she was left to provide for herself and the infant largely on her own.

She lived at first on the family farm outside town and then in Warsaw itself, working at a variety of jobs—as a waitress, in a glove factory, in an electrical coil manufacturing plant—and taking care of young Tommy with whatever help she could find. When her mother gave up the farm and also moved to town to support herself with a job cleaning churches, she would sometimes take her grandchild along. At the Warsaw boardinghouse where Willodean and Tommy were living when he was about four and she was single again at twenty-two, she met a white-haired fellow boarder at least twenty years her senior named Cloice Metzger and they were married shortly after. Despite the fact that he belonged to a well-established Kosciusko County family, Cloice Metzger appears to have also been something of an outcast. Someplace along the line he had encountered a run of bad luck. There had been two previous wives, one of whom had been discovered in their bed with another man, and there had been a period of sorrow, drinking, and general dissolution evidently ended not long before he met Willodean when he found temporary salvation in helping a booming-voiced minister from out of town build a new Church of God. He had two other families nearby and a number of grown children probably about the same age as his newest wife. By the time he got together with Willodean, his darkest days were over, but he retained an emotional volatility that left him warm and loving one moment, mean and sometimes even violent the next. Nor was he as economically stable as was the Warsaw ideal. He had been a farmer, a rancher, and a livestock broker and was, like Willodean, working in the Gadke brake-lining factory when they met, but they moved around a lot, from town to farm to town again and twice to Florida, and by the time they settled permanently on the eight-acre property outside town that Tommy came to regard as his real home, the boy had been to eight or nine different schools. He was enrolled at school as "Thomas Linton Metzger," which is how he was always known, but he was not officially adopted by Cloice Metzger until 1963, when he was a married man.

What family happiness there was was periodically shattered by the arrival of a present from Thomas Linton in California, where he had started a new family and was rising to prominence as an engineer, just as Willodean's sisters had predicted. Linton worked for Cal Tech and the U.S. Naval Weapons Station at Seal Beach, held a number of patents, including one for a hydraulic apparatus for aircraft, and in his later years, coming to believe that the world would be better off using base-twelve rather than base-ten mathematics, became active in the Dozenal Society, formerly the International Duodecimal Society, for which he invented a base-twelve slide rule still available from the society today. He died in 1981. "You're no good!" "You're just like your father!" "Someday you'll run off to California and leave me just like he did!" were some of the charges Tom remembers being hurled at him by his mother whenever a gift from Thomas Linton would arrive in the mail. Her hurt and her anger were never-ending. Thomas Linton Metzger is not now and undoubtedly has never been a crybaby. When he thinks of his childhood he thinks of hunting, fishing, rafting, a dog—above all, of the sense of independence and freedom that came from having such ready access to the land. He was always properly housed, clothed, fed, and sent off to church on Sundays—even when the adults did not go themselves. From my many conversations with Tom Metzger, I believe he would be the last person to attribute any of his adult convictions to his childhood environment, and who is to say he would be wrong? But he was a bright and spirited child with a love of adventure, strong practical aptitudes, and the kind of intellectual rebelliousness that would prompt him to spout evolution just when the teacher was spouting God. What he probably lacked most was an audience.

In 1945, when he was in the second grade, the young Tom Metzger would sit for hours with friends beside the Pennsylvania Railroad tracks near his house, watching carload after carload of American soldiers returning home. They would wave at one another, the boys and the soldiers. Sometimes they would even salute. Where had

they been? the child wondered. Where were they going? It was
something he always wanted to know. His favorite subjects in school
were history and geography. At the time and in the place in which
Tom grew up, the greatest link between the individual and the outside world was radio. Television was just getting started. When a
customer on his paper route one snowy night around 1950 invited
him to come in and watch *Howdy Doody* live from Chicago, the
experience was so powerful that as he speaks of it now you can still
see him shaking off his boots in the doorway and following the blue
glow into the living room, transfixed. But radio was something you
could actually do. When another neighbor demonstrated a home-
built radio to his scout troop, setting up a black box with an antenna
and headset and tapping out his greetings in Morse code till they
reached as far away as Chicago and St. Louis, Tom fell in love. From
then on, his life revolved almost wholly around radio. He learned
Morse code, got an FCC operator's license, built himself a trans-
mitter and receiver, which he installed first in his room and then in
an outbuilding he set down next to the house, added an antenna—
and presto, at thirteen, he had a radio station. Whenever he could
be he was on the air talking to like-minded ham operators not only
throughout Indiana but gradually, as he built stronger transmitters,
across the continent and even in Europe. And the transmissions he
could receive! Not just Hoosiers sounding off about the same as they
would down at the hardware store Saturday morning or the sad
midnight poet somewhere in Wisconsin who read the same poem
over and over into his lonely microphone but the Voice of America!
Radio Moscow! London! illuminating what was really happening in
the world. And what was happening was so important! The Free
World was about to be overrun! By 1953, when Tom was starting
high school, children weren't the only ones who wondered where
the soldiers would be going next. World War III seemed right
around the corner and everyone thought it would begin the way
World War II had, at least for the United States: with a surprise
attack. In response, the air force organized the Ground Observer
Corps, which signed up 350,000 volunteers at fifteen thousand posts

around the country to scan the skies for the low-flying Russian bombers that America's Distant Early Warning radar system would fail to detect. The headquarters in Washington was linked to every region by telephone. But what if the telephone communication system was not working? A six-state Bell System telephone operators' strike in 1953 put U.S. defenses to the test. Into the crisis stepped the regional ham radio operators, fifteen-year-old Tom Metzger among them, remaining at his post at one point for a twenty-hour stretch lest a breach of the DEW line by enemy aircraft within his coordinates go unreported. The next year he helped build a communications center in the downtown courthouse and at sixteen was given the title of communications director of Kosciusko County. It was a heady life. There were photos in the newspaper, praise from adults, the respect of his peers. For his performance as a ham operator, doubtless including the civil defense component, he was awarded the A-1 Operators' Award by the amateur radio association, the American Radio Relay League, in 1955, one of the youngest people ever to receive the award. Ham radio is an alternative to regular channels of communication, what you use when regular channels are blocked, and considering his isolation at home, it is tempting to see it as a metaphor for something else in Tom's life, but it also offered important satisfactions. His country might need him at any moment! Says Tom: "I wanted to be Paul Revere."

The only rival of radio for Tom Metzger's heart when he was in high school was cars. Not that he was alone. From talks with some of his friends, I got the impression that all the passages of their collective youth could be marked by their possession of particular cars—in Tom's case, a 1937 Dodge, a 1947 Chevy Coupe, a 1949 Mercury, and a 1956 Austin-Healey convertible, not to mention a red 1939 Mercedes he had in the army that caused people in the little village of Donnersberg, Germany, where he was stationed, to call out, "There goes Herr Göring!" because Göring had driven the same thing. Sometimes cars and radios were intertwined, as with the black Dodge into which Tom installed a shortwave radio, and if you imagine a shy adolescent at the drive-in fiddling with dials and talking to guys all over the state while the girl beside him looks on either bored or not, depending on the girl, and the other couples in the cars around them are doing something else, you may have as true a picture of Tom Metzger as a teenager as it is possible to get. If there was anything else in Tom's life that distinguished him from other boys of the Warsaw Community High School Class of '56, it is hard to uncover it now. His own memories place him a shade closer to the others than theirs of him but that could be no more than the centrality we each have in our own recollections, together with a wish on the part of his classmates not to be associated too closely with the man he has become. More telling may be the fact that while Tom remembers himself as something of a hell-raiser, others remember him as quiet and reserved, suggesting that if he was indeed raising hell anywhere, it must have been at home. At the basketball games, the beach parties, the roller-skating rink, and the miniature golf course that were about all the places the Warsaw boys actually went in their cars, he was just one of the crowd. He was a good-enough student, he took part in a variety of afterschool activities, including operating the spotlight at school shows ("When Tommy worked the lights, they were right," says a friend who was in the band), and through a work-study program he was also an apprentice at the local radio and TV store, where he began to learn the trade that he would follow the rest of his life—and that paid for the radios and cars. "He was cooperative, intelligent, polite, open to suggestions, and easy to work with," an older man who worked in the store at the time says, echoing the opinion of every acquaintance of Tom's I talked with in Warsaw. "He was a good boy."

Immediately after graduation Tom joined the army, in part lured by a recruiter's promise that he could be trained as a TV technician, in part to see the world. The TV school did not work out—he was trained as a microwave technician instead—but the world did. There was Fort Leonard Wood, in Missouri, for basic training, his first experience of intimate contact with people from different back-

grounds. There was the Army Signal Corps School at Fort Monmouth, New Jersey, his first opportunity to see New York. And
finally, in June 1957, there was Germany, specifically a small army
telephone microwave relay station in the mountains about twenty
miles north of Kaiserslautern, where he lived for the next two years
with about a dozen other soldiers in a relatively informal compound
that also included German dogs, cooks, and cars. The function of
the post was to relay military communications back and forth
between Europe and the United States and, considering its location,
not far from the frontier of the Cold War, it would have been natural enough for it to have been a center of political discussion of a
sort the former director of civil defense might have found engaging,
but in those days the young soldier had more practical than ideological considerations on his mind. For one thing, there were many
opportunities for travel. Whenever there was space on a transport,
a soldier could simply climb aboard, and for Tom on his leaves there
were the Folies in Paris, the Tower in London, the Prado in Madrid,
and in Amsterdam, after the World Court and the museums, several
hours one day in a tattoo shop, where he received the etchings he
still displays—a boa constrictor and a panther attacking not just each
other but the veins of their host and a heart-piercing sword with a
twisted snake labeled "Tom." He also had to try to stay out of
trouble. He succeeded, but between the occasional brawls, botched
inspections, and assorted other instances when the something in him
that resisted regimentation spontaneously made itself felt, he had a
few close calls. Assigned to escort military prisoners on his way back
to the United States in June 1959, he felt that with less luck he
could have been on the other side of the bars. At home, he lived at
first with Willodean and Cloice in a trailer they now occupied on a
portion of their former land and then in an apartment over a TV
and appliance shop where he had quickly gotten a job, but he did
not find it very much fun. In Warsaw by the beginning of the decade
the winds of change that were gathering elsewhere in the country
were blowing those of Tom's friends who had not yet started families toward the West. Two, three, four at a time, they would throw

their belongings into a car and head for California, where they expected to find sunshine, jobs, and—it was rumored—sex. In June 1960, Tom and three others strapped a TV set onto someone's 1953 Plymouth and set off to check out L.A. Shortly afterward, he flew home, worked long enough at the appliance store to buy himself the Austin-Healey, gave his two-week notice, and hit the road. If he could take himself out of Warsaw, however, he could not so easily take the Warsaw out of himself. It retained a special place. In 1977, when he became the leader of the California Klan, he sent a packet of photos of himself dressed in robes to the Warsaw *Times-Union* with the polite note "As a former Warsaw resident I thought you would be interested in the attached material for your readers. Please send out a copy of anything printed." Later, when his position in the racial movement brought him in touch with the racist group known as the Order, which operated underground, he was sometimes known by the code name "Radio."

21

Tom moved into a two-bedroom apartment near Santa Monica Boulevard with three Warsaw buddies, got himself a job installing radios in cars at Chip's Auto Radio in Culver City, and opened himself up to a new way of life. Bliss was it to be a twenty-two-year-old boy from Warsaw, Indiana, in Southern California in 1962 and to drive was very Heaven! The girls . . . the beaches . . . the music . . . the sheer animal joy . . . it was not just a dream of their stopped-up Midwestern ids. It was real. There was plenty of it. They could do what they wanted. Of course, nothing is perfect. Chip's Radio, directly across the street from the MGM studios, was frequented by film people who could be as pleasant or unpleasant as they chose, and one day after a near altercation with a star who was being the latter, Tom realized he would have to move on. A new job would not be a problem. Through a roommate who worked at the Douglas Aircraft military and space systems division, he learned that the Santa Monica–based company needed people with electronics experience and he was hired as a technician in the materials-processing laboratory, testing circuit boards for combat and outer space. Soon he was promoted to a standards laboratory that was responsible for certifying the electronic parts to be installed in missiles. The lab was largely staffed by engineers, and despite the difference in their status, these now became Tom's friends. They ate, drank, and partied together after work, and when there was an opening in a house three of them rented across from the beach in Playa del Rey, they invited Tom to move in. The Warsaw boys were scattering, some heading elsewhere in the great wide world America at that moment seemed to be, some returning home. Tom himself was starting to do what one was supposed to do in California at that time or any time: discover himself.

In 1962, neither Douglas Aircraft nor any other defense contractor was simply in the business of selling equipment: it was also in the business of selling America. Our embarrassment at the Bay of Pigs, the construction of the Berlin Wall, the Soviet atmospheric nuclear testing program, the Cuban missile crisis, and constant other confrontations throughout the world all contributed to a national sense that the Cold War with Russia, like the wars of the past, was something to be won or lost. At Douglas there was literally a Sell America Committee, which used company space and projectors to show anti-Communist propaganda films such as *The Truth about Communism* and *Agents of Deception* that revealed step by stealthy step the elements of the Communists' long-range plan to undermine freedom around the world. Anti-Communist speakers made the same point. The incursions of the welfare state on individual liberties, which had been progressing since the New Deal, were not merely oppressive in themselves: they could prepare the way for actual enslavement in the future. The message was one that Tom Metzger instinctively found congenial. He had a strong streak of independence, a desire not to be pushed around. Not long after his promotion, the International Association of Machinists, which had recently organized the Santa Monica plant, began pushing for an agency shop clause and he was not only practically but politically offended. The idea that he could be forced to join the union or pay a service fee as a condition of employment violated his sense of himself as a trained technical worker who had won both his job and his promotion on his own. It was not only Big Government that was a problem: it was Big Labor, Big Business, Big Everything, and it appeared they were all in collusion. Although his previous political experience was limited to wearing an Ike button in 1956 and voting for Nixon in 1960, he flung himself into opposition so conspicuously and energetically that he was promptly offered a $30,000-a-year position organizing for the union—and he turned it down. Instead he joined the National Right to Work Committee and a newly formed Aerospace Workers for Freedom and participated with several other employees in a lawsuit against Douglas and the IAM for infringing on their right to work. A photo in the Santa Monica paper shows him looking on soberly, in suit and tie, as the employees witness an injunction being prepared in their attorney's office. When the suit was dismissed in late 1962 and he was summoned for a meeting with management and given a final opportunity to accept the union or leave the company, he quit. In the accommodation of labor and management, he sensed oppression. Others might preach anti-Communism and let themselves accept collectivization, if only for the sake of their paychecks, but not Tom Metzger. If you were for freedom, you were for freedom, word and deed.

One summer night while Tom was still living with the engineers, he staggered in from a round of barhopping, heading for the sink, only to find a tall blond girl following him into the bathroom asking if he needed any help. When he was done, she began unflinchingly cleaning up the mess: something she would do for him just as willingly in a variety of other ways for the next thirty years. Kathleen Murphy, then nineteen, came from a conservative Catholic family in nearby Westchester, where she had attended Catholic schools. A photo that is probably from her high school yearbook shows a somewhat long-faced, firm-jawed young woman with the stiff bouffant hairstyle of the day, not so much conventionally pretty as attractive, strong, looking as if she has a mind and will of her own. Kathy was working as an insurance claims adjuster and living in her own apartment. Not long afterward, Tom also moved into an apartment of his own on Manhattan Beach and they began seeing each other often for long walks and talks and barbecues, usually also having Sunday dinner with Kathy's parents. One of the many things that drew Tom to Kathy almost from the beginning was her Catholicism. However much he had balked at the enforced devotions of his Indiana childhood, part of him yearned for the sense of order and stability that only religion could bring, and that yearning grew greater as the combination of the sixties and California brought all the flux and flotsam of the dawning New Age right to his doorstep. When he recalls that time now, it is almost with a shudder at the rootlessness and transience that might have become his way of life. In those days, one could become a Catholic merely by taking a few lessons with a priest, and in the summer of 1963, after a brief period of instruction, Tom converted. In October 1963, he and Kathy were married in a Catholic service attended not only by Willodean and Cloice Metzger but, to Willodean's dismay, by Tom's father, Thomas Linton, whom Tom, with the help of Kathy's insurance network, had located in nearby Garden Grove. The couple traveled across the country with Willodean and Cloice to a large reception in Warsaw in a new 1956 Pontiac station wagon presaging the many children to come and went on to honeymoon in New York. When they returned, they lived first in Hermosa Beach in a house they rented and, soon afterward, in Redondo Beach, in a house of their own.

When Tom left Douglas, he did not leave his new political interests behind. He continued receiving mailings from the Sell America Committee and found himself increasingly drawn to its message. He was now working for an independently owned radio and TV shop of the kind he had worked for in Warsaw, he and Kathy were anticipating the birth of their first child, and with his new married life he might well have retreated behind the walls of his two-bedroom cottage and come out only to mow the lawn; but it was no longer the 1950s, it was the 1960s, and even though the president whose inaugural speech had asked what we could do for our country was dead, the idea of taking responsibility for life beyond one's doorstoop was still very much in the air. As the 1964 election took shape, Tom read Barry Goldwater's popular reinterpretation of constitutional principles, *The Conscience of a Conservative*, and plunged into working for Goldwater against the liberal Nelson Rockefeller in the critical California Republican primary, walking the precincts of Redondo Beach, South Bay, and Torrance handing out Goldwater literature and talking about the issues until he had literally worn out a pair of shoes. He was hardly unique. Eight thousand other citizens of Los Angeles County also volunteered for Goldwater that year, along with hundreds of thousands of citizens elsewhere across the country—an enormous outpouring of support for the articulate and dignified standard-bearer for the long-marginalized conservative position that government was doing too much. But too much of what? That was the important question. Farm support, welfare, aid to education, and the host of other New Deal programs that Goldwater believed should not be the province of the federal government had all been around a long time. What was new in 1964 was the demand for yet another kind of federal intervention: to guarantee the implementation of new civil rights laws and to protect the lives of civil rights workers in the South. Hidden as it was in the traditional American language of federalism, race was not overtly the central issue of the 1964 campaign, but it was in the background. More obvious was the issue of the nature of the American right, which, particularly after Goldwater's famous "Extremism in the defense of liberty is no vice! And moderation in the pursuit of justice is no virtue!" dictum, was emerging from the various closets to which decades of liberalism had consigned it. What was respectable conservatism and what was far-right extremism was a subject of intense debate both among conservatives and in the country at large. Tom considered himself a respectable conservative and he resented the Democrats' attempts to confuse the one with the other. When

Goldwater's "In your heart you know he's right" became Johnson's "In your guts you know he's nuts," Tom thought it was unfair. When Goldwater was accused of wanting not only to destroy Social Security but to blow up the world, Tom thought it was practically crooked. The idea that if Goldwater lost the country would remain in the hands of the man who commissioned such lies was particularly distasteful. Reading J. Evetts Haley's influential campaign diatribe *A Texan Looks at Lyndon: A Study in Illegitimate Power*, Tom learned that LBJ had previously been involved in dubious election practices in Texas and dubious other practices besides. The Goldwater-Johnson campaign was not the first in American history to caricature issues and candidates, nor was it the last, but if it was your first direct encounter with American politics outside the textbooks it could look pretty scurrilous. Whether it was the murder of President Kennedy, the gathering racial struggle, the fear of a new and final war, or simply another spin of the wheel of history, by 1964 the bonds of trust and allegiance that had united Americans through the crises of depression and war were wearing thin. You might think Tom could have waited a little longer before coming to grand conclusions, but he was not alone. Like so many others of his generation—and at the same moment—Tom ended his first involvement with the political process disenchanted.

In late 1964, at the invitation of a reporter he had met at the Goldwater campaign office, Tom attended a meeting of the five-year-old John Birch Society and he liked what he saw. Ten or so ordinary people from his own neighborhood looking the menace of Communism straight in the face and attempting to do something about it: if the ordinary methods of American politics were going to be so unsatisfactory, there was no other way. At the time Tom became interested, joining the John Birch Society was not something one would do lightly. Ever since the much-quoted utterance of Birch Society founder Robert Welch that one of the most beloved American leaders of all time, Dwight David Eisenhower, was a "dedicated conscious agent of the Communist Conspiracy," prominent embarrassed conservatives from William F. Buckley Jr. to Goldwater himself had been attempting to distance themselves from "The Founder" as best they could, and to join now, when the organization was under attack by conservatives and liberals alike, was to risk being branded forever with those great scarlet letters of American politics: E-X-T-R-E-M-E. While the conservative leadership was protecting its reputation, however, the grass roots was flinging itself into the cause. In December 1964, the month after the election of Lyndon Johnson, about five hundred new Birch Society chapters were started nationwide—the biggest single period of growth in the organization's history, before or since—and within a few months there were an estimated ten thousand members in the Los Angeles area alone. The great convenience of the John Birch Society from the point of view of its converts was that it had an explanation for everything. Whether the subject was such world historical events as the French Revolution, the Bolshevik seizure of power, the world wars, or the founding of the United Nations, or such specifically American developments as the Federal Reserve system, the graduated income tax, the direct election of senators, or the breakdown of civic values, it was all part of a capital C Conspiracy, beginning with the Bavarian Illuminati, to destroy individual freedom, a Conspiracy so old and so vast that the Communist movement itself was only one wing of it. The ultimate beneficiaries of the Conspiracy were members of a two-hundred-year-old secret circle called the Insiders, a vague worldwide assemblage that assumed different guises at different times and places but whose purpose was "always, and by all means, to reduce the rights and responsibilities of individual citizens, while steadily increasing the quantity, the reach, and the potential tyranny of governments"—and if you wanted to know where to find Insiders now, according to Birch dogma, the tax-exempt foundations, with their independent billions and their behind-the-scenes role in shaping international policies, was a good place to start.

But the John Birch Society was not only a coherent set of ideas:

it was an effective organization. Modeled after the Communist Party, which Welch had studied in detail, it combined small local chapters with centralized direction in a way that gave its members a sense of exercising their individual initiative and participating in a large, important national movement at the same time. Beyond the cells, there were society "fronts," both temporary and permanent, mass petition and letter-writing campaigns, a series of carefully stocked reading rooms that developed into a chain of American Opinion bookstores, and the society magazine, *American Opinion*, itself—all copied from the Communist source. The John Birch Society was one of the greatest meeting points of ordinary Americans on the right since the New Deal and it was the seed of much that followed. Many of the most important leaders of the far-right revival—Willis Carto of the Liberty Lobby, Robert DePugh of the Minutemen, Ben Klassen of the Church of the Creator, Colonel Jack Mohr of the Christian Identity–Christian Patriot lecture circuit, and William Pierce of the National Alliance, author of the politically inflammatory 1978 novel *The Turner Diaries*, whose future readers would include Oklahoma City bomber Timothy McVeigh—all passed through the Birch Society at one time or another, along with many dedicated followers, and it provided at least some of their basic political educations. Contrary to the later direction of these early members, the stated policy of the Birch Society was to exclude all manifestations of racism and antisemitism, which Welch maintained only created diversions under cover of which the Insiders could conduct their machinations. His name for these racist and antisemitic spoilers was the Neutralizers. In lectures, which became pamphlets, which became videotapes, which in time constituted an entire library, Welch criticized the Neutralizers in such authoritative detail that in the case of the then little-known racist and antisemitic Christian Identity movement, for example, he was in effect spreading their word. It is difficult to read about Insiders and Neutralizers without becoming conspiratorial oneself but if you were a Bircher schooled in Welch's famous "Principle of Reversal," by which everything is the opposite of what it appears, you would have to wonder why he advertised them so much. While the Insiders were practically incorporeal, the Neutralizers were right at hand. As a chapter leader, Tom Metzger himself had to expel two elderly women who repeatedly brought up "the Jewish question," but you can almost sympathize with the confusion of the poor dears—because the Neutralizers were such a prominent presence, while the Insiders were never named. Whether or not Welch intended to leave the racist and antisemitic legacy he in fact did leave is not possible to say—and many people still believe Robert Welch was an honorable man—but the roster of Birchers who became Neutralizers is impressive. If the Birch Society did not offer its members a direct outlet for racism and antisemitism as such, it delivered them panting to the door.

On a hot August night in 1965 Tom was standing outside his Redondo Beach house when he saw the skies turn suddenly red with the fires of one of the greatest racial conflagrations ever to strike any American city: Watts. The Metzgers were not immediately endangered by the ghetto rebellion but the deaths, the destruction, the militarization of a portion of the city were not just television images, they were close at hand. Another California watershed that bothered Tom was the United Farm Workers' strike and grape boycott, also close at hand. The California Supreme Court's endorsement of a controversial bill outlawing discrimination in the sale of property, which he believed violated his right as a property owner to sell to whomever he chose, was a third. Moved by a sense that the country was in such dire condition that ordinary citizens had to remain politically involved, he supplemented his Birch Society work by volunteering in the 1966 gubernatorial campaign of Ronald Reagan, but once again he was quickly disillusioned. Not only did Reagan soon abandon the fiscal principles on which he had campaigned by raising state taxes and expenditures after he took office, he was also more of a social liberal than he had acknowledged, promising to use the military to enforce the United States Supreme Court's decision on busing to promote school integration, if necessary, and raising the number of minority employees in California state government to its highest level ever. In such a demoralizing set of political circumstances, it was hard to know where to turn. In late 1966, Tom and Kathy began to talk about leaving the turmoil of the city and raising their family in the country, where at least it would be quiet and safe. Weekend after weekend they set out from Los Angeles for long drives through the bustling communities of Orange and Riverside Counties until at last they alighted on Fallbrook, an unincorporated rural village of a few thousand people in the northernmost corner of San Diego County between San Diego and L.A. Called the Avocado Capital of the World, it had miles of blooming farmland, great rolling canyons, and a small, old-fashioned one-street business district lined with family-owned retail stores that, except for the palm trees, could almost have been in Warsaw, Indiana. Not far from Main Street they found a modest two-story, five-bedroom house on a large lot and soon they had made their decision: this is where they would settle down. They had two young children, Carolyn, born in 1964, and Dorraine, born in 1965, and there would soon be two more, John, the only son, born in late 1968, and Lynn, born in 1969. Much later there would be another two, Rebecca, born in 1983, and Laurie, born in 1984. Moving day was July 4, 1968, and they felt at once they had made a good choice. The house was big enough for everything. From that time on, the headquarters both of the flourishing Metzger family and of the flourishing racist organizations that followed would be an unexceptional California dwelling with the cheerful unpolitical address of 308 Sunbeam Lane, Fallbrook.

22

In the summer of 1968, Tom Metzger was not the only one who thought his country might be coming apart. Disasters abroad, disorders at home: it sometimes seemed that for every one of the more than 500,000 uniformed Americans in Vietnam there was another

in the streets of Washington or New York or Chicago beating someone up. Nominally in charge during an uncontrollable year whose
events ranged from the North Vietnamese military offensive in the
winter to the assassinations of Martin Luther King and Robert Kennedy in the spring, with countless protest demonstrations, urban
riots, and student rebellions in between, was a political establishment as self-enclosed and self-referential as any in the history of the
republic—and that included both parties. With the Democrats too
disgraced by their inability even to hold a civil convention and the
Republicans compromised by the nomination of Richard Nixon, a
politician whose ability to inspire mistrust was legendary even then,
the moods of "alienation," "disaffection," and "disenfranchisement"
so endlessly noted at the time were not confined to student radicals
or blacks alone: the third-party campaign of Governor George Wallace of Alabama, who was attempting to create a new populist
movement where "ordinary" people who felt left out of the political
process could find a home, won nearly 10 million votes. Newcomer
though he was, Tom opened a storefront Wallace for President
office immediately after settling in Fallbrook, and he continued his
involvement in the American Independent Party spawned by the
Wallace movement for several years. He also joined a local chapter
of the Birch Society. The fact that Tom Metzger was a Wallace
worker in 1968 does not automatically mean that he was a racist at
that time—an assumption he then resented—and the evidence supports him that he was not. Along with joining a Catholic parish
whose worshipers included many Hispanics, Tom and Kathy sent
their older children not to public school but to a Catholic mission
school on the Pala Indian Reservation, about twenty miles from Fallbrook, where they were among very few whites. Picnics, fiestas, and
other mission celebrations found the family mingling naturally with
the rest. Tom also served the area's mixed population in his TV
repair business with no discomfort and he must have served them
well, for until it became a sideline to his politics rather than the
reverse, the business expanded steadily, eventually involving three
locations and several employees.

What Tom was, what many of the other 13.5 percent of the electorate who voted for Wallace that year were, was worried. In spite of his personal ability to provide a life for his family that could have left them insulated from political cares, as an American he was deeply troubled. What could have brought a great nation to this sorry passage? Reading incessantly, he found himself drawn to a number of right-wing classics forbidden by the John Birch Society that explored the relationships between Communism, Judaism, and the international banking system and that pointed inexorably to the Jews. *Pawns in the Game* and *Red Fog over America*, by Guy Carr, *The Rothschild Money Trust*, by George Armstrong, *The Federal Reserve Hoax*, by Wickliffe Vennard, *Tragedy and Hope*, by Carroll Quigley, *The International Jew*, by Henry Ford—gradually he began to piece together a new intellectual understanding. As reconstructed in an unpublished as-told-to biography of Tom put together by San Diego journalist Jack Carter, one night a representative of the Massachusetts headquarters of the John Birch Society addressed a meeting of Fallbrook area chapter leaders and announced that henceforth any member found reading any of the books in a stack he had placed beside him would be banned. He held up the first title, *Pawns in the Game*. "I've got that one," Tom declared. "Oh?" said the man. "Why don't you tell us about it?" "*Pawns in the Game* describes how New York's Kuhn-Loeb bank gave Russian revolutionary Leon Trotsky millions of dollars to finance the Russian Revolution," recited Tom. "They hid Trotsky with some Communist Jews who were living on the Lower East Side, then sent him off with the money to Canada. From there they figured he could easily get back to Russia, but Canadian authorities learned of his illegal entry into the country and detained him. Then Washington intervened and had him released." Next the representative held up *Red Fog*. "I've got that one too." "And—?" "Basically it tells how the United States was conned into fighting World War II." There was a third, Alfred Jay Nock's *Our Enemy, the State*—"a critique of the danger of statism," Tom reported—a fourth, a fifth, they were all on his shelves, and almost before he knew it his cumulative dissatisfaction with the vaporousness of the Birch Society came pouring out, and he said, "Nobody tells me what books I can or can't read. Not you, not Belmont, Massachusetts, not even Robert Welch! . . . If you're talking about Jews, say Jews. If you're talking about someone else, say so. But for Christ's sake, say something! Don't hide behind your so-called Insiders!" He quit the Birch Society soon after.

It was not only the Birch Society that Tom found wanting as the 1960s drew to a close: it was also the Catholic Church. Joining after Vatican II, when religious practices that had been in place for centuries were suddenly in flux, he soon found himself in a world where the very ceremonies he had been moved by during his conversion had little place. To hear the Latin Mass, the Metzgers had to go all the way to San Juan Capistrano, about an hour's drive. Nor was the liberalism merely liturgical. Vernacular masses were one thing, but when Fallbrook's St. Peter's actually brought in guitars and showed a film about Cesar Chavez during Mass one day, Tom and Kathy simply gathered up the children and walked out. But in religion, as in politics, there is always an alternative, and sometimes the two are the same. Literally on the fringes of an anti–Vietnam War demonstration featuring Jane Fonda at President Nixon's estate at San Clemente, where he had gone with a group of Birchers not only to protest the war's body count but to denounce Fonda, Tom encountered for the first time a world of rightists more racist, antisemitic, and militant than those he had previously known, and one of their auspices was a church. There was J. B. Stoner, cofounder of the National States Rights Party, which had been involved in violent action against the civil rights movement in the South, hawking his antisemitic newspaper, the *Thunderbolt*, to which Tom was immediately attracted. There were right-wing tax protesters, easily as against the government and against "the system" as any on the left. And there were followers of an influential preacher named William Potter Gale, whose Ministry of Christ Church was part of a burgeoning racialist-religious-political movement known as Christian Identity. Shortly afterward, at a meeting at San Diego's Onira Hall, where he had gone to hear a tax protester, Tom heard Gale preach for the first time. In Tom's words, "Gale's speech . . . lifted me out of my chair, spun me around, and set me back down again. [He] showed me the light."

Christian Identity is the theological inspiration of a substantial element of the contemporary far-right racist movement, a credo limited in numbers of adherents but large in political implications. Beginning as a belief within small nineteenth-century English Protestant circles that the descendants of the ten lost tribes of Israel expelled from the Northern Kingdom by Assyria in 722 B.C. were not Jews but Englishmen—a belief that led to an assumption of brotherhood with the actual Jews, whom they regarded as descendants of related tribes—the doctrine, then known as British- or Anglo-Israelism, traveled and darkened over the years until it emerged in America, after its acceptance by some of the major antisemitic preachers of the Depression era, as what has authoritatively been described as "the most . . . anti-Semitic belief system ever to arise in the United States." More a loose affiliation of like-minded worshipers than a hierarchical organization, the Identity movement has no texts other than the Bible and its ministers can preach as they choose, but its central tenets, shared by Gale, are that it is modern Aryans, not Jews, who are descendants of the lost tribes; that Jews are literally the children of the Devil, the offspring of a union of Eve with Satan in the Garden of Eden, which produced Cain; and that the world is nearing a final battle between Good and Evil, with the Aryans representing God and the Jews representing the Devil, a battle that must be won by Aryans for the world to be saved. Nonwhites are considered not fully human but part of a separate line of creation that preceded Adam and Eve, "Pre-Adamite" or subhuman "Mud People," believed to be governed by Cain; lacking capabilities of their own, they are instruments of the Jews in the battle, used to try to miscegenate the Aryans out of existence.

Identity holds that when God told Jacob that his children would form "a company of Nations," he was referring to the white nations of Western Europe, whose descendants would in their turn find the land of milk and honey in the United States—and for several of Identity's leaders, Gale included, the prophecy turned out to be true. Following a successful army career that ended in 1950, when he was in his midforties, he retired to Los Angeles, where he had a second successful career in business, first with Hughes Aircraft, then with the brokerage house of Waddell and Reed, and later with a securities and insurance firm of his own. He lived comfortably in Hollywood, in a house once owned by Lucille Ball, where one of his daughters, a Disney Mouseketeer, often brought Mouseketeers and other stars of the younger set to rehearse at their house. "John Wayne's son, Pat, used to come over every day. . . . My son's girlfriend was Gordon MacRae's daughter. Bob Hope's wife used to come over all the time. [And] Audie Murphy was one of my closest friends," he once recounted to an interviewer. "Colonel" Gale, as he was usually known, was part of a Southern California social and political network that took its Cold War responsibilities seriously, and it was politics that eventually led to his departure from Waddell and Reed, for in addition to running for governor and other electoral ventures, he also founded an underground paramilitary group called the California Rangers. When one of its members was arrested for selling machine guns to Treasury agents, in 1963, his employers did not like the headlines. Introduced to Christian Identity in the early 1950s, Gale was immediately at home with its blending of religion and politics and was ordained as a minister in 1956 by one of its leading figures, the Reverend Wesley Swift, himself a close associate of perhaps the best-known American Christian antisemite after Father Coughlin, the Reverend Gerald L. K. Smith. In 1957, Gale incorporated his own church organization, operating first in Hollywood, later in Glendale, and eventually from a hundred-acre ranch in the foothills of the Sierras near Yosemite named, after the lost tribe headed by the son of Joseph—and the seal on the one-dollar bill of the United States—Manasseh. Ranches were not unusual in Christian Identity circles—Swift had a ranch in Kern County; Richard Butler, another Swift initiate, whose Church of Jesus Christ

Christian so neatly conveys the Identity precept that Christ was not a Jew, was shortly to establish the Aryan Nations compound in Idaho—but Manasseh was particularly functional. With its modern campsites, which included shower facilities and a pleasant lake, it was ideally suited for the series of private summertime National Identity Seminars begun by Gale in the mid-1970s at which many of the most radical antigovernment and antisemitic projects of the next two decades, including the Posse Comitatus and the Committee of the States, were either furthered or hatched. Through a "tape ministry"—tapes of his sermons sent to Identity followers all across the United States and frequently broadcast by radio station KTTL-FM in Dodge City, Kansas—Gale's influence was extended nationwide. Why Tom Metzger was so taken by the man and his doctrine we will never truly know for it happened in some private chamber of the heart where internal and external forces suddenly come together, and as it turned out, Christian Identity was only a starting place, but it was Gale who presided over Tom's one lasting conversion: to racism. He would never see the world the same way again. After first hearing Gale, he began to steep himself in Identity literature and he was ordained as an Identity minister himself by Identity writer Bertrand Comparet, who was also a prominent San Diego attorney, in 1974. From the notes of an FBI informant who was present on many occasions, we can see Tom as he was at the beginning of his journey: a modest disciple, a "Communion Steward" at the regular meetings held by Gale in San Diego, teaching "Communications" or helping out with video demonstrations at the ranch. But however far he would travel from his roots in Christian Identity, the key work had already been accomplished. From the Klan to the skinheads, Tom's later alliances were never matters of conviction. They were matters of strategy.

Christian Identity and an escalating right-wing tax protest movement aimed at curtailing the powers of the federal government went hand in hand, and it was through the tax movement that Tom had his first taste of what he would always like most about political life: doing something. Not only did he join in a number of mass actions against the IRS, such as gathering with hundreds of other disaffected protesters singing out "God Bless America" at the top of their lungs at the sheriff's sale of a small Los Angeles waterbed business undergoing foreclosure, but from 1971 to 1975 he was a tax rebel himself, maintaining his noncooperation even after the IRS posted his property and capitulating only when further delay would have put him in jail. But while it was zest for action that brought Tom into Gale's circle initially, it was the same thing that drove him away for, more than anything else, what Gale himself liked to do was talk. Within a short time Tom had loosened his ties to Gale and begun working with another Swift disciple, James Warner, pastor of his own New Christian Crusade Church, whose opinions on the proper relationship of theory and practice Tom found more congenial. Some years before Warner had attached himself to Swift, he had had another leader, indeed a Leader, indeed a Fuehrer: Commander George Lincoln Rockwell, USNR, founder of the postwar American Nazi Party, at whose Arlington, Virginia, headquarters in 1958, in his own words, "the Swastika first flew in America after fifteen years of being trampled in the mud and slime of Jewish lies"—a swastika sent to him by none other than Warner himself—and here we must pause for another "begat" before returning to Tom because Rockwell's place in the political genealogy of contemporary American racism is so central that the movement cannot be understood without him.

George Lincoln Rockwell is probably the single most underrated figure in the history of the American right—an introduction he would have relished for it coincides so precisely with his own estimation of himself. Born in 1918 to a lesser vaudeville comedian known as "Doc" Rockwell, whose Jewish friends included such other vaudevillians as Walter Winchell, Fred Allen, and Groucho Marx, Rockwell was brought up, after his parents' divorce, in Maine and Rhode Island and admitted to Brown University in 1938. He left in 1940 to enlist as a navy pilot, in time becoming a lieutenant com-

mander in charge of a large squadron of scout and observation aircraft based at Pearl Harbor. Presentable, intelligent, a respectable
artist, and an articulate writer, he graduated from Pratt Institute on
the GI Bill and did a variety of work in Washington, D.C., and
Maine, none of which, however, either paid well enough for him to
adequately support his family, which came to include eight children
from two marriages, or was compelling enough to ward off a long-
felt dissatisfaction with the world as he found it, a sense that somehow, somewhere, things were deeply awry. The mounting evidence
of a Communist conspiracy high in the reaches of the federal government was one possible explanation, but apart from Joe McCar-
thy, whom he appreciated from afar, nothing he encountered in the
way of postwar anti-Communist individuals or organizations
brought him relief. In 1950, he was recalled to active duty because
of the Korean War and sent to San Diego, where through a chain
of association that led from an attempt to join in a defense of General Douglas MacArthur after his firing by President Truman to a
speech by Gerald L. K. Smith to the *Protocols of the Elders of Zion*,
Rockwell discovered *Mein Kampf*. "Reading *Mein Kampf*," he wrote
in his autobiography, *This Time the World*, "was like finding part of
me":

> Chaos and disorder and mental "grayness" are immensely frustrating
> to me and I had suffered for years trying to fathom the bottomless
> philosophical, social and political mess in the world and the even
> messier explanations offered by religion and sociology. Over and over
> I had said to myself, "There must be some sense, some logical causal
> relationship between social and political facts as to how they got that
> way!" But no person, no book, nor my own mind had been able to
> discover head or tail to these things. I simply suffered from the vague,
> unhappy feeling that things were "wrong," without knowing exactly
> how and that there must be a way of diagnosing the "disease" and its
> causes, and making intelligent, organized efforts to correct that
> "something wrong."

In *Mein Kampf* I found abundant "mental sunshine" which bathed all the gray world suddenly in the clear light of reason and understanding. Word after word, sentence after sentence, stabbed away into the darkness like lightning bolts of revelation, tearing and ripping away the clouds of more than thirty years of darkness; brilliantly illuminating the heretofore obscure reasons for the world's misery.

I was transfixed, hypnotized. I could not lay the book down without agonies of impatience to get back to it. I read it walking to the squadron, I took it into the air and read it, propped up on the chartboard, while I automatically gave the instructions to the other planes circling over the desert. I read it on the Coronado Ferry. I read it into the night and resumed the next morning. When I had finished, I started again and reread every word, underlining and marking especially magnificent passages. I studied it, thought about it and wondered at the utter, indescribable genius of it.

How could the world not only ignore such a book, but damn it and curse it and hate it, and pretend that it was a plan for "conquering" the world, when it was the most obvious and rational plan for saving the world which has ever been written? Had nobody read it, I wondered, that people went around saying that it was the work of a mad "rug-chewer"? How could sensible people get away with such monstrous intellectual fraud? Why was it so hated and cursed? I could see why the Jews would hate and curse it, but why my own people?

I re-read and studied it some more. Slowly, bit by bit, I began to understand. I realized that National Socialism, the iconoclastic world-view of Adolf Hitler, was the doctrine of scientific racial idealism, actually, a new "religion" for our times. I saw that I was living in the age of a new world-view. Two thousand years ago there had been a similar rise of a new approach or world-view, called a "religion"; a world-view which shook and changed the world forever. I realized that this new and wonderful doctrine of scientific truth applied ruthlessly to man himself, as well as to Nature and inanimate matter, and that it was the only thing which could save man from his own degradation in luxury, self-seeking, short-sightedness and racial degeneration. The doctrine of Adolf Hitler was the new "Christianity" of our times, and Adolf Hitler himself was the new "savior," sent by inscrutable Providence recurrently to rescue a collapsing humanity.

Rockwell's portrait of his epiphany—still widely read—goes a fair way toward explaining his influence: he was a natural dramatist with an innate flair for the alternations of language and image that would help him turn his experience into myth. Some years after this first illumination—years spent in dissatisfaction with the refusal of traditional right-wing organizations to admit that "Communism is Jewish" and follow their anti-Communist premises to their inevitable antisemitic conclusions—Rockwell had another revelation: that the correct response to the "ultimate smear of the Jews," namely, "You're a Nazi!" was "You're damned right we're Nazis, and we shall shortly stuff you Jew-traitors into the gas chamber!" By being "an open, arrogant, all-out Nazi," he reasoned, "I would not only make an end of the filthy 'silent treatment'—for they could never ignore Nazis with Swastika armbands and talk of gas chambers—but I would also force the Jews to publish my propaganda in their press!" His tactic worked. With the founding of the American Nazi Party, the establishment of a compound in Virginia across the river from the nation's capital, a series of small but controversial demonstrations there and elsewhere in the late 1950s and early 1960s, and even a run for the governorship of Virginia in 1965, Rockwell broke through a tacit compact against the open expression of antisemitism that had somewhat sheltered America's and the world's Jews in the period after the liberation of the concentration camps and began to attract widespread news coverage. He also attracted a following. Among his initial hundred or so early storm troopers, in addition to Warner, were several other young men, including William Pierce, on his next stop after the Birch Society; Ralph Forbes, a mentor of Louisiana racist David Duke; Roy Frankhauser, an adviser to sometime presidential candidate Lyndon LaRouche; and Matt Koehl, head of the ANP's successor, the National Socialist White People's Party (NSWPP), through all of whose work the word of Adolf Hitler started reaching new generations of Americans and who were among the principal instruments through which traditional American racism, with its emphasis on blacks, and systematic Nazi racialism, with its emphasis on Jews, began to converge.*

Tom Metzger never Sieg Heiled George Lincoln Rockwell, who was assassinated in 1967, but he shook the hands of many who did. Tom saluted him in other ways. After Rockwell's death his followers took two paths, some maintaining a distinctly Nazi connection, with their brown shirts and swastika armbands and little Hitler moustaches, some dissolving into other racist organizations or movements, most discreetly Christian Identity. In the Identity circles in which Warner and Tom now traveled, the effectiveness of the Nazi mantle in the American political context was a subject of constant debate. "Most of the principal leaders [of the New Christian Crusade Church] were once involved with the American Nazi Party," the FBI informant reported at one point. "They are now smart enough to disdain the Swastika because they realize that promotion of such a hated symbol is futile. However, they fully if secretly believe in what the Swastika represents." Metzger said "the Swastika is just one of the forty versions of the Christian Cross but it is time to use one of the other versions; the Swastika had its application in its time but not in ours," the informant also noted. In the name of Warner's New Christian Crusade Church, the word *Crusade* was not chosen lightly, for it captured exactly the spirit of militant holy war that Warner intended to convey. In 1974, he made Tom head of a special "action arm" of the church whose purpose was to carry its message into the streets. "Remember the glory of the valiant Crusaders as they crushed the Turkish occupation of Jerusalem?" Tom asked in a flier announcing the new organization. "Remember the chivalry of old when Christian Knights defended Europe against

---

*White supremacists whose identities were formed in the World War II era did not universally welcome the convergence. "You don't have to be a Nazi to be an antisemite," a Klan leader explained to me as late in the process as 1989, by no means a singular position. In part out of the same residual patriotism, when neo-Nazi skinheads began attending racist gatherings in the mid to late 1980s, they were often shunned, with some older leaders refusing to share platforms with them or to shake their hands. Such resistance has now all but disappeared.

Asiatic hordes? Well they are back and they are called the 'Crusaders.'" Further described as "an action organization that stands for the Aryan race of peoples, . . . also base[d] on the message of the truly chosen people of God," the "Christian Crusaders" were a perfect expression of the underground blending of theological and ideological antisemitism that made the Identity movement such a choice location for the continuation of Nazism by other means. On the Crusaders' letterhead was the motto JESUS DROVE THE MONEY CHANGERS OUT OF THE TEMPLE—LET US DRIVE THEM OUT OF THE U.S. OF A. and a drawing of an angry Crusader dumping over a table laden with treasure while Jews looked helplessly on. The Crusaders' symbol was the four-armed Jerusalem cross. In spite of their large aspirations, the Christian Crusaders were a short-lived organization of a handful of men who held three or four polite demonstrations in Southern California in 1974 and 1975 where, dressed in identical red jackets marked with the Jerusalem cross, they gave out leaflets explaining the "Christian viewpoint" on such matters as racial tensions in the schools. For the most part, the organization is notable more for its clues to the development of Tom Metzger than for the mark it left on the world. But there was one exception. On December 8, 1974, Tom and about fifteen other red-jacketed Crusaders held a peaceful "Border Watch" at the San Ysidro–Tijuana border crossing that may well have been the first action in the rising tide of national feeling against immigration that has not yet come to a stop. "WANTED," read Tom's announcement in a leaflet that is one of the earliest political appeals in his own hand. "PEOPLE WHO ARE *NOT AFRAID* TO PICKET":

Fresh from successful encounters in 3 California cities with anti-Christians and their sometimes unwitting allies THE NEW CHRISTIAN CRUSADERS are going to picket the Mexican Boarder at Tijuana. Thousands of illegal alien mixed-bloods are entering our country. Your immigration service has no backing whatsoever from the kosher conservatives.

60,000 illegal aliens attend L.A. schools right now. L.A. could close six schools at least by cleaning up this situation. Immigration law says the first offense is punishable by six months in jail.

Our liberal, Jew, race-mixers know what they are doing.

Let us be the first organized unit to demonstrate for American nationalism and complete deportation of all illegal aliens, or close the boarder. We will have an audience of thousands of people, plus news and television . . .

In fact, the 1974 Border Watch, like other actions of the Crusaders, drew little public attention and was scarcely noticed by the busy immigration officers who went about their usual duties undisturbed; but for those who follow the movement of ideas from the fringes to the center of American life, it might be tempting to imagine that the action was not unnoticed by later anti-immigration politicians such as Governor Pete Wilson of California, who was mayor of San Diego at the time. To the FBI informant, it was obvious that Tom was on to something. "This group does not automatically get adverse responses from the public," he reported to his superiors. "Many passersby indicated support for their aims." In 1974, Tom Metzger was only a small television repairman with a lot of mouths to feed, but his antennae were sensitive. As the informant also concluded after watching Tom in action, he was a natural leader.

In the same period that Tom Metzger was starting to find ways to take the political message of the Christian Identity movement into the streets, dozens of other small racist, antisemitic groups and anti-Communist groups around the country were doing the same thing. At a national meeting in Missouri called in September 1974 by Robert DePugh, founder of the underground anti-Communist militia known as the Minutemen, and at regional meetings later, leaders of like-minded organizations ranging from units of the American Independent Party to various Southern Klans to offshoots of the American Nazi Party met to ponder ways of working together to break out of the narrow channels that had left them, each with their own

mailing lists, on the outskirts of American political life. A February
1975 meeting of the "West Coast Patriotic Leadership Conference,"
sponsored by Warner's New Christian Crusade Church at the May-
fair Hotel in Los Angeles, was probably typical. There, in a long,
narrow hall draped with large blown-up photographs of such heroes
of the far right as Francis Parker Yockey, author of a postwar antisemitic tome called *Imperium*, Charles Lindbergh, and the poet Ezra
Pound, an audience of about 150, inspired perchance by the music of
Wagner they had heard on the way in, listened to a welcoming
address in which Warner defined their common purpose as getting rid
of the Jews. "If I'm killed by Jew devils while leading this movement,
take revenge! Kill every Jew rabbi you can get your hands on!" he
screamed. J. B. Stoner, attending from Georgia, was just as wild.
"Jews are out to destroy Christianity and the White Race. . . . Adolf
Hitler failed to solve the Jew problem. . . . The alleged six million are
in the United States and own Los Angeles. . . . Every time a nigger
commits a crime, Mr. Jew is responsible!" Stoner cried.

Among the many speakers at the 1975 Patriotic Leadership Conference, none was more eagerly awaited or more fervently
applauded than a handsome young Southerner barely out of college
who brought new hope to the veteran racists on whose tired shoulders the battle for white survival had rested for so long—David
Duke. At twenty-five, Duke was already the man of the hour.
Raised in New Orleans in a troubled middle-class family, he had
discovered racism through Carleton Putnam's *Race and Reason* at
thirteen in 1964 and had led himself on his own directly from there
to *Mein Kampf*, soon immersing himself so intensely in the world
of Nazism in both its German and its American manifestations that
when George Lincoln Rockwell was assassinated a few years later
he called up a White Citizens' Council staff member he knew and
sobbed into the phone, "The greatest American who ever lived has
been shot down and killed." At Louisiana State University in Baton
Rouge, which he entered in 1968, he was so active and conspicuous
a Nazi that in 1970 he was invited to address two NSWPP-
sponsored gatherings near Washington, D.C., by Rockwell's succes-

sor, Matt Koehl, who was attempting to link up with student anti–
Vietnam War feeling through Duke's message that "National Socialists want to smash the System" too. Gradually, after several explicitly Nazi organizational tries, but without changing his beliefs, Duke
concluded that a Nazi party as such was doomed to insignificance
on the American political scene and he invented—simply invented—
a new Klan for himself, the Knights of the Ku Klux Klan, through
which he hoped to give a more distinctively American flavor to his
Nazi convictions and energize the entire racist movement in the
process. He named himself national director. Well-dressed, well-
spoken, with a debating style honed in LSU's Free Speech Alley and
arguments he had learned by heart in adolescence, he could move
smoothly between a crowd of two thousand working-class Irish
Catholics protesting forced busing in Boston and the staid mock
drawing rooms of the national TV networks, comfortable in both.
"I'd always thought of the Klan as being a bunch of old fogies who
were concerned with yesterday. But you're intelligent, articulate,
charming," his first national TV host, Tom Snyder of the *Tomorrow*
show, told him in 1974, a compliment that would echo through the
years. In 1974 and 1975, Duke was constantly on the road speaking
not only to gatherings of the faithful but to new audiences such as
college students, and wherever he visited, applications to the KKKK
invariably followed. After his February trip to Los Angeles, in
which, in the name of "the white race, civilization, and culture," he
said things like, "We're going to make sure that all Jews are equal—
equally dead," and told of a restaurant in the South that stayed
segregated by posting a sign in its window, "All proceeds go the
KKK rope fund," James Warner, Duke's host, received over three
hundred letters. In the circles in which he traveled, David Duke was
unmistakably a phenomenon. "Unless I am a very bad judge of character Duke will someday carry things much farther in the Far Right
than any of his predecessors were able to do," an FBI informant
wrote.

By early 1975, the relationship between David Duke and James
Warner was very close. Tom was a part of it. With Tom at his side,

Warner guided Duke on a two-day visit to San Diego in April that included a day-long "inspection" of the Mexican border, followed by an evening visit to one of the Onira Hall meetings that Identity minister Bertrand Comparet held every third Saturday. When the decorous old Comparet chastised the vigorous young Duke for turning his religious service into a Klan meeting by soliciting Klan applications then and there, Duke immediately apologized, but Warner, Metzger, and their Crusaders, offended, walked out. "[Comparet] is not likely to receive further support from any of them," the FBI informant said. On his next visit, Duke let it be known that he wanted to start a California Knights of the KKK chapter and Tom was one of about thirty new members inducted at a July 1975 ceremony held in Warner's garage. The disappearance of God and religion as the foundation of his political beliefs seems to have given Tom little pause. Like the Crusaders themselves, they simply vanished without a trace. Joining an organization that was almost universally regarded as subversive was so much more radical an act than any Tom had yet undertaken that for a time he found it necessary to keep his membership secret, but he joined anyway. He was swept away. At about the same time that David Duke created the California Klan chapter, he made another decision that affected Tom. Following the example of George Lincoln Rockwell, he decided to enter electoral politics, running as a Democrat for a Baton Rouge state senate seat for his first effort. Duke asked Warner to manage his campaign. In a letter that perfectly captures the exaltation of David Duke in racist circles in 1975, Warner wrote to his congregation that only a crucial historical opportunity could have persuaded him to abandon California. "Five years ago," Warner wrote,

> I met a young man that was the leader of an organization based in New Orleans. . . . He was a good speaker and showed a lot of promise. In the past three years he has become one of the best orators and debaters in the United States. He has been able to win over countless thousands of White Christian Americans to our cause. . . .
>
> I have been in the "right wing" movement for eighteen years and

attended patriotic meetings from coast to coast. . . . [At these meet-ings] many of the "old guard" would sadly bemoan the fact that very few young people [were in attendance] or were in the "right wing." They would ask me "Why aren't we getting the young people?" I couldn't answer them.

Now—I know the answer.

Religious and political movements are built around leaders. Huey Long was a leader . . . Father Coughlin could get up to 150,000 people at his rallies . . . Many patriots believed that the late George Lincoln Rockwell was a great leader . . . [but without these leaders, their movements died.] . . .

THEN there was this young man that showed so much potential and had most of the qualities of a good leader. He had been in the right wing since he was fourteen years old. When I met him I knew if anyone could win this fight for Christianity and the White Race— he could do it. He was a leader of one faction of the Ku Klux Klan and had a lot of young followers all over America but very few "old guard" fighters to help mold these people into a real movement.

Believe me—I love California and all the patriots there.

After years of hard work I finally had a decent home to live in. I had always wanted to be pastor of a real Church and not a store front Church—and now we had our own Church buildings. I now had most of what I had worked for for many years.

Then I was confronted with this hard decision. This young man COULD be the salvation of our race and nation—and his success or failure could hinge on the help he received IMMEDIATELY and not at some distant time in the future.

I always said that if a potential leader came along I would be will-ing to put our race, nation, and movement ahead of my personal life and follow.

And there he was, just like that, in Louisiana. The 1975 David Duke state senatorial race was not about Louisiana politics: it was about national power. No sooner had he got there than Warner phoned his lieutenant Tom to ask him to come to Louisiana to manage the campaign staff while Warner himself handled the national press, and in a short time Tom was beside him again, driving across the country in Warner's old VW with the San Diego Identity friend who had brought him to the San Clemente antiwar rally only a few years, but already a long political era, before. Duke lost, but he won a third of the votes, and for everyone involved with the campaign the national exposure and the thrill of working day and night for a cause they all believed in were almost as good as victory. "Over 11,000 people went to the polls and voted for my ideals," Duke announced jubilantly afterward. "The movement has just started."

Tom was not the only one excited about loosening the bonds of religion: so were his children. Other than rare outings to Manasseh, from the children's viewpoint Christian Identity consisted mainly of being dragged to San Diego to squirm through meaningless, dry-as-dust sermons, while the Klan, with its dramatic costumes and secret cross-lighting ceremonies, in which families were always included, was fun. There were also dietary advantages. The choices may have been as much budgetary as religious, but to the children Christian Identity seems to have been associated with a puritanical natural diet high on dried fruits and low on sugar cereals. The Klan had a lot of picnics. The Klan was also an improvement for Kathy. She had long been doing the clerical work that Tom's meetings, demonstrations, and other political activities often required, but with an effort to improve the position of women an important part of Duke's plan for bringing the Klan up to date, she now had more respect. Any private feelings she may have had about the changes that had led her from her conventional Catholic girlhood to the outskirts of society within a few short years are not available. She showed nothing but support. The only one Tom recalls as registering dissent when his Klan membership was made known to her was his mother, Willodean, in Warsaw, who roundly disapproved. Other than the radicalization of his political outlook since he had moved to Fallbrook, Tom Metzger was much the same as before. His business was good, his marriage was strong, his children were healthy. There were so many of them that things were sometimes a little tight, but with neither parent very interested in money in the first place and Tom able to fix whatever broke, the financial situation was not a problem. They lived a casual, economical, and, as far as we know, happy family life, usually with enough extra left over for a pizza party at the end of the week. In 1976, about six months after the Louisiana election, Tom, Kathy, and their four children attended a twenty-year reunion of the California-based members of the Warsaw High School Class of 1956. Photos show an ordinary, relaxed, utterly Southern California–looking family standing on someone's beautifully landscaped terrace with Tom in a leisure suit—but perhaps things were a little too ordinary. Summing up for a pamphlet called *More Tracks We've Made*, which a classmate had put together and which otherwise contained the usual reports of children, degrees, jobs, and moves, Tom kept the fact of his Klan membership to himself, but its spirit was just waiting to burst out. "I am an independent small businessman slave," he reported.

My wife Kathleen is a kitchitonal engineer, secretary, warden, lover, mother and bookkeeper. I've been to the School of Hard Knocks where I obtained the degrees of Black and Blue. John is 8, Lynn is 7, Dorraine is 10, and Carolyn is 11. I'm a ham radio operator and radical right-wing fanatic trying to break this mess up and start all over again. Tax resistor-demonstrator-county central committee American Independent Party which is good for a cup of coffee along with a quarter. Have just renewed old friendship with [a classmate] who lives near me. We plan to march on Washington soon and demand immediate surrender. Toastmasters. National Director of Crusaders dedicated to the Preservation of an Endangered Species: The Whiteman. Minister of new Christian Crusade Church of Escondido. Don't get too excited. We allow a little beer now and then (mostly now) and lipstick too. In fact [the friend] and I may get a little drunk and call the group, if we can reverse the charges. Keep smiling. Motto: If life is boring, risk it!!

23

In late 1976, following a yearlong debut as underground head of the California branch of David Duke's Knights of the Ku Klux Klan—a period in which a newspaper was started, some twenty-five new chapters were formed, and the KKKK's California ranks increased perhaps tenfold, from about three hundred to about three thousand members—Tom found himself facing a major political decision. Immediately west of Fallbrook on a large tract of California paradise containing its own mountains, rivers, and seventeen miles of prime oceanfront, lay the U.S. Marine Corps base, Camp Pendleton, and there on the night of November 13, after a period of mounting cultural tension between black and white marines that came to a head over the issue of soul versus country music on the commissary jukebox, fourteen black marines attacked a roomful of white marines they thought were Klansmen and beat the shit out of them—an act less gratifying than it might have been because, as it turned out, the Klan marines, who had indeed played their part in the mutual harassment of black and white that was a staple of Pendleton life, were in another room. Hoping to control the disturbance, the Pendleton command attempted to break up the Klan unit, which they had previously ignored, by isolating its members from their barracks and shipping them off to other bases as soon as possible. Feeling themselves wronged, since they had not been involved in the actual incident, the Klansmen turned to Tom. Their call placed him in a delicate situation. Self-respect, leadership, and sheer political opportunity all required that he publicly support the young Klansmen, who, though part of a different Klan organization, were operating largely on their own, but to do so would expose his own position in the Klan. Fearful of the consequences for his family, Tom at first described himself to the press only as the Klan's "Spiritual Advisor," but before long he was ready for the further revelation that the mild-mannered, civil-libertarian Christian Identity minister speaking for the Klan soldiers was—a Grand Dragon! As it turned out, he need not have worried. At a Christmas party soon afterward, Kathy told a friend that of two hundred letters received after the disclosure, only four were hostile. As for business, it actually improved.

From the time he came out of the closet as a Klansman until the time he went back in a few years later, Tom's California Klan branch was much on the move. There were other Klans active in the area, but Tom's was the one in the news. The Pendleton case itself had a long press run. Jesse Jackson came, David Duke came, and beyond the immediate furor, the Marine Corps's separate but equally unconstitutional treatment of the black and white marines brought the intervention of the ACLU on both sides—for the Klan, at Tom's direct request—an instance of First Amendment impartiality that elicited further headlines as several members of the Southern California ACLU board resigned in protest, the National Lawyers Guild denounced the "poisonous even-handedness" of the civil liberties group, a "Free the Pendleton Fourteen" committee was formed on the left, and the case became a test of liberal principle versus progressive politics that is argued to this day. Next came a "Border Watch" in October 1977: Tom and David Duke swoop down out of the sky at San Ysidro in a rented helicopter before a large press to commission Klan patrols to ferret out aliens slipping through the brush and report them to the INS. The Klan is opposed by leftist demonstrators. The pictures circulate round the world. The bulk of the Klan's publicity is about street fights, but freedom of speech and freedom of assembly are also important themes . . . Oxnard, July 1978: A few dozen Klansmen in riot gear led by Tom in a three-piece suit and shield enter a community center for a legal showing of *Birth of a Nation* over the violent opposition of a contingent from the Progressive Labor Party, who, outmaneuvered by the Klan, battle instead with the police. Inside, the victorious Klansmen barricade themselves amid broken glass and busted fixtures while on-screen their hooded forbears ride to the rescue once more . . . Castro

Valley, August 1979: After an appearance in San Francisco at a state commission investigating violence against minorities, which hears their testimony about violence against themselves, a group of black-jacketed Southern California Klansmen head to a rally at an American Legion Hall across the bay, where, without benefit of police, who are on strike, they fight an unimpeded street battle with waiting members of Progressive Labor and the Committee against Racism, and win . . . Oceanside, March 1980: a controversial, much-publicized Andrew Jackson Day Klan demonstration and leftist counterdemonstration at John Landes Park ends in riot as the police stand by and let the two sides battle it out with sticks, rocks, bats, bottles, concrete, and pieces of fence until the violence overflows the park into the surrounding community, when they move in to stop it at last. Police, press crews, Klansmen, and leftist demon-strators all sustain injuries. A Klan attack dog named Bear, a Dober-man, dies.

And there was more. It is hard to disentangle truth from myth in the history of the California KKKK both because the dispropor-tion between the scale of the incidents and the news coverage was so great and because the rhetoric was so overblown. What did these warriors think they were doing as they assembled time after time at the barricades? Defending Western civilization. Never mind that many of them were low-income, low-status males so bloated with beer that an ad for "Robes by Susan" in the *California Klan News* cautioned, "Please note if waist is larger than chest"—they would shoulder the burden. And what did Tom think he was doing? Pre-paring for the seizure of power. That helicopter swooping down from the sky at San Ysidro was not an original gesture: he was copy-ing Hitler. Eventually, both his understanding of American politics and his historical reference points would broaden, but for the moment the impact of the Nazi example on his thinking was enor-mous and he believed that the period between assembling a band of street fighters and taking the White House would be short. Whether it was the words of Hitler speaking directly to his heart or the influence of a Nazi friend named Don Musgrove, at whose Oakland house George Lincoln Rockwell had written his autobiography and who was now one of Tom's closest companions, the Nazis had a place in Tom's political imagination matched by nothing else. The fact that the enemies were "Communists" only made the struggle loom larger. "The Communists," too, expected imminent revolution. "The capitalist class was on the defensive at the International Border at San Ysidro/Tijuana," reported Progressive Labor's newspaper of its own picket line. It saw the Klan as the advance guard of the racist state. The killing of five members of the Communist Workers Party in Greensboro, North Carolina, in November 1979 by a Klan-Nazi alliance virtually under police protection was a sign to both sides that they were on the right track. There was even a Greensboro song to the tune of "Sixteen Tons" written by a California Klansman who was a friend of Tom's:

> They shot fourteen Reds and five of them died
> If you're gonna be a Commie better run and hide
> When a White man talks he uses fire and steel
> And if the Nazis don't get you a Klansman will
> A Klansman will.

Another popular number sung when the boys got together was "Gas 'Em All":

> Gas 'em all.
> Gas 'em all.
> The long, the short, the tall.
> We are coming to power
> We'll gas Jews every hour
> Oh, what the hell, gas 'em all.

In November 1979, during a major national Klan leadership meeting in New Orleans, Tom and a number of other key members of the Knights of the Ku Klux Klan acknowledged to themselves what it would take outsiders much longer to learn: that Imperial

Wizard David Duke was a weak, untrustworthy leader who could not be counted on to lead them very far. Dissembling to the public was one thing; deceiving his own kinsmen was something else. Duke's recently exposed pseudonymous authorship of a sex manual for women and a self-defense manual for blacks, as well as his money-grubbing sale of the Klan mailing lists to a competing Klan leader—without cutting the rest of them in on it—were all fundamental matters. Nor was he good in a pinch. At an encounter with police during a cross lighting that week, Duke had urged Klansmen to throw their Klan ID cards into the fire, while a much cooler Tom told them to keep their cards in their wallets, talked calmly to the officers, and enabled the ceremonies to go on. Four years earlier, observing Duke's harsh treatment of his staff toward the end of his election campaign, Tom had doubted whether Duke had the necessary qualities to keep people working together, but now he knew. When Duke appeared onstage before three hundred people at the close of the week dressed only in a bathing suit, delivered a speech about physical fitness, and began lifting weights, it was the end. Tom and Grand Dragon Louis Beam, an influential Texan, looked at each other across the room and rolled their eyes. Back home, Tom sent Duke a letter of resignation citing their "moral differences," rechristened the California KKKK chapter the California Klan, and was on his own.

The 1979 Klan conference was important for another reason: the idea of gaining power through the electoral process, first outlined by George Lincoln Rockwell, was one of its principal themes. Tom himself had already run for two local offices in 1978—the Fallbrook planning board, for which he won nearly five hundred votes, and the San Diego County Board of Supervisors, for which he received more than eleven thousand votes, nearly 11 percent of the total— but now, carrying out the spirit of the meeting, he was ready for a bigger move. Looking around and noticing that the popular three-term Republican representative of the Forty-third Congressional

District, Clair Burgener, was effectively running unopposed against a token Democratic candidate who had won the honor by losing a coin toss, he decided to run as a Democrat himself. The story of Tom's 1980 congressional election campaign cannot be told without beginning with the crucial anomaly that the campaign manager, bodyguard, and general factotum who carried Tom from a narrow 392-vote victory in the June primary to a 46,383—14 percent— showing against Burgener in November was a San Diego Police Department reserve officer named Doug Seymour, working under-cover in the Klan. It was Seymour who provided the final signatures required for Tom to qualify for the primary by the official deadline; Seymour who supplied much of the food, drink, transportation, and other niceties needed to turn the unanticipated primary win into a real campaign; Seymour who protected him from the rocks and cans thrown by angry mobs at many of his campaign appearances; Sey-mour who, on an occasion when the weapon was not a rock but a gun, probably even saved his life. That the other major figure in the campaign was Rockwell supporter Don Musgrove—whose principal distinction besides being a Nazi was reputedly being the oldest living cystic fibrosis patient in the United States—only makes the situation more weird. Weirder still was Tom's later claim that he knew Sey-mour was a cop from the time he joined the Klan in 1979 and ignored the fact not only because he liked Seymour but because who else had a $200,000 house in Escondido, a well-stocked bar, an infinite supply of radios and walkie-talkies, a Winnebago, a Lin-coln Continental, and above all a license to carry that made this dangerous business of politics just a little safer? What Tom's cam-paign might have come to without the help of the San Diego Police Department we have no way to know, but between an informant who—as he is now the first to admit—at times lost his bearings, a card-carrying member of the National Socialist White People's Party, and an irrepressible candidate who believed that he was pull-ing the strings, whether or not he was in fact pulling all of them, it was quite a team.

Apart from its curious foundation, however, Tom Metzger's

campaign for Congress was a genuine phenomenon, for it represented the one time in his career that he had the opportunity to go
beyond the racist movement and become a figure with a real following in the country at large. He was a natural campaigner. Genial, unpretentious, and energetic, he was a good listener as well as
talker, he learned quickly, and when he appeared on the hustings,
especially dressed in his three-piece suit, he was likely as not to
leave with more friends than when he arrived. The Forty-third
Congressional District was a vast chunk of California that included
most of the coastal and inland communities between San Diego and
San Clemente, the dry, agricultural Imperial Valley to the east
running all the way down to the Arizona border, and a portion of
the rural areas southwest of Riverside, and he took it on seriously,
traveling sometimes hundreds of miles a day to make himself known
to the voters and hear what they had to say. Early in the campaign
he even nominally dissolved the Klan, creating instead a White
American Political Association (WAPA), with which he hoped to
broaden his appeal. While not concealing his racism, Tom's campaign emphasized not only "reverse discrimination," busing, and the
"swarms" of Cuban and Asian refugees entering the United States
but the exportation of American jobs, dependence on foreign oil,
and the buying up of American corporations and property by foreign
investors, in a way that had as much a populist as a racist cast.
Whether you were a retiree in Palm Desert or a barber in Temecula,
it was easy to find something in common with him. "He's against
the invasion of this country by illegal aliens, which is lowering our
wage scale and putting Americans out of work. I'm against that
too. He's against people on welfare that can work getting money.
I'm against that too," said a well-dressed businessman in one of the
many man-in-the-street interviews featured in the press and TV
during the campaign. "I think the policies that he's espoused need
to be heard, reviewed, and assessed by the entire country," said a
man in a cowboy hat in another town. A speech at San Diego State
that began with a violent attack on Tom as he was on his way in
ended quite differently in a quiet classroom with the students lis-

tening, if not in agreement, at least in respect. After a speech at a Sears store in La Jolla, a store manager told a reporter, "I'm favorably impressed. I think Mr. Metzger's ideas coincide with some of mine." He was also a paragon of flexibility. In the Imperial Valley he worked with an old Jewish anti-agribusiness activist who was trying to help small farmers get their fair share of loans and water. In El Centro he met with members of the Mexican American community who shared his views on illegal immigrants and who, when the returns were counted, appeared to have been impressed enough with his integrity to give him their votes. Others were less easily swayed. The list of people who came out against him and appealed to others to do the same ran from President Carter in Washington to almost the entire establishment of San Diego and beyond— Governor Jerry Brown, Mayor Pete Wilson, police chief Bill Kolender, Urban League chair Clarence Pendleton, Bishop Leo Maher, the San Diego Ecumenical Council, the San Diego Rabbinical Association, the San Diego Evangelical Association, and more. Democrats throughout the state endorsed the Republican Burgener rather than be associated with Tom. The only California politician who seems both not to have been afraid of contamination by Tom and to have known exactly what he was looking at was the former Democratic governor, Pat Brown. At a Democratic fund-raiser in Palm Springs at which Tom had made an unwelcome appearance, Brown greeted him openly, shook his hand, and said aloud what all observers of the campaign knew in their hearts to be true: "Tom, you make a hell of a politician. If you changed a few of your ideas you could go far."

Tom's shunning by the establishment during the primary campaign only increased afterward. The entire Democratic apparatus closed its doors. As the candidate he was entitled to several seats for himself and his appointees on various state and local Democratic committees, but when, after numerous lesser affronts, he tried to take his place at a Democratic Central Committee meeting in Sacramento, he was forced from the room. Tom's public reaction was, of course, political—he claimed that his constitutional rights were being violated—but his expulsion must have been personally galling as well. News clips show him seated alone as if none of the other delegates can bear to be near him, he is denounced with ministerial righteousness by the chair, and as he is finally led away by an armed California state trooper he looks and sounds like nothing so much as a small boy forced for the moment to surrender to authority but vowing to return another day. In spite of Tom's disclaimers that his election bid was only part of a national Klan strategy, I believe that his encounter with the electoral system was in fact of deep personal and political importance to him. At the least it raises a number of questions that deserve to be stated, even if they cannot be fully resolved. The first is: Did the political route suggested by Pat Brown ever hold any real temptation for him? Were there seductions of power that might have led him to a different course? While there is no evidence for this and Tom claims otherwise, the answer is, "How could there not have been?" Power is power. "I found before the primary that my parents, who were visiting from Indiana, were upset by my Klan activities and they went home in a huff, but after I won it was a whole different story; people worship power," Tom told a reporter. He noticed. What's more, he had the prime ingredient central to a successful American political life: he enjoyed it. Ideological content aside, there was a rapport between Tom and his audiences that is the stuff of which political careers are made. And his family could have stepped out of a campaign handout. A second question is: Did his public rejection affect his later political development? Here we are in even more private territory, but I suspect that there was an echo in it for him of his constant denunciations by his mother for the sins of his father when he was a child. My contact with Tom's mother has been limited to a brief telephone call, but when she asked me what the people I had been speaking to in Warsaw were saying about Tom and I replied, "I have to tell you that nobody here has a bad word to say about him," she exploded, "That's just the trouble," which struck me less as a criticism of Warsaw's failure to condemn his racism than as a cry of frustration that she and and she alone had known all along he was damned. If any theme runs through Tom's interviews with reporters over the years it is: I'll be as bad as they say I am. "The more people yelled, bitched, and threw things at me, the more I became the things they said I was," is one of his typical formulations. "When people called me a racist when I wasn't, finally I just stuck out my chin and said, Well, if you want it that bad, I will be, and I'll be the loudest one you ever saw," he told me in 1989, in our first conversation, still piqued at what he felt to be the unfair characterization of the 1968 George Wallace campaign. "If you think that was bad, how about this?" is one of his instinctive responses to threat or challenge, and, without reducing a movement-wide political evolution to personality, it is worth noting that his White American Political Association was first renamed White American Resistance, then renamed again White Aryan Resistance, an escalating "badness" as well as an escalating distance from the social and political mainstream. The hardest questions are these: What is the relationship between Metzger's political positions and his moral character? "I'm Tom Metzger, Evil One," he would introduce himself affably to the Portland jury. Is he? Does everything he has stood for, particularly in the years since the *A* in WAR became "Aryan," automatically make him a "bad" person, or must "badness" involve "acts" beyond "words," or must the "words" themselves be considered "acts," which they sometimes are and sometimes are not, according to which way the First Amendment winds are blowing at a particular time? If Tom Metzger had become a conventional politician subject to the moderating forces of the American political process rather than a movement politician subject to the reverse, would we be speculating about his "character" at all? While no one would claim that it is impossible for a conventional politician to be a "bad" person, what about the opposite? Is it possible for a racist politician to be "good"? How "bad" is Tom Metzger personally? How far would he actually go? According to the police infiltrator Doug Seymour, who was often present, Tom knew about the ugly actions in which his Klan boys were often engaged, but when there were fights to be settled, debts to be paid, or people to be threatened or intimidated, he didn't participate himself, drawing a line around himself—for the sake of . . . his conscience? . . . his family? . . . his business?—that would protect him from a moral reckoning. That he never intentionally violated a law is one of his favorite claims. Instead he took up the plaintive cry of politicians everywhere who do not wish to get their hands dirty, the Henry II–Thomas à Becket strategy: "Will no one rid me of this man?" When someone in a white neighborhood told a Klansman that a black person had moved in next door, Tom hinted that "It would sure be too bad if someone wrote 'KKK' all over that house." When something illegal was going to happen during a particular meeting, he stayed away. When the Klan planned a night ride to the home of a black city council member after a cross-burning ceremony in Fontana, Tom went home first.

Any moral accounting of Tom Metzger would be remiss if it did not also note that throughout his entire political evolution he would remain a good father and husband. No one who has felt the venom of his racist and antisemitic ideas or heard the thrill with which he has long uttered such phrases as "Turd World" or "Martin Lucifer Coon" could fail to sense that beneath his political line is a human disturbance for which such politics must be a release, but evidently it is release enough, for whatever anger and regression it contains were not imposed on his family. There he was a model of maturity. No matter what strains he was under, he stayed on the parental job, checking on schoolwork, making sure his daughters were behaving themselves, attending Little League games with John, and if, leaving the field, he would throw his arm around the boy, mingling his praise with the consolation that, after all, there were too many niggers or Jews on the other team, both items have to be entered in the ledger. Nor was he controlling about his politics. "My dad specifically told me that if I believed everything he said because he said it, he wouldn't respect me," Lynn Metzger, Tom's third daughter, a mainstay of a WAR offshoot called the Aryan Women's League, told me, and John, who became Tom's closest political ally, has told me the same. This is not to say participation was not rewarded—"I got a quarter for each hundred envelopes I licked," says Lynn, recalling the communal activities in which the business of WAR actually got done—but it was not a condition for acceptance. The only one of the four older children who is not a racist—the second daughter, Dorraine, a music teacher—is not otherwise estranged, her photo and her children's photos carried in Tom's wallet with the rest of the family's, and when he boasts like any father that one of his two younger girls was admitted to a major university on full scholarship he sounds proud of her intellectual independence. In addition to his strong relationships with his children, Tom Metzger was also faithful to his wife. He and Doug Seymour are as one in recalling that when Tom could have had a prostitute at the New Orleans Klan meeting in 1979, he turned her down. There, too, his loyalty was requited. Coming home from the hospital where she had given birth to their fifth child prematurely a few weeks after rocks had been thrown through their bedroom window, Kathy gave an interview to the San Diego paper describing their life together that was a very paean of wifely appreciation. According to John and Lynn, as well as to household visitors, she was the picture of solidarity. Tom has also never lacked for friendship. The nature of the relationships he shares with his ever-present male followers is not open to this writer's inspection, but they appear comfortable. Doug Seymour himself told me that when, after a traumatic exposure, he subpoenaed Tom to testify at his lawsuit against the San Diego Police Department for having left him in such an impossible situation for so long to begin with, Tom seems to have genuinely understood his dilemma. Tom has a natural fellow feeling, an instinctive sympathy for others, that has no place in his political rhetoric. When Whoopi Goldberg asked him on her short-lived TV show what he would do if he saw a black child left in the street by a hit-and-run driver, he replied he would stop his car, gather up the child, and take it to the hospital, and

I think he would. Where there was a contradiction between his instincts and his ideology, he dismissed it with a joke. He liked the Mexican Americans he met with in El Centro and they liked him, and when they actually made a small donation to his campaign, he turned to Seymour and said, "Mark this down. Gas them last." He also liked Clarence Pendleton, the black head of the San Diego Urban League, later head of the U.S. Civil Rights Commission, who treated him more civilly than most, and after Pendleton greeted him normally the night of his primary win, when the rest of the political figures at the Election Watch were in shock, he said, "He's not such a bad old Uncle Tom. Gas him last." I sometimes wondered during the course of this book what Tom made of me. We had many good conversations and a few good meals over the years, we cooperated in obtaining his FBI files and on other things, and I often felt that he enjoyed our contacts, as I did. Once I thought he had forgotten I was a Jew. Until I wrote this chapter I did not understand how he resolved the conflict but now I think I know the answer: "She's not such a bad old kike," I can hear him saying to himself. "Gas her last."

24

In the early 1980s, Tom began looking for something new. Electoral politics required too many compromises. When a 1982 run for a U.S. Senate seat netted only 3 percent of the votes in the state Democratic primary, he brought his political career to a close. WAPA, the front-style White American Political Association, which had succeeded the Klan for such purposes as staging public meetings, went too, as we have seen, to be replaced first by the more obviously militant White American Resistance and then, when that proved too tepid or even ambiguous—for there were those who persisted in believing Jews were white—by its frankest, most revolutionary form yet, White Aryan Resistance, a network of racists with origins in the California Klan whose name meant exactly what it said. About the same time, Tom read a newspaper report about public access requirements being built into franchise regulations for the newly emerging cable TV technology, and he saw at once something WAR could actually use. He had already begun making audiotapes of his public appearances and marketing them, along with other items, through the *Klan News*. Perhaps he could create a series of videotapes and market those too. Within weeks, John, now a technically competent teenager, and a number of Tom's other followers had started to use the Orange County cable company Group W's studio on the campus of California State University at Fullerton to produce a TV interview show first called *Race* and shortly renamed *Race and Reason* for cable access. Soon John and about a dozen others had taken part in the free training in production techniques sponsored by Cox Cable in San Diego as well.

That a man with Tom Metzger's lifelong involvement with television should have seen the possibilities for the racist movement in public access TV seems natural enough after the fact, but it was quite a feat of imagination when it happened. With cable just beginning and access audiences literally too small to be counted, envisioning a clumsy, locally produced "talk show" as a resource for a national grassroots political network took an understanding of the power of the media few people had. Twice a month, dressed in a three-piece suit and tie, he would smile into the camera, introduce his guest, usually a significant person in the racist movement, say, "Hi! This is Tom Metzger, your host for *Race and Reason*, that island of free speech in a sea of controlled and managed news," steer the conversation through the points he wished to have made, and presto! suddenly he was a talk show host, accepted as one both within the movement and without. His use of public access television also took an understanding both of the meaning of the First Amendment and of the way it worked. Like it or not, *Race and Reason* was exactly what public access was designed to protect. He was on strong ground. From the news of its production in a public university facility to its unpopular content, *Race and Reason* created outrage wherever it became known, and wherever there was out-

rage, there were the real talk show hosts, relieved to find in Tom
Metzger a competent, professional spokesman for the "other side."
There was something about being a "talk show host," like being a
"former congressional candidate," that was reassuring. He was a nice
guy. Before long Tom would be catapulted from public access to
prime time, appearing with increasing frequency on both local and
national programs up to and including *Oprah* and *Geraldo*, debating
the constitutional issues raised by *Race and Reason* before vast audiences and becoming practically a respectable figure in the process.
Within his own circles, too, the show offered numerous opportunities. As the movement developed, the selection of guests automatically left Tom in an influential position to emphasize certain
directions and downplay others. *Race and Reason* helped define the
agenda. It also offered Tom more personal benefits. When visitors
from out of town such as Richard Butler of the Aryan Nations or
Ben Klassen of the Church of the Creator were scheduled, Tom
would often pick them up at the airport, bring them home, swap
ideas and experiences, learn what was on their minds. With the
locals he often went out for beer. For younger guests in particular,
an appearance on *Race and Reason* became a badge of honor,
rewarding not only in the excitement of production but in the
knowledge that the show was part of an informal neo-Nazi curriculum with Tom as instructor that would help spread the message
of the movement nationwide. *Race and Reason* was an extraordinary
political creation. Out of his own experiences, from his emergence
as a Klan leader at Pendleton to running for political office, Tom
had thoroughly grasped the wisdom of George Lincoln Rockwell:
the shortest route for an American Nazi into the minds of the American people is the Bill of Rights.

Along with his new forum, Tom also had new ideas. The insecu-
rity of the blue-collar workers and small business owners he had met
during his campaigns, his own struggles with the Internal Revenue
Service and the Democratic Party, perhaps even his reading of the
leftist newspapers distributed at his political appearances all led him
to a conclusion that would shape his further direction as much as

racism itself: a racial worldview was not enough. There were larger forces at work than he had previously realized. There was a System. Turning to books, he discovered the work of such American historians as Charles Beard, who told the story of the country from an economic viewpoint, and he fused their analyses with his own. A vision of the Civil War as the mutual slaughter of white men for the benefit of the business classes of both sides is a case in point. He was enthralled by the anticapitalism of Major General Smedley Butler, a disenchanted former marine—"I helped make Honduras 'right' for American fruit companies in 1903. I helped make Mexico safe for American oil interests in 1914. . . . I brought light to the Dominican Republic for the American sugar interests in 1916"—and he quoted Butler's famous "War is a racket" speech many times. As he moved toward a larger picture of American history and politics, nothing interested him more than the early-twentieth-century struggles of labor against capital, with their great working-class leaders, Big Bill Haywood, Eugene Debs, and above all that fiery California intellectual Jack London, whose own racism, embedded as it was in a socialist framework, enhanced Tom's conviction that he could combine both as well. "I am a Socialist, a revolutionary Socialist, an up-on-the-hind-legs fighting Socialist Labour Party man . . . but above all else I AM A WHITE MAN," London wrote, according to a New Zealand pamphlet called *Radical Origins of Racial Nationalism* Tom quoted in the WAR newspaper. In London's powerful 1908 novel *The Iron Heel*, which tells of a future socialist revolt crushed by the oligarchy, Tom found a new political metaphor that would serve him for a long time to come. He did not jettison Nazism, but he found among the early followers of Hitler the radical brothers Otto and Gregor Strasser, the one in exile after 1930, the other murdered in the 1934 purge, new mentors whose idea of a "Third Position" between Nazism and Communism allowed him to keep both his old racialism and his new socialism intact. "You say, 'The government is too big, we can't organize,' " Tom once berated his followers. "Well, by God, the SA did in Germany and if they did in Germany in the thirties we can do it right here in the streets of

America!" Tom was not a theoretician, he was a man of action, and the exact mix of rationality and irrationality in his new program is ultimately beside the point, but in leading the racist movement beyond its narrow origins in the right toward the broader economic analysis normally associated with the left, he was creating a political space for it potentially greater than any it had occupied for some time. Compared with the rest of the Aryans out there, he was a political genius.

On December 3, 1983, Tom Metzger of WAR, Richard Butler of the Aryan Nations, and about a dozen other assorted Klansmen, members of the American Nazi Party, and freelance racists attended a cross burning in a neigborhood called Kagel Canyon in the San Fernando Valley. Planned as a white supremacist unity meeting, the gathering also included a couple of informants and a fair number of protestors from the Jewish Defense League. The cross burning caused Tom endless difficulties. Busted by the Los Angeles Police Department and prosecuted through numerous challenges by the L.A. city attorney as a fire code violation, it became after eight years of litigation the only offense for which he ever went to jail, a conviction for "misdemeanor unlawful assembly" that coincided with the lowest ebb of his fortunes in other respects, as we will see later on. But the Kagel Canyon cross burning, as it came to be known, was important to Tom for another reason. For rightly or wrongly— and the point has never been proved—it has long been understood as a tacit salute to the initiation of the most genuinely radical group the racist movement had yet produced: the underground terrorist organization known as the Order.

Thanks to a vast FBI investigation, a federal trial in Seattle in 1985–86 that put all its members in jail, and several books, the story of the Order is undoubtedly the best-known chapter in the history of the American racist movement in the 1980s. Established at his rural home in Metaline Falls, Washington, by Robert Jay Mathews, a young romantic, former Arizona tax protester with a gift for persuading others to follow him, the Order did what no other organization on the racist right had done on a sustained basis: it acted. "I, as a free Aryan man, hereby swear an unrelenting oath upon the green graves of our sires, upon the children in the wombs of our wives, upon the throne of God almighty, sacred be His name, to join together in holy union with the brothers in this circle," swore the twelve founding members, Sieg Heiling over a borrowed Aryan baby in October 1983. "From this moment, I have the sacred duty to do whatever is necessary to deliver our people from the Jew and bring total victory to the Aryan race." What was remarkable about the Order was not merely its stout Aryan rhetoric but its seriousness. It was a revolutionary organization. "We declare ourselves to be in a full and unrelenting state of war with those forces seeking and consciously promoting the destruction of our faith and our race," concluded a "Declaration of War" issued when the FBI was literally at its doors. There was even a "Principles of War and Rules of Engagement" promising to abide by the Geneva Convention but defining anyone who cooperated with the Zionist Occupation Government—that is, the government—whether with a local police officer or a member of the armed forces, as a combatant. The immediate aim of the Order was to provide the leadership and funds required to turn the scattered white supremacist movement into a unified revolutionary army. Its ultimate goal was its own territory, a White American Bastion, aka the Pacific Northwest. Inspired by *The Turner Diaries*—the guide to underground action and organization written in the form of a novel by William Pierce, the founder of the neo-Nazi National Alliance, who was one of Mathews's principal mentors—members of the Order counterfeited money on a press at the Aryan Nations, robbed banks in Seattle and Spokane, and held up an armored car at a Seattle shopping mall and a Brinks truck in Ukiah, California, all between November 1983 and July 1984. They also bombed a Boise synagogue, killed an Aryan Nations member suspected of having a loose tongue, and murdered the popular Denver talk show host Alan Berg along the way. Traced through a gun left by Mathews himself on the floor of the van during the Brinks robbery, the group finally became the subject of an epic federal manhunt greatly aided by the betrayal of Mathews by a follower named Thomas Martinez, who, caught passing the counterfeit money, turned informant and agreed to help the FBI set him up. The setup failed. Ambushed at the seedy Capri Motel in Portland in late November 1984, the wounded Mathews leaped over the balcony and made his way first to Brightwood, Oregon, near Mount Hood, where the Order had previously established five safe houses, and then, with the Brightwood group, to Whidbey Island in Washington's Puget Sound, where they had rented several more. Now the FBI was not far behind. It mounted a major military operation. On December 7, 1984, neighbors were evacuated, shipping lanes shut down, air traffic suspended. Surrounded by about a hundred agents, some of the Order members surrendered, some were captured, but Mathews held out. "White men killing white men, Saxon killing Dane. When will it end? The Aryans' bane," he asked in a florid final testament about the white agents he observed in his gunsights but forbore to shoot. He did not forbear long. A one-man armory, he withstood a major tear-gas attack, held his own in a gun battle with agents who stormed the house, and fired a machine gun at a helicopter gunship hovering overhead. On the evening of December 8, flares were lobbed into the house, which the FBI knew in advance would set it on fire. Mathews stayed inside. About all that was left when the house cooled down enough to be entered the next morning was the gold *"Bruders Schweigen"*—for "Silent Brotherhood"—medallion worn by all members of the Order melted into his chest. One member of the Order had already been captured in the Capri shootout; the rest were soon rounded up. In spite of the fact that many members of the Silent Brotherhood later talked, most of the $5 million stolen by the Order for its war chest has never been found.

Coming as it did when the Reagan era, the worldwide economic recession of the early 1980s, and the cumulative effects of the racial reforms of the 1960s and 1970s were already unleashing a new surge of racism and antisemitism across the country, the revolutionary Order was the greatest political challenge either Tom or any other racist leader ever had to face. To distance oneself from it was to be exposed as a mere talker: to assist it risked at the least going to jail: to position oneself between the two poles required considerable balance. How close Tom actually was to the Order is an unresolvable question. It was, after all, clandestine. Following the confession of one of its no longer silent members that Tom had received as much as $300,000 from the group, the FBI began a major investigation that identified a moment in 1984 when Mathews was in San Diego that a transfer of funds could theoretically have taken place, but no evidence was ever discovered and the allegation was later withdrawn. More important than cash is whether Tom was part of a larger racist circle that may have influenced the conception of the Order in the first place or provided underground support later on. He probably was. For several years Tom had been calling for the formation of underground cells to counter police infiltration such as that he had already experienced himself; while he did not have direct ties to Mathews, he was close to Frank Silva and Randy Evans, two California Klansmen who were Mathews's recruits; he was knowledgeable about communications and security; and it seems more natural that he would have given technical assistance than that he would not. On an Order memo found by the FBI assigning positions to various people after the revolution, Tom was designated as a "civil administrator" slated to take charge of a portion of the West Coast. On another was his code name: "Radio."

What is clearer is that as soon as the Order died, Tom was at great pains to revive it, not as an action group but as a myth. He had an instinctive feeling for the usefulness to the racialist movement of an updated list of Aryan martyrs and he officially or unofficially took on the job of creating one, identifying himself so closely with the fallen organization that at times the line between where the Order stopped and WAR started became blurred. Shortly after Mathews's death Tom took his cable TV crew on a pious journey to Washington for an "In Search of Robert Mathews" *Race and Reason* special. At the Mathews's fifty-three-acre farm he interviewed Bob's widow, Debby. "I know Bob's death wasn't in vain from all the letters I've received," Debby told him sorrowfully.

Tom: (Gently) That's for sure.
Debby: It's not going to be extinguished until we have ultimate victory.
Tom: (Ditto) Course it won't.

He also praised the Aryanness of Bob's adopted son, neatly skirting the well-known fact that Mathews had lately deposited his Aryan seed in the womb of a mistress who had, alas, produced a girl; traveled across the state and took "the big ferry" to Whidbey Island, where he camped "on the spot where [Mathews] fought his last fight"; filmed in the light of a car headlamp; and evidently got sick in the process, because it is a very sniffly *Race and Reason*. As the WAR paper developed, Tom devoted page after page to the group, tracking who was talking and who was not, publishing the myriad communications of the faithful, and eventually creating a regular "Prisoners of War" feature giving their prison addresses and asking readers to support them with donations and news. When he placed a trailer on some property in Rainbow, California, to hold WAR meetings, he named it Mathews Hall, and on several occasions taped telephone speeches by Order members, including Frank Silva and David Lane, one of the participants in the Berg killing, rang out across the land. Both on the television show and in the paper there were frequent tributes to Mathews himself. In time these venues reached all across the world. Bob Mathews was not the only Aryan martyr of the moment—there was John Singer, a Utah Mormon shot by police in a struggle over his refusal to send his children to public schools in 1979; Gordon Kahl, a North Dakota farmer and tax protester belonging to a group called the Posse Comitatus, incinerated, much like Mathews, after a gun battle with federal marshals in a hideout in Arkansas in 1983; and Arthur Kirk, another Posse farmer, killed in a gun battle with a Nebraska SWAT team only six weeks before Mathews himself—and these martyrs also found a place in Metzger's pantheon, but Mathews was best. He was everything a propagandist could want. Young, idealistic, and brave, he smiled out from the many photos reproduced in WAR, now in hard hat and work clothes outside the Metaline Falls zinc mine where he worked, now snuggling with his son and his dog, the perfect combination of strength and soul. He was even a poet. At the same time, Tom knew exactly how far he could go. To join the Order was one thing. To praise it was something else. Federal authorities in the heat of the Order and subsequent investigations were continually frustrated by Tom's adept use of the First Amendment. "He does not attempt to conceal his involvement and beliefs in the white supremacy movement [but] he has been careful to give the appearance of being law abiding, however extreme his personal views," reads a typical report. "In spite of the fact that [he] is careful about his public comments . . . he stated [on a talk show] that the incarcerated Order members were 'men ahead of their time.' When the host questioned how he could say that considering these men were convicted of robbery, murder, counterfeiting etc., Metzger simply reaffirmed his statement that they were men ahead of their time. During the same program he also stated that although he would not kill a Federal official or marshal who was attempting to collect taxes, he was certainly glad there were people who would (referring to Gordon Kahl). Metzger added that he hated Federal agents." Tom Metzger never lacked physical courage, but he did have a life to lead. He was the first to cry out from behind the thick safety glass of the American Constitution a call now uttered by neo-Nazis all over the world whenever they get together: "HAIL BOB MATHEWS! HAIL THE ORDER! HAIL VICTORY!"

A HUNDRED LITTLE HITLERS

WAR believes that if it works, use it. If it doesn't, try something else.

—TOM METZGER, 1988

25

What Tom learned from his observation of the Order was: it is time to get on the move. In fact, the idea was a movement commonplace. "We, the older and less active spokesmen for the folk and faith are being replaced by the young lions," proclaimed the Midwestern white supremacist Robert Miles in late 1984. "These dragons of God have no time for pamphlets, for speeches, for gatherings. They know their role. They know their duty. They are the armed party which is being born out of the inability of white male youths to be heard." Tom concurred. From twenty years of experience he sensed that the economic dislocation of all but the rich that was the mark of Reaganomics would create new political opportunities for the racist movement, but with his own generation content to sit around at Miles's place in Michigan or Butler's in Idaho and repeat the same slogans and his own followers an unambitious lot content for the most part to drink and talk, he did not know how the movement could make use of them. Among the younger people Tom had met in his appearances on the California hustings, one in particular stood out, an enterprising Sacramento racist named Gregory Withrow. Withrow, twenty-three, had admired Tom for years. He had joined the California Klan in 1979 when Tom was Grand Dragon, followed him through its development into the White American Political Association and WAR, and thrilled as only a young man can when his own initiatives brought him to the notice of the great man. The reader may perhaps recall Greg Withrow. He is the one who told a TV reporter in the summer of 1987 that he had left the movement for love, was found soon after outside a Kmart, his hands nailed to a board, his throat cut, and survived his "crucifixion" to tell the story over and over again, to other reporters, on television, and on film. He is also, in or out, the most Nazi-like person I talked to in the course of this work, not in the sense of present political allegiance but in the sense of a deep mystical feeling for "the race" as a force in history that would not have been out of place in Himmler's castle. That a boy born in California in 1961 should be so steeped in racialism is not as impossible as it sounds. According to an unpublished autobiography titled "Child of the Fourth Reich," which is the source of much that follows, he had been given *Mein Kampf* as a birthday present when he was seven years old. Son of a drunken small-time Nazi sympathizer bent on grooming the fruit of his loins to be the Fuehrer he could never be, Greg not only participated from an early age in an assortment of underground neo-Nazi activities occurring throughout the state but continued his training at home, forced by his father to such triumphs of the juvenile will as beating up a black boy who had become his friend and killing his own dog. Nor did such acts of fealty get him what he wanted, for

Greg Withrow's father had nothing to give. He was pitiless and pretentious both. Trying to extract from his son the full measure of respect for his authority denied him elsewhere in life, he refused even to be called "Dad" or "Daddy," insisting on "Father" or "Honored Father." He called his offspring "It"—or else the offspring has a remarkable imagination. The mother, the custodial parent after her separation from the father when Greg was three, was not much of a countervailing force. Greg's political history and his emotional history are hard to separate. From the age of ten, when he began doing drugs he pocketed by helping sweep up the Sacramento nightclub where his father worked, his life was a succession of internal eruptions and external confrontations that shared the essential characteristic: pain. What is singular about Greg Withrow is not the miserable record of drugs, arrests, detentions, mental hospitals, and escapes—twenty-four are cited in his book—that filled the years between 1973, when he was twelve, and 1979, when he was eighteen: it is the way his criminality and his politics came together. Somewhere between the correctional tortures of the state of California and the random desperation of the streets, he had not so much a revelation as a kind of spiritual awakening: His father was right! That slimy Jesus-spouting queer who wanted to seduce him stood for all the hypocrisies of Judeo-Christian civilization. What a fraud! One moment he was part of a loose band of street brothers complete with fake blind men and cripples sleeping under newspapers and cardboard in Chinese Park and eating from trash bins. The next he was transforming these experiences into a new political understanding: the tired, poor, wretched, tempest-tossed derelicts of the streets of San Francisco were white! The opposite side of the coin was also true: those gangster Crips who had scared and humiliated him during a stint at a California youth home in L.A. were black! The whites needed a leader! Putting together his childhood images with ideas gleaned from more recent readings of Nietzsche and Hitler in the San Francisco Public Library, he arrived at the idea that it was time to take things into his own hands. Before long he had engaged in his first act of political—as opposed to random—

violence: beating up a gay man who whistled at him in Golden Gate Park. With a few other boys he formed what may well have been the first neo-Nazi youth gang in the United States, the League of Aryan Assassins, which rolled black and Mexican drunks for their welfare or disability checks, hit up the point men for Chinese drug dealers, and mugged Japanese tourists. The League of Aryan Assassins was not quite as streetwise as it thought. According to Greg's autobiography, a longhaired, poncho-wearing drug dealer sleeping it off in a San Francisco doorway with his pill bottles exposed and an expensive camera on his lap was a police decoy. It was December 1977 and Greg was sixteen and a half years old. For the umpteenth time he went through a cycle of arrest, detention, and hospitalization, ending up remanded to the custody of his similarly unrehabilitated father, but the vision held: "Wandering a drearily littered street in San Francisco with three other enraged and disillusioned young men . . . I vowed to create the largest, most violent white supremacist group this nation had ever seen."

In 1980, after finishing his GED, he was ready to put his vision into practice. Excited by the example of Allen Bakke, whose famous charge of white discrimination against the University of California Medical School in Sacramento had done so much to reinflame black-white relations, he enrolled at a Sacramento junior college called American River College (ARC) and began organizing a White Student Union (WSU). In spite of his years on drugs, Greg Withrow was smart, he could be rational enough when he had to, and he was a good actor. With his bright red hair and red moustache, he was a conspicuous figure. He was also an instinctive strategist. From his deceitful interviews with fellow students whom he was asking to sign a simple petition in support of the WSU's right to exist to his secret tie-breaking vote against himself at a meeting of the Inter-Club Council in order to create the appearance of repression, he developed, step by step, a classic front-style political organization as surely as if he were using a Communist handbook from the 1930s. The purpose of the front structure was twofold. One level— "overt"—would be a group of moderate collegiate recruits who in modeling themselves after the black, Hispanic, gay, and other student organizations on campus were demanding only "Equal Rights for Whites." The other level—"covert"—would be a cadre of street fighters who would ultimately take the movement in the violent direction Greg meant for it to go. The first would be a lure for the second. Nor was this only a matter of theory. The strategy worked. On the one hand: the local papers were full of news and letters about the struggle over freedom of expression at ARC, reports that gave Greg considerable personal publicity in the form of radio and television appearances, newspaper interviews, and so on between 1980 and 1983. On the other hand: the publicity helped him not only to attract and identify students prepared to carry the white constitutional rights banner on campus but to reach out still further to create the militant underground Aryan Youth Movement (AYM) that he says was part of his plan from the beginning. The White Student Union, the Aryan Youth Movement, and a group of Sacramento skinheads emerging at about the same time were part of the same conception. How the parts made a whole is shown by two Northern California deaths that occurred during this period for which Greg, in his autobiography, claims credit, one in Oroville, north of Sacramento, the other in Davis. In Oroville, an adult Nazi who had been using Greg's White Student Union literature to attract young people murdered a seventeen-year-old recruit who had confessed to the police who and what was behind the racist leafleting at his school. In Davis, a Vietnamese high school student was killed in a fight with a white student during a flare-up of racial tension undoubtedly heightened by a nighttime propaganda assault by Greg's Aryan guerrillas about a month before. The second death could perhaps have happened in any case, but the defiant we-are-still-here leafleting of the high school campus on the day of the boy's funeral and the littering of his grave entitled the young Aryans to claim it as their own. As he looked around at the start he had made toward implementing his vision of violence, Greg Withrow had every reason to feel satisfied.

To Tom, watching the news on television, it was obvious that Greg had a quality too often lacking in the racial movement: drive. As for Greg, Tom held an exalted position somewhere between Adolf Hitler and his father. They kept each other in sight during Greg's early years on the scene—a letter here, a phone call there, moral and practical support in both directions—in the spirit not so much of teacher and student as of two comrades marching side by side. In February 1984, when Tom was ready to produce his cable TV show, Greg Withrow was exactly what he wanted. Inviting Greg down from Sacramento, Tom paid his plane fare, housed him overnight with the family in Fallbrook, and hauled him off next day to the Fullerton studio where the first taping was about to begin. Greg Withrow's performance on a show that would take its place as one of Tom Metzger's major assets in his campaign to attract the young was strikingly polished. He was straight, to the point of being stuffy. Gone were the bizarre history, the criminal record, the Nazi image. In their place was a quiet, legalistic college student forced by the capitulation of American River College authorities to aggressive minorities to take appropriate action to protect the rights of whites. Tom also was no slouch of a performer. With his skillful probing of the precise sequence of events on the Sacramento campus, he elicited not only the justifications but the blueprints. Afterward, at the airport, Tom popped a question Greg had been hoping to hear: Why not work together? Not only did they share the same aims, they shared an instinct for the tactics of respectability they had just put so smoothly into practice. They were two of a kind. John was just as eager as his father. At sixteen, he had gone from being a kid in a Klan robe to a racist in his own right; he had admired the twenty-three-year-old Greg from afar, even writing him for advice on starting a WSU at Fallbrook High School, and he was ready to find his place in the movement. Greg could choose the materials for a tabloid-style White Student Union newspaper in Sacramento, John could put it together in Fallbrook, it could be distributed inside the WAR newspaper, and a national version of the same two-level strategy Greg had improvised spontaneously in Sacramento would be on its way. It would be several months before the first issue of the WSU paper would actually appear, but beginning with their initial meeting, Greg Withrow and John Metzger had a strong working relationship.

The linkage of WSU-AYM and WAR opened up a period of momentum for both organizations. What the WSU lacked in numbers—it consisted at first only of Greg's group in Sacramento and John's in Fallbrook—it made up in mobility. Night riders that they were, the small units were able to blanket several schools or neighborhoods in one evening with their racist "literature hits," drops that produced anger that produced news that produced recruits for both WSU and WAR. "[Our] opponents must be made to believe we are everywhere," Tom had written Greg before they met, and sometimes it could seem that they were. And WSU-AYM had an asset that WAR itself did not have: the bluntness of youth. Asked in public whether he hated blacks, Tom would sometimes equivocate, rambling on about the distinction between "supremacist" and "separatist" until a newcomer would feel he had better look elsewhere for action. Greg would say, "Yes, we hate them all and we want to see them die horribly." He wore his violence on his sleeve. He called his project the "Hundred Little Hitlers" program. With start-up kits assembled by Greg and John mailed out on request, small WSU-AYM chapters sprouted up all through California, perhaps as many as a dozen "overt" and two dozen "covert" units over the next two years. On Martin Luther King's birthday in January 1985, forty schools in four parts of the state had their lockers stuffed in one evening. Between Christmas and New Year's the next year, the total, in an area ranging from San Diego to Sacramento, was ninety-two. Another time, thousands of copies of an old issue of the WAR paper were distributed in Ukiah, California, in memory of the Order Brinks robbery there. On Easter Sunday 1985 at a large gathering of racists at Tom's new meeting place in rural Rainbow, Mathews Hall, Tom introduced Greg to the assembly as a new leader, praised the WSU, and warned, "You old people like me better watch out because they're coming on strong." Greg got a standing ovation. The following summer Greg joined Tom, John, and Tom's oldest daughter, Carolyn, for the drive to the annual Aryan Nations meeting in Idaho. The 1986 Aryan Nations Congress was a particularly important gathering. The previous meeting had been canceled because of the Order setback and it was the first time since then that the movement had raised its collective head. Greg Withrow was the man of the hour. A film of his speech made by an infiltrator shows him as fanatic, Hitlerian, bold, bringing the movement new hope with a wild high-pitched oration ending, "THE WHITE YOUTH OF THIS NATION SHALL UTILIZE EVERY METHOD AND OPTION AVAILABLE TO THEM TO NEU-TRALIZE AND QUITE POSSIBLY ENGAGE IN THE WHOLE-SALE EXTERMINATION OF ALL SUBHUMAN NON-ARYAN PEOPLES FROM THE FACE OF THE AMERICAN CONTI-NENT!" Bald men rose to their feet Sieg Heiling, reborn in the determination of the young. At the congress that summer there was introduced for the first time a little dog-tag medallion in honor of the Order that would later make its way throughout the movement: "Should you fall, my friend, another friend will emerge from the shadows to take your place." To those who heard him it was clear that Greg Withrow was already such a friend.

Eight days after the Aryan Nations Congress, Greg Withrow's father died of cancer, and step by step the life Greg had built for himself out of his father's demons began to fall apart. His own health, too, was poor. Drugs, fights, and a painful unnamed intestinal ailment all took their toll. His guard down, as he tells the story, he let himself be comforted by a waitress at the casino where he worked, and in her arms he made a surprising discovery: he was a human being.

Almost before he knew it there were intimate conversations, romantic dinners, walks on the beach, and a live-in soul mate who came complete with so much stuff for the apartment that he had to dump out piles of WSU-AYM literature when she moved in. They even had cats and goldfish. Watching this development from Fallbrook, Tom became somewhat concerned. The love of a good woman was one thing, but a man had to stay on the job. At a time when, partly thanks to Greg himself, a youth movement seemed actually to be taking off, someone had to open the mail! Then, just as Greg began loosening his commitment to the movement, his girlfriend began loosening her commitment to him. Six months after they set up housekeeping, she was gone. Now he was completely unmoored. Hoping to revive his flagging spirits, he hopped a Greyhound to Fallbrook, but for the first time Tom's ambitions for a worldwide white revolution seemed to him merely mad. Heading north together, he and John stopped near Palo Alto to drop off ten thousand copies of the latest WSU-AYM newspaper to a fresh young recruit named Dave Mazzella, who had begun to be in the news. Photos of the meeting show Greg every inch the Leader sitting in a Mountain View pizza parlor in his shirtsleeves with a map marking the latest WSU-AYM units across the country while John, Dave, and a handful of other intense-looking young men look on, but in truth, the Sacramento national headquarters was closed. At home Greg became suicidal. In June 1987, in an interview in the *Sacramento Bee* prompted by Dave Mazzella's controversial WSU-AYM "literature hits" in the Bay Area, Greg made the tearful confession— "I don't want to hate anymore"—that allegedly led to his first beating by the Sacramento skinheads who had been his earliest followers. Two months later, after a television interview, came the second alleged skinhead attack, the "crucifixion." Greg Withrow's dramatic exit from the movement in August 1987 was not the end of his contact with the Metzgers. He wrote them several letters explaining that his departure was not what it seemed. Sometime in the spring or summer of 1988 he sent a "Last Communique," beginning, "When the lion hunts, it must first leave the pride. The lion hunts alone," and ending, "In the desperate gamble of the hunt, soul and reputation are surrendered toward the stakes the lion seeks . . . ultimately for the pride," and the Metzgers may be understood if, throughout all the public celebration of Greg Withrow's redemption, they privately expected to see him one day marching beside them once more. They were not particularly disturbed. The Hundred Little Hitlers program was doing fine. There were now dozens of WSU-AYM chapters across the country. The lion had left the pride, but he left his cubs behind.

26

In 1983, when he was a freshman at Fallbrook High School, John Metzger had found himself in a difficult position. His history curriculum included the Holocaust, and he had to watch a film called *Kitty: Return to Auschwitz*. Even for someone familiar with the death camps, *Kitty* is a brutal experience. A British X-ray technician who as a Polish Jewish teenager spent several years incarcerated at Auschwitz, Kitty Hart returns with her grown son and a cameraman to bear witness, which she does in unflinching detail. In one part she shows how a single bowl was all the prisoners carried—the same bowl for eating, washing, and shitting. How did you clean it, asks the son, now a doctor in Canada. We didn't, she replies. We used the urine for washing ourselves. Later, there is more excrement: shots of the long benches of open latrines and a graphic demonstration of the work of scooping out under the holes, putting the shit in two buckets strung across the back, and walking out into the open air—a rare privilege—to dump it. As the film unfolds, you come to understand how it is that Kitty Felix Hart, as well as her mother, survived Auschwitz. All those terrible things that the Jews who remained after the war wished had never had to be done—she did them all. When inmates died in her barracks she stripped off their thin layers of clothing and added them to her own, searching the pockets for an extra ration of leftover bread. When she worked as a Sonderkommando she filched through the piles of corpses, storing away pieces of gold or jewels to trade for advantage later. The only rule she followed was the rule of the dead: never take anything from the living, but the dead are fair game. Almost any normal American teenager would find watching *Kitty: Return to Auschwitz* an unsettling experience, but a teenager whose father's beliefs included doubt that the Holocaust ever happened was bound to find it more so. Kitty Hart is a defiant, unattractive figure. Her own son trails beside her throughout the film practically mute, either from being in Auschwitz or from being led through it by Kitty, many of whose stories he has clearly already heard too often. But the film's harshness is inseparable from its power. No one would tell those things about themselves if they weren't true. Until that point, John had been relatively protected from his father's politics. A rebel himself, a man who understood himself above all as an independent thinker, Tom was not about to provoke rebellion in his children by dictating what they should think, and he left them to find their bearings on their own. True, there were all those dull Identity sermons in San Diego, but that was only because Tom and Kathy would never leave their children home alone on a Sunday. As for the Klan cross lightings, they were simply good wholesome family fun. There was also the matter of getting by in Fallbrook. "You have to sleep somewhere," was the family's view of the need for keeping the peace in town. Just as his parents had mingled comfortably with the other families on the Pala Indian reservation where he and his nearest sister, Lynn, started school, so John continued to have Mexican playmates in the neighborhood and in the public elementary school, which he began in third grade. Summers he spent mostly at the Fallbrook Boys and Girls Club playing video games and hanging out with whatever mixed crowd happened to be around. When he pitched the—mixed—Little League All-Stars two years in a row, his parents were always there. But however much John might have wished for an extension of his fun-filled childhood, gradually it came to an end. As his schoolwork acquired more and more content, the background noise he had been hearing around the house his whole life and what he was learning in the classroom began to collide. Particularly through his social studies and history classes he began to grasp that there was his father's view and there was the world's view and the two were at odds. A thoughtful boy, he wondered why his father kept trying to change people's minds about things, especially when he wasn't getting anywhere, and he even tried to talk to Tom about it—gently, so as not to hurt his father's feelings— but he did not press. *Kitty* is about as convincing a record of Auschwitz as any American schoolchild in the early 1980s would be able to have. If John believed *Kitty*, he would have to challenge his father. If he did not believe it, he would have to challenge society. Tom and John Metzger had a close father-son relationship. The only males in a six-female household, they relished each other's company. After he outgrew baseball, John began helping Tom summers in the TV repair business and doubtless learning more about the political business as well. Like his father, John Metzger was far too independent a thinker to take so important a matter as the truth of the Holocaust on faith, nor would Tom have wanted him to, but when John read for himself the revisionist history books he attempted to donate to the high school library, he found he agreed with them. Faced with a choice between *Kitty: Return to Auschwitz* and Tom Metzger's White Aryan Resistance, he chose his dad.

When John told his father that he wanted to start a White Student Union at Fallbrook High School, Tom was not overjoyed. A meeting of minds was one thing—conspicuous public leadership was something else. Over the years Tom had withstood many death threats as well as many outright attacks. They were not what he wanted for his son. On the other hand, Tom was not about to say no. It was an idea whose time had come. On the Fallbrook High School campus, John's White Student Union never really took off, moving from the "overt" to the "covert" stage almost before the authorities had a chance to prove that Greg Withrow's strategy of provoking repression was right, but on the streets it did. Many of the high school locker stuffings that brought in so much publicity in 1985 and 1986 were John's doing, as was a method of distributing WSU-AYM newspapers by placing them in plastic bags and tossing them onto people's lawns from a pickup truck, paper-route style, a method he and Greg called "the John-boy system." John was efficient in other ways too. Comfortable with computers, he helped Greg, who was not, set up a computer system in Sacramento; he took part in all the basic movement-building activities, such as keeping track of the doings of various chapters and answering mail; and he played a major role in getting out the newspaper. When he and Greg had been working together about a year, in January 1985, Greg, who had always designated himself president, gave John the title of vice president of the White Student Union–Aryan Youth Movement. In May 1987, in a succession planned well before his departure, Greg named John president. John Metzger's story made him a natural candidate for press coverage. In June 1985, he was the subject of his first major independent publicity, a two-page spread in the San Diego *Times-Advocate* that featured not only his yearbook photo but so much information about the WSU, including its address, phone, and computer contact numbers, that John and Greg were able to use it in their next recruitment kit. John, Greg, and the White Student Union were also the subject of a favorable article in *Instauration*, a racist and antisemitic journal published in Florida, that Tom was able to reprint in the WAR paper. Soon there were more. In spite of his name and title, John Metzger was more than just the son of his father. With his collegiate style, he would often be mistaken for what one of his father's more aggressive admirers derisively labeled "a generic person," but in fact he carried his own weight. Equally content to be in front of or behind the cameras, he had a firm set of beliefs and a range of abilities that served the movement well. In the multitude of television appearances from *Larry King Live* to *Donahue* that followed Greg's leaving and brought in more than six hundred letters of interest in WSU-AYM and WAR, he seems right at home. When Tom and John were condemned by interviewers who thought the apple had fallen strangely close to the tree—Tom for being a sinister corrupter of his own child, John for being a tool—it did not bother them very much. In their hearts, they knew they were partners.

27

Nightimes were always the hardest. Daytimes he could forget his worries by flinging himself onto his skateboard and racing, leaping, flying through the sweet-smelling California air, but alone in his room they all came back: the anger, the shouting, the fighting that had finally made his mother make his father move out. "Who will take care of us now?" Dave Mazzella asked his mother the day his father left. There was no good answer. The life he had lived for his first ten years in the small town in the northern Sierra foothills where his mother was a room mother and his father coached soccer and he and his sister would come back from school and do their homework in the appliance shop his parents ran in the village was simply over. It was the beginning of the 1980s. Now there was not only no marriage, there was no business, and soon there was no father either, for Dave Mazzella Senior returned to Southern California near where he had worked as an airline mechanic when Dave Junior was born, and even though he promised he would write, send presents, stay in touch, he rarely did. A new stepfather, a Jew, only made things worse; a volatile character, sweet one moment, violent the next, he sometimes beat his own children, and although Dave's mother was involved with him for three years before they divorced, she was always moving in and out. In seventh grade Dave went to four different schools. Two things reached him as he made his way through some lonely, miserable years. The first was music. On a visit to his father's in Newport Beach he encountered the "mod" scene: longhaired, pot-smoking, Vespa-driving teenagers with British flags on their jackets. Near his mother's, closer to the Bay Area, there were "wavos," punks, and malls. The other thing that interested him was Nazis. Watching war movies on late-night TV he became fascinated by the contradiction of them. They were so good-looking, clean-cut, disciplined—yet they always lost. At his father's he carved a swastika into his arm and his father bought him a Nazi flag: more a paternal than a political indulgence, according to the son. On a college campus not far from his mother's was a radio station that played punk music way into the night, and, tossing in bed, Dave would often switch it on, not changing stations when the music was followed by a talk show that regularly chewed over the events of the day. The Order was one of its many subjects. In spite of a bad record at school, Dave Mazzella was not slow; he was a curious boy who wanted to know more of the world. Often as a youngster he had sent off for material about things that had captured his fancy and he did so now. When the talk show host told her listeners they were welcome to write for more information about any of the things discussed on the program and gave her address, he reached for the notepad on his night table and wrote it down.

Soon he was in the midst of the action. From the names provided by the talk show host, Dave had contacted the National Socialist Vanguard's Rick Cooper, who still lived in Salinas, and by reading through the contact lists in back issues of the National Socialist Vanguard *Reports*, he had discovered Greg Withrow. Of all the recipients of the White Student Union starter kits designed to further the Hundred Little Hitlers plan Greg had in mind, Dave Mazzella seemed the likeliest to succeed. He was so enthusiastic. No sooner had Greg sent him a stack of the latest White Student Union newspapers than he wanted more, and the same was true of the stickers and leaflets he began plastering up at schools all around Palo Alto, sometimes zooming about by skateboard, sometimes by bus. Which routes passed the greatest number of schools in the shortest amount of time was something he knew by heart. Dave was also a good collector of names. Whenever Greg checked the post office box in Sacramento, he found lists from Dave of more people to send WSU information to and Greg was always ready to oblige. That was how the movement would grow. Soon there were chapters not only in Mountain View, where Dave lived, but in Sunnyvale, Cupertino, and Los Altos, and Dave was making a name for himself on both sides of the bay, frequently in the news for his confrontations with school authorities over such issues as the right of a student to wear a White Power T-shirt, singled out in the WAR paper, a promising addition to the established circles of older Northern California racists through whose hospitality he attended his first Klan rallies and meetings of the San Francisco unit of WAR. In 1987, when he met Greg Withrow and John Metzger at the Mountain View pizza parlor where they snapped the picture of the WSU-AYM high command poring over a map, it was as if the three of them had always been working together.

But success in the movement was the opposite of what was happening at home. There he was always in trouble. For one thing, he was never actually in school. Between politics and drugs he was suspended often, kicked out for good when he was in eleventh grade. His mother had married a permanent husband, a straight, rock-solid military sort who was willing to stay up all night if need be to help a kid with his homework but had no tolerance for a kid on the loose. Soon they were in a state of war. "The eggs," his mother remembers. "I never could keep any eggs." A punk, not a skinhead, Dave would bring the eggs out to the cabana of their condominium to do up his hair, part of his ambassadorial portfolio to the world he was trying to organize. That was not all he brought. Every day racist trash would pour into the family mailbox, and if his mother didn't get it first, Dave would haul it down to the pool. Once his stepfather went down and cleaned out two overflowing garbage bags full. Another time he brought it back to the house and lit a fire. No matter what they did or said the stuff kept coming. It was in his closet, it was under his mattress, it was everywhere. Eventually he got his own mailbox. Then there was the problem of lies. One summer when he was supposed to be in an alternative school, he didn't go, leaving the house with his lunch at the appropriate hour and returning on time but spending the hours between on his political work. When his stepfather found out, he was furious, at one point actually landing a blow. Dave fled the house, only to return a short time later in a police car with a smirk as big as the Ritz on his face, accusing his stepfather of assault. When his parents had tried to get help controlling Dave from the juvenile authorities some time before, they had had no such luck. In late 1986, when he was seventeen, Dave was invited by TV station KGO in San Francisco to represent the White Student Union on a session of its morning talk show *AM/San Francisco* devoted to the topic "What Do Racists Want?" The other guests were a man from an organization favoring a constitutional amendment limiting U.S. citizenship to non-Hispanic whites and Tom Metzger, representing WAR. Without telling his parents, Dave cut school and joined Tom, whom he had not previously met, a few blocks from his house for the trip across the bay. Dave's performance on what turned out to mark the beginning of a short television career was not particularly impressive. With his goopy hair, denim jacket, and plaid shirt, he looked more like a greaser than a Nazi and he talked so fast and so recklessly he made Tom Metzger look like an elder statesman. What the WSU wanted was "pure white racism" and "it would utilize any method necessary to accomplish it," said Dave. "Any method?" pressed the host. "What does that mean?" "Tire chains, guns, knives, whatever it takes." "So you would use violence?" asked the host. "Would you kill?" "That has yet to be seen," replied Dave, at which boast the host was so incredulous that he quickly moved the conversation on. Even more incredulous was Dave's stepfather, who, summoned to the TV lounge by his coworkers at the golf club he managed in the East Bay, phoned KGO in a rage, demanding that Dave be asked, "What about your Jewish great-grandmother? What about your great-great-great-great-grandmother who was a Cherokee?"—facts about his family tree Dave had known his whole life—but the questions were never aired. Delivered by Tom back to the corner where they had met, Dave was soon confronted with the sight of his belongings on the sidewalk outside his house, for his stepfather, for the moment, had had enough of him, but he shrugged it off. Overall it had been a good day.

The more he read, the more he believed. That white people are dying faster than they are being born: that the United States is an endangered country: that white people created lightbulbs and telephones and television and cars and the only thing that blacks ever created was peanut butter: he thought about these things day and night. Then there was the Jewish Question. That the Holocaust was made up to create sympathy around the world for the "return" of the Jewish people to Israel: that the government of, by, and for the Jews in Washington, D.C., was giving everything away: that the Jews masterminded everything: all this he also believed. Once he had got the Word he could not rest unless he was passing it along. If there were newspapers to be distributed, leaflets to scatter, a soul to be converted, he had to go. If he so much as stopped to see a movie he felt guilty. It was all so urgent. Later he would say there were three stages in the development of a racist skinhead: hatred, which came naturally; education, which had to be cultivated; and violence, which was the point, but his own racism did not begin with hate. Growing up in the suburbs he had never had any difficulties with blacks. His best friend for years was a black kid, also named Dave, with whom he was still hanging out even as he was distributing racist material. Another friend was a Vietnamese refugee. The problem was not with today, it was with tomorrow. However easily he and his friends could talk about black pride versus white pride, when the race war started they would have to go. He would shoot them himself. There was nothing personal about it. If a million white supremacists at the birth of the new order each made an exception for his one black friend, there would be a million whites and a million blacks right from the beginning and we would be back where we started. Only the race mattered. Like the victims of other revolutionaries whose firing squads have left their bloodstains on the walls of modern history, "blacks" for Dave were more a theoretical than an actual enemy. They were not so much a reality as an abstraction.

But the white racist movement was more than a set of ideas—it was also a brotherhood. Each time a member was added to the underground units making up the Mountain View chapter of the White Student Union it was like adding a secret comrade. Nationally, too, brotherhood was increasingly a reality. Even a youth in California had access to older racists around the country like Texas Grand Dragon Louis Beam and North Carolina White Patriot Party leader Glenn Miller, with both of whom, along with Tom, Dave now established contact. By any conventional measure, Dave Mazzella was lost. His relations with his mother and stepfather were terrible. He was permanently expelled from school. Even a stint in the army was a failure, for with white power engraved in several versions not only in his heart but on his body, he was thrown out of Fort Benning not long after he arrived and was back on his parents' doorstep in a short time. From his own point of view, however, he was found. The locker stuffings, spray paintings, and other protests he was starting to organize might be small in themselves but they were part of a worldwide campaign to save the greatest race humanity has ever known. He was serving the people. He not only had an occupation: he had a calling.

Among Dave's "brothers" in the movement, the one to whom he was closest was an intense young Klansman named Clinton Sipes, who lived across the bay in the southern Alameda County town of Dublin. At twenty, Sipes was already an experienced racist. Taken by a Klansman grandfather to one of Louis Beam's rallies against Vietnamese fishermen in Galveston Bay at age nine, he had been thrilled by the display and later, an embattled white kid in the Oakland ghetto, he remembered the power of collective action, first joining a local racist paramilitary street gang and eventually progressing to the Klan. Other things in his life did not go as smoothly.

Raised by a violent stepfather and a frightened mother, he was a wild and desperate child repeatedly in trouble with the law who spent most of his teens in the hands of the California Youth Authority for crimes that included shooting an Oakland black child in the head. When Dave and Sipes met, at Tom Metzger's suggestion, in the fall of 1986, Sipes had just been paroled. The Klan that Sipes had chosen after investigating various possibilities was the American Knights of the Ku Klux Klan based in Modesto and headed by a large, beer-bellied, theatrical character named Bill Albers, who with his great gray beard, pointy hat, and flowing robes looked bound almost by fate to play the role of Imperial Wizard into which his politics had cast him. Sipes was Albers's "Kleagle"—a high-ranking officer—in the Bay Area. The fact that Sipes was part of the Klan and Dave was part of WSU/AYM did not limit their political partnership. They were both free agents. Nor did it affect their activities. One night they might go to a private meeting of the San Francisco WAR chapter where twenty to thirty middle-aged men would listen to Tom Metzger, up from Fallbrook, talk about how liberal race traitors were giving everything away to the blacks. The next night they might go to an open Klan rally in Modesto, driven by some of the very same men they had met the night before. Everything was part of the same thing. WAR might be into theory, the Klan practice; WAR might be fluid, the Klan rigid; WAR might start from the bottom up, the Klan from the top down, but the differences were less important than the commonalities. Sipes—not Dave—made a big, controversial, and headline-gathering push to get Tom's *Race and Reason* aired on the Viacom cable channel in the East Bay. He thought of himself as a member of WAR. Dave—with Sipes—appeared on the San Francisco TV talk show *High Voltage* as a spokesman for the Klan even though, under eighteen, he was too young to belong. "From the KKK we learn our heritage as a white man," he said. Whether they were talking to punks in the suburbs or rednecks in the valley, they took both their wares, knowing that some customers leaned to swastikas, some to robes, and wanting to be ready to oblige. Such competition as there was between them they both thought was fine. While Clint was making headlines on one side of the bay with *Race and Reason*, Dave was matching them on the other with the WSU. "WHITE SUPREMACISTS WIN TEEN CONVERTS" and "WHITE SUPREMACIST LEADER SAYS, 'I'M PROUD TO BE A RACIST,' " proclaimed front-page stories on Dave and his activities in the San Jose *Mercury News* on Easter Sunday 1987, and there were more. The two talked to each other often, planned to live together, and shared the organizer's dream of filling a van with literature and driving across the country, hitting every little city and town until the literature was gone. But it was not to be. At a small rally they staged at an East Bay police station in August 1987, with Sipes wearing his hood and robes and Dave in Klan fatigues, Sipes was arrested for violating a parole restriction against associating with Klansmen and was returned to jail. A few months later, Dave joined Albers's Klan himself, inherited Sipes's position as Kleagle, and got robes of his own. From then on he carried both their wares.

In the fall of 1987, on a trip to New Haven, Connecticut, with Tom and John for a Sally Jesse Raphael show about young white suprem-acists—his first national television appearance—Dave Mazzella received the title of vice president of the White Student Union–Aryan Youth Movement, succeeding John, now the president. Dave also received a new look. Riding up in the motel elevator soon after their arrival, Tom had looked at Dave's stringy hair, said something like, "Why don't we just shave it off—?" and then it was gone. Tom even paid for a barber to do the job. The title and the haircut were both overdue. Even before Greg's publicity-generating exit, Dave had become the informal WSU-AYM spokesman in Northern California, and afterward he stood out more, responding to questions from the press, defending WAR from rumors that Tom and John were involved in Greg's "crucifixion," and generally shoring up morale. "It's sad to see an Aryan warrior fall on his face. But [even] with Greg out of it, it's not going to stop. There are a lot of racists out there and we're growing rapidly," Dave told the San Jose *Mercury News*. As for the haircut, he had more or less been specializing in skinheads already. They were his natural constituency. All around the Bay Area small groups of teenagers were expressing their alienation with school or the punk scene or life in general by shaving their heads, and wherever there were skinheads, there was Dave, trying to provide the political education that would help them make the leap to racism. If some resisted, holding on to the interracial solidarity that had marked the earliest skinheads in England, it was not for lack of effort from Dave Mazzella. That the ghettoes are hellholes not because people are poor but because they are black: that blacks have declared war on whites in the form of crime: that for every black woman raped by a white there are thirteen white women or girls raped by blacks: these were the things he wanted skinheads to understand. Hate is not enough, he would tell them at the slightest expression of racial feeling. Here. Read this. For the teenagers Dave was recruiting, the Withrow drama was not necessarily a turnoff: in fact it was something of the opposite. Whether it was the ideas or the violence that offered the attraction, with appearances by Tom and John on *Larry King Live* and *Donahue* in the aftermath of the "crucifixion," inquiries to WAR soared. Skinhead incidents all over the Bay area from Berkeley to Redwood City testified that something new was going on. A few months before his elevation to the vice presidency, Dave was hanging out with some skinheads in a park in San Jose when four of them intercepted a black woman crossing a footbridge with her dog and informed her she had to pay for the privilege. "Niggers pay tolls!" and "We're going to string you from that tree!" is what they said. Terrified, the woman ran, helped to safety by a Hispanic stonemason who was standing nearby. Dave was not one of the skins on the bridge, but he was part of a larger group standing beneath it. Immediately he became the chief commentator on the event, interpreting it to the press, claiming that the skinheads were members of a new underground chapter of his Mountain View WSU-AYM organization although it is not clear that they actually were, and generally reaping the rewards. "Skinheads are our front-line warriors," he said in a phrase Tom liked so well he subsequently made it his own. "They roam the streets and do what's necessary to protect the race." The San Jose story was an enormous boost to WAR. With the "front-line warrior" phrase repeated all across the country, the episode brought still more publicity. At the end of 1987, the Anti-Defamation League, which had been watching the emergence of the racist skinhead movement with rising concern, issued the first in what would become a number of publications on the subject, a six-page bulletin titled "Shaved for Battle—Skinheads Target America's Youth," in which Dave received prominent mention. For Dave, it was his best-ever report card. For the first time, he was getting good grades.

28

WAR was an innovation in racism. "WAR wears no uniform, carries no membership card, takes no secret oath. WAR doesn't require you to march around a muddy street. WAR works the modern way, with thousands of friends doing their part behind the scenes, within the system, serving their race," Tom said, one way or another, many times. It was exactly how he wanted it. In the years he had been active he had learned a thing or two, and one of them was that if you raise your head too far out of the trenches, you get smashed. If you cross the line between legal and illegal activity, you go to jail. Whether it was the overdose of violence that had accompanied the Klan demonstrations, the toll of duplicitous friendships with people like Doug Seymour, the dead end of electoral politics, or just plain middle age, Tom Metzger, nearing fifty, was enjoying his new approach. By the end of 1985 he had made eighteen half-hour *Race and Reason* television shows featuring guests ranging from the body-guard of George Lincoln Rockwell to the editor of the Holocaust revisionist *Journal of Historical Review*. By the end of 1986 the num-ber was thirty-one. The market was also expanding. From the first shows aired only around Southern California in 1984, the program had grown in two years to over twenty venues, including Northern California, New York, Pennsylania, Idaho, Arizona, Georgia, Tennessee, Virginia, and Texas, provided to the stations in every case by a "WAR associate" who, according to the rules governing cable access, had only to make the request and supply the videotape in order for the program to be adopted. WAR associates were also responsible for another means of communication, the WAR message lines, commentaries usually recorded by Tom in Fallbrook and played on simple telephone message machines in an increasing number of cities across the United States. "Attention, all patriots of the white race. . . . We are the generation who will decide if the world will belong to us as it has through all recorded history or if [it] will diminish to the brown races and the blondes become human sacrifices to their gods," began one such message in 1986. Computer bulletin boards, engineered partly by John, were another form of direct instant communication with like-minded people across the country. Last but not least was the WAR paper, a bimonthly tabloid-style grab bag of racist analyses, cartoons, news, and opinion, much of it reprinted from other newspapers around the country where the free speech controversies invariably stimulated by *Race and Reason* were making news.

The agenda of the moment was outreach. If it was white and it moved, Tom wanted it. "WE NEED EVERY ONE OF YOU," proclaimed an editorial note in the WAR paper in early 1986. "We need Christian-Identity, we need Odinists, we need southern white separatists, we need European Strasserites and orthodox National Socialists. We need every branch of fighting, militant whites. We are too few right now to excommunicate each other . . . because, let's face it brothers and sisters, the only thing that counts is what works. Whatever will save our Race is what we will do." Frustrated by the sectarianism that left each racialist group involved mainly with itself, Tom wanted to try to bring them together. He also wanted them to go further. "Ku Klux Klowns," as he often called

them, "Hollywood Nazis"—groups for which he had a string of denigrating tag lines such as "kosher conservatives," with the emphasis
on the "con"—they had no idea what they were really up against.
He did. As his continuing self-education in American history constantly reminded him, the enemy was not simply Jews or blacks; it
was the Iron Heel. Building on his deepening identification not only
with Jack London but with less well-known racialist radicals such
as Denis Kearney, founder of the Workingmen's Party in late-
nineteenth-century San Francisco who agitated against the rich and
the Chinese both, Tom wanted to create a revolutionary white
working-class movement that would overthrow the Jew-dominated,
white-forsaking, black-embracing system and—in a program uniting
the best of the Bolshevik and Nazi revolutions—usher in a new
dawn of economic and racial justice at the same time. Nor could
such a revolution be merely national any longer. The System had
grown. "International capitalism seeks the establishment of a global
factory unhindered by racial and national boundaries, with the free
flow of capital, labor, and technology," he editorialized. The "pimps
and fatcats of international finance capitalism who are selling us
down the tubes in the interest of marketing strategy" and the "white
race traitors who are our number one enemies" were one and the
same. The reason for the failure of previous racialists has been "their
inability to recognize that white power and white racists come in
many forms." The time for such provincialism was over. "Whether
white men or women have long hair or short, wear jeans and sneak-
ers or suits, believe in Christ or Odin, live in tribes in the hills of
Colorado or in the ranks of the grunts of the Soviet Army" was less
important than "overthrowing the totally corrupt capitalist system
that is strangling all life among all people on this planet and . . .
building a radical, futuristic, truly revolutionary new order of white
people. Any non-Jewish white man or woman who shares this
objective and is committed to the cause is welcome. The revolution
is on! Smash the system! Build the movement!" he frequently
exhorted.

• • •

But rhetoric was not revolution. The response to *Race and Reason*, the WAR newspaper, and his increasingly frequent national television appearances all told Tom there were troops out there somewhere but they were not coming together. While his high-flown Third Position racism attracted a few recruits from the left—most importantly the publisher of a racist Trotskyist newsletter called the *Democratic Socialist—Voice of the New Aryan Left*, Wyatt Kaldenberg, who would soon become managing editor of the WAR paper—and the low-flown gut-level racism frequently visible beneath his three-piece suits attracted others, the mass of unattached young white men that the experience of the Order suggested might be ready for mobilization had not yet consolidated. What Tom perceived as he listened to the messages on his answering machine or leafed through his mail was the statistical truth about to be exposed by conservative economist Kevin Phillips in his best-selling populist *The Politics of Rich and Poor: Wealth and the American Electorate in the Reagan Aftermath*—that the rich were getting richer and the rest were getting screwed. During the Reagan era the country experienced a shift in income "away from the bottom 80 percent of the population toward the most affluent fifth," with "the less affluent segments slipping downward even as the top strata were enjoying a major surge of . . . wealth"—an intensifying contrast between "proliferating billionaires and the tens of millions of others who were gradually sinking." Among those sinking fastest were young white males. Between the early 1970s and the early 1980s, the average earnings of males between twenty and twenty-four dropped by 30 percent, and the drop was highest among those who had not been to college. With the loss of manufacturing jobs to the Third World and the attack on unionization by business and the Republican administration, young men who in the recent past might well have found good lifetime jobs in the manufacturing sector under full union protection were entering the low-wage, low-benefit service sector instead. "Newspaper writers from Appalachia to the

Iron Range wrote more or less the same story," noted Phillips. " 'Once blue-collar sons could follow their fathers into the plants and make $13, $14 an hour. That meant the middle class, a car, maybe a little cabin on a lake, a chance for kids to go to college. Once, but not anymore.' " "Reduced earnings . . . may signal a drop in the standard of living over a lifetime," said *Dollars and Sense*, reporting the same phenomenon even earlier. "The prospects for wage growth over time are dim." Add to that the fears of competition from affirmative action and immigration, and it is no wonder that Tom Metzger, with his markedly "less affluent" constituency, sensed a stir. "Under the superficial economic glitter of *Lifestyles of the Rich and Famous* . . . powerful polarizing forces were at work," wrote Phillips. From the lessons of Tom's library to the evidence of his senses, everything supported his opinion that "the system" was reaching a breaking point, but it was happening so slowly.

Far off, in England, he thought he saw a vanguard for a white worker revolution. There the group of dislocated young men gathered around the shaved-headed, bull-bodied leader of the band Skrewdriver, Ian Stuart Donaldson, had aligned themselves with the national socialist political party, the British National Front. Their message was summarized in the title of their signature anthem, "White Power," a call for the return of an all-white, all-powerful Britain. "We're letting them take over, we just let them come," they protested, and their words were meant to be heard. Heavy and intense, they thudded up and down the dance floor to a simple rock beat— "pogoing"—slamming into one another in the pit, men re-creating in dance halls the camaraderie of the barracks of the lost empire in which they so poignantly misremembered their place. "Race and Nation," "I Don't Like You," and "Free My Land" were some of their other numbers. Tom had been in contact with Skrewdriver since 1983, featuring British National Front soccer thugs on *Race and Reason* when they were visiting this country, trying to help arrange an American concert tour, and otherwise offering support. An album cover inscribed by Donaldson "To Tom Metzger, Racial Regards" and the band's dedication of a song to "the men and women of White

Aryan Resistance and director Tom Metzger" at the 1987 BNF "White Noise" rock festival were among the most treasured accolades of his career. The more Tom learned about the relationship of the skinheads to the British National Front, the more he envied his British comrades. American skinheads were so standoffish. Weekend after weekend saw them gathering in small knots all over California to brawl and party, but they had no ideas. Try to organize them and they immediately identified you with their parents, a hopeless situation. By any standard known to history, American skinheads were as plausible a vanguard for a racial revolution as was likely to emerge in the near future, but they didn't know it. They lacked consciousness. How to reach them: that was the question.

Toward the end of 1987, having been thrown out by both the army and his mother, Dave Mazzella moved to Costa Mesa in Southern California to live with his father. A casual, nonjudgmental fellow possibly making up for past neglect by present acceptance, his father seems to have taken Dave more or less as he found him, program, haircut, and all, distancing himself from the racism, which he did not share, but praising the leftish social and economic attitudes, which he did. The geographical closeness to Tom only enhanced Dave's sense of mission. Just as in the Bay Area, skinhead gangs with names like Death Squad Skins, Gestapo Skins, or merely Crazy Fucking Skins were appearing throughout Southern California with white power symbols plastered all over their jackets, but except for a few individuals who had independently made contact with Tom they were not part of anything larger. It was prime territory. Tom, too, knew an opportunity when he saw one. Unlike more old-fashioned racists who saw the rising skinheads as the very satanic force they proclaimed themselves to be and were fearful of association with them, Tom saw skinheads as a symptom of the break-down of capitalism, and he ushered them into the ranks. As diplomatically as befit the father of so many teenagers, he tried to cultivate them, sensationalizing the WAR paper with crude, easy-to-read stickers and cartoons, downgrading the language of his mes-sages, interviewing the few skinheads he knew on *Race and Reason*, where, in the form of questions like "So aren't we in a white civil war?" he could make the points he wanted to make, whatever their answers—but he had to be careful. Having gone to such lengths to assert their independence, most skinheads were not about to be co-opted by a grown-up. Nor was John much better placed, for just as kids in general looked hard at Tom for being old, so skinheads looked hard at John for being straight. Handsome, buttoned-down, the picture much more of "Likely to Succeed" than of "Likely to Overthrow," he was incorrigibly clean-cut. Dave Mazzella was exactly what was needed. Where Tom and John were weakest was just where Dave was strongest—on the street. Always moving, he turned up here, there, everywhere throughout the cities and towns of Southern California in his van, bullshitting with one group, "jumping in" with the next, trying in his own fashion to deepen their racial education and lead them toward WAR, a bridge between alienation and organization. Sometimes John came along, becoming more comfortable with skinheads and the skinhead scene all the time. By now there were a few thousand skinheads in at least two dozen American cities, tentatively making contacts with whatever outcroppings of the larger neo-Nazi movement they happened to have heard of, but apart from Clark Martell, founder of the Chicago Area Skinheads (CASH), who also tried to unite local skinheads under the WAR umbrella, no one introduced as many skinheads to WAR as Dave Mazzella did, simply by keeping going. It was Dave who, with his friend Mike Barrett, started the Southern California WARskins to advertise their connection with WAR, an initiative that was later dropped because its implication that some skinheads were closer to the source than others rankled some of the others but that got a lot of mileage along the way; Dave who introduced Tom to a formidable San Francisco racist skinhead known as Baxter the Pagan, who became a mainstay of the WAR organization; Dave who first brought Robert Heick, founder of the San Francisco–based American Front, a particularly influential skinhead, down to Fallbrook. With Dave in the picture, the skinheads' suspicion of adults and adult authority gradually lost some of its edge. What Tom really made of Dave is another matter. He had been in the movement for so long that the arrival or, for that matter, departure of any particular individual would hardly affect his assessment of the revolutionary moment one way or the other, but clearly this kid was an asset. Too experienced to mistake a manic teenager for a mature organizer yet too wise in the ways of skinheads to attempt to control him directly, Tom knew how to let things happen. If Dave talked so fast you could hardly understand him, if he exaggerated so much you could scarcely believe him, if he got in too many fights, he was still moving things in the right direction. With Dave bringing in troops, John managing the office, and Tom in the background dispensing political and ideological instruction, they had a great recruitment system. Nobody planned it that way, but it worked.

On January 17, 1988, Dave was stalking a Martin Luther King Day march in Fontanta, California, with a van full of skinheads when he was busted on an illegal weapons charge. Besides a gun, police noted the bats and balls that were standard skinhead issue for possible confrontations but also noted that the baseball gloves that usually provided cover were missing. Dave's afternoon in the Riverside holding tank awaiting the $2,500 bail put together by a combination of his father and WAR was a singularly depressing moment. Large as he might loom on the street, in the tank he was just a small, insignificant white kid and he was scared. If the bust was personally humiliating, however, it was nonetheless politically useful. Following the local publicity, Dave and a few others were asked to pose for a *Time* photographer, and though it was ultimately a snarling Mike Barrett rather than Dave himself who graced the feature titled "A Chilling Wave of Racism," it left the skinheads even more widely known. Immediately after the appearance of the *Time* article, the WAR skinhead contingent received the magic call that

marks the division between obscurity and fame in America: a sum-
mons from Oprah Winfrey's producers. The importance of the February 4, 1988, *Oprah Winfrey Show* to the skinheads around Tom
Metzger can probably not be overstated. It was the biggest thing to
happen to them so far. As guests of the show, they received the
usual plane tickets, cabs, hotels, and expenses and they took full
advantage of it all, throwing a big racist party in the hotel, visiting
long-time Chicago Lithuanian antisemite Joseph Dilys, cementing
their ties with the members of Clark Martell's CASH. Photos in the
AYM paper show them Sieg Heiling through O'Hare Airport, smiling out of the backseat of a limo, planning their strategy, adjusting
their microphones onstage, all with a kind of swaggery energy that
looks like pure existential joy. The show itself was even more exhilarating. With Dave, John Metzger, Mike Barrett, and a Fallbrook-
area skinhead named Brad Robarge (who later married Tom's oldest
daughter) on the panel, and Tom himself, Carl Straight, a former
American Nazi Party member who had become Tom's informal
bodyguard, and Marty Cox, another of Tom's skinhead followers,
in the audience, surrounded by large numbers of antiracist skinheads, members of the militant John Brown Anti-Klan Committee,
horrified blacks, and aghast whites, the stage was set exactly as the
producers intended—for a shocking outpouring of racial ugliness—
and the WAR group was happy to oblige. The threat of violence
was palpable throughout. In one scene a camera-stealing Tom rises
and in a theatrical finger-pointing gesture exposes the antifascist
John Browns as "Marxists" in tones worthy of a street-fighting 1930s
brownshirt, while Marty Cox menacingly mutters, "Communist
scum!" in the aisle. Another time Tom seizes the floor with his
radical theme that the enemy is not blacks, "it's the creeps on Wall
Street and Washington of our own race," for "we are in a white civil
war!" In a scene shown round the world, Oprah confronts Cox, who
has responded to a comment from a black audience member that
God has the last word on who will sit where in heaven with a
muttered "I don't sit with monkeys."

Oprah: I just heard what you said. You said, "I don't sit with mon-
keys." You think because she's black, because I'm black, we're
monkeys, is that—?
Cox: It's a proven fact.
Oprah: That's a proven fact? It's a proven fact that I'm a monkey?
Cox: Could be—

at which his right arm shoots out in a Nazi salute in her face, Oprah
pushes it down, he begins to vilify the Anti-Defamation League, she
interrupts—

Oprah: No, I want to talk about this monkey stuff—
Cox: The ADL—
Oprah: No, no, no, I want to talk about the monkey business, I want
to talk about the monkey business—

and reaches out to touch his arm with her hand seemingly to settle
him down when he yanks it away and glares down at her with such
physical revulsion that you feel he is about to run from the studio
to wash away the contaminating touch; and Oprah, realizing at last
this is not for show, drops the case and moves on up the aisle to
the literally brown-shirted, Hitler-moustached Will Linebarger of
the American Nazi Party of Chicago, who, indignant that anyone
would think he would actually want to put his ideas into practice,
is the very picture of moderation in comparison. After further abu-
siveness during a break, Cox is asked to leave and they all walk out.
Four empty chairs on the stage where the skinheads had sat and a
shaken Oprah confessing "This has been somewhat out of control"
are an eloquent tribute to their victory. Fresh from *Oprah* the group
flew to New York for an appearance on another important program,
The Morton Downey Jr. Show. The *Downey* performance, unlike the
Oprah, was a thoroughly crafted production. Opening with a reasonably civil discussion between Downey, Tom, and Roy Innis, the
black chairman of the Congress of Racial Equality, it first added
John to the mix; moved on to the staged entry of Dave, Mike Bar-

rett, and Carl Straight, who marched single file into the spotlight, turned toward the audience, and Sieg Heiled; threw in a rabbi; got wilder and wilder as it went along; and ended, believe it or not, with Mort conducting his thoroughly incited audience in a rousing chorus of "America the Beautiful" while Tom chanted his own anthem, "Gas 'Em All," sounding a bit like Polly Wolly Doodle, sotto voce on the side. A second *Downey*, filmed at the Apollo Theater in Harlem, was even more heated from the beginning. What is important to grasp about *Oprah*, *Downey*, and all the skinhead shows that preceded and followed is that they did not happen only once. Rebroadcast, videoed, sold, spliced into other videos, such as a six-hour history of WAR, they became a vital organizing tool, proof of the kind America trusts most that the neo-Nazi skinhead movement was already big-time. It was as if WAR had hired a high-priced public relations firm. In a self-absolving comment toward the end of one of the shows, Downey addressed the publicity problem, saying, "For every one person who rises in their defense, ten thousand are alerted to the enemy," but it was Tom who counted the mail—hundreds, sometimes thousands of letters after every major exposure. And Dave? Dave was in the center of things. The fastest mouth in the house, a master of interruption, he was second only to Tom and John in getting his words out, frequently leaving the slower skinhead panelists behind, and if his talk consisted mainly of such round nonsensical utterances as "We don't come to the crime rate; the crime rate comes to us" or "They tell you to go out overseas and kill the Communists but if you try to kill one over here you go to jail," it really didn't matter very much: what mattered was that he was there. According to some of the other people near WAR, Dave Mazzella was not a very respected fellow. He was a "parrot," says Robert Heick of the American Front. "He didn't know what the hell he was talking about. He would have made a good foot soldier—if only he had had any feet." Wyatt Kaldenberg, editor of the WAR newspaper, agrees: "He was always a nobody. He didn't write or read. He never understood ideology. His whole concept of the race movement was nigger this, nigger that." What he was was available. When some of the more mature skins in the entourage, such as Robarge, stopped going on television because they lost their jobs or suffered other consequences, Dave continued. Whether he was taken seriously by an inner circle was less important than that he appeared to be. As Kaldenberg, a sharp observer of the interplay between the movement and the media remarked, "TV is where reality is made." There Dave was a star.

29

On Easter Sunday 1988, the birds and the beasts asleep in their nests near Lake Elsinore in the Cleveland National Forest were awakened at sunrise by sights and sounds never before heard in those woods: the first-ever California Aryan wedding. The groom was Dave Mazzella, eighteen. The bride was Sylvia Rowe, twenty-one. Tom officiated. In a ritual said to be taken from old Aryan sources, there was a sermon of sorts, there were Odinist blessings, there was an arch composed of about twenty Sieg Heiling skinheads through which the couple walked three times, and then it was done. More of a bash than a sacrament, the celebration had actually begun the day before when scores of skinheads and other warriors began arriving at the campground in cars, trucks, and vans from up and down the state. They spent the night watching Skrewdriver and other white-power videos on a large generator-run TV provided by Tom and drinking beer cooled in huge trash containers—so much beer, in fact, that when the time came to Hail the New Dawn as planned, some of them were not awake to hail it. Unfortunately for WAR, those asleep included John Metzger, who had intended to videotape the ceremony for its archives. The only members of the wedding party who were not part of the movement were Dave Mazzella's father and his new wife. In the time Dave had lived in Costa Mesa he had often brought friends to the house to share a beer or watch a ball game or spend the night, and his father was popular. He even bought most of the beer.

The couple had met the previous summer on the day of the "nigger toll" incident in San Jose—Sylvia was one of the skinheads in the park—and as Dave's fame rose over the next months, so did Sylvia's fondness. When he moved to Costa Mesa, she followed. The marriage was mainly her doing, and it almost didn't happen, for shortly beforehand she had let slip in the presence of some WAR followers that she was close enough to a particular Native American woman to regard her as a "sister"; the remark, understood as referring to a biological tie, was reported to Tom, and Tom refused to perform the ceremony until Sylvia could be certified white, which was accomplished by bringing him photos of her parents. After the wedding the couple moved back north to Hollister, where Sylvia was from, and Dave took up his usual organizing activities, beginning by converting Sylvia's female skinhead group, American Fringe, into the WARskin Girls. Sylvia's brother, James Rowe, was also a skinhead and a WAR convert, immediately proving his usefulness by drawing what became one of WAR's staple recruiting images: a primitive, almost cavemanlike skinhead with a bat in one hand, a razor in the other, and "WAR," "Blut und Ehre," an iron cross, and a swastika among his multiple tattoos. Other recruits followed, and soon there was an active WARskin chapter with a post office box, a new leaflet, and, grandest of all, a sweatshirt, whose black background and red lettering against its owner's white skin was meant to suggest the Nazi flag. Whether it was the family element or some other reason, the Hollister WARskins seem to have been particularly close-knit. Besides the usual Sieg Heilings, a photo album that is one of Dave's favorite possessions shows the same handful of skinheads in a variety of playful activities from clowning around in one another's apartments to partying at a local hotel. There is even a photo of an immense cake decorated with thirteen-eyelet Doc Marten boots—also in black, red, and white—to celebrate the birthday of Mike Gagnon, a floating Northern California skinhead whose girlfriend and baby son lived in Hollister and who was around much of the time that summer. However congenial the Hollister skins were as a group, however, the relationship between Dave and

Sylvia was largely empty. Outside of a single photo of them with Dave's mother at a family reunion—Dave, for once, in a dress shirt and tie—and the fact of a pregnancy, there are few signs of a marriage at all. Such signs as there are are negative. In a July 15, 1988, letter to Portland skinhead Ken Death, who had contacted his group in Salinas, Dave described his wife of three months as a "bitch."

They split in the summer and Dave moved on to Salinas, where he lived with his sister. There he continued working with some of the Hollister WARskins and recruited more. It was a busy group that quickly got attention by widespread distribution of the WAR paper and other racist material on people's lawns. "The most active and best-organized Skinhead group in California is the WarSkins . . . led by Aryan Youth Movement vice president Dave Mazzella," said the Anti-Defamation League in an updated assessment called "Young and Violent: The Growing Menace of America's Neo-Nazi Skinheads," which came out a few months after his move—another good report card. The action in Salinas was part of a major surge of neo-Nazi activity nationwide. The previous spring, in April 1987, the Justice Department, attempting to follow up its prosecution of the Order, had indicted fourteen prominent racists—including Louis Beam of the Klan, Richard Butler of the Aryan Nations, and Robert Miles of the Mountain Church of Cohoctah, Michigan, for "seditious conspiracy"—and in April 1988, after a bungled trial in Fort Smith, Arkansas, lost the case, emboldening the very movement it was intending to suppress. Tom was not one of the "Fort Smith Fourteen," for the FBI, despite strenuous investigation, had been unable to find sufficient evidence against him, but he championed those who were and when the victory celebrations began after the trial, he was well positioned to share the spoils. Energized, exultant, he threw himself into his expanding activities with even more relish than usual. One big event that spring was a May 1—May Day—

"White Workers' Day" march in San Francisco organized mainly by Robert Heick and his American Front but with Tom supplying much of the political education, and reaping many of the political benefits, along the way. Another was a San Francisco TV talk show called *People Are Talking* with Tom Metzger pitted against Tom Martinez, the turned Order member who had cooperated with the government and was now promoting his book, *Brotherhood of Murder*. With about thirty skins mobilized by Dave and Heick in the audience and Dave himself on camera much of the time, the show was yet another demonstration both of the WAR-skinhead alliance and of the skinheads' growing sophistication as agitators. The WAR paper was increasingly high-pitched, filled with in-your-face headlines, drawings, photographs, the names and addresses of a growing number of skinhead and other Aryan "prisoners of war," and much movement news.

As WAR reached out and became better known, so did Dave himself. When *Rolling Stone* was looking to capture the movement's dynamism for a photo feature called "Skinhead Nation" being written in the summer of 1988, the representatives they chose were Tom and John in Fallbrook, Robert Heick in San Francisco, and Dave in Salinas. He was on a first-name basis with skinhead leaders all around the country, whose particulars he carried in a neatly kept address book, and they often exchanged pictures and letters. In Salinas things were getting pretty hot. In early September, Dave went to a house party where he attacked an eighteen-year-old white boy who was trying to talk a fifteen-year-old white boy out of rejoining WARskins. Charged with assault and battery and disturbing the peace, he failed to show up for his court date at the end of the month, and a warrant was issued for his arrest. Even before the assault, Dave had been thinking about leaving Salinas. His sister was moving elsewhere, his relationship with Sylvia was over, and in spite of the fact that he was soon to become a father, he saw no reason to stick around. Other WARskins were also thinking about relocation. Mike Barrett, in trouble for vandalizing a synagogue in Redwood City, and Mike Gagnon, who was charged along with Dave in Salinas and who also faced the problems of fatherhood in the form of the girl-friend and baby in Hollister, were both ready to make a move. One idea was to go down to Southern California. Another was to head for Milwaukee or Dallas, where the Skinhead Army and the Con-federate Hammerskins, respectively, were among Dave's many con-tacts. Still another was Portland, where he had exchanged racial greetings with the East Side White Pride skinhead Ken Death only shortly before. In California skinhead circles that summer, there was a lot of talk of Portland. News that the city had a flourishing skin-head scene had made it down the coast; at a combined rock festival and political rally in Oklahoma called the Aryan Fest, Tom and John had met a few members of Portland's POWAR and heard about their rivalry with East Side White Pride; Rick Cooper had published a notice on POWAR's behalf in his National Socialist Vanguard *Report* that "other skins are wanted in Portland" and that housing was available for them until they could find jobs; and, best of all, the POWAR skinheads were known to be largely—girls! A fair level of hospitality could be taken for granted among skinheads anywhere, but this was exceptional. The more Dave thought about it, the more a move to Portland looked good. In the rumored competition between POWAR and East Side White Pride, perhaps he could lend a hand. At the least, it was worth a try. Besides the political oppor-tunities, the idea made personal sense. Not only was moving across the border not as much of a break with his present life as the Mid- or Southwest, but with his mother herself now living in southern Oregon, he would still have a place to fall back on. In the end, his companion was Mike Gagnon. They had a fine drive north on Inter-state 5, through the valley and then the forests, past lakes and mountains, past Mount Shasta, and finally up through the Siskiyous into Oregon, and it only got finer along the way. The clearness of the air, the greenness of the trees, the whiteness of the people—it was so refreshing. They stopped for a time at Dave's mother and stepfather's new house in Ashland. On Friday, October 7, 1988, in early afternoon, they reached Portland.

• • •

When Dave Mazzella told John Metzger he had decided to move to Portland, the news did not make much of a dent. Dave was always moving somewhere. Leaving behind a pregnant wife was not the first thing he had done that caused the Metzgers to raise their eyebrows, but they were not about to second-guess him either. That was not the way the movement functioned. Tending to business in Fallbrook when Dave and Mike were already on the road, John announced their impending arrival to the Portland skinheads. "East Side White Pride—Wanted to drop a line and let you know we would like to open up communications with your group," he wrote.

> You'll get a feel of how we work when you meet Dave Mazzella and Mike Gagnon soon.
>
> A.Y.M.s been around for almost 10 years. We changed our name from White Student Union a few years back for the more militant A.Y.M.
>
> Rolling Stone will be featuring an interview with A.Y.M./Skinheads/W.A.R. in their October issue. Also "Reporters" will be doing an interview with us soon and a French TV crew will also be doing an interview with us in a week.
>
> We have about a 700 list of supporters, members, etc. and we have 10 chapters around the U.S.
>
> We work with any pro-White, anti-drug, White group as long as they do not talk.
>
> Racial Regards,
> John Metzger

Found in a shoe box at Ken Mieske and Julie Belec's apartment by detectives investigating the death of Mulugeta Seraw only a few weeks later, it was a letter John would see again—in court.

30

Oregon was not California. San Francisco and Los Angeles were part of a national culture loosely defined by the *New York Times*, men-

tion in whose pages generally conferred status at home, but Portland, where until 1982 the *Times* could be gotten only by individual
arrangement, was the proverbial province. When local writers or
artists participated in the larger world by, for instance, writing for
the Sunday *Book Review* or showing their paintings in Soho, the only
people who could be counted on to notice were family and friends
in the unfamiliar territory known to Portlanders as "back East," even
if they had never been there. When Dave Mazzella came to Portland
in the fall of 1988 he was in just that marginal position: his credentials didn't matter. Like Portlanders in general, the skinheads of East
Side White Pride were interested more in their own world than in
the world beyond them, and in most things their principal frame of
reference was themselves. They knew "Tom Metzger" as a leader in
a distant racial movement of which they were dimly becoming
aware, but as to the scope and structure of that movement and its
internal hierarchies they had little idea. If Dave had brought with
him a thread from the shroud of George Lincoln Rockwell himself
it would have had just as little weight as the letter to East Side
White Pride from John Metzger, which in fact arrived after Dave
did. In other ways, too, Dave's position in Portland was more difficult than it had been in California. There, whether north or south,
he was at home, but here he was an outsider. He knew Rick Cooper,
the former Salinas Nazi who now worked in Portland, he had talked
with Ken Mieske a few times on the phone as well as having once
written him a letter, but he had no strong personal connections. In
his own mind, the tension between East Side White Pride and
POWAR might tend to weaken the skinhead movement nationwide,
but for the skinheads actually involved it was local. Whatever else
they might be individually, the members of East Side White Pride
were, collectively, satisfied. They had built ESWP together out of
their own ideas and experiences and most of what they wanted to
do they were already doing. It was true that over the last few
months the Portland racial scene suddenly seemed to be going places
and themselves with it, but they did not take themselves too seriously. Just as the best-known Portlander in any field is more apt to

be found on a weekend at the mountains or the coast or gathering with family and friends than at work, so the members of ESWP liked to keep things in their place. Sure, they wanted to go out and fight on Saturday night, but there were other things in life besides that.

The visitors stopped first at the basement apartment of Ken Mieske and Julie Belec in Southeast Portland, where Dave staged an ambassadorial phone call to Tom Metzger in Fallbrook, grandly handing the phone over to Ken for a personal introduction, then headed downtown to Cascade Blueprints, where Kyle Brewster gave them the keys to the apartment he shared with his friend Prick near the Hawthorne Safeway. When Kyle came home they rounded up a few of the other members of East Side White Pride by phone and began to get acquainted, a process that involved starting a fight with some other white guys in the Safeway parking lot. They won. In spite of their welcome by East Side White Pride, Dave and Mike Gagnon were under a handicap from the moment of their arrival: they had nothing to do. True to their "white working class" identities, the skinheads of East Side White Pride had jobs, apartments, girls. Dave and Mike had nothing and no one. What's more, they were broke. For the basic necessities of food, gas, and beer they had to sponge. To make matters worse, Dave and Mike got into a fight with each other within a few days of their arrival and Mike went back to California, leaving a cryptic "Don't trust Dave!" warning behind him. Whether it was politics, money, or girls they were not to trust him about the members of ESWP didn't know, but Dave made them nervous. Reputation or no reputation, some members even thought if he was going to hang with them he should be "jumped in," and he had to talk them down. In the absence of any personal life, Dave fell back even more on his politics. It was what he had. He wrote to several skinhead friends in California describing the bright racial future of Portland and urging them to join him. He called Fallbrook to freshen his connections with Tom and John or simply to listen to the WAR hot line to get the Word. Once he actually signed a letter to Sylvia "Racially, Dave." As often as possible, he relived his moments of glory on national television via videos, showed off his Klan robes, and—mainly—talked, using all the arguments he could think of to get the local skins to be more active. It was not a very comfortable relationship. The homeboys of East Side White Pride had things they had always done and ways they had always done them and they were not about to change at a nod from a stranger from California. Night after night they would head for Kyle and Prick's for beer and conversation but when it came time to actually do anything other than fight, they were too drunk. From Dave's point of view, they were downers. From theirs, he was much too intense. From day one the modus operandi of ESWP had been a little politics and a lot of beer and here he was trying to reverse the proportions.

After two weeks at Kyle and Prick's, Dave moved to suburban Tigard with two other members of ESWP, Pogo and Steve Strasser, facing down a hail of taunts about "abandoning the racial struggle in the city" as he moved out. In fact, the move had no such political implications. Pogo, who came from a comfortable suburban family, was willing to accompany Dave on a classic California-style "literature hit," and they had a fine time distributing some of the AYM newspapers from Dave's van at the suburban high school that was Pogo's alma mater and leaving them on people's lawns and cars. They even had a chat with Pogo's old history teacher about the material, though he did not invite them, as they were hoping, to debate his class. Other things picked up too. With the presence of Dave adding an extra pair of boots to their usual brawling, there was a dramatic provocation of a carful of white guys at Rocky Butte, an impressive intimidation of a Hispanic man at Laurelhurst Park, and other gratifying battles. Thanks to Dave's telephone calls to Tom, there was also a word of praise from that quarter: the remark in Tom's taped phone conversation with Rick Cooper on the progress of racial consciousness in the Northwest quoted earlier: "Unofficially, the fights and attacks against the race-mixers and some of the race traitors and the racial scum has been picking up because of the new warriors moving into the [Portland] area. When it comes out it will be all at once." What was not okay in Tigard was the apartment, which was a wreck. Heedless both of the neighbors and of the property, the skinhead tenants argued with the people below them, stuck their feet through the walls, and filled a bedroom with empty cigarette packages they had saved for that purpose. On one occasion the entire roster of ESWP held a giant rubber band fight— at which point the Mexican neighbor who came up to complain was lucky to escape with his life. The original landlord had been a friend of Steve Strasser's but the new one asked them to leave. Pogo's mother was co-owner of a small manufacturing plant in Southeast Portland, and, using her name, Dave and Pogo had both gotten jobs on the graveyard shift. Steve worked in Tigard. On November 1, a loose group including Dave, Steve, Pogo, Pogo's girlfriend, and a couple of others whose relation to the lease was ambiguous took an apartment at 1301 Nehalem Avenue in Sellwood. Dave and Pogo began work.

In Sellwood the situation was better. Dave was still broke, living off nineteen-cent boxes of macaroni and cheese that he bought at the convenience store across the street and trading soda cans for cigarettes, but so were the others, they shared, and gradually he was becoming part of the group. Mike Barrett would be coming up from California to join him shortly and he was glad he would be living with a friend. On November 3, 1988, two days after the move, Geraldo Rivera, in New York, gave Dave Mazzella, in Portland, a stronger boost than anything he had been able to muster himself. "ON-CAMERA BRAWL . . . HE STARTS WHERE OPRAH STOPS," ran the ad for Geraldo's most famous program, and so he did. On *Oprah* nine months earlier the violence was potential, but on Geraldo it was real. At the taping of a show called "Young Hate Mongers," planned to coincide with the fiftieth anniversary of Kristallnacht, John Metzger of the Aryan Youth Movement called Roy

Innis of the Congress of Racial Equality an Uncle Tom; Innis, with Geraldo's encouragement, rose, went over to John, and began to choke him, Wyatt Kaldenberg, from the audience, threw a chair, which hit Geraldo's face and broke his nose, and the rest is television history. "By the time the tapings were over, the studio was crawling with reporters, attracted to the scene by the police . . . and by the efforts of . . . [my] publicist," Geraldo wrote in his 1991 autobiography, *Exposing Myself*:

> Tom Brokaw broadcast a two-minute clip of the riot on NBC *Nightly News*. By eleven that night, all the TV stations and CNN were running with the riot. "Isn't this awful?" asked the commentators. "It's so awful, why don't we see it again, this time in slow motion?" It was shown repeatedly over the next few days, not only in America, but around the world. I later received newspaper clippings from France, Australia, Holland, Japan, and Argentina. The next Monday, the day before the Presidential elections, *Newsweek* put me on its cover. I guess the riot was bigger news than George Bush's coming rout of Michael Dukakis. The headline screamed "Trash TV—From the Lurid to the Loud, Anything Goes." Like the rest of the media *Newsweek* had condemned me, while simultaneously profiting by prominently displaying that which had offended them. (Isn't he awful? Buy this magazine and read all about it.)

While Geraldo, like other talk show hosts, justified the show by claiming it focused attention on "the rapid growth and spreading influence of neo-Nazism," it was also, as he cheerfully acknowledged, "great television." For one week—until the famous *Oprah* where she revealed her successful diet—it actually held the record for the single most-watched daytime TV talk show ever, and over the next months Geraldo's program became the fastest-growing talk show in the land. In Portland, some of the stardust rubbed off. John Metzger was president of the Aryan Youth Movement. Dave Mazzella was vice president. The attention was bound to make his life a little easier. Ever since he had arrived, Dave had been trying to get East Side White Pride to help him get rid of the stacks of AYM newspapers mildewing in his van. This time they agreed. At the meeting at Nick Heise's the day after the *Geraldo* show was broadcast in its entirety for the first time, they made their plans. As we have seen, East Side White Pride's literature distribution effort downtown was not exactly a great political breakthrough. Except for the racist admirer who handed them the short case of beer for their efforts, not much happened. Dave did most of the talking. Back at Nick and Desiree's, he was still talking, while the others were longing for their girls. As they stood on the corner of Southeast Thirty-first and Pine after Desiree threw them out, the sight of most of the couples going off together into the night must have given Dave pause. As far as he was concerned, the evening had a mixed rating. November 12, 1988, fifty years and two days after Kristallnacht, the racist skinheads of Portland's East Side White Pride, led by Dave Mazzella of the Aryan Youth Movement of Fallbrook, California, had held their first Boys' Night Out. That was an achievement. But Boys' Night Out or no Boys' Night Out, he was still going home alone.

If Steve Strasser had been a Greek messenger bringing back tales of far-flung catastrophes he could not have been more dramatic than when he burst breathless and drunk into the shabby apartment in Sellwood at 3:30 A.M. on Sunday, November 13, 1988, Heidi at his side, relating the details of the beating of Mulugeta Seraw to the skinheads who had left before the fight. So often and so excitedly did he tell the story in the hours and days that lay ahead that to those who heard it again and again it was as if they had been there themselves. It was Steve's story that Dave and others would tell the detectives, Steve's story that the detectives would tell the district attorneys, Steve's story that the district attorneys would tell the public and the county court, Steve's story that the lawyers of the Southern Poverty Law Center would ultimately tell the jury so that in the trial of Tom Metzger nearly two years later jurors would still see Ken Mieske standing over Mulugeta Seraw in the street with a bat and bringing it down once, twice, maybe more, with a powerful right-to-left motion: "Like chopping wood." Steve's story was not particularly coherent but it was graphic. There was the fountain: "The blood coming from his head was like a fountain." There was the embryo: "He was lying in the gutter like an embryo." There were kicks, twenty or thirty. Shattered car windows. There was a "pool of blood." As his recitation became a prosecution, it was revised, amplified here, contracted there, with Steve himself coming to play a lesser role. But always there was the central image: "chopping wood."

About 6:30 the same morning, Rick Cooper, carpet cleaner, storm trooper, publisher of the National Socialist Vanguard *Report*, Nazi by day, medical transcriptionist by night, was sitting in his office at Emanuel Hospital, in the middle of black Portland, typing a report just dictated by the consulting neurosurgeon. A black man thought to be Ethiopian had been assaulted in a racial disturbance earlier that evening. He had been found in a large pool of blood. According to the ambulance workers, he had "respiratory effort" right up till the time of admission, but none was observed later. His body was cold. He had a large skull fracture. The lower two-thirds of his brain looked like "ground glass." He was warmed in the ICU to determine whether he had any brain function but it appeared to the doctor that he had a "fatal brain injury brought about not only by concussive forces but also by possible hypoxia. (He is coated with dried vomit.)" In other words, he was as good as dead. Twenty-five minutes later the telephone rang in Rick's office. It was Dave Mazzella calling from the apartment on Nehalem to tell the only adult Nazi he knew in Portland that there had been a serious fight. "I know," said Rick. "The guy died. "Oh," said Dave. And then he said, "Uh-oh."

PART TWO

LAW

To discover the Devil—in a sense both literal and meta-phoric—was, after all, their chief goal from the start. Through Elizabeth's possession, they confronted the evil (the "promises," the "temptations") which plagued them all. There were many levels of resonance. There was the naming, the locating, the making tangible, of what had hitherto seemed obscure. There was a certain kind of tast-ing—a vicarious indulgence of forbidden wish and fantasy. And there was, at the end, a decisive act of repudiation: *The Devil is in Elizabeth, not in me . . . The evil is there, not here . . .* Thus did the beholders sound their own depths, sorting the good from the bad. They emerged—one imag-ines—with a stronger, sharper sense of themselves. They were cleansed.

—JOHN DEMOS
Entertaining Satan

THE CASE AT LAW

Part of every case at law is the state of the world at the time the case arises.

—CHARLES REMBAR
The Law of the Land

31

To readers accustomed to the racial politics of larger American cities, Portland, Oregon, is likely to seem uncommonly placid, if only because its black population is so small. There were exactly 54 blacks in the entire Oregon Territory in 1850, and in the city itself, where most came to live, there were approximately 500 blacks in 1900, 2,000 in 1940, 22,000 in 1970, and still only about 34,000 in 1990, the census closest to the death of Mulugeta Seraw. About 25,000 blacks had moved to the area during World War II to work in the shipyards, but perhaps half of these left when the war was over. At the time of our story, Portland was probably the whitest big city in the United States. Even with its growing Asian, Hispanic, and Native American populations—about 42,000 combined—84.8 percent of its 1990 population of 371,123 was white. The 2000 census puts the white percentage of an expanded population of 529,121 at 77.9. The secret of Portland, which continues to be well kept even from most of the people who live there, is that the racial politics and the smallness of the black population are one and the same. As Darrell Millner, former chair of the Black Studies Program at Portland State University and the leading authority on the experience of black people in the state once put it, "It is not that blacks didn't like rain."

If the members of East Side White Pride were looking for ancestors who shared their values, they did not have to look as far away as Germany: the history of Oregon would do very well. Admitted to statehood in 1859, a year of intense polarization between North and South over the issue of slavery, the Oregon Territory was infused with racial consciousness or—not to put too fine a point on it— white supremacy. "Niggers . . . should never be allowed to mingle with the whites," said N. V. Holmes, a member of the territorial legislature that was debating such questions in 1855:

> They would amalgamate and raise a most miserable race of human beings. If niggers are allowed to come among us and mingle with the whites, it will cause a perfect state of pollution. Niggers always retrograde, until they get back to that state of barbarity from whence they originated. . . . I don't see that we should equalize ourselves with them by letting them come among us. They never *kin* live with the whites. The Almighty has put his mark on them, and they are a different race of human beings. Let any gentleman read the history of a physician that has dissected a nigger, and see what you will find: their very brain is tinctured with black.

"His feet stick out too far; his forehead retreats too much; his smell is too strong," another legislator complained. The little-discussed fact of Oregon history that is responsible for the racial pattern of the state today is that from 1857 to 1926, when it was amended, the Oregon state constitution not only excluded slavery: it excluded blacks.* Indeed, the exclusion began even earlier. While the 1843 organic law of the Oregon provisional government prohibited only slaves, the constitution of the Oregon Emigration Society of Iowa the same year prohibited any "Black or Mulatto person," slave or free, from joining the wagon train, and an 1844 amendment to the organic law provided that any free black who arrived anyway depart within a specified time or "receive upon his or her bare back not less than twenty nor more than thirty-nine stripes," such "stripes" to be inflicted every six months until the interloper got the idea. In 1850, federal law further curtailed the incentive to black settlement by offering "to every white settler or occupant of the public lands" 320 free acres for each single man or 640 acres for families. In the 1857 constitutional ballot, more people voted against blacks than against slaves, a vote not so much against "human servitude [as] against the Negro," an early historian concluded. What is striking about the racial debates that occupied Oregon's formative period is not only the universal presumption of white superiority but the sheer disinclination on the part even of the antislavery forces to live among blacks. Indeed, the high-mindedness of the antislavery forces is so tainted by fear of association with blacks that it is hard to pry them apart. "Making Oregon a free state [is] the best and only means of securing it to the white race," the founding convention of the state Republican Party declared in 1857. Politician George H. Williams, an influential judge and author of an article known as the "Free State Letter," whose rational economic and political arguments against slavery are thought to have been an important factor in the vote, also believed that

> Negro slaves . . . are an ignorant and degraded class of beings [who] will vitiate . . . those white men who are compelled to work or asso-

---

*Three other states—Illinois, Iowa, and Indiana—also excluded blacks, but Oregon was the only state admitted to the Union with an exclusionary clause in its constitution.

ciate with them. Moral difference, like water, seeks a common level and therefore if white men and negroes are brought in contact without that perfect subjection and rigid discipline which prevail among the slaves of the south, the white men will go down and the negroes up, till they come to resemble each other in the habits, tastes and actions of their lives.

It was "selfish policy," not "moral principle," that dictated the outcome of the slavery debate in Oregon, the secretary of the American Antislavery Society decided in 1859.

The attempt to control the presence of blacks did not end with statehood. While the North and South fought over slavery, politicians in Oregon began laying the foundation for a white-dominated social order that would later be known as Jim Crow: blacks would pay a poll tax (1862), they could not serve on juries (1863), and there would be no intermarriage (1866). Why they would intermarry where they could not live and why they should pay a poll tax when they could not vote—along with many other legal contradictions—were not explained. At war's end, the state disdained to support the historic Reconstruction amendments to the federal Constitution, ratifying and then repealing ratification of the Fourteenth Amendment, which granted black citizenship under equal protection of the law, and refusing to ratify the Fifteenth, which endorsed black suffrage. (It was finally ratified by the centennial legislature in 1959.) With white supremacist attitudes institutionalized not only in the state's official policies but also in popular unofficial bodies such as the paramilitary Knights of the Golden Circle, which wanted to create an independent "Pacific Coast Republic" based on slaves, why any blacks who were free to go elsewhere would come to Oregon and why any blacks who were free to leave there would stay are good questions, but a few hundred did. Concentrated in what is now downtown Portland side by side with the equally despised Chinese population, they lived within a

nexus of understood rules neatly captured in a 1905 newspaper editorial supporting the right of a theater to refuse a box seat to a black
plaintiff: "It is not a question as to whether a white man objects to
sitting next to a [black man]. It is simply a well-known fact that he
does object."* "White labor only," "White trade only," or even flatly,
"No people of undesirable colors and kinds" policies were sometimes
articulated, sometimes unstated, but always implied. Excluded from
the commercial growth that preoccupied the new town, blacks
lived in a world apart, venturing out for such work as bootblacking,
stable cleaning, houseboying, or other menial service to whites,
returning when the day was done to a kind of Bantustan that in
time came to support a variety of institutions of its own—newspapers, churches, a hotel, barbershops, beauty parlors, restaurants,
boardinghouses, and so on. Thanks to the practice of the railroads
of employing black men as porters and to the importation from the
South of numerous highly trained black waiters to staff the dining
rooms of the fancy new Portland Hotel, there gradually emerged
something of a black leadership with a modicum of economic security, as well as links to black communities throughout the country.
Following a visit from W. E. B. Du Bois in 1913, they established
an active branch of the NAACP. Whatever promise there may have
been in the years before World War I, however, was swept away in
its nativist aftermath. In the early 1920s the state was more or less
taken over by the Ku Klux Klan, whose platform of opposition to
"Koons, Kikes, and Katholics" reflected the postwar mood. The
mayor of Portland, the governor, hundreds of lesser politicians
across the state, and an estimated 15,000 other Oregonians—10,000
of them in Portland—all belonged. The feeling behind the Klan

---

*The full flavor of white supremacy in Oregon cannot be grasped without including the
experiences of the Chinese, Japanese, and Native American populations, which are outside
the boundaries of this narrative. Parts of these stories—such as the internment of Japanese
citizens during World War II—are well known. Others—such as the massacre of thirty-one
Chinese miners in Hells Canyon in the eastern part of the state in 1887—have been virtually
secret for more than a hundred years. The new Western historiography is only now beginning
to explore these issues. Jews, on the other hand—mainly German Jews—were relatively integrated into both business and public life from the outset and included two early mayors of
Portland as well as a New Deal–era governor.

sweep was in fact more anti-Catholic than antiblack but the blacks got the message. There was more tension, more general unpleasantness, and in a state that had formerly implemented its racist ideals more by word than by deed, there was more violence: a lynching on the coast, two near lynchings in southern Oregon, a fourth in Oregon City. At the same time, both housing and job opportunities declined, with the Portland Realty Board for the first time formally forbidding its members to sell property to blacks or Orientals in white neighborhoods and the Portland Hotel, among other businesses, now reserving to whites the same positions it formerly offered blacks. Not surprisingly, black people's interest in Portland also declined. Where the black population of every other major city in the western United States grew substantially in the decade between 1920 and 1930, the black population of Portland grew by exactly 3—from 1,556 to 1,559. The white population grew by 44,000. In 1940, after the Depression had further displaced blacks for the sake of whites, the number of blacks in Portland was still only 1,931—an increase of only 375 people in twenty years. From the numbers alone there can be no doubt that the word had gone out from the first generations of black people to live in Oregon to their friends and relatives: Portland is a good place to be out of.

World War II changed everything. In early 1941, the famous industrial contractor Henry J. Kaiser began building three vital shipyards just north of the city, and Portland, the least of the major West Coast urban areas, "became a high pressure defense city" overnight. By the beginning of 1943, the black population numbered at least 20,000, more than ten times the 1940 figure; soon it reached 25,000. With whites also pouring into the city in record numbers, the essential whiteness of Portland was never really challenged, but the atmosphere was different. To the people who had been there beforehand—old-time blacks as well as whites—the new situation was alarming. Where was everyone going to live? A week after Pearl Harbor, the City Council created Portland's first public housing authority, a decision was made to construct an instant city for war workers on a floodplain of the Columbia River between Portland and Vancouver, Washington, near the shipyards, and lo and behold! there came into being "Vanport," completed in less than two years, the largest public housing project in the United States and the second largest city in Oregon, displacing Eugene. It eventually housed about 42,000 people, including about 6,000 blacks, in segregated sections. A second wartime project run by the Housing Authority at nearby Guilds Lake also took blacks, about 5,000. Other public housing did not. A critical wartime problem was racial discrimination on the job. Sixty-five percent of the shipyards' workforce was controlled under a closed-shop agreement by the Boilermakers and Shipbuilders Local 72 (AFL), which was determined to confine blacks to unskilled positions. Resisting integration in spite of pressure not only from black workers and the federal government but from Kaiser himself, the boilermakers instead created black auxiliaries in which, in return for paying the same dues as whites, black members got no privileges whatsoever and indeed experienced the indignity of being governed by whites in yet another setting. "It is . . . a serious question whether [such an] auxiliary constitutes an improvement over complete exclusion," a commentator reported in 1944. The union leader put it more crudely. He would "pull the place down" rather than give black people equal rights in the shipyard, he said. Both the longshoremen and the laundry workers unions, which had nondiscrimination policies at the national level, attempted to refer black workers to their Portland locals, only to have the Portland locals refuse to take them in. What distinguished the wartime situation from Oregon's earlier racial history was the increasing political awareness of the blacks. Against the backdrop of a war against fascism to which they were expected to contribute on an equal basis, the absence of equality at home plainly stood out. "No line of demarcation can be drawn to separate the philosophies of the 'white supremacists' who foster poll-tax, lynching and Jim Crowism, from those of Hitler and his followers in Europe who are intent on enslaving the free people of the world and establishing 'Aryan superiority' over the face of the globe," wrote William H. McClendon, editor of one of Portland's two black newspapers, in 1943. Justice was a particular sore point. Not only were blacks ruthlessly treated by a white police force, it seemed the police were always right. There was not a single case between mid-1943 and the end of the war where a black person brought before a white jury was not convicted. The exoneration of two white detectives who killed a black father of five in his own home at Guilds Lake while looking for another man and the refusal of clemency in two controversial death sentence cases were widely resented. Just at the point that the new black population was beginning to create the institutions that might strengthen its place in the larger community, the conditions that brought it to Portland came to an end. As war production shut down, thousands of shipyard workers lost their jobs, blacks first. Many left—but many remained, subsisting on a patchwork of welfare and unemployment benefits and roaming the streets along with the later-dismissed white workers, looking for jobs. What would happen at Vanport, where 5,000 blacks lived side by side with a declining number of whites, was a source of rising public concern. Then on Memorial Day 1948 the dike separating the rushing waters of the Columbia River from the Vanport community broke, there was a terrible flood, and again lo and behold! even more suddenly than it had come into being, the city literally disappeared. Vanport was not egalitarian, but it was the one place in the Portland area where blacks and whites could naturally mingle at schools, churches, stores, bus stops, and sometimes even dances in anything approaching a human manner. Now it was as if it had never been.

The flood finished what the war began. Contrary to the intentions of its founders and the will of its citizens, Oregon was to be an interracial society. By 1950, even with the departure of thousands of blacks, the black population of Portland was about 10,000, a difference of nearly 400 percent from ten years before, largely confined to a single square mile east of the Willamette River whose density was six times greater than that of the city as a whole. It was known by the name of a nineteenth-century village that had preceded it on the site, Albina. Another 2,000 or so blacks lived scattered throughout the state. Perhaps the best way to summarize the shifting relationship between white conscience and black consciousness as the decades advanced is to trace the tone of a series of influential reports on race relations published by a progressive civic organization known as the City Club, reports that can be successively characterized as benevolent (1945), perplexed (1957), fearful (1968), and "correct" (1991). From the condescension of 1945's "Scientific men have proven by careful research that fundamentally there is but one human race" to the deference of 1991's "[These] reports . . . are not intended to be studies *of* minority groups . . . [but rather of] the ways in which the institutions, programs, attitudes, and behaviors of the majority community in Portland affect majority-minority relations" is a change in rhetoric intelligible largely in terms of the powerful civil rights movement that lay between. What the reports cannot reveal in spite of the goodwill of their authors is the sheer daily pain of being black. Talk to blacks who were there in those years and what you will hear about is the Coon Chicken Inn on Sandy Boulevard, entered through a thick-lipped wide-grin mouth in a black face—the equivalent for a Jew of entering a delicatessen through a hooked nose—the suspicious "Are you lost, boy [or girl]"? if they were seen in certain parts of town, the visceral revulsion of whites at the prospect of any physical contact with blacks, whether at sports events, at recreational facilities, or on the street. With petition campaigns, cross burnings, and even house burnings accompanying many attempts on the part of black people to move out of the ghetto, the wartime reputation of Portland as "the most prejudiced city in the West" remained intact. In 1949, the passage of the first benign racial legislation in the state's history—a Fair Employment Practices Act—marked the beginning of the construction of an official legal framework within which the advancement of black people could theoretically take place, but popular attitudes lagged behind. In Portland, a Public Accommodations Act passed by the City Council in 1950 was defeated in a referendum at the polls. Of even more consequence to the black community than its psychological or legal status was its physical status, which was repeatedly threatened. Whatever life it made for itself around the edges of the white society was not allowed to develop. Three times the black community was displaced by the forces of "urban renewal": in 1955, for the building of a sports arena, the Memorial Coliseum; in the early 1960s, for the construction of the federal highway, Interstate 5; and finally, in the later 1960s, for a planned expansion of Emanuel Hospital, some of which has not even yet taken place. In addition to a total of close to a thousand homes, the black community lost many of the landmark churches, cafes, businesses, medical offices, and other significant black-owned gathering places that had helped give the neighborhood its life. From the ghetto there was nowhere to go. In spite of the formal recision of the Portland Realty Board doctrine that "Negroes depress property values," the 1957 City Club report found that more than 90 percent of the brokers in town would not sell or rent to black people elsewhere in the city, even when they could afford it. "In confining a majority of its Negroes to a restricted section of the city, Portland has forced them to live in . . . ancient, unhealthy, and wholly inadequate dwellings," the report stated. "Overcrowding, below-average living conditions, and the generally lower economic level of Negroes have conspired to produce disquieting symptoms of social disorganization." In other words, the racism that created the ghetto in the first place soon made it worse.

As the 1950s turned into the 1960s, blacks in Portland, like blacks elsewhere, changed. Breakthrough events such as the Supreme Court's ruling outlawing segregated schools in Topeka, Kansas, in 1954 put the daily unpleasantness of life in Portland in a new light, and the Montgomery bus boycott a year later suggested for the first time that you did not have to be a lawyer to fight back. The generation of children born to the shipyard workers who had remained after the war was ready to leave the ghetto and move on. Along with the proper Urban League, which had joined the NAACP as the voice of the black community after World War II, suddenly there were Muslims, Panthers, CORE, and other more radical people and organizations willing to take their protests to the streets. Compared with other West Coast cities such as Los Angeles and Oakland, which were in the vanguard of black protest throughout the decade, Portland was still a backwater, but it was on the map. There were even Portland-sized riots among black youth in 1967 and again in 1969. The central issue for black people in Portland during the 1960s and 1970s was the schools, and for good reason: almost three-quarters of the city's 4,800 black students were enrolled in nine of its ninety-four elementary schools, nine schools whose quality can best be gauged by the fact that, despite the vast increase in Portland's black population since before the war, the number of blacks entering college actually went down. It was out of a lengthy struggle against the unpopular desegregation plan that actually increased the isolation of black schoolchildren that the militant new grassroots coalition known as the Black United Front was formed.

The 1980 victory of the Black United Front in forcing the ouster of the white school superintendent most closely identified with the failed desegregation plan and his replacement by a strong, black former military officer who became not only the most important black but the highest paid public official in the state of Oregon opened a new chapter in the history of race relations in Portland. There was more than just a power shift, there was an ideological one. Blacks were not so certain about integration anymore. They wanted justice. Whites were puzzled and lost. The progression from supplication to self-determination on the political agenda of Portland's blacks created a level of black-white tension never before present in the city. Even among whites who had stood with the blacks at all the stages of their rising hopes and expectations there was a new sense of distance. Friends who had poured one another's coffee at all-night strategy sessions in church basements and shepherded one another's children at demonstrations now barely nodded in the street. As every personal transaction and every social and political institution was inspected for racism, none was found more wanting than the police force, which was 94 percent white. It was now, in 1981, as long-standing complaints by blacks about police brutality and harassment grew more insistent, that the officers from the North Precinct threw the dead opossums on the stoop of the black-owned restaurant in the midst of the ghetto. "UPPITY NIGGERS—WE ARE STILL IN CHARGE HERE!" is what they meant. For several years after the "possum incident," relations between the police and the black community in Portland continued at an angry simmer, each side waiting for the other to do something wrong. Then, on April 20, 1985, at 11:30 P.M., a thirty-one-year-old black security guard and father of five named Lloyd Stevenson was killed by police responding to a report of a shoplifting at a neighborhood convenience store where Stevenson, who was merely a bystander, happened to be doing an errand. Attempting to subdue Stevenson, for reasons that remained unclear, an officer had applied a carotid artery "choke hold" a little too long or too hard. When the police chief promptly banned the controversial hold, two officers produced and sold T-shirts bearing the slogan "Don't Choke 'Em, Smoke 'Em" in their precinct parking lot and the Police Athletic Club—on the day of Stevenson's funeral. Quite a number were sold. Stevenson was the fourth black man killed by the police in the ten years since 1975 and reaction in the black community was intense. Where the possum incident had brought about two hundred black people into the streets, the death of Lloyd Stevenson brought hundreds more. In demonstrations, in newspaper and radio interviews, and at the corner barbershop, the situation of blacks in Portland was linked to the situation of blacks in South Africa. The police were identified with the Klan. Six months after the killing, when the T-shirt officers were

reinstated through a binding arbitration—as the officers in the possum case had been—outrage erupted again. Nor were the blacks
altogether alone. However many aspects of racism blacks believed
whites would never understand, homicide was no longer one of
them. There was also a public relations factor. It was hard to imagine more of an embarrassment to a growing city openly in pursuit
of Asian trade than the original possum incident but the police had
managed to find one. An increasingly liberal and cosmopolitan local
establishment, influenced in part by the civil rights movement,
believed the police were out of control. Nothing marks the movement from racism to guilt in the city's racial politics better than the
reactions of its officials to the exoneration of the T-shirt officers.
"I came back feeling very good from lunch. Now I feel like going
home sick," said Portland's populist mayor, Bud Clark, when he had
to announce the arbitrator's decision. Mike Lindberg, a leading
member of the City Council, and Portland's female police chief,
Penny Harrington, were also disturbed. "It's almost an unsupervis-
able police force at this time," Lindberg said. The killing of Lloyd
Stevenson revealed how tender relationships between black people
and white people in Portland had become, and particularly the hostility between the black community and the police, but it also
revealed the emergence of a new, if elementary, consensus that
would strongly affect the events to come. It was: Cop or no cop,
no white man is going to kill a black man in Portland, Oregon, for
no reason anymore and get away with it.

32

When Portland police detectives Tom Nelson and Mike Hefley
arrived at the corner of Southeast Thirty-first and Pine before dawn
on Sunday, November 13, 1988, they felt as if they were entering
an empty theater. A yellow street lamp haloed in the dampness
illuminated the crime scene with a ghostly glow. Partway across

Southeast Thirty-first Avenue, about ten feet north of the intersection, was a large pool of blood with some vomit in the middle. There were two buttons, a gray loafer, a bloody pink shirt that seemed to have been cut off the victim by the emergency crew, two piles of auto glass, one from a windshield, one from a taillight, an empty beer can—that was all. The players had vanished, some into a hospital, others off into the night. The audience had pulled down its curtains and gone back to sleep.

According to the officers who had answered the call, they had been rushing toward Southeast Thirty-first and Pine in response to a report of gunshots when they were flagged down by a screaming man with a foreign accent who told them a friend was injured nearby. At the corner they found another man running around bleeding. A third man lay crumpled and dying in the street. They called ambulances for the two injured men and attempted to learn what had happened from the third but he was "hysterical" and hard to understand. At the suggestion of a resident of the building at 3101 Southeast Pine who thought the attackers might have come from an apartment where some skinheads had earlier been having a party, the officers had also attempted to talk to the skinhead couple who lived there but were told by Nick Heise and Desiree Marquis that their only guests that evening had been two girls who had left before midnight. From Emanuel Hospital the officers learned that one of the victims was not expected to last the night and they put in the call that had roused the homicide detectives on regular rotation—Nelson and Hefley—from their beds.

Picking up where the uniformed officers left off, detectives Nelson and Hefley finished processing the evidence, then went over to Emanuel Hospital for an update. An Ethiopian man named Mulugeta Seraw was brain-dead but had been placed on life support to see if his brain function might return. If not, the machines would be turned off in a few hours. His blood alcohol level was .073 percent, just under the legal definition of intoxication, .080. A second Ethiopian man, Wondwosen Tesfaye, still in the Emergency Room pending overnight admission, was in too much pain to say much, nor could he say much the next day other than that they had been attacked by three or four white males wearing military clothes and boots, that Seraw had been assaulted first and he next, and that after being knocked to the ground he had rolled under a car for protection but had been stomped on his legs and groin area many times. He had heard girls yelling, "Kill him!" or "Kill them!" He said "he had been drinking beer and gin at the party earlier and in fact had a plastic cup with him in the car that he was drinking from as they drove." His blood alcohol level at 4:15 A.M., almost three hours after the fight, was .190, more than twice the legal limit. A third Ethiopian man, Tilahun Antneh, who had driven himself over to the hospital to join his friends, was also in the Emergency Room. He said he had had a glass of gin at the party but he had not been drunk when he left. He did not have to be admitted to the hospital and his blood alcohol level was not tested. As Antneh described it in accounts that turned out to be so at variance with the evidence that neither the Portland criminal prosecutors nor, later, the Southern Poverty Law Center would want him on a witness stand, the fight had occurred in front of Seraw's apartment building at 212 Southeast Thirty-first Avenue. He said the assault was "totally unprovoked and it appeared to him as if it was a racial attack." He had been sitting with two friends in the car outside the apartment when another car stopped in front of them, the doors "flew" open, and three males and two females got out. He heard two white females yelling "Kill him . . . kill him . . . kill the damn nigger." "As the driver . . . got out . . . he reached down in front of the seat and pulled out a three to four foot long piece of wood [which] did not appear to be a baseball bat but was some type of clubbing instrument." The front-seat passenger also had a club. After being clubbed on the back by the driver, Antneh had gotten back into his car and driven off. According to Antneh, the driver was white, male, about twenty-two, about six feet tall, 185 to 200 pounds, with very short hair, wearing a military jacket with a zipper on the upper arm, blue jeans, and black lace-up boots. It was he who went after Seraw.

By the time the detectives left the hospital, it was late enough

Sunday morning for them to begin talking to neighbors. Many residents of 3101 Southeast Pine knew that a skinhead couple lived in number 6, that there had been a gathering in the apartment that afternoon, that there had been a second gathering that evening that ended just before the struggle in the street. There had been commotion on the stairs, an angry woman's voice telling people to get out, a car with a busted muffler that had woken almost everyone, other cars, other voices—in short the events of the last hours had not gone unobserved. From other buildings people had heard shouts like "You fucking son of a bitch, you're a dead man!" Others had heard "squishy or thudding sounds" or "pops." Someone had looked out of a window and seen a man standing over another man at the intersection kicking. Another had heard a man cry that his friend was dead. Several had seen a car backing down Southeast Thirty-first Avenue to pick up the attackers and heard the words "Just get back in the car!" One had seen a white male with a club jump back in. After listening to the neighbors, Nelson and Hefley reinterviewed Nick Heise and Desiree Marquis in number 6, who had already told their story to the other officers, but their claims seemed even more improbable than before. There had been no visitors. They had not had a party. At about 2 A.M. they had heard screaming in the street and had gone down to look but had seen nothing before the police arrived. As for the girls Desiree Marquis had earlier told the other officers had driven her home, she would not give their names. According to a distinguished member of the Portland bar who observed the case at a distance, "the shaping of the story always begins in the mind of the [investigating] officer," and this was no exception. A dead black man. Lying skinheads. Abusive shouting. What the Ethiopians said and what the neighbors said appeared to converge. Tom Nelson and Mike Hefley are systematic professional investigators and they do not leap to conclusions but they do form impressions. The report by Tom Nelson reflecting their initial interviews summarized the fight as a "Racist Attack on Three Ethiopian Males by Three Alleged Skinheads." That was clearly where their investigation would be headed. A different description would have been "an unplanned fight between (white) skinheads and (black) Ethiopians, undoubtedly intensified but not caused by race, that ended in an unplanned death," but it was not one that would ever have a chance to materialize.

A few blocks from where Nelson and Hefley were conducting their canvass another group of Portland police officers was monitoring a different situation. Ballot Measure 8, the divisive measure ending a ban on discrimination against homosexuals in state employment that Ken Mieske himself had endorsed at the Pine Street Theatre not long before, had passed in the general election the previous Tuesday and gay-rights activists were protesting it. On Wednesday about sixty people had demonstrated, and eighteen been arrested, for blocking a major route across the Willamette River, the Burnside Bridge. Today, Sunday, more had gathered at the Portland Foursquare Church, where a minister who had prominently supported the antigay measure was preaching a sermon denouncing "works of the flesh," by which he plainly meant homosexual sex. Outside the church, the demonstrators refused the parishioners' offerings of coffee and pastry, shouting, "Justice, not donuts." Inside, they interrupted the service. The police were there to keep order. Sensitive to the bigotry that linked the two occurrences, a police officer at the church told the demonstrators what had happened. Reporters were also present. "SKINHEADS BLAMED IN MAN'S DEATH," the first *Oregonian* headline about the killing announced Monday morning. While Nelson and Hefley were beginning the quiet, methodical inquiries that would enable them to identify particular skinheads and build a case against them, the press was already crying, "Read all about it!"

33

The city was in an uproar. The first bulletins were followed by such intense news coverage it was almost as if racism itself, and not only the skinhead movement, was being discovered. Monday's "SKIN-HEADS BLAMED IN MAN'S DEATH" was followed by Tuesday's "DEATH PROMPTS OUTRAGE," Wednesday's "FBI JOINS INVESTIGATION OF BEATING DEATH," Thursday's "SOURCES SAY GRAND JURY PROBES PORTLAND KILLING," and so on until the arrests the following weekend. At supermarkets, bus stops, and lunch counters the incident was the talk of the town. *An innocent black man was walking across the street when he was beaten to death by three skinheads with bats:* that is the way the killing was generally represented. Portland had had a lynching! Beside the bats, the main thing that seemed to distinguish the killing of Mulugeta Seraw from the homicides of other black men in Portland that year was the nature of the Ethiopians. They were so—foreign. Whenever you turned on the TV, there they were: Mulugeta Seraw, in suit and tie, his sweet, open, smiling face so ready and eager for life. His uncle Engedaw Berhanu, a professional social worker, forcing himself through the pain of interviews to plead with the city to find out what had happened and why. Beautiful women in Ethiopian dress weeping at Mulugeta's apartment and later in church. The other victims were also in the picture. Tilahun Antneh, the driver of the Ethiopians' car, bringing his arms down in a chopping motion right to left demonstrating the attack, explaining in his charming English, "They have stick and they kick him and he lay down and after that they kick me and broke the car and . . . then they run away." The young passenger, Wondwosen Tesfaye, in a hospital gown, pointing to his injured groin. But at the same time the Ethiopians were exotic they were so—American. Their previously invisible Ethiopian Community Organization had suddenly appeared out of nowhere complete with a well-dressed, articulate spokesman named Betra Melles who took his place alongside the traditional representatives of Portland's black community with such assurance it was almost as if he had been there all along. Nor was the Ethiopians' concern limited only to themselves: they were acting for the sake of others. "If this could happen to him, it could happen to anyone," said Engedaw Berhanu, calling Mulugeta's death a "sacrifice." That Mulugeta could have been any black person was a point made again and again. All through the week public feeling continued to mount. Press conferences and demonstrations built around the Ethiopians but supported by other black organizations occurred all over town. A recessive fact-finding body known as the Metropolitan Human Rights Commission began sounding practically aggressive. The militant Black United Front was constantly in front of the mikes. On the Thursday after the killing, there was a tense meeting at a hall in the black community named for Martin Luther King where several hundred people heard from representatives of the police, including the new chief, Richard Walker, that a white supremacist movement was indeed on the rise. The next day there was an antiracism rally at City Hall, organized chiefly by Somali students at nearby Portland State University but attended spontaneously by hundreds of city and downtown workers and other passersby. The governor, Neil Goldschmidt, was among them. He would have closed down state offices to allow all public employees to come if he had known about the rally beforehand, he said. "WE'RE GONNA RUN THOSE SKINHEADS OUT OF TOWN!" was one of the watchwords. "DEATH TO THE SKINHEADS! DEATH TO THE KLAN!" was another. Besides the local clamor, national and even international press interest was making itself felt, bringing to Portland a level of publicity more typically reserved for such natural catastrophes as the eruption of Mount St. Helens. In spite of the sincere revulsion of Mayor Bud Clark at the death of Mulugeta Seraw and his determination that the Police Bureau be seen decisively to have separated itself from its old ways, the undercurrent of doubt that the police would even care about such a killing, let alone be able to solve it, was very strong.

For detectives Tom Nelson and Mike Hefley, whose job it was to find the actual killers, the situation was far from being an ordinary one. The pressure was enormous. From the first appearance of the word *skinhead* in the press—"Boom!" as one of them put it in one of our conversations—the investigation was hard to control. By Sunday evening the Ethiopian community spokesman, Betra Melles, had already called them, threatening to bring the case before the City Council. The next thing they knew, he had phoned the U.S. attorney, who brought in the FBI. On Tuesday they were personally urged by Police Chief Walker please to solve the killing by Thursday so he could announce the arrests at the community meeting. They were also told at first to report to a superior officer every three hours, which would have interfered with their ability to find the killers at all. Because of the furor, they were given additional manpower to answer the telephones, do surveillance, and conduct some of the interviews and searches, but the help itself was sometimes unwieldy. With so many people involved, it was hard to track what was going on. Thanks to intelligence officer Larry Siewert, who pulled out his skinhead files going back several years to give them a crash course in Portland skinhead history, and Gang Enforcement Team member Loren Christensen, who also had skinhead contacts, the detectives quickly confirmed a rumor that their suspects had probably come from a skinhead group called East Side White Pride, but which members might have been involved and how to get to them was much less clear. The most obvious link between the mug shots in the intelligence files and the events of the evening was Nick Heise, the unforthcoming artist-skinhead outside whose apartment the killing of Mulugeta Seraw had taken place, and it was there that the detectives returned for a third visit as soon as they could with the express purpose of forcing Nick and Desiree to cooperate. They conspicuously brought Nick's probation officer along. When the couple continued to maintain that the only guests at their apartment that evening had been the strangers who drove them home from downtown, they were subpoenaed to a grand jury quickly convened by Deputy District Attorney Norm Frink in part to support the investigation but in part also to reassure an inflamed public that the authorities were taking action. For Tom Nelson and Mike Hefley, calling a grand jury in the face of a large number of suspects whose loyalties were not yet known was a problematic maneuver. The line between getting and giving information was too thin. When Nick Heise was asked, "Do you know . . . Mieske? Do you know Brewster?" and he said he didn't, "We got him in the lies but it also told him that we know who was involved," Tom Nelson recollected later. "We were concerned that everybody was going to go ten different directions, not stay in town." The calling of the grand jury was the first instance of the political intrusion that would affect every aspect of the Seraw case. It was one thing to calm the city, but demonstrating civic virtue and unraveling a homicide were two different matters.

34

"I love you very much—I'm proud of you," Heidi Martinson congratulated Steve Strasser as they raced back up Southeast Thirty-first Avenue together to the car after the fight. He was eager to hear it again. "Did you like that?" he asked her when they were lying in bed the next morning. "Yes," she replied, smiling. "You really liked that," he said—a statement rather than a question this time—and Heidi looked at him, and she said, "Yeah."

•

"Fuck, I think I killed him," Ken Mieske said as they got in the car and drove away from Southeast Thirty-first and Pine. Then he said it again. Kyle Brewster had a busted lip. Steve Strasser was giddy. Patty Copp was mad. Heidi Martinson was drunk. Julie Belec laughed. They were all reassuring. "You can't kill someone with a baseball bat," said one. "He'll just go to the hospital and get some stitches," said someone else. They finished the evening—and the beer—at Patty's, talking of other things. Later she drove them home. At 3 P.M. on Sunday when Ken woke up and turned on the football game the first thing he saw was the Ethiopians' car with the taillights he had battered the night before. "Three unknown assailants . . . brutally murdered . . . shaved heads . . . military boots and clothing . . . ," the newsbreak said. He woke up Julie, sound asleep in their waterbed. "I had a feeling that guy was going to die," he told her. "Brutally murdered!" They were terrified. They had no idea what to do. "I was outta line," Ken told a friend that afternoon. "I hit him too hard. I didn't mean to kill him." Maybe if they pretended it hadn't happened it would go away. "Hey, I was at the coast this weekend," Ken said on the telephone to the skinheads at 1301 Nehalem for the benefit of any authorities who might already be listening. "Any parties?" But Dave Mazzella had immediately started calling him "Batman." The alibi would be no use.

•

Patty Copp was frantic about the bat. Not only was she the driver of a getaway car, the bat had her father's name on it, for Christ's sake! It was his bat! Monday morning Kyle brought it to the basement of her apartment to cut it up but he was such an asshole he refused to use the table saw without goggles! What did he think this was—shop? Finally she sawed it up herself and stuffed it under her passenger seat in a paper bag while she tried to attend her morning college classes, but she could not stop thinking about it. Cutting her eleven o'clock, she reached Ken Mieske and arranged to pick him up, but he was almost as dumb as Kyle. A Dumpster was his first idea. Great security in that. The barbecue pits at Laurelhurst Park. Another great idea. Practically at the scene of the crime. They had to destroy it. With seventy cents change from bottle returns they filled a small can with gasoline and drove to a deserted hangout along the Columbia River known as Dittler's Beach. "[Ken] took the bat and dumped the pieces out on top of the paper bag and poured gasoline over it. He . . . lit the baseball bat and periodically threw more gasoline on it. . . . The bat burned for approximately 20 minutes. They then found a plastic lid to a cooler, placed water on top and dumped it on the fire. [He] . . . stomped the burning bat, scooped up the pieces on the cooler lid and dumped them into a nearby fire pit on the beach." Days later there were still some bat shards on the fire pit.

•

Dave Mazzella was attempting to be a leader. He met with Rick Cooper. He called Tom and John Metzger in Fallbrook, alerting them to the crisis and passing along to as many East Side White Priders as he could their standard advice in such situations: "Don't talk!" He scribbled ideas to himself about possible "Relocation Services" for the three skinheads involved in the killing ("Kyle— Oklahoma," "Steve—Oakdale, California," "Ken"—this one was blank) though who would receive them at their far-flung destinations he did not note. Reached through Rick Cooper by a TV station looking for a skinhead reaction to the killing, he even prepared for the interview by writing out his position in advance—"The media is blowing this way out of proportion. . . . If this is a racial matter it is an isolated incident. . . . Blacks [kill] whites every day, so why should we feel any remorse for him and his friends?"—and no doubt dusting off his dark glasses, bomber jacket, and boots as well. "Did the skinheads beat Mulugeta Seraw to death?" the interviewer asked him on Wednesday.

> Dave Mazzella: I don't believe so, no I don't . . .
> TV interviewer: You don't believe, or you don't know?
> Dave Mazzella: I don't believe, I just really don't believe it. We've talked to quite a few skinheads on the street, and no one, ya know, we've been looking around and ya know we haven't been able to find, ya know, it's just one of those things, no one knows who it was and ya know, we have skinheads coming in from Seattle, everywhere, ya know, it could have been anybody.

It was the climax of his career as a skinhead. Shortly before the interview, intelligence officer Larry Siewert had learned from his sources that a prominent California skinhead named Dave Mazzella was in Portland and that he had an outstanding warrant from an assault in Salinas two months earlier, which meant he could be brought in. From the television station, Siewert now knew where to find him. The day after Dave's TV appearance—on Thursday, November 17, at 1:15 P.M.—he was picked up by two Portland officers at 1301 Nehalem and brought to the Central Precinct. There was an interlude that felt very long. Waiting for the detectives, Dave thought not so much about the great and glorious future of the white racial movement but about the sad and lonely present of Dave Mazzella. About the fact that he was broke. That he would soon lose his van. That he was estranged from his family. That his own son would soon be born and he would be estranged from him too. He thought of the "Keep this away from me!" tone in Tom Metzger's voice when he had called to tell him the news. Who was he really connected with, anyhow? Who could he count on? Who were his friends? At 3:30 P.M., he met with Tom Nelson. Slowly, professionally, the detective started to lead him back through the evening of November 12, beginning with the gathering of the skinheads in the parking lot of the Hawthorne Safeway about 9:00 P.M. How many cars had there been? Who was in which car? What did they do downtown? Where had the girls gone? Evidently the pace was too slow. Only minutes into the interview when Tom Nelson asked Dave Mazzella to tell him what had happened after the skinheads left downtown, Dave stopped and looked up at him. "Why don't we skip all this and get down to the part you want to know?" he asked in return.

"Racial Greetings!" Dave wrote East Side White Pride from the Multnomah County Jail about two weeks later:

> What has happened [here] has been very tragic, some good people in jail, and I can guess for quite along time. This is also a time that you should all pull together or you will all fade to oblivion.
> To quote SKREWDRIVER "When the storm breaks which way will you run!!!"
> Don't let Z.O.G. intimidate you. The police have a lot of respect for the Skins now. Somehow they can see through the propagandiz-

ing of the whole situation! The Jews used this isolated incident for a week and a half in the paper. It was a stepping stone for themselves, the public never makes this much hassle when white's are murdered, raped, and maimed on a daily basis, without this kind of exposure.

The Movement is still pulling for you guys. Give Tom Metzger a call at (619) 728-9817. His phone is tapped so pick your words wisely.

As for myself, I've been trying to rush my extradition back too California. I really doubt I'll do more than a month if that! I'll probably just get probation!

The D.A. and the Homicide Dept. of the police were trying to get me to testify against Kyle, Ken, and Steve, they claim I knew something, which of course I denied!

Save my mail for me will ya. . . . I'll be moving back up here after I pay my dues to Justice.

Stay strong and keep the faith.

Racially Sincere,
Dave Mazzella

"What was his reason for talking so freely?" I asked the detectives later. "My impression of Dave Mazzella is he is on the side of whoever he's with at that particular time," Nelson replied. "He likes all the attention, he likes being involved in things, and he was getting all this attention from the police." "So he wasn't at all hostile to you?" I inquired. "He wasn't hostile at all. He was just totally cooperative. Friendly as can be," Nelson said. "I've been a crook and I've worked for law enforcement and either one by itself is not enough," remarks Gary Gilmore's informant cellmate "Gibbs," in Norman Mailer's *The Executioner's Song*. Dave Mazzella was not exactly a "crook" nor did he exactly "work" for law enforcement. But you get the idea.

•

Dave Mazzella was not the first informant in the Seraw case. From Sunday on, wherever skinheads or people who knew them clustered around the city, the talk was of little else, and a few had actually called in tips. On Tuesday, Tom Nelson and Mike Hefley received a call from a young man close enough to those involved in the killing to have talked about it on the phone with one of them, who let it be known that, in return for a $10,000 reward for Seraw's killer posted by the Jewish Defense League that he had read about in the *Oregonian*, he was willing to give up his friends. From the time he called until their meeting a few hours later, the detectives were worried that he would change his mind, but the young man materialized. He did not want to tell them who he was—though they soon knew—asking to be known by a code name. He said he would never say publicly what he was saying now. He would never testify in court or be named in any legal document. But he correctly identified Ken Mieske, Julie Belec, Kyle Brewster, and Patty Copp as four of the six people in the fight at Southeast Thirty-first and Pine, and it was the first breakthrough. When Dave Mazzella identified Steve Strasser and Heidi Martinson two days later, it was the second. Because his refusal to be named withstood intense pressure from the district attorney and hindered the investigation at a later point, the "Confidential Informant" never did get the JDL money, but he did get protection. His name has never been disclosed.

35

The citizen entering the world of a police investigation for the first time is entering a strange moral universe. Not only do suspects lie so routinely you would think the police would be bored waiting for the alibis to stop and the real conversations to begin, the police lie too. "So and so has already talked." "We know what happened, we just need you to fill in a few gaps." These are the tools of the trade. The purpose of an investigation is not only to find out the facts, as in science, but to decide which of the supposed facts will make a compelling story, as in art. The investigation and the resolution of a case are closely tied. While it is no secret that trial lawyers are storytellers, it is less well understood that the police interviews from which the lawyers draw most of their stories are themselves rough drafts within which many other plausible stories could also be found. These drafts are open to revision and indeed are often revised. Tom Nelson and Mike Hefley are among the most effective detectives in the history of the Portland Police Bureau: 88 out of 110 homicides solved during a ten-year collaboration that spanned both sides of the Seraw case, 88 killers—including a baby killer, a prostitute killer, and a serial killer—off the streets. Calm, methodical, as unlike the oversize characters who staff the station houses of TV police shows as it is possible to be, the two are model partners: they have a common memory bank, they finish each other's sentences, in our conversations the most frequent word out of either of their mouths was "We . . ." Both observant Christians, they lead strong domestic lives in suburbs far from the grim circumstances in which they work, and their thoughts are filled with their families. Driving home after a long night to show up for breakfast, taking a kid to school—all this is part of their talk. The same decency that Nelson and Hefley bring to their personal lives they try to bring to their work. Their word matters to them. Appalled by the bloodbaths whose details reveal truths about human nature most people never have to see, they take deep satisfaction in getting their killers convicted, but—apart from the universal post-*Miranda* practice of keeping their suspects out of the hands of lawyers as long as possible—they would not cut legal corners to do so. Yet for all their scruples, Tom Nelson and Mike Hefley are professionally relentless. In solving a homicide their job is to account for what they see in front of them, not to consider other ways it might have come about. In their brief interviews with the Ethiopians at the hospital and after, the detectives asked little that would challenge the victims' self-protective versions of the fight. The Ethiopians' share in the provocations that led to the death of Mulugeta Seraw was never followed up. The importance of the one-sidedness of the police investigation is that Antneh's and

Tesfaye's statements to the detectives are the only ones the two Ethiopians ever had to make. Their statements were the foundation of much that followed, not only in the criminal cases but in the civil case as well. The Ethiopians would never be questioned by the defense attorneys because the attorneys never got that far. They would never be cross-examined at trial because there never was a trial. That there might be "another side to the story" would never be publicly explored.

•

    Tom Nelson: We chose Patty first because . . . she was [a middle-class college girl] working for a chiropractor. . . . We figured if anybody's going to break down [she is]. She doesn't have any criminal record, she's going to . . . cooperate with us to keep from getting involved and being arrested herself. The other girls had . . . records.

    Mike Hefley: [We] try to take the weakest first. Went through this scenario and tried to psychologically profile who would be the easiest to interview. . . . We were trying to pick them off one at a time which was interesting because—

    Tom Nelson: We picked her first thing and she turned out to be the most bullheaded of the group. She wasn't going to budge.

Tom Nelson: "I asked Patty Copp [in a convenience store parking lot Wednesday night] where she was on Saturday night 11-12-88. She stated she went out that night with her boyfriend Kyle Brewster [to a] Chinese restaurant. . . . She stated that they got home at approximately 8:30 P.M. where they remained all that night. She stated they watched TV and did not leave the residence. . . . I asked her if Kyle Brewster was associated with the Skinheads and she stated that he had been in the past but that he no longer associates with them. She stated that she has been sick for the last couple of days and that Kyle has been sick also. She stated that he has not been going to work. According to Patty Copp, she and Brewster remained at her house all day Sunday watching TV and Brewster also spent Sunday night with her. I asked if she knew a girl by the name of Desiree Marquis. She stated that she did not. . . . I asked her if she knew a guy by the name of Nick. She stated that the only Nick she knew was a Nick Lindsay. I asked her if she knew a Nick who lived in the apartments at SE 31st and Pine. She stated that she did not. I asked her if she has ever been to the apartments at SE 31st and Pine. She stated that she never has. I asked her if she was there Saturday night or Sunday morning. She stated that she was not. . . . I asked her if she knew very many of Kyle's friends which belong to a Skinhead organization and she claimed again that Brewster was not part of that organization anymore. She stated that she met a few of his friends in the past but did not know any of their names."

•

Tom Nelson: "So [after our interview with Dave Mazzella] we knew about Heidi Martinson and we knew that she was probably going to be our next target . . . but we didn't know where to find her. . . . The very next morning "Pogo" shows up on his own. His father [dragged] him down there. . . . His father's an attorney and he brought another attorney. [He's] concerned that this is a serious crime. He knows his son hangs around this group and he's talked with him enough to know that he's not involved but he knows who is. . . . "Pogo" was reluctant at first to talk, but with the encouragement of his father and the attorney, he finally broke down and told us what he knew about it. He [also] told us where we could find Heidi."

> Tom Nelson: So we went out to where Heidi worked and . . .
> Mike Hefley: Got her in the car and . . .
> Tom Nelson: Realized right away that we were in trouble because she's got a very belligerent attitude . . .
> Mike Hefley: Got her downtown and advised her and she invoked right off the bat.
> E. L.: Could she have been subject to a murder charge too?

Tom Nelson: Not to the same extent [as Patty] because she wasn't driving . . . but she [admitted] she was out of the car and we knew someone—

Mike Hefley: Some girl.

Tom Nelson: Some girl was out of the car yelling, "Kill him!" and that was enough for us [to use].

Mike Hefley: So [we got her in] a little after four and it wasn't till after ten that she'd got her attorney down there and we were ready to sit down and start talking. So we were with her essentially from 4:00 P.M. till about 2:30.

Tom Nelson: But remember, we took a break? Her parents came down and we let her talk to them [with] the attorney. They all got together and huddled. Then we went back in and concluded the interview. She told us where she was and who was driving and [that part] coincided with what we had heard before but she also told us some stuff we didn't know—that Strasser was involved in stomping on one guy and that Mieske was the one with bat.

•

Mike Hefley: [So] it's Friday night, we just spent eight hours with Heidi, we're dead tired, we just want to go home and get some sleep. Okay. We'll come back tomorrow, we'll come up with a probable cause to arrest these guys based on what Heidi just told us. . . . And it's like 2:30 in the morning and we're walking out the front door and the uniform guys come in and say, "Oh, Hefley, Nelson, where are you? We got Mieske in custody."

Tom Nelson: And we're, "Oh, jeez, just what we need right now," because we didn't ask for him to be arrested yet. We had surveillances set up on their houses and uniformed did a routine stop on [an] old beater car because of the noise and the guys were [checking IDs] and realized, "That's one of the guys we were looking for. The detectives are interested in him. Better bring him in." Julie was with them.

Tom Nelson: "Detective Hefley and I interviewed Mieske in the interview room located next to the Robbery Office. . . . I told [him] we were investigating the homicide [of] the Ethiopian male . . . at SE 31st and Pine. . . . He said he knew about it because he had been reading about it in the paper . . . and watching it on the news. I asked him if he was involved in that homicide and he told me that he did not hear anything about who was involved in it. I asked him if he could tell me where he was [at the time it occurred]. He said he was with his girlfriend Julie Belec at her brother's residence. . . . He said they had dinner [there] between 8 and 9 P.M. and they stayed the night. . . . I asked Mieske if he was familiar with any Skinheads and he stated that he knows several of them because they come to "Our shows." . . . I asked him if he had ever been a Skinhead and he told me that several years ago he had shaved his head but that he was never in any kind of group. I asked him about the East Side White Pride Skinhead group and he told me he knew some people in that group. I asked him who that would be and he [named a few names]. . . . I asked him if he knew of a member of the East Side White Pride by the name of Nick. He said he did know of a guy by the name of Nick and he said that he has 'Seen him around.' He then told me that [a friend] had told him that the homicide . . . involving the Ethiopian male had happened over by Nick's residence. I asked him if he had ever been to Nick's house or apartment and he told me that he 'Never' has been. I asked him if he knew where Nick lives and he told me that he did not. . . . I asked him if he knew a guy by the name of Kyle Brewster. He said he did because Kyle was in a band a few years ago called 'Junk.' He said he has not seen Kyle Brewster since November 4, 1988, which was the last show he played in with his group 'Machine.' I asked Mieske if he knew a girl by the name of Patty Copp. He told me he has never heard of her. I asked him if he knew a girl by the name of Heidi and he told me that he doesn't know any girls by the name of Heidi. I asked him if he knew a guy by the name of Steve Strasser and he told me he did not know Steve Strasser. I told him that we needed his cooperation in solving the death of the Ethiopian and he said 'I think it's bullshit, someone killing some innocent man from Ethiopia.' I told him I agreed with him and I asked him who he thought did it. He told me that he did not know who did it. He then asked me if we had any leads in the case and whether we knew who did it. I told him that we did. He asked me who and I stated 'You did it.' "

•

Tom Nelson: "After talking with Mieske, Detective Hefley and I interviewed Julie Belec. . . . I asked her where she was on 11-12-88 and in the early morning hours of 11-13-88. . . . She stated that her brother picked them up in his car and took her and Mieske over to his house for dinner that night. She stated that they had spaghetti at his house and they ended up staying all night. . . . I asked Julie Belec if she was present in the vehicle that Patty Copp was driving when this incident occurred and she told me that she had nothing to do with it, nor was she in Patty Copp's vehicle. . . . She stated that she was not at Nick's apartment last Saturday night nor did she know anything about the incident which occurred there."

Mike Hefley: "We were running on three or four hours' rest a night. . . . Talk about sleep deprivation. . . . More than any other investigation we've done, we were exhausted. [The DAs] want to write a search warrant for the houses . . . but all the information's in our head because we haven't had any chance to write any reports. And . . . we were so rummy, [we could barely remember anything]. . . . They were . . . asking things questions [like], 'What did Brewster do?' and we're going, 'Brewster? Brewster? Who's Brewster?' "

•

The pressure on Patty Copp was mounting. Even before her lies to Tom Nelson and Mike Hefley in the parking lot, she doubted that she would be able to maintain her story, and afterward she knew she could not. From the moment of her first interview with the detectives, the police did not leave her alone. They told her she might be indicted on a murder charge. They subpoenaed her to the grand jury. They searched her car. They also went after her father, who owned the building where Patty had her apartment and had become her confidant. On Thursday, the day of the grand jury hearing, she contacted a public defender, who helped her navigate repeated interviews, including the recovery of the bat, but her mood was desperate. Kyle, who had been staying with her, felt terrible. His presence was not making things any easier. After one of her encounters with the detectives, "Patty went to her apartment and obtained [Kyle's] clothes and dirty laundry [and] other possessions and put them inside two bags. . . . She and her father discussed what to do with Brewster's property and they did not know what to do." Clearly Kyle should split, but the utilities had been turned off at the apartment he had shared with Prick, so where should he go? Toward the end of the week, he left Patty's to stay with a friend in a neighborhood not far from where he had grown up—a fact reported to the police by the "Confidential Informant," this time looking for a smaller sum from an evidence fund—and he went back to work. When he was picked up on the Sunday after the killing, he was wearing a fleece-lined denim jacket, a black crewneck sweater, an Oxford button-down shirt, and a green baseball cap from his job at Cascade Blueprints. He looked sad and young. "I have the right to remain silent, right?" was about all he said to the police.

•

Detective D. E. Tuke: "On 11-20-88 at approximately 1220 hours I was assigned with Detective P. J. Nelson to escort Mr. Mieske to the jail from the Detective Division holding cell. I handcuffed Mr. Mieske and led him to the custody elevator and rang the 'down' bell. As it happened, his co-conspirator, Kyle Brewster, was on the elevator coming up to the Division. As the doors opened, the two faced each other. Brewster immediately looked away, but Mieske continued to stare at him, shaking his head left to right indicating a 'no' head shake. He discontinued this when he got on the elevator and Brewster was out of his line of sight. Brewster would not look him in the face. As the elevator doors closed, Mieske turned facing front and said 'Fucking snitches must die.' I responded 'What?' He then said, 'Whoever snitched us off is dead.' Mieske made no further comment or statement and we continued on to the jail where he was booked."

•

D. E. Tuke: "On 11-20-88 at apx. 1100 we received info that [Steve Strasser] was at the Edgewood apts #7 at SW Bonita and Hall in Tigard. We went to the front door and knocked. Strasser answered the door in his underwear. We told him we were the police and asked him if he would mind coming downtown to talk about a problem. He said he would come if we would let him get dressed. Det. Barr and Tuke watched through the open front door as he got dressed. He then locked the front door and came with us. He did at no time ask what we wanted him for nor did he ever protest anything concerning our meeting. We told him he would have to be handcuffed for the ride, he didn't object. He was transported to dets. and turned over to homicide."

Steve Strasser was positively garrulous. From shortly after eleven in the morning till after eleven at night he was with the detectives, and the longer he was with them, the more cooperative he became. Who was in East Side White Pride . . . their activities the previous Saturday, beginning with the gathering at the Safeway . . . the distribution of literature downtown . . . the party at Nick's . . . who did what in the fight . . . what was the conversation in the car after the killing . . . whom had he talked with since and what did they say— whatever the detectives wanted to know they had only to ask. He also expressed his views on race. "He told me that he thinks everybody should be proud of their own race. He said blacks should be proud of their race and whites should be proud of theirs," reads Nelson's report. In midafternoon, after a short break, "I pointed out to Strasser that I had talked with individuals who had heard him give an account of the killing . . . in more graphic detail [than he had given it to them so far and] asked him if he had described the blood as coming out of the victim's head like a fountain. [Strasser] told me he was exaggerating when he told that story," Nelson recorded. The implications of Steve Strasser's subsequent hours with the detectives are best seen in Nelson's summary: "In our interview with Strasser, he admitted to being involved in the assaults which occurred at SE 31st and Pine, but stated that he fought with only one of the victims, the one that was not killed"—a version of his role very different than the one he had given his roommates. His kicks had vanished and, with them, his direct responsibility for the death of Mulugeta Seraw. The long conversation also had a further effect. About 5:00 P.M., after remarking that Strasser had neglected to mention stealing beer from the convenience store on the way back to Nick's, Nelson "pointed out to Strasser that he had [also] totally left out any suggestion that this incident had anything to do with the victim's race. . . . I told him that it was my opinion that race had something to do with this incident because I knew of the philosophies of their organization. I asked him if it was not in fact true that they knew there was some black guys sitting in the car on the corner before they even went around the corner. He admitted that they did. He stated he knew this because Ken Mieske had said before getting into the car that 'there's some monkeys around the corner.' " About 9:30 P.M., slumped in the interview room in his jacket and cap, morosely flicking ashes into a Styrofoam cup, he repeated this information for the video camera:

Nelson: Who was it who made the comment about some guys in a car around the corner?
Strasser: I believe it was Ken . . .
Nelson: What did he say?

Strasser: He said somethin' to the effect of, you know, monkeys, uh,
    I can't remember the exact quote.

Nelson: Okay, but what was he referring to?

Strasser: Apparently there was somebody around the corner.

Nelson: Can you remember what he said. [Long pause.]

Strasser: Not right off.

Nelson: Well, I'm not asking you to remember the exact words . . .
    but what was he referring to?

Strasser: I imagine he was referring to somebody. I didn't know these
    gentlemen were around the corner until . . . we went around the
    corner.

Nelson: I realize you didn't have anything to do with that part, but
    there was some black guys around the corner and Ken had made
    reference to them. What did he say?

Strasser: Okay, told ya he said somethin', monkeys or somethin'.
    They were around the corner.

Nelson: Who did he make that comment to, was it just to you or
    to the whole group?

Strasser: Well, he said it, it's basically a matter of who heard it.

•

Three days later, "based on what [Steve] said, we went back to
Heidi and said, 'Isn't it true . . . ?' and she corroborated what
[Steve] had said," Nelson told me. The scene is the interview
room. Heidi, in suburban sweater and skirt, rises to illustrate her
points at a diagram of the intersection of Southeast Thirty-first and
Pine like a pupil reciting her lessons. The interview is prenegotiated
with her attorney:

Martinson: Anyways, Kyle starts to stray off and . . . he says, uhm, "Is
    that a nigger?" or "Is that a fucking nigger?" He's over by himself
    saying something to the effect like he sees a black person some-
    where. So, you know, everyone's . . . standin' around startin' to get
    in the car . . . and we all stop and we're . . . I said, "Where?" or
    "What?" . . . or "We wanna . . . what're you talking about Kyle?" . . .

Hefley: Did the other people ask the same question?

Martinson: Yeah, we were all kinda looking over, going, "What're you talking about Kyle" . . . I don't know if . . . they . . . saw what Kyle saw or, or what, but uhm, you know, I, I was questioning where, what're you talking about and, uhm, he pointed out that there was a man standing up here that, uhm, it was under a street light and he knows that he was black. . . .

Hefley: Were the people in the car black also?

Martinson: I don't . . . you . . . I can't tell from here.

Hefley: At that point you cannot tell?

Martinson: Yeah. No. Uhm. . . .

Hefley: What's being said in the car now?

Martinson: Uhm, uh, Ken refers that, says he, basically Kyle says, "Let's go over there, let's—," you know, "Let's go check it out" . . . referring that he wants to, you know, go over there . . . and Ken, uh, there's a bat, uh, a baseball bat in the backseat and Ken's, uh, er—says that he's got a bat and uhm. . . .

Hefley: All right, you're getting in the car.

Martinson: Yeah, we're getting in the car, uhm, Kyle's, you know fussin' around saying "Let's go up there," Ken's going, you know, everybody in the car's kinda going, "Let's go check it out," 'cause Steve's all, you know, "Let's go . . . see what they're all about . . . Let's, let's go see if we can fuck 'em up," whatever, you know, I mean, everybody's—

Hefley: Who says that? "Let's go fuck 'em up"?

Martinson: "Let's go fuck 'em up"? uhm, all three (3) of 'em say it, in a way, leading to the same thing, what they're saying, do you see what I mean, they're all kinda saying that in the same way, uhm—

Hefley: They all wanna go confront—

Martinson: Right.

Hefley: —those people, right?

Martinson: That when it comes down to it—

Hefley: Get on 'em then.

Martinson: Kyle spotted 'em . . . they all wanna go check it out.

Hefley: What do you mean by check it out? . . .

Martinson: I mean, check it out. They wanna go up there, see, see
    if they could start something.

Hefley: Alright.

The interviews with Steve Strasser and Heidi Martinson are the decisive moments in the investigation of the death of Mulugeta Seraw. They were the only ones who fully cooperated with the police. Neither Ken Mieske nor Kyle Brewster ever did, and though Patty Copp and Julie Belec were interviewed many times, neither would consistently say what the district attorney would have liked them to say: that the skinheads had seen the Ethiopians up the street in advance. Patty Copp passed a polygraph test and was still insisting two years later that she had "no recollection of having seen the black guys before [she] pulled up on SE 31st" and that at first she "didn't even know they were black." Julie Belec said much the same. "I had to take a lie-detector test and I failed it, but I was telling the truth," she told me. "It was because I knew what question they wanted the answer to. They wanted to know if it was preplanned, and I said no, it was not. And so they . . . said I was lying. And they were, you know, really hard on you and they—I guess they made you almost want to lie and say what they wanted to hear so they would leave you alone . . . and some of the time I ended up having to do that. I mean, not really stretching the truth, but just so they'd let you alone." Heidi Martinson herself told a friend "that she had had three very long interviews with the police . . . [of which the] second . . . lasted nine hours. [She said that] that was the time when she got frustrated with the police and decided to tell them what they wanted to hear. This was also the time she made the videotape [quoted above]."

•

The nonfiction writer attempting to capture the truth of a police interrogation can only envy the novelist. " 'Did [the district attorney] make any promises to you for giving him that confession? Did he say something like, well, you tell us you killed Josie and we'll let you go?' " asks a defense attorney of a boy who has just given a false confession in Jim Thompson's *The Criminal.* " 'Well' "—he hesitated—'I kind of felt like he did. He said that if I'd do the right thing, he would; that he knew I didn't really mean to do it and it was just a mistake and he didn't believe in punishing anyone for—' 'But he didn't make you any kind of outright promises?' 'No—not exactly, I guess. I mean it kind of seemed like he did, but . . .' " Something of the same must have been at work here:

> Tom Nelson: We went through a pretty long interview before and then you . . . agreed to put this on tape. . . . Now has anybody made you any promises today? . . . Did we threaten you in any way, did we coerce you to talk to us? . . .
> Steve Strasser: Yeah. We talked. There was–
> Tom Nelson: It was on your free will?
> Steve Strasser: Well, you guys seemed angry, and you know you guys didn't—but I know what you're saying.
> Tom Nelson: . . . Nobody coerced you. . . . You're making these statements voluntarily, is that right?
> Steve Strasser: Yeah.

"I don't see any reason Strasser would have said that [about seeing the Ethiopians up the street] if it didn't occur," Tom Nelson told me later. "It was real low-key at that point, there wasn't any pressure." Low-key for him. In my own acquaintance with them during the writing of this book, Tom Nelson and Mike Hefley were such candid and unintimidating gentlemen that it is hard for me to imagine them otherwise, but the fact of the matter is they are not defense attorneys, and they are certainly not civil libertarians—they are part of the prosecution. Not only did they know what to get into the record, they knew what not to get in. The Ethiopians had to be wholly blameless. In the heated week that followed the death of Mulugeta Seraw, the other victims were briefly reinterviewed, but the inconsistencies between Wondwosen Tesfaye's, and particularly Tilahun Antneh's, recollections of important details and the evidence were never questioned, and the Ethiopians disappeared from the investigation. In my 1992 conversations with Tom Nelson and Mike Hefley, Tilahun Antneh's belief that the fight occurred in the middle of the block outside Mulugeta Seraw's apartment rather than at the street corner, where his body was found, was ascribed to "confusion." "Confusion" was also the detectives' explanation of Antneh's perception that it was the driver who wielded the bat, a claim that would have made the killer Patty Copp.

> E. L.: If [the interviews with Heidi Martinson and Steve Strasser] hadn't taken place, how would it have affected the DA's case? Could he have done a "racial motivation" case without it?
>
> Tom Nelson: Basically, that's all we had to show that this was a racially motivated incident. That they knew beforehand that these guys were black when they got involved with them. You can still go with when we saw them in the car, obviously we knew they were black, and it started from there. But seeing them beforehand and going to the car with the specific purpose of having some kind of confrontation with them is obviously a lot better than just meeting them haphazardly on the street.

The brutal killing of an Ethiopian man by white supremacist skinheads was terrible enough even if it began "haphazardly" in the chance confrontation of a car carrying drunken Ethiopians and a car carrying drunken skinheads on a crowded street at the end of a long Saturday night, but the detectives provided more. Not only to separate lies from truth but to weave out of a conflicting welter of real memories, false memories, lies, and bargaining chips a narrative of the killing that would be just what the district attorney needed: that was the role of the police investigation.

•

"The Police Bureau constantly deals with the senseless loss of life in our community whether it is from a traffic accident or the homicides and other acts of aggression that people commit," read a statement from Police Chief Richard Walker accompanying the announcement of the arrests on November 20, 1988, one week after the killing. "This particular homicide has had a tremendous impact on the entire community as the motive involves something that is so distasteful to the way almost all of us think. Even though an arrest has been made . . . we must not forget that bigotry and racism do exist. We need to build on this tragedy to encourage better understanding and work to eliminate this type of intolerable behavior." The initial charges were murder for Ken Mieske and Kyle Brewster and second-degree assault for Steve Strasser, shortly afterward upped to murder for Strasser as well, as legal maneuvers continued. They all pleaded not guilty.

36

In the months that followed the arrests of Ken Mieske, Kyle Brewster, and Steve Strasser, public agitation over the death of Mulugeta Seraw only increased, and for good reason. Skinheads were coming out. Contrary to the pattern in most communities, where, after a widely publicized racial crime culminating in arrests, racial violence tends to go down, in Portland it went up. Suddenly skinheads were everywhere: In Wendy's, leaving a note for a black employee telling him to "Beware!" and burning a pile of napkins as they fled. On a Tri-Met bus, assaulting a fellow passenger, who had to be taken to a hospital. Downtown, beating and kicking a man who interrupted two of them breaking into a newstand. In neighborhoods on both sides of the Willamette River, slipping fliers such as "WHITE MEN BUILT THIS NATION—WHITE MEN ARE THIS NATION" under windshield wipers and stapling them to telephone poles: all this made known by Gang Enforcement Team member Loren Christensen, who was now the chief spokesman for the Police Bureau on the subject of skinheads. Far from being reviled, Ken, Kyle, and Steve were viewed as leaders and had so many visitors in jail they did not have enough visiting time to see them. "SUSPECTS

IDOLIZED," one *Oregonian* headline reported. The impact of these local incidents was greatly magnified by increased news coverage of skinheads and neo-Nazis elsewhere. When a skinhead was arrested in Corvallis or Spokane: when skinheads and neo-Nazis gathered in commemoration of Robert Mathews on Whidbey Island: when Reverend Butler issued a call for a national skinhead conference to be held at the Aryan Nations on Hitler's birthday: it was big news. Anxiety was heightened still further by reports from the Anti-Defamation League and the Northwest Coalition against Malicious Harassment that racist and antisemitic incidents were on the rise nationally and that the area was contributing more than its share. The *Seattle Times* headlined a gloating front-page article, "PORTLAND: A TROUBLED CITY." Faced with a killing that meant so much more than itself, the white citizens of Portland reached the collective civic opinion not merely that such a thing must never happen again in the future—but that it had never even happened in the past. "Racism is un-Oregonian," said a politician. "Our country is built on no division between the races," said a civic leader. "A man has been killed because of his race!" said a judge. The black citizens could scarcely believe their ears. "What else is new?" "It is the quiet racism of the larger society that permits such a loud act to happen." "The only thing different about the skinheads is their suspenders" were some of the comments from black spokesmen. But for whites the skinheads' racism was original sin. A thick wall of righteousness simultaneously depressing in its self-delusion and touching in its goodwill was now found to be separating "Us"—the good people—from "Them"—the bad skinheads. From small community meetings to a large gathering in Pioneer Courthouse Square where black and white citizens looped themselves together in a shining yellow ribbon, there was a burst of antiracist feeling. New organizations and new coalitions of organizations, most importantly the Coalition for Human Dignity, sprang up overnight. The only way to capture the spirit of Portland in the period after the death of Mulugeta Seraw is to borrow the term of the British sociologist Stanley Cohen: "moral panic." I know because I shared it.

. . .

What was true in the community was just as true in court. The ways in which "the state of the world" shapes the "case at law" may be hidden, but they are real. Here the mood was so hostile to the defense that there might as well not have been any. In intermittent pretrial hearings that began in January 1989, any intimation on the part of the skinheads' court-appointed counsel that Seraw's death might have resulted from a spontaneous act rather than an intentional one—the difference between manslaughter and murder— elicited a reaction almost of vilification. Motions to suppress evidence that were in fact routine seemed, instead, suspect. When the lawyers attempted to exclude the propaganda found in the skinheads' apartments on the grounds both that few of the items could be definitively linked to a particular defendant and that in any case they were too general to demonstrate a specific "intent," the attorneys seemed just as racist as their clients. Why else attempt to protect a client from revealing *that?* Some of the defense efforts were indeed ridiculous. One defense lawyer characterized the skinheads' white-power tattoos as "comic book art." Another described the picture of East Side White Pride on Ken Mieske and Julie Belec's wall as "a bunch of friends together under an American flag." But even had they been less ridiculous, the reaction would have been the same. Either you were with "Us" or you were with "Them." Every little thing counted. When one defense lawyer said, of a protracted discussion, "Let's not beat this to death," when another referred to the Ethiopians as "Boys," those of "Us" in the courtroom raised our eyebrows at one another as if to say, "How bad can it get?"

The weakness of the defense was underscored by the strength of the prosecution. "Proof of intent and motive can only be accomplished through scrutinizing the life and thinking of the man; his associations, his readings, his writings, his self-identification, his politics, his fascination with violence and institutionalized examples of violence and the unifaceted quality of his interests and activities," reads part of a lengthy brief from the state, later described to me by a Portland lawyer as one of the best prepared he had ever seen from the Multnomah County district attorney's office. The state also argued for volume. "It is only when the fact finder is faced with the *magnitude* of material generated, received, preserved, disseminated and displayed by defendant [Mieske] that the true picture of the man emerges," the brief continued.

> Defendant is a radical, white supremist. He is a Nazi. He advocates violent enforcement of his views. He views blacks as "subhuman." He knows no moral obstacle to racial violence; it is good. He was prepared for it, armed for it, and primed for it; defendant acted on his white supremist beliefs on November 13, 1988. As a direct result, Mulugeta Seraw died. The facts of November 13, 1988 must be viewed against that backdrop. To do less is to perpetuate a fraud.

The judge concurred. As the evidence of "the life and thinking" of the skinheads through which the reader of this book has already met them circulated in the courtroom and beyond, trying the skinheads for who they were as well as what they did seemed not only permissible but necessary. It was precisely who they were that was on trial. The most chilling item was a sheet of paper in Ken Mieske's handwriting containing the lyrics to a Machine song called "Senseless Violence" found during the search of his and Julie's apartment—"Victims all around me / I feel nothing but hate / Bashing their brains in / Is my only trade. / Senseless violence is the only thing I know / Piles of corpses never ending watch them grow / Kill my victims for pleasure and for fun. / Beat them over the head. Shoot them with my gun"— words that Ken would repeatedly say he had not written but merely copied but that to anyone who encountered them seemed damningly to prefigure the death of Mulugeta Seraw. And the evidence was still coming in. In jail, Ken in particular enjoyed the mantle of stardom in which his skinhead followers enveloped him and wrote numerous rabid letters that, intercepted by prison authorities, also found their way into the state's case. "Greetings, Comrade," he wrote to another inmate at the time of the hearings:

Well it is good to hear from those who share the same feelings as me. Yes I am being charged with 1st degree murder, 2 counts of assault, 3 counts of intimidation and another count of Assault 1 [from the Safeway incident] for stabbing and puncturing a black SUBHU-MANs lung. As you can tell, these Zionist whores and the media are allready accusing me and Kyle of being guilty. We would have never got caught but some weak wanna be white scum turned us in for the J.D.L.'s 10,000 reward.

'For Faith, Race, and Nation, Your Brother!!!! KEN DEATH, A Hero to the White Race!!!" was how he signed the letter. "P.S. Explain to me about Kristallnacht. Who or what is it?" he added. The more the press and public followed the prosecutors into the roiling underground from which the defendants seemed suddenly to have materialized like a primeval force, the harder it was to see them as human beings. Those dull, unrepentant faces we saw staring out at the proceedings seemed to have come from a lower world. When the skinheads sat at the defense table "snacking on salted peanuts," as the *Oregonian* reported one day of Ken, it was as if Satan himself were pouring the salt.

If I am deliberately fusing the substance of the proceedings with the atmosphere, it is because I think the two were inseparable. The wall that we are taught is supposed to exist between them was permeable. Everyone involved played his or her part well—the judge, Philip Abraham; the prosecutors, Deputy District Attorneys Norm Frink and Jill Otey; the court-appointed defense lawyers, Randall Vogt for Ken Mieske, George Haslett for Steve Strasser, and William Park for Kyle Brewster, the latter soon replaced by privately retained Pat Birmingham—but I think that no matter who had been in those positions, the outcome would have been the same. It is hard to imagine any court in Portland at that moment limiting the case against the skinheads to what the state's brief called "the individual threads of evidence which comprise the circumstances of the event" rather than "the fabric of the [men themselves, their] racist essence" or redefining the issue to include not only whether the killing of Mulugeta Seraw was indeed a "racist attack on three Ethiopian males by three alleged skinheads" but whether, if it was, those racist skinheads could get impartial treatment. Of the myriad motions, including an attempt on the part of the defense to move the trial out of town, virtually every ruling the court was called upon to make was decided in favor of the state. As many times as I have reviewed the documentation, reconsidered my interviews, and reread my notes, my conclusion is always the same: from a legal standpoint, what happened in the pretrial hearings did not add up to much. They were beside the point. While most of the decisions were intended to provide a framework for an actual trial rather than to stand by themselves, the result, if not the intention, was to raise the stakes. At the end of the hearings the death of Mulugeta Seraw seemed an even worse crime than before.

Then, about six weeks before the May 8, 1989, date set for the big trial and a week after rejecting a similar motion from the defense, the presiding judge granted the state's request that, instead of being tried together, the three defendants be tried separately. With the defense argument that because Ken Mieske, Kyle Brewster, and Steve Strasser had each had a different role in the actual homicide they were bound to incriminate one another now joined by the DA's argument that, because of continuing changes in the statements of Julie Belec, Patty Copp, and Heidi Martinson about whether or not they had seen Kyle Brewster and/or Steve Strasser punch or kick Mulugeta Seraw, he had withdrawn their immunity and could no longer accept the "evidentiary limitations" of a joint trial, the severance was probably legally inevitable, but it was politically disappointing. A joint trial was intrinsically more significant. Not only was the skinhead movement itself bound to be more central to a joint trial than it was likely to be in individual ones, but as even the minimal argument that had been heard in court so far made clear, the use of ideological evidence to establish "intent" raised First Amendment issues that would also loom larger if the defendants were tried together.

The cancellation of the political trial to which the preliminaries had seemed to be headed downgraded the Seraw case to an ordinary criminal proceeding and left it subject to the ordinary tactics of criminal proceedings: deals. While collectively the defendants had always maintained that—their racism to the contrary—the death of Mulugeta Seraw had been an accidental occurrence and they would not plead guilty to "racial motivation," individually they would be likely to be more pliable. That was just what the prosecution wanted. As the date for what was now to be the first of three trials neared, it began to be clear that not only was there not going to be a joint trial, there were not going to be any trials at all. What the district attorney was really after was plea bargains. It was not that the state was fearful of losing—but neither was there a guarantee that the state would win. "We would have prevailed, but there would have been dicey moments," lead prosecutor Norm Frink told me candidly much later. "There were significant issues." A bat is "not inherently a death-dealing object." The killing was supposed to have taken place outside Mulugeta Seraw's apartment in the middle of Southeast Thirty-first Avenue after the skinheads had seen him standing outside Antneh's car, but he was found at the corner of Southeast Thirty-first and Pine, so he had been down the street. The testimony of both Antneh and Tesfaye was self-serving and incoherent. The statements of both the defendants and the girl-friends contradicted not only each other but themselves. Ken Mieske had said in the car afterward that he had not meant to kill Seraw. And more. "The case got made into something it wasn't," Frink reflected. "It looked like a roving band of skins went out to kill a black person [but] that wasn't what happened. It became an image as opposed to a real case." With what took place at the corner of Southeast Thirty-first and Pine and the public "image" of what had taken place so much at odds, as the DA knew: with the first-rate criminal defense attorney now representing Kyle Brewster eager to expose the soft spots to a jury: with a loss certain to further inflame the community, why take risks? Ninety-five percent of the criminal cases in the country were settled by plea bargain every year. Why not the death of Mulugeta Seraw? In addition to local factors, the federal Justice Department had also entered the case, and it needed a strong result. Officials from the Civil Rights Division, startled both by their loss in the April 1988 sedition trial of white supremacist leaders at Fort Smith, Arkansas, and by the continuing growth of the racist movement nationwide, were beginning to grasp what was actually happening in the streets and had begun to investigate a skinhead group in Dallas called the Confederate Hammerskins as well as East Side White Pride. In closed-door sessions with the Portland defendants and their lawyers, representatives of the Justice Department pulled together the assault on the Safeway security guard in September 1988 with the killing of Mulugeta Seraw two months later and threatened to charge Ken, Kyle, and Steve with federal civil rights violations carrying life sentences without possibility of parole, in addition to the state criminal charges, if Washington was not satisfied with the outcome. A more informal presence was the Southern Poverty Law Center of Montgomery, Alabama, which made it known to both local and federal officials that it was interested in mounting a civil suit in the Seraw case similar to its much-admired 1987 case against the United Klans of America for a lynching committed by UKA members, an initiative that would be directly tied to the criminal results, for if the killing was not established to have been motivated by racism in the first place, it could not be linked to any racist organization.

On May 1, 1989, in a plea bargain that his lawyer described as "the result of complex and very tough negotiations with the Federal government," Ken Mieske pled guilty to first-degree murder in the Seraw case. He also affirmed what he had always denied: that "on November 13th, 1988, I unlawfully and intentionally killed Mulugeta Seraw because of his race." His sentence was life with a minimum of twenty years, later raised to thirty by the State Parole

Board.* In the courtroom at his subsequent sentencing were Mulu-geta's uncle, Engedaw Berhanu, who asked the judge for the death sentence, and Portland trial lawyer Elden Rosenthal, said at the time to be representing the Anti-Defamation League. In early September, Kyle Brewster, who had also been charged with murder, likewise capitulated, pleading guilty to the lesser charges of first-degree man-slaughter (for "aiding and abetting" the killing of Seraw) and second-degree assault (for fighting with Antneh) and "no contest" to two charges of racial intimidation, in spite of the fact that his private attorney had sworn he would never plead. Convinced that his client's degree of guilt was being exaggerated, the lawyer described the pressures to plead as the most intense he had ever faced and said that if Kyle chose to resist them, he would represent him for free. Kyle received a twenty-year sentence with a ten-year mini-mum. The next month, Steve Strasser followed, pleading guilty to first-degree manslaughter (for "aiding and abetting" the killing of Seraw) and second-degree assault (for fighting with Tesfaye) and "no contest" to two charges of racial intimidation. He, too, was given a twenty-year sentence, but with a minimum of nine years.

The reduction of the Seraw case from moral panic to done deal occasioned very little comment in the community. To the white public in general, it was mainly a relief. Among the principals, everybody was satisfied: the district attorneys because they believed they had gotten the strongest possible results: the Justice Depart-

---

*The addition of charges from the Safeway stabbing in September 1988 to the Seraw charges—a first-degree assault and intimidation charge for Ken Mieske and an intimidation charge for Kyle Brewster—made the pleadings even more complicated. In spite of federal agreements not to prosecute, the Justice Department was still looking into the possibility of charges in the Safeway case many years later. Besides the principals, several other people were eventually charged for matters growing out of the Seraw case—Nick Heise for perjury before the grand jury, Julie Belec and Patty Copp for hindering prosecution, and Heidi Martinson, who lost her immunity when she "could no longer remember seeing Steven Strasser kick Mulugeta Seraw," for intimidation. Heise served six months, and all the girls much shorter periods.

ment because its role as a political force was explicitly acknowledged: Engedaw Berhanu because he understood the importance of Ken Mieske's "racial motivation" plea both for criminal sentencing and for possible civil litigation. About the only dissidents were some members of the black community, including other Ethiopians, who had always wanted the cases to come to trial and held three days of demonstrations in the district attorneys' offices to tell them so but had been overruled. This saga of the devolution of the criminal prosecution of the Portland skinheads is so familiar that were it not for what followed it would hardly be worth recounting in such detail, but it was not the end of the story—for the day after Steve Strasser's plea bargain, the Southern Poverty Law Center and the Anti-Defamation League filed a joint lawsuit in federal court in Portland charging Tom Metzger, John Metzger, and WAR as an organization, along with Ken Mieske and Kyle Brewster, with civil liability in the death of Mulugeta Seraw. Portland would get a political trial after all, but its target would be Tom Metzger.

CAKES AND CAUSES

We run our business like a business. Whether you're selling cakes or causes, it's all the same thing, the same basic process—just good, sound business practice.

—MORRIS DEES, 1991

37

Sometime in the early 1970s, I began to get fund-raising appeals from a new organization in the deep South, the Southern Poverty Law Center. At that time, mail solicitation for political causes was not the filler of recycling bins it is today. In fact, it did not exist. The mailings were hard to place. Unslick, seemingly amateurish, they appeared to be direct personal pleas from a backwoods Alabama lawyer named Morris Dees, whose signature was scrawled

across the envelopes, for help in stamping out one after another
dreadful instance of continuing racial injustice in the South. His
picture of a South where white-sheeted Klansmen marched in the
streets while poor black prisoners faced the death penalty for rape
seemed practically quaint. In those years, so much closer to the
divided 1960s, I still had the illusion common to the radical movement that if anyone was on the right side of the great struggles for
peace and justice I would already know about them. Whatever else
"the movement" of the 1960s was or wasn't, it had always been
something of a club. As an involved journalist, I had my own private register of who in the legal profession was on the front lines of
civil rights work, and Morris Dees was not on the list. Not only
that—there was something off about the mailings in spite of the
gravity of their claims. I didn't believe them. This "Morris Dees"—
unlikely name—this "Southern Poverty Law Center"—whatever
that meant—they did not fit in. Fortunately for the Southern Poverty Law Center, others who received its original mailings were not
as heartless. From all across the country, thousands—in time, hundreds of thousands—of people responded. Between 1982 and
1992, the period most relevant to this story, the SPLC's income
from contributions alone rose from about $2.5 million to about
$11.4 million yearly. Its 1992 assets of $48.1 million were more
than three times both the combined assets of the ACLU and the
ACLU Foundation—$14.3 million—and the NAACP Legal
Defense and Educational Fund—$16.9 million. It had $44.2 million in reserves. Besides its work in the courts the SPLC had
become a major force in the field of monitoring the far right. Its
Intelligence Report, a bimonthly account of white supremacist activity prepared primarily for police agencies, had become, along with
publications from the national ADL and the Atlanta-based Center
for Democratic Renewal, the chief source of information about the
neo-Nazi movement. The *Intelligence Report* was published by a
department of the SPLC known as Klanwatch that had come to
give its name to the entire growing phenomenon of far-right-
watching of which I too, through my investigation of the neo-Nazi

movement for the *Nation*, had become a part. We were all Klanwatchers.

"The Morris Dees Story" has been told so often by Morris Dees that it is difficult to tell it independently. In radio and television interviews, magazine profiles, speeches, an autobiography, and a full-length NBC made-for-TV Monday Night Movie, he has recounted the same events so often they have achieved an eternal form. I personally have read or heard so many of them so often I know them by heart, and the reader who has been in his audience more than once will have heard them too. There is the time he sassed a black field hand who was leading him on a mule and he was whupped around the barnyard by his daddy. Moral: No five-year-old kid is gonna call an old black man "nigger" in this family. The time he watched his daddy drink water from the same dipper as a black woman. Moral: Whatever they do elsewhere in the South, in this place we gonna treat the black folks as human beings. The time he tried and failed to defend a black neighbor from a drunk-driving fine wrongly leveled by a justice of the peace. Moral: Ain't no justice for black people from white people, least-ways in this part of Alabama. The trouble with most of these Morris Dees Stories is that they belong to an oral tradition. Their authority lies not in documentation but in repetition. From his very name, Morris Seligman Dees, Jr.—said to have been given first by his grandfather to his father in honor of a Jewish merchant in Montgomery who befriended him—to his moment of truth in 1968 when, snowbound in the Cincinnati airport, he reads Clarence Darrow's *The Story of My Life* and decides to devote himself to civil rights, his self-presentation is one uncorroboratable anecdote after another. Take, for example, the oft-told story about the Sunday in September 1963 when he stood before the congregation of the white Baptist church in Montgomery where he led the Sunday school and asked for donations to rebuild the black Baptist church in Birmingham where four little girls had been killed in the bombing the weekend before, a story that ends with the rest of the congregation filing out and Morris and his then-wife Beverly at the front of the sanctuary, praying alone. "Years later, Beverly would look back on this day and say, 'That was the beginning. You knew your life was going to change and you had to go on with it,' " reads the finale to this passage in Dees's 1991 autobiography, *A Season for Justice*—but what Beverly told a newspaper reporter in 1994 was, "I wish I'd been there to see that." "Mr. Dees did ask for donations, but the scene at the church was less dramatic than the one . . . described in his book," the reporter added.

For the writer trying to provide an accurate introduction to Morris Dees it would be useful if every such anecdote carried the parenthetical tag (F) for Fact or (L) for Legend or, as in this case, (F, L) for the probable mixture of both, but, alas, they do not. The Fact-and-Legend problem is compounded by what might be called the Hero-or-Villain problem: that the opinions held of him by others are so extreme. For every Brotherhood Award with its intimation of sainthood, there is a poisonous letter accusing him practically of demonic possession. To some extent the argument is about Morris Dees himself. When a man so professionally righteous is found to have had four previous wives, a multimillion-dollar estate, and a whatever-it-takes-to-win attitude both in and out of court—people talk. More important, however, the argument is about the organization he created, for the Southern Poverty Law Center is not only about racism and justice, it is about money and power, a combination that plants in some minds the nagging question: Which is the end, which is the means? In attacks that have appeared in newspapers and journals from *The Truth at Last*, on the right, to *CounterPunch*, on the left, with a recent mainstream stop at *Harper's* along the way, Dees has been criticized for many fund-raising offenses, most of which fit into one of a trio of "Bads," namely "Bad Faith," taking in much more money than he needs, under false pretenses; "Bad History," claiming too central a place for himself and his litigation in the broad record of attempts to integrate the South; and "Bad Taste"—"I'm sure the implied linking of Jefferson Davis to Klan lynchings will stir the juices of ignorant Yankee contributors, but it pisses me off," Jimmy Carter's press secretary, Jody Powell, wrote Dees at one point.

The main difference between Morris Dees and some of his critics has to do with the relationship between selling and law. While to some critics, at least, law is about discovering truth and selling is about telling lies, to Morris Dees they are parts of a whole. "Raising money for the SPLC is no different from selling birthday cakes or political fund-raising," he told *Newsweek* in 1977. "In direct mail, you have to find people who will donate; you drop test packages and calculate your chances for a greater return. It's the same way you try to sell different members of a jury different aspects of your case. Then they go off and sell the rest to each other." Selling is what he is doing all the time. A good example is the Morris Dees story about a bleak moment in his career, in 1975, when a judge in the much-publicized murder trial of North Carolina black prisoner Joan Little for the death of her white jailer accused Dees of suborning perjury from a state's witness and ordered him dismissed from the case and arrested. His only hope of saving his reputation lay in getting the corroboration of the sheriff of the distant county in whose company he had heard the witness's testimony in the first place, corroboration that would leave the sheriff, a state employee, testifying against his own side. It is a dramatic story, complete with a flight across North Carolina in a chartered plane, darkening clouds, and a pilot anxious about the weather. On the scales are the sheriff's electoral career, on the one hand, and the sheriff's soul—and Morris Dees's legal career—on the other. An affidavit must be secured in two hours or less. "I can't remember what else I said," Dees writes, about the sheriff's initial reluctance. "All I remember thinking is that I had spent my whole life selling, and if I ever had to make a sale, now was the time."

> We talked for the next hour. Time was running out to fly back to Raleigh, but I couldn't leave. We talked about everything on earth and beyond—philosophies of life, the Bible, Jesus. We laughed, we

cried, we prayed. When we finished Sheriff Davis stood up and took a long look at the pictures of his kids. When he finally turned to me, tears were running down both sides of his face. "Morris, I'll sign your affidavit," he said.

"I learned everything I know about hustling from the Baptist Church. Spending Sundays sitting on those hard benches, listening to the preacher pitch salvation . . . why it was like getting a PhD in selling," he once said, in a frequently cited remark. He was clearly a good student. Whether his selling or his other tactics are truly different from those of other lawyers or he is merely better at them, it is hard for a nonlawyer to weigh. But they may be what a law professor who taught both Morris Dees and his original partner, Millard Fuller, was thinking of when he told a reporter that although both had made a lot of money and done a lot of good with it, "Millard [who founded Habitat for Humanity] gave all of his to the Lord. Morris used his to do what the Lord would do if he was a lawyer."

Morris Dees was born in December 1936 in a cotton-farming area about ten miles east of Montgomery. Neither "white trash" nor "society," his family occupied a social niche he describes as "wealthy poor." They had no land and little money—the houses they rented had no water or electricity—but neither were they the sharecroppers of Walker Evans and James Agee's *Let Us Now Praise Famous Men*, which describes the same time and place. Status or no status, it was a good way to grow up. "There was nothing I liked more than sitting out front of Pinkston's store with Daddy," he writes in his autobiography,

> unless it was . . . racoon hunting in the oak and palmetto swamps
> along the Tallapoosa . . . with T. J. Henricks, a black farmer; . . . or
> riding my bike to [my grandmother's] house and [spending] the night

in her big featherbed; or hiking the mile and a half to Solomon's Pond and fishing for bream with Momma and an old superstitious woman we called "Rat," who claimed her secret for success was that she spit on her hook and worm before she threw in the line . . . or swimming naked with little Buddy Orum in the hole under the . . . railroad trestle; or terrorizing Mount Meigs' spinster postmistress . . . by riding my pinto pony down [the road] faster than she was driving her 1932 Chevy; or working behind the counter in my uncle Lucien Dees' country store; or listening to Johnny Ford, an aged black hand, play the blues on an old guitar using the neck of a broken Red Dagger wine bottle . . . or greeting Big Jim Folsom, our populist governor, when he came out to the house on Sunday afternoons . . . to escape from favor-seeking politicians.

As rich as it was in pleasure, however, the life of the Dees family was poor in independence. Several times before 1948, when his father was finally able to buy some property for his own cotton operation, the family was forced to leave rented houses and land. This seems to have particularly bothered Morris Senior. When, in high school, Morris Junior began speaking at Baptist revivals and thinking about being a preacher, his father discouraged him. Preaching didn't pay. Make a living at something else and save religion for the weekends, his father advised him. He took the advice. Even as a young child he had sold watermelons and other items grown on a small patch his father had given him near their house. Now, with money saved from picking cotton at two cents a pound, retrieving Coke bottles from the roadside for one cent apiece, and a paper route, he bought a calf from a neighbor for fifteen dollars, mated it with a bull of his father's, and started a herd. He did the same with pigs, feeding them with scraps from the school lunchroom given to him in return for bringing back the fifty-gallon cans clean every day. He bought the pigs at 80 pounds for five dollars and sold them at 245 pounds for forty-five. He also raised chickens, doing all the work himself and selling about 250 every week to nearby stores. By graduation from high school in 1955, he was named Star Farmer of Alabama by the Future Farmers of America and was earning about five thousand dollars a year.

At the University of Alabama, where he was both a prelaw student and a husband, for he had eloped with his high school sweetheart—Beverly—the year before, his talent for moneymaking flourished. When his mother mailed him a cake for his first birthday away from home, he realized that other students must be just as lonely as he was and other mothers just as eager to cheer them up. "Why [not] write each student's parents and offer to deliver a freshly baked birthday cake?" he asked himself. He did. Evidently he wrote a winning letter for by the next year he was delivering about 350 cakes a month made by a local bakery to fellow students at a profit of about three dollars per cake. Even more valuable than the money was the experience in direct mail. "Thousands of postal employees delivered my sales message, all at once, all over America," he wrote in 1991, still exultant. "I learned to write sales copy, to design an offer and to mail at the opportune time." With the help of his equally enterprising partner, Millard Fuller, the 'Bama Cake Service soon expanded into marketing an assortment of fund-raising items to clubs and organizations in thirty-two states, and "we did it all by mail." With profits from direct mail they bought an old barracks near the university and converted it to student apartments, which eventually netted them over twenty thousand dollars apiece. The two ambitious young law students were close friends as well as partners, and as graduation approached in 1960 they were hoping to find a way to remain together but they did not quite know what or where it should be. Should they "stay in Tuscaloosa and be businessmen or return to Montgomery and become attorneys"—that was the question. Influenced in part by Morris's father's belief that business could be as uncertain as farming and in part by the fact that they both now had families to support, Morris Dees and Millard Fuller finally decided that they would not, after all, make a choice. Fuller & Dees of Montgomery, Alabama, would be a business and a law firm both.

. . .

If any city in the United States can claim the title of "The Birth-place of the Civil Rights Movement," that city would have to be Montgomery. It was in Montgomery, in December 1955, that Rosa Parks refused to move to the back of the bus. It was in Mont-gomery, in January 1956, that the young pastor of the Dexter Ave-nue Baptist Church, Martin Luther King Jr., went to prison for the first time. And it was in Montgomery, five years later, that the first Freedom Riders arrived at the Greyhound terminal fresh from the burning of their bus in Anniston, only to be ambushed by a group of white vigilantes in a violent attack that left several people hospitalized. Like all other Montgomery whites, Morris Dees and Millard Fuller had to decide whether to side with the blacks attempting to integrate interstate buses or with the whites attempt-ing to resist, and like most Montgomery whites—with a few distin-guished exceptions—they chose the whites. "Fuller recalls agonizing privately with Dees over that shameful spectacle but they concluded that 'it would be bad for business if rising young lawyers spoke out for social justice and equality,' " one writer reports. They even rep-resented one of the white men involved in the assault, their fees paid by the White Citizens Council and the Klan. Gradually, how-ever, in the struggle between reputation and conscience, conscience began pulling ahead. Although Dees's previous political stirrings had been mild at best, he knew from his childhood neighbors that the principal difference between white people and black people was that whites, as a rule, had more money, and he could not support what was happening. Sometime after the rejection by his own con-gregation of his efforts to aid the bombed Birmingham Baptist church, whatever its exact form, he began turning away from the church of his past toward a newly formed Unitarian fellowship in which he became very active. Some members of the fellowship were also members of the local American Civil Liberties Union, and he was introduced to another side of Montgomery. Millard Fuller was a serious Christian and he, too, was dismayed by the violent resistance to change. In 1964 their burgeoning mail-order firm held an integrated office Christmas party in a Montgomery hotel, which may have been the first such event in the history of the city. In March 1965, they both took part in their first civil rights activity, driving people to Selma for the start of the Selma-Montgomery voting rights march. Later they sat on the lawn outside the State Capitol and heard the speeches, a small step toward action in itself because the authorities had asked the city's whites to stay away. By that time, the successful marketing partners had each taken home their first million dollars. When one of Morris's uncles, a heckler, threatened them both with a .38 and called them "nigger lovers," they could afford to feel "So be it." For Millard Fuller, 1965 was a year of decision. Shocked by his wife's declaration that in spite of her closetsful of clothes and shoes all she really wanted was the good Christian man she had originally married—and that she was leaving him—Fuller chose with her to renounce their wealth and enter Christian service. By the end of the year he had sold his share of the business to Dees, stripped himself of his possessions, and given away over $2 million. The couple lived for a time in the Christian community of Koinonia Farm in Americus, Georgia, and also served as missionaries in Africa. In the 1970s, Fuller started Habitat. For Morris Dees, the timing was different. Named one of the ten "Outstanding Young Men of the Year" by the Junior Chamber of Commerce in 1967, he was beginning to receive national attention for his business abilities, but by then his own attention was flagging. Soliciting the favorite recipes of home economics teachers and selling the collection to Future Homemakers of America clubs as a fund-raising product might be profitable, but it was hardly compelling. Many of his other projects were just as mundane. With the country still in turmoil and new civil rights laws generating new opportunities for litigation, surely the more interesting work ahead would be in law rather than business—but the business was so successful he had had to give up his practice. He was restless in other ways as well. A country boy at heart, he had begun buying land outside Montgomery on which he could raise horses and cattle, and he was even riding rodeo on weekends. By 1968 there was also a new wife, a Georgia beauty queen, replacing the high school sweetheart and taking charge of the estate he named Rolling Hills Ranch. In 1969, shortly after his oft-recalled awakening by Clarence Darrow in the Cincinnati airport, Morris Dees sold Fuller & Dees to the Los Angeles Times-Mirror Company for $6 million. With no more financial concerns, he could focus on civil rights.

By the early 1970s, when Dees shifted direction, the momentum of the civil rights movement was indeed in the courts. For the new federal civil rights laws to take effect, test cases had to be mounted, cases that required a host of courageous and committed plaintiffs, lawyers, and judges throughout the South. In these lawsuits, the Southern Poverty Law Center, established in 1971 by Morris and a fellow Montgomery lawyer, Joe Levin, took its place alongside older organizations such as the NAACP Legal Defense Fund and the ACLU in undertaking what were essentially civil rights class-action suits whose reach would be broader than the immediate instance at hand. One important case, begun while the partnership was still known as Levin & Dees, involved the desegregation of the Montgomery YMCA, which had gone to great lengths not only to avoid integrating but to help the city do likewise, through secret agreements replacing the city's public recreation facilities with the Y's private recreation facilities, which both thought would not come under the laws. Another case involved the integration of the whites-only Alabama State Troopers. Still another challenged Alabama's voting districts in a way that led to the first black representation in the legislature. Yet another ended the exclusion of blacks and women from the Montgomery County jury pool. Outside court, too, the innovative young businessman-lawyer was starting to make a mark. From the outset, the founders of the SPLC had agreed that the new firm would finance itself by the same means that had made Dees financially able to found it in the first place—direct mail. Their first 25,000-person mailing—about a black defendant charged with murder in a case in which the judge had declared beforehand that the man would get the death penalty—brought a return two and a half times what they expected and left the center with a base of five hundred donors. A different fund-raising letter, on behalf of Montgomery black civil rights leader Fred Grey, who was running for the legislature as a result of the redistricting suit, was so effective that when it reached Gary Hart, who headed the fledgling 1972 antiwar presidential campaign of his fellow senator George McGovern, Hart invited its author to Washington to meet with them both—"heady stuff for an Alabama boy like me," Morris remarks. He subsequently became the finance manager of McGovern's campaign. The saga of Morris Dees's introduction of direct-mail solicitation to the 1972 presidential race has been told so many times it is probably the quintessential Morris Dees story. How he wrote a seven-page personal-sounding letter beginning, "You are one of a number of people whose help I am asking in the most important effort any American can ever undertake." How the McGovern staff dismissed it as six pages too long and told him to send out their edited one-page version. How he did not do what they said because "I had tested one-page and four-page letters selling books, and four pages always beat one." How he incorporated their changes into an improved seven-page version he sent to 300,000 people at his own expense without telling the staff. How a nervous McGovern received a letter from an adman on Madison Avenue denigrating Morris's letter as "so amateurish, so bald, so badly conceived, so incompetent" it would surely "bomb"—only to find a few days later that the responses had started to roll in, "boxes and boxes of contributions," an unprecedented 15 percent return rate, resulting both in a feature article in the *New York Times* and in the respectful observation of the conservative fund-raising master Richard Viguerie that "someone in the McGovern camp knew what he was doing." By the time the campaign was over, it had raised $24 million, and it ended with a surplus. When Morris Dees returned from Washington he was in a unique position. Not only did he have the list of McGovern's nearly 700,000 donors and a return offer from McGovern for future fund-raising support for the SPLC in his pocket—he had the attention of powerful politicians all over the country who had not previously known his name. In 1976 he raised money for Jimmy Carter, in 1980 for Ted Kennedy, in 1984 for Gary Hart, and he evidently continues. According to a current story, not so much by as about Morris Dees, when he appeared not long ago at a gathering of senators and representatives at the Capitol, the room fell to silence in awe at the presence of the Alabama miracle worker known in all their prayers as the God of Direct Mail.

As the 1970s became the 1980s, the United States was once again in a new racial era. At the top was an administration that took every opportunity to make clear its conviction that the civil rights movement had gone too far. At the bottom was an outcropping of white supremacists such as the reader has met in the first part of this book, still separated into isolated organizations but groping toward becoming a movement. What's more, as we have also seen, the supremacists were starting to act. In 1978, Klan rallies in Decatur, Alabama, brought thousands of Klansmen into the streets for the first time in more than a decade. In 1979, an alliance of Klansmen and neo-Nazis resulted in the killing of five labor organizers in Greensboro, North Carolina, and the killers were later acquitted. In 1980, Klan members shot five black women in the streets of Chattanooga, Tennessee. In 1981, Grand Dragon Louis Beam led his Texas Klan in an open campaign of intimidation against Vietnamese shrimpers in Galveston Bay. Nor were these stirrings limited to the South. In 1982, Richard Butler hosted the largest Aryan Nations Congress so far in Idaho. In 1983, Robert Mathews founded the Order in Washington. In 1984 the Order assassinated Jewish talk show host Alan Berg in Colorado. And so it went. How much Morris Dees then sensed of the long-term political implications of these developments is hard to say, but he understood their financial implications promptly. "You can't raise money through the mail for just any candidate," he once said about his fund-raising strategies. "You've got to have [someone] who's way out on the extremes—a Reagan, a Wallace, a McGovern, a Goldwater. The people who will give big money through the mail are either on the far right or the far left. They're true believers. You can't fire them up with a middle-of-the-road cause or candidate. You've got to have someone who can arouse people." Or some thing. In 1980, after losing the defense of a black man accused of attacking a Klansman in the Decatur marches, Dees decided to redirect the energies of the Southern Poverty Law Center away from the broad-based litigation it had previously undertaken toward the Ku Klux Klan, creating the new unit known as Klanwatch, which would help educate the public, monitor Klan activities, and try to hold the Klan legally responsible for its actions.

The founding of Klanwatch could not have been better timed. With the collapse of the FBI's counterintelligence program following the congressional investigations of the 1970s, federal efforts to track the far right were at a standstill and those of local law enforcement bodies were minimal and scattered. The Anti-Defamation League monitored "extremist" activity across the left-right spectrum and shared its information with authorities but did not take on litigation. The press knew nothing, and the same was true of academics. By 1981, with the initiation of the bimonthly *Intelligence Report*, officially aimed at law enforcement agencies but unofficially available to journalists as well, Klanwatch had become an indispensable source. And not only its timing was auspicious; so was its structure. The "good, sound business practice" Morris Dees referred to in the quotation that heads this chapter includes creating and meeting need. Just as the makers of medicines first dramatize our ailments and then sell us cures, so the Southern Poverty Law Center dramatized the racial illness of the 1980s and then offered a remedy— the Southern Poverty Law Center. To learn the background of, for example, North Carolina White Patriot Party leader Glenn Miller, you had to turn to Klanwatch publications. To learn what was being done about him, you had to look at Klanwatch litigation. To gauge the significance both of Miller and of Klanwatch's successful prosecutions against him—again, Klanwatch. All roads led to Klanwatch.

Not by itself but together with other factors operating both inside and outside the movement, the transition of the Southern Poverty Law Center from "Poverty Law" to "Klanwatching" contributed to the changing nature of the white supremacist movement. All that Klanwatch publicity not only told the world about the movement: the publicity told the movement about itself. In the language of the 1960s, Klanwatch raised the movement's consciousness. The very Klan that the Law Center later put out of business, the United Klans of America, heralded the foundation of Klanwatch with a front-page spread in its newspaper, *Fiery Cross*, as if it had just won a blue ribbon at the county fair. The SPLC changed too. The more its pursuit of the Klan provoked a Klan response, the better known and better funded the center became, soon finding itself with more money than it could spend. In fact, the effect was circular. A 1983 arson fire in the center's office was set by a Montgomery Klansman with whom the SPLC had had numerous run-ins. Dees's and the staff's several frightening confrontations with Louis Beam were connected with the Texas Klan–Vietnamese fishermen litigation. Thanks to Morris Dees's instinct for mailing "at the opportune time," no sooner would something happen than a letter would go out about it, contributing to the momentum of the center and the momentum of the movement at the same time. There is no doubt about the reality of the danger. Seven of the attempts or threats of attempts on Dees's life ended in court. Dees was the number one target on the Order assassination list of which the dead Alan Berg was number three. (The man in the middle was TV producer Norman Lear.) The center's 1985 move from its original storefront to the expensive building that earned it the nickname "Poverty Palace" and speeded the departures of young staff lawyers committed to the ideals of the earlier years was undoubtedly necessary for security. But the enormous attention in the center's fund-raising mailings to its need for protection from the Big Bad White Supremacists broadcast the problem and the solution simultaneously. Ever since the era of George Lincoln Rockwell, when the American Jewish Committee and others had debated whether to ignore or oppose the American

Nazi Party's demonstrations on the Washington Mall, the opinions of community leaders across the country had been divided on whether exposure heightened the influence of little-known groups that would otherwise decline—a question that perhaps may also be asked of this book—but for Morris Dees the problem did not seem to exist. If he had any reservations about publicity, they are a well-kept secret. As for the white supremacists, the truth is, they liked the attention. Clearly the Klan was doing something right. A powerful Klan needed a powerful Klanwatch to oppose it. And vice versa.

The case that best established both the threat of the Klan and the merit of Klanwatch was undoubtedly *Beulah Mae Donald et al. v. United Klans of America et al.*—"the most important case of my life," Morris Dees has said many times. To summarize: On March 21, 1981, shortly after the late TV news announced that in Mobile, Alabama, a jury of eleven blacks and one white had declared itself unable to reach a verdict in the trial of a black man for killing a white police officer, a black nineteen-year-old technical student named Michael Donald left his Mobile home to buy cigarettes, only to be abducted by two local Klansmen, who, angered by the hung jury, forced him at gunpoint to enter their car, drove to a remote spot, beat him, strangled him with a rope, and slashed his throat, stringing his body from an elm tree near the Klan meeting place when they returned. In spite of the fact that, between the dangling body and the cross burned at the Mobile courthouse that same night, the killing was practically signed "KKK!" Mobile authorities professed to think otherwise and arrested some drug dealers, whom they quickly had to release. After that, they did very little. An initial FBI investigation also got nowhere. In 1982, as a result of continued black protest and the efforts of two black Mobile lawyers, brothers, one a state senator, the other an assistant U.S. attorney, the Justice Department authorized a new FBI investigation and, eventually, a grand jury. In June 1983, one of the two Klansmen—James Llewellyn Knowles, known as Tiger—broke, and the two were indicted on federal civil rights charges. Jurisdiction over the second, non-cooperating defendant—Henry Hays—was returned to the state, and in December 1983, he was tried and convicted for the murder. Tiger Knowles, who had pled guilty to federal charges in return for immunity from the state, went to prison.

To Morris Dees, who had followed the Donald case from the beginning, the linking of the Klan to the murder suggested a new legal opportunity. The Klan lawsuits he had brought so far involved individual remedies for individual wrongs. They did not affect the institution. One could keep suing particular Klansmen for particular crimes forever and the Klan would go marching on. Furthermore, most Klansmen were what is known in the trade as "turnips." You couldn't get blood from them. "Any lawyer could . . . file a civil rights or wrongful death suit against [Knowles and Hays]" for the Donald killing, but it would do no good. It was the Klan itself that had to be stopped. Every time the South seemed about to transcend its past, there was the Klan again, swinging black people from trees. "When the Klan connection [in the Donald case] was finally confirmed . . . I alerted the staff [to] a potential lawsuit," Dees later wrote. "I didn't know whom we would sue or exactly what our theory would be, but that really didn't matter. This was the most gruesome racially motivated murder in twenty years. We'd find something." Almost by instinct, he arrived at the idea that just as a corporation could be held liable for the acts of its agents, a Klan could be held liable for the acts of its members. Staff lawyers argued against him, but he persisted. With the cooperation of Beulah Mae Donald, Michael Donald's mother, an ailing but strong-minded woman who had been unable to make herself sit through the criminal trial but who was now ready to try to find some public meaning in her son's death, in 1984 he filed a civil suit whose main target was not the Klansmen who murdered Michael Donald but the Klan organization to which they belonged.

To judge from accounts both by Morris Dees and by his chief investigator, Bill Stanton, the prosecution of the Donald case was an exhilarating experience. To begin with, the legal territory was largely fresh. To establish that a national Klan based in Tuscaloosa was liable for a lynching in Mobile, the lawyers would have to prove, first, that the murder was not the act of Knowles and Hays alone but reflected a conspiracy within their units; second, that their Mobile "Klaverns" were effectively subordinate to the national Klan organization, the United Klans of America, to which they belonged; and, third, that the UKA had an official policy of using violence to achieve its ends—elements of "agency" law that had rarely been used in a political context. The development of evidence to support these claims also presented novel challenges. While the criminal files readily supported the conspiracy claim, and Klan files initially charmed out of Grand Titan Bennie Hays, Henry Hays's father, by Morris Dees and later subpoenaed, documented a "corporate" relationship, evidence that violence was Klan "policy" required intensive sleuthing. A telling find was a drawing published in the UKA newspaper in 1979 and unearthed by Stanton in the files of the ADL that was particularly useful for the violence-as-policy argument. In the first panel a white man says, "It's terrible the way blacks are being treated! All whites should work to give the blacks what they deserve!" The second shows the head of a black man hanging from a rope, his neck twisted into the same position as Michael Donald's. Even more critical were the depositions of two turned Klansmen who, pried out of the Federal Witness Protection Program by Klanwatch investigator Joe Roy, described firsthand the racist violence in which the UKA had taken the lead from Birmingham, Alabama, in 1963 to Childersburg, Tennessee, in 1979, a history from which the "policy" could be readily deduced. The ultimate in exhilaration was the trial. Greatly aided by the fact that the individual Klansmen were representing themselves and that the lawyer for the UKA so underestimated the case against the Klan as an organization that he literally did not put on a defense, the jury embraced the SPLC's vividly supported analysis of the crime. The individual Klansmen had decided in advance of the trial of the black killer of the white officer that, in the words of Grand Titan Bennie Hays, "if a black

man could get away with killing a white man, a white man should
be able to get away with killing a black man": they conspired. It was
as members of two Mobile Klaverns, which in turn owed allegiance
to the national United Klans of America, that they made their plans:
there was a corporate relationship. And the United Klans of America had long been the most violent Klan in the country: it had a
corporate policy of violence. But the real exhilaration in the Donald
case was not the legal victory, it was the moral victory. When Tiger
Knowles, who had confessed to the killing of Michael Donald, told
the all-white jury:

> I know that people's tried to discredit my testimony. . . . I've lost my
> family. I've got people after me now. Everything I said is true. . . . I
> was acting as a Klansman when I done this. And I hope that people
> learn from my mistakes. . . . I do hope you decide a judgment against
> me and everyone else involved.
>
> [Sobbing and shaking. Directly to Mrs. Donald.] I can't bring your
> son back. God knows if I could trade places with him I would. I can't.
> Whatever it takes—I have nothing. But I will have to do it. And if it
> takes me the rest of my life to pay it, any comfort it will bring, I
> hope it will—

and when Beulah Mae Donald, who had spent the entire trial rock-
ing silently back and forth, looked Tiger in the eyes for the first
time, and said:

> I do forgive you. From the day I found out who you all was, I asked
> God to take care of y'all, and He has—

it was as if not only the Donald killers but the South itself and perhaps all of white America had received her benediction. "There was
not a dry eye on the jury, nor at the bench, nor at the counsel table,
nor in the audience," Morris Dees says when he tells this story, and
by the time he finishes telling it, there is not a dry eye in the audience he is telling it to either. The $7 million verdict was never the

point. "History would show that an all-white Southern jury had held the Klan accountable after all these years," he wrote. That was the point. *Beulah Mae Donald v. UKA* was one of those rare cases where the facts of the killing, the theories of the lawyers, and the characters of the participants come together in an extraordinary pageant in which the demands of heavenly and earthly justice seem satisfied at the same time. It was as much about redemption as it was about politics. The law does not get any better. It was a great case.

It was also great business. Thanks to its many renditions, the Donald trial has become such a staple of American folklore that it feels rude to say so, but the fact is—as the SPLC's critics often point out— that while Beulah Mae Donald received a total of about $52,000, mainly from the much-heralded sale of the UKA headquarters building in Tuscaloosa, the center received nearly $10 million in donations during the period between 1985 and 1987 when the case was the centerpiece of its fund-raising. Clearly the "extremes" strategy worked. How to follow it up was an important decision. By the time the Donald trial was over, the federal government had begun its sedition case against the fourteen national white supremacist leaders who would be tried at Fort Smith, but it had hardly made a sweep of the movement. The most "extreme" of the leaders not caught in the government's net was Tom Metzger. Indeed, he had never been stronger. He was frequently on national television. His cable program, *Race and Reason*, was being shown in about twenty-five cities. His WAR newspaper had a rising circulation. And he was deliberately identifying himself with a new and violent section of the racist movement that was fast supplanting the Klan, the—increasingly neo-Nazi—skinheads. "One of the most openly revolutionary leaders of the white supremacist movement," Klanwatch called him in a special report on the history of violence and racism first published about this time. Yet so far he had eluded prosecution. The failure of the FBI to link him criminally either to the Order or to the alleged Fort Smith seditionists only confirmed what agents observing him for years had often reported: he was deliberately inflammatory, but he stayed within the law. As told in Morris Dees's *Hate on Trial: The Case against America's Most Dangerous Neo-Nazi*, the beginning of the center's case against Tom Metzger was something like this: Shortly after the death of Mulugeta Seraw, Klanwatch investigator Danny Welch brought to Morris's attention newspaper reports mentioning that WAR followers Dave Mazzella and Mike Barrett had been in Portland at the time of the killing and suggested that this might be a chance to get Metzger. Morris was skeptical, countering that since neither Mazzella nor Barrett had been charged with the crime there would probably not be a strong enough connection to hold Metzger liable. Probing further, Welch contacted the Portland Police Bureau, where he reached intelligence officer Larry Siewert, whose work made him familiar with the results of the searches of the skinheads' apartments and who understood just what Welch was looking for. One item in particular came to mind, a piece of paper detective Mike Hefley had found in a shoe box in Ken Mieske and Julie Belec's apartment not long before—the letter from John Metzger introducing Mike Gagnon and Dave Mazzella to East Side White Pride—and Siewert passed it along. In a different telling, credit for alerting the SPLC to John Metzger's letter is given to the research director of the Anti-Defamation League, Irwin Suall, who had heard about it during the criminal proceedings, which would place the origin of the case a little later. Either way, or neither, the letter was critical. Soon would come the plaintiff, the witnesses, more evidence, and all the remaining elements of a case that would rival *Beulah Mae Donald v. UKA* in terms of both the Law Center's reputation and its fortunes, but the letter from Fallbrook to Portland was the key. It was not exactly the boxful of charters, constitutions, and other legal materials that had documented the national UKA–local Klavern relationship in the Donald case. But it was a start.

38

Engedaw Berhanu was a driven man. His grief would not let him be. A few months after his nephew was killed, he had had to go to an Ethiopian wedding in Los Angeles and he sat bitterly on the sidelines, alienated not only from the others' joy but from himself for his inability to share it. He had too much on his mind. Uppermost was his own responsibility. If not for him, Mulugeta would never have come to America. Engedaw was Mulugeta's closest relative. They were "brothers." Now Engedaw was alive with a wife and a child and a job and a house and Mulugeta was dead, dissolving into the earth under a small stone in Portland, Oregon, far from everything he had ever known. He would never see Ethiopia again. Smile his wonderful smile. Serve his sizzling Ethiopian dinners. Race for a soccer goal. Then, too, Engedaw was responsible to the family at home. He was the one who had to explain the incomprehensible fact that Mulugeta was killed by people who didn't know him for no known reason other than that he was black. It was so irrational. There was every family in Ethiopia longing for their sons to leave the country to escape death in the army or on the streets and here was Mulugeta, dead in America. None of it made any sense. In addition to the weight of Engedaw's responsibility there was the sheer importance of Mulugeta's story. However much Mulugeta might seem to outsiders just another INS statistic, to Engedaw he was part of a long chain of hands reaching out across the oceans and continents, pulling people out of the abyss of Ethiopia to a better future in the United States. Just as Engedaw had helped bring Mulugeta, Mulugeta was helping bring one of his sisters, who was to be next to come. Someday he had hoped to bring his son. Mulugeta had such dignity. Promise. His life had to be remembered. Besides what he was suffering inside, Engedaw was also struggling with other Ethiopians. In the chaos immediately following Mulugeta's death, the local Ethiopians had urged the Portland public to send contributions to an Ethiopian community fund for the burial, which had in fact been paid for by the DA's victim's assistance program, and there had never been a proper accounting. To make matters worse, it was unjustly rumored throughout Ethiopian communities up and down the coast that Engedaw was somehow benefiting from the donations himself, gossip that spread back home and made his attempts to communicate with the family even more painful. He also clashed with the Portland Ethiopians about the criminal case. He had followed the proceedings closely, often attending hearings in person; he appreciated the deference shown him as the representative of the family by District Attorney Norm Frink, and he trusted Frink's thinking about the wisdom of plea bargains, but some other Ethiopians did not. Apart from his wife and small daughter, he felt completely alone. Almost as soon as Mulugeta was killed, friends and strangers alike began making sure Engedaw knew that he did not have to remain a mere bystander. In America, there were things you could do. Sue. An idealist, a man of principle, Engedaw Berhanu was not interested in money, but he did want to honor Mulugeta. The world should know his true story. In time Engedaw contacted a California office of the NAACP and began exploring the possibility of a civil lawsuit. It was spring 1989, less than a year after the Donald case. At the suggestion both of the NAACP and of an Ethiopian lawyer friend in Oakland who worked in the same firm as a former United States attorney who was familiar with the SPLC, he also put in a call to Morris Dees. We're already investigating that case, Morris told him immediately. We're interested. A few weeks later, Morris flew to Oakland and sat in Engedaw's lawyer friend's office for hours, listening to Engedaw's life story. A representative of the ADL was with him. It was a long, sweet, sad afternoon. There were many tears. When it was over, Engedaw Berhanu had a lawyer and Morris Dees had a plaintiff.

39

"It's really sad to see 3 go down for 1—it was a fair fight 3-on-3 and the Nigger was weak so he fell!" Dave Mazzella wrote San Francisco skinhead leader Bob Heick from the Salinas jail where he had been extradited on his assault warrant after a few weeks in the Multnomah County jail in Portland. It was January 1989, rumors were traveling throughout the movement that he had snitched on East Side White Pride, and he was trying to head them off. "I'd rather do life in jail than testify against my race," he wrote to one of his ESWP friends about the same time. Scared that his cooperation with the Portland police would lose him his status as a leading skinhead, he fell back on the most easily available psychological and political defense: denial. He blamed the rumors on an informant cellmate he claimed to have had in the Portland Justice Center and on the police themselves. "I sincerely believe they are trying to destroy the movement in Portland and my reputation with the skinheads," he continued. "ZOG will do anything to disorganize a direct threat to their very existence." He even planned to return to Portland after his short Salinas sentence to continue working with the city's skinheads just as if nothing had happened. "When I return I will . . . mold [East Side White Pride] with [POWAR] as 'War-Skins.' I was giving E.S.W.P. the time to find out there group wouldn't work before I turned them into 'War Skins,' now I believe the idea will go well and I think I have the cooperation from both parties!" he wrote Rick Cooper. And he did go back. From mid-February to mid-March 1989, Dave Mazzella was in Portland again, along with Mike Barrett and a few other California skinheads, once again working the territory. He contacted some suburban skins he had met on his previous tour of duty. He helped Rick Cooper put out the latest National Socialist Vanguard *Report*. He hung out with Julie Belec and her newest boyfriend, also named Ken, one of Dave's California friends. But it was a difficult time. Between the outbreak of skinhead violence after Seraw's death that had finally mobilized both the community and the police and the continuing headlines about the court cases, the skinheads did not have the same run of the streets. Personally, too, Dave was on the defensive. With papers beginning to circulate as a result of the discovery process confirming what had previously only been guessed about the extent of Dave's outpourings to the police, his position was increasingly insecure.

In late February, Dave and Mike Barrett were interviewed by KATU-TV's Troy Roberts, a knowledgeable black reporter who had been tracking the white supremacist movement for some time and who was particularly interested in the WAR-sponsored skinhead music festival known as Aryan Woodstock about to take place in Napa, California. The interview could have been titled "In Praise of Metzger." Zeroing in on the fact that Dave and Mike's youth movement seemed to have a lot of adult leadership about it, Roberts goaded them about their domination by the man who appeared to be masterminding it all, but even in the face of his goading, they defended him. The Tom Metzger of the interview was a family man who never egged them on, who lectured them when they went wrong, whose own children were actively involved:

> Roberts: But aren't you his tools? Isn't he taking it over?
> Mike: We all respect him. We don't mind if he did take it over.
> Dave: He's the father of the whole thing.
> Roberts: But Tom hasn't done time—you two have.
> Dave: In jail, we're not forgotten. We're political prisoners. It's for an ideal. We believe in this.
> Roberts: How much are you willing to sacrifice for this movement?
> Dave: I've already sacrificed my education, the army . . .
> Mike: My life.

As it turned out, that was Dave Mazzella's final tribute. About two weeks later, after a skinhead stabbing of a black man in Pioneer Courthouse Square, the skinhead house in which Dave, as well as the stabber, was living was raided by the police, who failed to find them—they were hiding in the basement behind a door concealed by trash bags—but returned the next day with dogs who sniffed them out. Again, Dave spent two weeks in the Justice Center jail in Portland, and again he was extradited to Salinas, this time for

violating parole by allegedly recruiting a young girl for the skinheads. About two weeks after that, the charge was thrown out by
a Salinas judge and he was released. By now it was spring 1989.
Faced with his perennial question—where to go next?—he stayed
for a few weeks with his mother and stepfather in southern Oregon,
where he cashed in some securities to buy himself a car, then headed
down to Southern California to live with his father in Garden
Grove. His loyalties were very uncertain. On the one hand: he
expected to return to Portland to testify for the district attorney in
the not-yet-canceled trial of Ken, Kyle, and Steve and he even gave
a further interview to the local police and FBI about the state of
the skinhead movement in Portland and elsewhere. On the other
hand: he wanted to stay in the movement. The Southern California
skinheads were his friends. He knew word of his cooperation with
the Portland police had now reached well beyond East Side White
Pride throughout the movement at large, undoubtedly even to Tom
himself. Things were tricky. One afternoon around the middle of
May, Dave joined a group of about fifteen to twenty skins partying
near a river when what he had long been fearing finally came down:
he was jumped from behind by a supporter of Tom's named Marty
Cox who had heard the stories. Marty Cox was a tough and intimidating skinhead. An early WAR follower best known as the one
who called Oprah Winfrey a "monkey" on TV, he had also appeared
on two segments of *Race and Reason*, been jailed on a gun charge
following an Aryan Nations Congress, and had otherwise made himself useful to the movement. Along with Tom's bodyguard, Carl
Straight, another Southern California skin, no one was closer to
Tom outside his family. Dave had to think fast, which he did:

> I told Marty, well, I just talked to Tom cuz he was all "You snitch,
> you," and he's all saying "Tom told me you snitched up there." And
> I'm like "No, no, I just talked to Tom a little while ago." I was lying to
> him. Then he stopped. He apologizes. "I'm sorry. I'm sorry." Then he
> wanted me to party with him that night at his house. He said, "Yeah,
> we'll go back to my house and kick back and call Brad [Robarge]

and talk to Tom." "Okay. That sounds good. I'll just get in my car and I'll follow y'all over there, I want to change" and I went home, and went, "Whew, close one!" So it was kinda a messed-up situation.

It was only then, sore in body and soul, that Dave Mazzella truly began to grasp what he had done to himself: destroyed the only life he had ever really enjoyed. No one would ever trust him again. Six months earlier, in his encounter with the Portland police, he had thought mainly of the immediate moment. Now his understanding was larger. Counting his assets, he did not like what he saw. His wife and child were gone. His parents and stepparents were sick of him, and the feeling was mutual. All he had to look forward to was a series of low-paying jobs that he was good at talking himself into but poor at keeping. What he did have was information. Among the first entries in Dave Mazzella's address book, after "Bill Albers," head of the American Knights of the KKK, the "American Klan," and "Aryan Nations," was the listing for the Anti-Defamation League's Orange County office, scribbled down long ago from the WAR hot line, where it was given to inspire harassment, and he thought of it now. He had even driven around the building in Santa Ana a few times, with Brad Robarge, wondering if it was vulnerable to attack. Casting back over his years in the movement, he remembered Clinton Sipes and the favorable press he had gotten when he left the Klan. Greg Withrow and his appearance on *Donahue* after his defection in Sacramento. Tom Martinez, Robert Mathews's betrayer, now touring the country with his *Brotherhood of Murder* about the Order. He, too, could write a book, with his mother doing the typing. There could be life on the other side. Racism was not the issue. The death of Mulugeta Seraw was not the issue. Survival was the issue. What followed was such extraordinary good luck, even for Morris Dees, that it is hard to believe nothing has been left out—and from time to time Dees has said, "We put out 'feelers' " or "We encouraged Dave to come in"—but in early July 1989 Dave picked up the phone, dialed the ADL number, and said to the receptionist something like, "My name is Dave Mazzella, I am trying to get out of the Aryan Youth Movement, I would like to come in and talk." He was transferred to a staff member, who said she would get back to him shortly. She put in a call to Irwin Suall, the ADL research director in New York, who in turn put in a call to the Southern Poverty Law Center in Montgomery. When she called Dave back, she made arrangements to meet him at a Santa Ana motel in a few days. "A friend might be with me," she told him, and one was. The "friend" was Morris Dees.

40

Fall 1989 found Tom Metzger at the top of his form. The world was going his way. Between attacks on immigrants in Germany and France, the rise of Pamyat in Russia, the emergence of WAR or WAR-like movements in South Africa and Australia, white people seemed finally to be waking up. Contemplating the success of *Race and Reason*, the new, improved WAR newspaper, his many prime-time TV appearances, he had every reason to be pleased with his own contributions to the cause, and his latest alliance made the future look even better. While old-fashioned racists stuck on World War II were pushing the skinheads away because of their swastikas and violence, Tom knew a good thing when he saw it. "WAR feels it has set its sights at the correct age level," he enthused in one of his messages. At home, too, life was good. The oldest children were now out of the house, leaving Tom, Kathy, and the two littlest girls, Rebecca and Laurie, a mere household of four, but the family itself was intact, with three of the four oldest actively supporting the movement—Carolyn, whose skinhead husband, Brad Robarge, had lost his job after his appearance on *Oprah*, behind the scenes; Lynn as a leader of the Aryan Women's League; John with WSU-AYM. Even the nonracist, Dorraine, was still in the family fold. On the evening of October 20, Tom was sitting in his basement office expounding his views to a San Diego freelance writer named Jack Carter, who was considering writing his biography, when the telephone rang. Kathy answered from the kitchen, upstairs. "Tom, I think you'd better come up," she called. It was another reporter. "We've got problems," Tom said when he returned. "The uncle of that Ethiopian kid who was killed in Portland has filed a suit against us."

The filing of the SPLC-ADL lawsuit did not exactly make Tom crumple up with fear.* In fact, he was—almost—gratified. Sieg Heiling from the door of the federal courthouse in Seattle during the Order prosecution, cheering on the defendants at Fort Smith, he had loyally played a supporting role in the trials of other white supremacists, but he was never at the center of the action. This time he was the action—something he had always enjoyed. What's more, the press attention could be a boon. Media-wise as always, Morris Dees had filed the lawsuit in federal court in Portland with maximum publicity for the Southern Poverty Law Center—which meant maximum publicity for WAR as well. Faster than Tom received the papers, which were sent by regular mail, there were stories in major newspapers from the *Los Angeles Times* to the *New York Times* and accounts on both local and national TV. His phone was ringing all the time. Even more satisfying to Tom than these immediate advantages was his sense that the case had historic importance. A deliberate propagandist who liked to say he "came as close to the line" between legal and illegal speech as he could without stepping over it—"sometimes I spit over it," he would boast—he knew his First Amendment. Furthermore, he did not see himself in the complaint. WAR was not an "organization . . . [seeking] to achieve the goal of a white supremacist revolution through the use of violence and intimidation against black citizens and others who disagree with [its] racist aims." It was not even an "organization." He did not send "agents" to Portland to "organize and guide East Side White Pride . . . to pursue white supremacist goals by violent means." He did not even have agents. He

---

*The ADL was the SPLC's official partner in the lawsuit and had a lawyer in attendance at the trial but played very little role in the case.

had never met the two members of East Side White Pride—Ken Mieske and Kyle Brewster—whom the SPLC had named as codefendants in the lawsuit.* Nor, prior to the killing, had he ever heard of Mulugeta Seraw. If this was a "conspiracy," he was not a member of it but its victim. As Tom understood the lawsuit, the issue was purely and simply free speech. Whatever WAR literature the skinheads might have seen was protected by the Constitution. By the same logic that Morris Dees could sue Tom Metzger for the death of Mulugeta Seraw, anyone could sue anyone for anything—rap bands for the rampages of their fans, gun magazines for the violence of their readers, even churches for the bombing of abortion clinics by their believers. Just recently a case he had followed in which *Soldier of Fortune* was successfully sued for publishing a help wanted ad for a hit man had been overturned on appeal. Whatever might be his views in some distant Aryan future, for now he believed in the Bill of Rights. Tom was not only politically but also personally offended. He was not a common criminal, he was a political radical, and the same was true for John, who was also named in the lawsuit. However ugly might be such racist antics as John's "I get so tired of Uncle Tom here sucking up, trying to be a white man" to Roy Innis on the famous nose-breaking, record-breaking *Geraldo* that brought in so many troops, they were still First Amendment business as usual. The SPLC was actually belittling them. "If we were to desire the death of Ethiopians, I would not settle for one, I would incinerate the entire Ethiopian population in their native squalor and turn the land to Aryan production," Tom thundered in one of his messages. The case was nothing more than the latest sob story of the "Southern Millionaires' Law Center," which, he learned, had filed the court papers and mailed its first fund-raising appeal based on the case almost simultaneously. If it fell to him to expose all this, fine. Not long after he learned of the lawsuit, I talked with Tom Metzger by phone for the first time and I found him in good spirits. "I look at the courtroom as just another

---

*Hoping to secure Steve Strasser's cooperation, Morris Dees had omitted him from the lawsuit but Strasser's cooperation never materialized.

battlefield," he told me. "Whether you're in the foxhole or the court-room, it's the same fight. I relish it—almost."

But relishing a legal battle was one thing: dealing with it would be something else. From the outset it was clear that the SPLC was not going to make things simple. In fact, pretrial courtesies routinely extended a conventional opponent were ignored here. Not only did the SPLC neglect to inform the defendants about the case before calling the press, but in November, about a month after the suit was ceremoniously filed in federal court, it was withdrawn and the case reentered in state court in Oregon, leaving Tom and John, who had just begun to prepare their responses in the federal system, off balance. With the law so specialized and a plaintiff who clearly knew exactly how to use it, most defendants would immediately move to arrange good representation for themselves, but for the Metzgers finding a lawyer was not a straightforward matter. The ACLU, approached by Tom through its Southern California chap-ter, which referred him to Portland, turned them down. The nation-ally known private civil liberties lawyers who might have been inclined to take on such a potentially significant case pro bono tended to be either leftists or Jews or both, and Tom and John did not bother to pursue them. The few ordinary lawyers they contacted who were willing to consider the case at all mentioned starting fees ranging from $25,000 to $100,000—sums not only beyond their personal means but beyond anything the movement was likely to be able to raise. They had a problem. But maybe it was an oppor-tunity. From Socrates onward, public "show trials" had provided revolutionaries of all kinds with their greatest political forums. Why sit back and be silent while some spineless nonentity from a third-rate law school mangled your politics and ideas? A movement law-yer named Kirk Lyons, in Texas, was willing to provide background advice. A few others across the country made it known that they would be available by phone and fax. Tom and John had law books. Computers. Brains. Energy. Guts. They even had senses of humor. What more did they need? Not lightly but with a great deal more "relish" than their opponents probably imagined, the father-and-son team of Metzger & Metzger decided to represent themselves. If they went down, at least they would go down in style.

In the same conversation where Tom Metzger told me he was ready to take on the lawsuit, he also told me the following story. Not long before—mid-December 1989—he had received a call from a man who introduced himself as a reporter for the *San Francisco Chronicle* planning to write a "fair" exploration of his racial views. The caller was particularly genial. Not only would he pay for the interview, he invited Tom to join him at a Fallbrook restaurant for dinner and suggested he bring John and Kathy along. At the dinner Tom remarked that the *Chronicle* had never heard of him. "I said the *Examiner*," replied his host, reaching into his briefcase for some of his previous articles, only to straighten up with a practiced flourish: "Mr. Metzger, you have been served!" When he left, an entourage of four or five other men—presumably bodyguards—left with him. This furtive service of the Oregon court papers on a man who had lived at the same address for twenty-two years and was as much a part of the Fallbrook landscape as any of the other local businessmen he in so many ways resembled was beyond Tom's comprehension. While most lawyers would consider it routine, to Tom it was a sneak attack. His overreaction to a move that was essentially standard made an apt beginning for a lawsuit that was "civil" in only a technical sense. The more he felt enmeshed in a series of procedural maneuvers acceptable to the law but contrary to common sense, the more extreme—at times hysterical—became his response. This effect was not accidental. "When we filed this lawsuit, we had a choice between state and federal court," Morris Dees told the *National Law Journal* when the case was over. "We chose state court because Oregon discovery rules are quite different than the federal rules. You can do trial by ambush in Oregon. You have no interrogatories, no production of evidence; you don't have to give the other side your documents." Oregon lawyers would argue against

both this interpretation of the state's discovery rules and the attri-
bution of the legal outcome to the forum rather than to Tom Metzger's home-style lawyering, but they would not argue with the
military metaphor. "Outwit" is what you do to an opponent.
"Ambush" is what you do to an enemy.

The enmity between the Southern Poverty Law Center and WAR
did not start with the lawsuit. Just as Klanwatch had been monitoring
Tom's message lines for several years, Tom had watched them back.
A 1988 WAR editorial titled "Poverty Is Where the Money Is"
attacked Klan and Klanwatch alike—the Klan for being such an easy
target, Klanwatch for taking advantage of it. But the case brought the
hostility to a new level. For both sides, the stakes involved were high.
For Tom, win or lose, much as the case was a political tribute, it was
also a private trouble that could result in the loss of his house and
everything else he owned. For the SPLC, having brought the suit with
such fanfare, it stood to lose not only face but financial contributions
if it failed. Worse, a loss would leave WAR and the racial movement
in a stronger position than before. Underlying the practical stakes
were personal feelings. For much of Morris Dees's career as a civil
rights lawyer, his opponents had been practically his neighbors.
Whether he was suing the Montgomery establishment or the KKK,
the people on the other side were people with whom he had worked,
played, or prayed his entire life, and if they had not been able to
change with the times, as he had, that was something he understood.
Even when he brought cases elsewhere in the South, beyond Montgomery, the casts of characters remained pretty much the same. Tom
Metzger was far from being a Southern homeboy. The shared joke,
the hand on the shoulder, the appeal to God, the invitation to Rolling
Hills Ranch—all tactics that had greatly improved Morris's win/loss
record—would never work. In fact, they seemed to have the opposite
effect: increasing contempt. For one thing, Tom was not only a cynic,
he was now an atheist. For another, such were his politics that he was
not merely against blacks, Jews, or Vietnamese, like most of Morris's
other adversaries, he was against rich WASPs like Morris Dees. And

his insidiousness! Tom did not personally create the violent Order, whose hit list had played a major role in invading Morris's—as well as his family's and his associates'—peace of mind, but he had certainly promoted it. Then there was Tom's political seduction of children. According to the analysis that underlay the lawsuit, Tom's leadership was what gave the skinhead movement its energy. The man was practically snatching rootless, fatherless children off the streets and turning them into Nazis overnight. He was evil. The revulsion Morris Dees felt for Tom Metzger was also shared by his colleagues. For SPLC legal director Richard Cohen, a liberal Southerner previously associated with Alabama civil rights lawyer Chuck Morgan and an exceptional theoretician who countered all of the Metzgers' briefs as thoroughly as if he expected to be arguing them in the Supreme Court: for Danny Welch and Joe Roy, the investigators, former Montgomery police officers committed to the work of the SPLC to the point of sometimes risking their lives to carry it out: for the staff members behind the scenes who worked indefatigably to provide the public figures with the research and other support they needed at every point: this was why they had joined the SPLC in the first place. The same was true of the two attorneys from outside the SPLC who completed the legal team. Elden Rosenthal, a Portland trial lawyer who had agreed to help Morris develop the case even before it was filed, was the son of a rabbi who had fled Europe shortly before the Holocaust. Of rabbinical cast himself, he seemed to carry the entire burden of Jewish history on his shoulders. James McElroy, a trial lawyer who had made himself available in San Diego, was in part a product of the 1960s, a Midwestern Irishman and longtime admirer of the SPLC whose opposition to racism and other forms of political reaction was deep and instinctive. He was appalled by the Metzgers. With so much moral energy behind it, the loathing that seeped through all of the SPLC pronouncements on the case was heartfelt. As for Tom, his loathing was real as well. How a Southern white boy like Morris Dees could make his living selling out his race was incomprehensible to him. Tom's limited imagination fed by his anticapitalist ideology, he could fathom no other motive than personal gain. The lies, the exaggerations, the heart-stopping photographs in the center's incessant mailings merely proved Dees's corruption. Nor was this corruption only political. Tom's Klan associates in Alabama had long since distributed divorce papers filed by Morris's second wife detailing sexual behavior that Tom found unsettling. From the fortress of his twenty-six-year-old marriage and six children—which he often mentioned—he lost no chance to attack Morris's personal life. There was also an antisemitic angle. It was one thing to be saddled at birth with the dreadful curse of that "Seligman" as a middle name, but now the man was literally courting the damn Jews, marrying a Jewish wife (his fourth), occasionally attending synagogue, and even flaunting the offending name on some of his fervid mailings—particularly the ones to Jewish zip codes. In the WAR newspaper and on his message line, Tom regularly referred to Morris as "Morris Sleaze Dees." The air was so thick with vilification on both sides that as the pretrial period progressed, the case pulsed not only with political but also with religious overtones. It seemed the ultimate stake would not be a monetary award: it would be eternal salvation or damnation.

The extent to which the two sides reviled each other in the abstract was soon matched by the extent to which they reviled each other in person. The more they saw of each other, the more they found to condemn. However adversarial, the pretrial period customarily elicits a certain amount of cooperation between opposing counsel. There are depositions to be scheduled, documents to be exchanged, the basic framework for the smooth disposition of any particular litigation to be argued out. Here there was mainly obstruction. When the SPLC team arrived in San Diego in January 1990 for Tom's and John's depositions, they found not only that John had filed a federal bankruptcy notice that day which would temporarily stay any lawsuits pending against him but that Tom intended to take the Fifth. A thick deposition consisting of little but "I refuse to answer on the grounds that it may tend to incriminate me" was all they had to show for their journey. What's more, the Metzgers used the deposition to have their hefty lieutenant, Wyatt Kaldenberg, serve notice on Dees that they in turn had charged him in a San Diego court with "malicious prosecution"—one grandstanding service evidently thought to deserve another. Now the Alabama team would not only have to come back to California to begin to develop the information they needed to try the case, but they would have to fight further legal battles as well. Unless they succeeded in getting the Metzgers' lawsuit dismissed, they, too, would be subject to deposition. Items such as phone records to which the SPLC was routinely entitled in its attempt to prove an "agency relationship" were similarly produced only after more than usual legal evasion, leaving considerable frustration among all involved. Tom, too, was frustrated, albeit the evasions he was facing were more subtle. On critical pretrial issues involving his right to see the evidence on which the case against him would be based—that is, "discovery"—his memoranda were so vaguely drawn that the SPLC team was able to withhold information he was legally entitled to without technically violating the rules. Just as the plaintiff, at trial, would have to link Tom and John Metzger to Dave Mazzella, Dave Mazzella to Ken Mieske and Kyle Brewster, and Ken Mieske and Kyle Brewster to Mulugeta Seraw, the defendants would have to unlink them, and without pretrial knowledge of what the evidence of the links was going to be, it would be practically impossible for Tom to dismantle them. He did no investigations on his own. In addition to his failure to obtain essential evidence, many of Tom's other legal gambits were also ineffective. He did win some minor arguments. His protest that the "agents" whom he was alleged to have sent to Portland had not been identified in the suit led to an amendment to the original complaint specifically naming Dave Mazzella, Mike Barrett, and Mike Gagnon, a disclosure that the SPLC had hoped not to make. Tom was also allowed to introduce into the pretrial record the fact that Morris Dees had been accused by a witness of suborning perjury in a Klan trial in the South, something else the SPLC would have preferred to omit. But most of Tom's efforts, from his several attempts to introduce the SPLC's and ADL's fund-raising practices, in order to establish their allegedly improper financial interest in bringing the lawsuit, to an attempt to judgment-proof his house by transferring title to his wife, went nowhere. Motions that required virtual mastery of a foreign tongue on the part of Tom and John before they could reach the court in the first place were circumvented or dismissed in an instant, strengthening Tom's belief that there was indeed a conspiracy and that it was specifically aimed at him. Neither before nor during the trial was the defense nonexistent but it was minimal. The legal truism that a case is won or lost on the basis of pretrial preparation seemed to elude him. Meanwhile, the demonization continued. So explicitly did Morris Dees represent himself as a prince of light battling a "prince of darkness" that he freely used words like *devil* and *monster* to describe Tom and the other defendants—for example, telling the lawyer for the *Seattle Times*, whom he successfully persuaded to bend the newspaper's usual First Amendment principle of withholding its reporters' notes from court proceedings, that the case was one of Good versus Evil. So primed was Tom Metzger for the propaganda benefit that his cup of bile practically overflowed. "In a desperate, grandstand, money-making move, the 'Anti-Defecation League' and their sweetheart, Morris 'I wish I wuz a Jew' Dees, of the Southern Poverty Law Center, have fallen into WAR's clutches," he sneered on the WAR hot line. "Dees, an alleged confidence man and sexual pervert, 'oh, nooooo,' have milked millions from the gullible. While talking about poverty, Dees, branch office of the Jew ADL, does almost nothing to alleviate poverty except to alleviate their own poverty." The WAR paper was full of the same. With headlines featuring WAR's countersuit ("WAR SUES FOR $10 MIL."), blaming the SPLC for an unsolved attack on the Metzgers' house with a high-speed arrow ("Assasination Attempt Fizzles—Southern Poverty Law Center supporters fail"), and screaming, "This Case Is Bullshit!" in one way or another at every opportunity, it was plain that the lawsuit made great copy. If Morris Dees needed any more evidence to persuade his supporters that the Metzgers were indeed "extreme," their reaction to the lawsuit more than supplied it. The catch was that, while the Metzgers were building their political case, the SPLC was preparing a legal one.

41

"Jeez, what have I done?" Dave Mazzella told me he thought to himself when he arrived at the Santa Ana motel on July 12, 1989, and saw—along with the woman from the ADL, whom he would never see again—Morris Dees. The man was public enemy number one! It was at his hands that some of the men Dave most admired in the racist movement, particularly North Carolina Patriot Party leader Glenn Miller, had met their downfalls. Now he was after Tom Metzger and he wanted Dave to help. Dave was floored. It was one thing to offer up tidbits to the ADL, which was all he intended, but this was betrayal! He had nothing against Tom and John Metzger, who had always treated him warmly. He liked them. A knife in his pocket, Dave knew he could, in a single move, kill Morris Dees, protect Tom Metzger, redeem his disgrace in Portland, and take his place alongside Robert Mathews and the other members of the Order as a hero of the white race—or he could listen. He listened. That curly-headed, crooked-smiled, ungrammatical preacher he had hated at a distance was oddly comforting in person. At the end of a long talk during which, after hearing Dave's life story, Morris shared some of his own experiences, his hopes for the trial, and the information that the Seraw killing was also the subject of a quietly ongoing investigation by the Civil Rights Division of the Justice Department, which just might take a favorable view of Dave's participation in the civil suit, Dave agreed to cooperate. The knife stayed in his pocket. The next day he signed a statement saying exactly what Morris wanted to prove: that "the three Skinheads who killed Mr. Seraw were pumped up on Tom Metzger's racist material," that Dave himself "was the prime motivator of the violence that led to Mr. Seraw's death," and that "I do not believe they would have been so violent if I had not come to Portland, organized them for Tom Metzger, and indoctrinated them with Metzger's philosophy." The role he would play in the trial itself was left unspecified. "Dave, you renewed my faith in people," Morris wrote him on his return to Montgomery immediately after their meeting. "Just when I think a new fad like Skinheads is threatening to cause serious and long term harm to innocent people, someone like you surfaces to let me know things will work out in the end." But "faith" was not exactly the word. Far too shrewd a reader of character in general and the character of potential witnesses in particular to be nearly as softheaded as he sounded, Morris grounded his faith in works, enfolding Dave in the net of a real relationship, writing him often, performing small services, such as helping him retrieve some personal belongings from Portland, hinting at the possibility of a book or movie based on his life. In October 1989, Morris brought Dave to Montgomery for a visit, introduced him to his family and staff, took him cotton picking and alligator hunting, and used the occasion of the forthcoming unveiling of the center's haunting new memorial to people killed in the struggle for civil rights to photograph him with his own daughter under the granite-carved words of the Prophet Amos, "Until Justice Rolls Down Like Waters and Righteousness Like a Mighty Stream," hoping Dave would get the message, which he seemed to do. Then Morris filed the lawsuit.

In November 1989, Dave moved from his father's house in Southern California to his mother's house in southern Oregon. "I've talked to a few ex-comrades [in California] what a joke," Dave wrote to Morris shortly before leaving. "Though I believe I've led a few of them to believe I'm still involved. My stupidity!" But whatever "involvements" he may have kept in California were nothing to those he developed in Oregon. He had barely settled in when he resumed the role of skinhead organizer, flashing his newspaper clippings, boasting about his toughness, hinting about his closeness to the Metzgers. Soon there was an SOS—Southern Oregon Skins—

complete with bomber jackets and patches, challenging and domi-
nating a previously existing local group known as the South Medford
Aryan Skinheads, or SMASH. What's more, he was dreaming about
an Order-style paramilitary organization. Unlike the gentle Rogue
Valley town of Ashland, home to one of the finest Shakespeare
festivals in the United States, where Dave's mother and stepfather
lived, nearby Medford, where he hung out, was the down-home
commercial center of the surrounding farm- and lumber-producing
areas, the kind of place where there are so many rifles strung across
the rear windows of pickups you would think they were an option
at the dealers. Even so, Dave's arsenal was outstanding. He had—
he told me—two AK-47s, machine guns, semiautomatics, and hand-
guns, including a $900 Baretta. His stepfather says that Dave and
the "kids he was running with had more firepower than the cops."
His behavior, too, was conspicuous. In February 1990, he was
busted for illegal weapons possession. He also threw a Jewish boy
he believed had stolen a hunting knife from his family's home into
freezing Emigrant Lake in the Siskiyou Mountains and drove away—
an incident Dave's mother believed had risked the boy's death. In
March he assaulted a fifteen-year-old, breaking the boy's jaw.
Besides these events—the ones that resulted in actual charges—
there were the ones the police didn't know about. Most nights he
would gather with his followers and try to set an example, driving
by the houses of black people, shouting epithets, stirring up trouble
outside a teen hangout, beating up kids who questioned his leadership. "Police in Southern Oregon . . . have recorded an increase in
Skinhead violence since Mazzella moved to Jackson County," the
Oregonian later reported. "When he came here, things started happening," said a Medford officer. There was action all the time. If
anything, the politics-to-violence ratio that characterized his activities favored violence even more than it had before. His mother and
stepfather were at a loss. They knew he was in touch with Morris
Dees and they knew he was in trouble in Medford, and they did
not know what to think. Dave was confused himself. "Once a skinhead, always a skinhead. There's no turning back," he told his new

friend Laura Dailey; but he also told her if Morris Dees contacted her "not to let Dees find out he was a skin." He had told Dees he wasn't, Dave confided, "but he wanted us to know it was just an act," Laura wrote later. It was the same double game he had been playing since he first talked with Tom Nelson and Mike Hefley in Portland, only now someone was actually watching him.

Minding Dave Mazzella became the SPLC's most delicate pretrial business. This half-skinhead, half-penitent centaur was their central witness. Clearly his conversion was not very deep. How much of his doings became known could be decisive at trial. What's more, Dave could have killed someone—or could be dead himself—by the time the trial started and be unacceptable or unavailable when he was needed. He had a knack for making enemies. There were no guarantees. Like directors lining up understudies for their leading roles, the SPLC auditioned a number of possible backups to Dave in case their star was unable to perform, but there were problems with all of them. Mike Barrett had been in Portland less than a week before the killing and was an inarticulate felon who would not make a good impression on a jury. Steve Strasser, insufficiently grateful for not having been named along with Ken and Kyle in the lawsuit, had now persuaded even himself that he was totally innocent of Seraw's death and refused to participate voluntarily lest he be further branded a snitch by his fellow inmates when he returned to prison. Stanley Hawkins, a San Diego police volunteer who had successfully infiltrated WAR in 1988–89, was ready but irrelevant—he had no connection whatever with the events in Portland. Greg Withrow, whom the SPLC located in Sacramento and housed in Portland during the trial, was also willing but unappealing. "Hold it, I have to go stir my soup," he interrupted a phone conversation with Morris Dees, who was later enlightened by Klanwatch's Danny Welch that he was probably talking about fixing drugs. No, the part had been written for Dave Mazzella. Only he could tie Tom Metzger to East Side White Pride to the death of Mulugeta Seraw. The

SPLC would have to try to keep him out of sight, both for his own good and theirs. The trial was set for October 8, 1990. Every time they learned Dave was in trouble, Danny Welch or Joe Roy or sometimes Morris himself would fly to Oregon, remind Dave of his higher calling, explain to local officials the importance of his participation in the civil suit, and try to smooth out his record a little bit. Once they helped him enroll in a truck driver school in Eugene just to get him out of town. Dave was always grateful and always apologetic—but there was always another incident.

Given Dave's unreliability, the question most debated by the lawyers was whether or not they should take his deposition. For: it would preserve his testimony so it could be read in court even if the witness himself could not be present. Against: it would be handing the Metzgers the script of the trial. If the Metzgers knew how he would testify, they could prepare their defense. The nos had it. Hoping "out of sight" would lead to "out of mind," the SPLC had already been using every device it could to make the Metzgers believe that Mike Barrett rather than Dave Mazzella was their prize informant, prominently attaching an affidavit from Mike elicited by Danny Welch after Mike's release from prison in February 1990, rather than Dave's statement to Morris in July 1989, to their successful defense against Tom's motion for dismissal at the start of the case. Now, June 1990, the SPLC scheduled depositions in Los Angeles for both Mike Barrett and Dave Mazzella, hoping to give Tom the idea that was where they were, then canceled them at the last minute, hoping to give him the impression the two had somehow got away. Tom seems to have been overwhelmed. His senses told him that something was happening in the Mazzella department but he did not follow it up. There was nothing to stop Tom from deposing Dave himself, and since he knew where both Dave's parents lived, he should have been able to find him, but with the indifference to investigation that characterized all his pretrial activities except for his own investigations of Morris Dees, he did not pursue him. In spite of being aware that Dave had already talked with the Portland police, Tom let himself believe that Barrett or the misleadingly unnamed Strasser would be in the witness chair.

When, only a month before the trial, he finally sent Dave a letter—which Dave turned over unanswered to the SPLC—his tone was casual. "Will you willingly make a statement, if I visit you?" he inquired mildly. He was worried but passive. The testimony of Dave Mazzella would be both the strongest and the weakest part of the SPLC's case against Tom Metzger, and he had missed his chance to "discover" it. As for the witness, whether or not he had given a deposition, he had still gotten a trip to California. "I had a really good time talking with you in L.A.," Dave wrote to Morris after the cancellation. "I've messed up so much since I moved up here. . . . I really want to clean up my act. I've hung out with the wrong crowd, and I've stepped on a lot of people, and worst of all, I've hurt my family and embarrassed them by my actions. . . . Besides my mother, you are the first person who didn't turn their back on me when I skrewed up, and I really mean that. You've given me a lot of inspiration and hope."

The first week in August 1990 was a hot time in the skinhead scene in Medford. Outside Night Lights, the teen club, Dave picked up three citations on Thursday night, all connected with recruiting—one for furnishing alcohol to minors, one for disorderly conduct, and one for trespass. Then, on Saturday, Dave and his friends in SOS were "jumping in" a white supremacist teenager named Anthony Bounds, when Dave went out of control. According to one of the members who participated, Leif Barge:

> We left [Bounds's] house drinking to Emigrant Lake in Ashland to the cemetery were more drinking went on. Than everyone got in a circle & Dave punched [him] in the jaw. Everyone jumped in. When Anthony hit the ground [it] went on for about 1 minute which seemed hours. Then I told every one to stop & Dave said "Don't stop until I say so" so it went on for about another minute. Then we stopped, but Dave kept kicking on him in the face until he was content.

"Dave threatened to shank [knife] us all if we didn't partake in the incident," a second SOS member later reported. "[He] kicked Anthony repeatedly in the head, face, and stomach. He shattered Anthony's jaw bone," said a third. Two days later Bounds pressed charges against Dave, and Dave alone. The others had all pulled back.

By now Dave's legal record was thick. There was the February weapons charge. There was jaw number one, in March. Bounds's was jaw number two. With the concurrence of the SPLC—Morris and Danny Welch had flown to Medford when they got the word— a judge revoked bail on the first jaw and set bond at $25,000 on the second, requiring that Dave come up with $2,500 bail, which they knew he would not be able to do. His mother, who had supplied the earlier bail money, this time refused. The consensus was that both Dave and the SPLC would be better off if he were in jail, an opinion with which the culprit seemed to agree. "All he had to do [was] eat, sleep, follow a few simple orders, and play cards all day," his stepfather told me. "[He had his] smokes and [his] candy bars and . . . [he] didn't have to do anything. He thought that was great." One thing he did do was resume his prison pastime of writing letters. "This stay here will at least give me the chance to get my priorities together. I really hope I'll be a better person when I get out of here," he wrote to Morris. "I've signed up for church services and the A.A. program and I'm averaging two books a day! . . . When am I going to be sent to Portland for the trial? I am still very gung-ho in helping!" "I've been recruiting a lot of people in here. I've got quite a following here in North Dorm. I've been giving out the P.O. Box to other inmates," he wrote to his lieutenant, Leif Barge, telling him to "MAKE THINGS HAPPEN" while he, Dave, was in prison. "Shit don't happen by itself," he added. In other letters he referred to what Morris was going to do for him when he got out, not concealing the fact of his impending testimony but giving it a self-interested twist. "Morris is so cool. He is probably gonna have all the charges on me thrown out. He is so fucking rich & he has all kinds of influential friends in the government and law agencies!" he told his friend Laura Dailey. "[Dave] also said that Seraw deserved to die," Laura herself wrote later.

42

October 5–13, 1990, was Dignity and Diversity Week by order of the Portland City Council. On Wednesday, October 3, the community was invited to the King Neighborhood Facility in Northeast Portland to pick up its rainbow-colored ribbons and bumper stickers. Two days later would begin daily events sponsored by organizations from the governmental Metropolitan Human Rights Commission to the grassroots Coalition for Human Dignity, ranging from a salmon bake to raise funds for Native American causes to a "Coming Out" program on the local community radio station. The call to honor diversity went beyond the week and beyond the city. Mayor Bud Clark named October Justice, Harmony, and Equity Month for Portland, while Governor Neil Goldschmidt gave the same designation to the last three months of the year. "Portland has been called the hate-crime capital of the world; we want to show there is another side to us," said the head of Oregon Ecumenical Ministries, which had developed the idea, at a ceremony attended by leading business and government representatives, another of the events of the week. With skinhead activity continuing its rise, with Portland still seen by skinheads all across the country as a center of action, it was important to authorities that the city become known as the place not only where the skinhead movement had come together but where it had been stopped. The centerpiece of Dignity and Diversity Week was a march and rally scheduled for Sunday, October 7, the day before the opening of the trial. The demonstrators would start in Laurelhurst Park, near Mulugeta Seraw's apartment, move past the corner where he was killed, travel down one of the city's main streets, Burnside, across the Willamette River, and end in the Park Blocks downtown. It was an extremely tense prospect. For weeks Tom Metzger had been using his message lines to urge his followers to come to Portland for "the greatest show trial since the Chicago Seven tore up Chicago." "The biggest fight will be in the streets," he threatened. At the same time, prominent citizens, among them the mayor, several city commissioners, and numerous other city, state, and federal officials, including District Attorney Norm Frink, who had prosecuted the skinheads, were expected to join the throngs. The police had no idea what would happen. To Loren Christensen of the Gang Enforcement Team, who was monitoring everything he could, it seemed possible that busloads of skinheads from Idaho or Seattle would indeed materialize to claim Portland as "the Aryan capital of the Northwest," just as Tom was demanding. Early on, the Police Bureau and the city's politicians had decided together that whatever the costs, whatever the dangers, the security of everything connected with the trial of Tom Metzger would have to be guaranteed. If there was trouble, Portland's reputation would never recover. That included the demonstration. Though the counterdemonstrators turned out to be few in number, at the event there were so many police flanking the marchers that at times it looked as much as if the police were themselves demonstrating as that the police were the demonstrators' guardians. Everything was just as the city wanted. That bad Californian who had sent his forces northward to corrupt our Oregon children had to be unequivocally repudiated. "METZGER'S RACISM GOES ON TRIAL," proclaimed an *Oregonian* headline the day of the march. This time Portland would not be judged. It would be the judge.

THE TRIAL OF TOM METZGER

E. L.: Isn't a lawyer like a writer? A playwright? You more or less write the script in advance?

M. D.: I could have put on five or six different "plays" about the Metzger case. Had that many in various stages of preparation. Then I went over it with [my colleagues], and one was chosen.

—MORRIS DEES, in conversation, Portland, 1991

43

The trial of Tom Metzger has got to be one of the stranger proceedings in American legal history. It takes place in the Multnomah County Courthouse in downtown Portland, opposite a park where militants gather daily, most loudly a mixed lot of black-booted, bomber-jacketed, tattoo-covered skinheads, most of them racist but some from an antiracist faction whose tattoos say something else. The mood is frightening. A bombing at the San Diego federal courthouse a few weeks earlier by a man claiming to be a WAR supporter is on everybody's mind. Outside, the courthouse is ringed by riot police. Helicopters circle overhead. Dark-uniformed sharpshooters with high-powered rifles loom from nearby roofs. Inside, K-9s scour the corridors. Spectators' bodies and bags are searched at repeated checkpoints, press included. Defendants, lawyers, judge, and, later, jury are brought to the fifth floor by a secure elevator usually used for keeping prisoners out of sight. In the courtroom itself, officers flank the far wall, rising instantly from their seats at any hint of disturbance and at every break. The windows are covered with butcher paper to discourage snipers. Everyone is afraid of everyone else. Once, an officer I have talked with often sees me reaching across the space separating the onlookers from the lawyers to try to ask someone a question and he bounds in front of me to shield them, his stare so cold it practically freezes me to the spot. Alone at the counsel table farthest from the jury sit Tom Metzger and John Metzger in business suits, their bodies bulking under bulletproof vests. Their codefendants, Ken Mieske and Kyle Brewster, have been brought to Portland from state prisons and housed in the county jail across the street but have not been brought to the courtroom. Ken testifies in the plaintiff's case as a hostile witness but otherwise he and Kyle are invisible in this trial. Behind the Metzgers sits their own security, straight from the pages of the WAR newspaper— Wyatt Kaldenberg, "Baxter the Pagan," Carl Straight—large, scowling, formidable-looking strongmen, as tense as the police. Portland's Rick Cooper and a handful of other neo-Nazi supporters are also usually with them. At the plaintiff's table are Morris Dees, somehow simultaneously casual and intense, Portland counsel Elden Rosenthal, who never smiles, and Engedaw Berhanu, looking exhausted and sad. In the small courtroom, Engedaw is literally an arm's length from the Metzgers. SPLC staff lawyer Richard Cohen, San Diego counsel Jim McElroy, Morris Dees's coauthor Steve Fiffer, other staff members, an ADL lawyer, and a jury consultant are also present but sit among the spectators, lest the size of the team be held against it. At the bench, by a turn of the judicial wheel that is not entirely random, is one of the circuit's two black judges, the Honorable Ancer L. Haggerty, an Oregonian born in Vanport to

World War II shipyard workers a few years before the flood, a thickly built former University of Oregon football player and highly decorated Vietnam War marine officer whose academic credentials, including Hastings Law School, are as solid as his physical ones. Like all other judges, he would prefer both parties to be represented by counsel, which would make his role simpler, but he treats Tom's lawyering, as he does Tom's racism, with professional aplomb. He is the calmest person in the courtroom. As he tries to steer this dangerous confrontation into conformance with the law, sitting back, chin on hand, to ponder the technicalities or leaning forward, over his desk, to explain, admonish, or rule, his stoic patience conveys the unmistakable signal: "I have heard all this before." It is Wednesday, October 10, 1990. The jury has been seated after a candid voir dire that provides its first introduction to the themes of this trial—a black and a Jew have been excused—and it has also heard opening speeches, Morris's a dramatic preview of the evidence he will use to link Tom Metzger to the death of Mulugeta Seraw, Tom's a defiant political autobiography, John's a vague attempt to explain the experiences that led him to his racial views. The jurors, with alternates, are ten men, one a Hawaiian, and four women, one a Japanese American, the rest white, and they are fearful. Following the speeches they ask for and receive a private meeting with the judge at which he reviews the procedures worked out between the police and the court for the jury's safety. The TV cameras televising the trial for local cable will never show the jurors' faces. Their addresses will be kept secret. They will meet in the mornings at a point several miles outside town and be bused to the courthouse. Their phone numbers have been coded into the 911 system to guarantee an instantaneous response from the police if they should need it. The police at the schools attended by the jurors' children will also be wired in. Alongside the special precautions come the standard injunctions. The jurors are not to blame either of the parties to the lawsuit for these conditions. They must ignore any information or impressions they may have gathered independently before the trial or may acquire during it. They must not even pay too much attention to the lawyers. Repeatedly, they are told by Judge Haggerty to decide the case only on the evidence they are about to hear in court. How they are to do that he doesn't say.

44

A juror who had hoped at the outset that the trial might center on such abstract questions as the distribution of civil liability for a criminal act between a person who could be shown to have commissioned it and a person who carried it out would have been brought down to earth with a thud at the opening of the plaintiff's case—the thud of bats. With the bat that killed Mulugeta Seraw existing only in photographs of its charred remains on the Columbia River beach where it had been burned by Kenneth Mieske and Patty Copp, the play begins with its proxies: four "bats" from the apartment of Kyle Brewster—technically one bat, one thick tree branch, and two clubs—and four more from the skinhead apartment housing Steve Strasser, Mike Barrett, and Dave Mazzella, the last four truly bats, with the initials of East Side White Pride carved into the sides. As the bats are identified by the detectives who found them, they are propped up against the table used by the court clerk and the court reporter, directly in the sight line of the jury, the gun in the first act we know has to go off by the third. The bats carry the meaning of the plaintiff's case. By the time Morris Dees says, in closing, "The bat that hit Mulugeta Seraw in the head started in Fallbrook, California," everyone in the courtroom will understand its trajectory.

The complaint under which *Berhanu v. Metzger* is heard goes like this. Ken Mieske and Kyle Brewster = "the Oregon defendants." Tom Metzger, John Metzger, and WAR = "the California defendants." WAR, as we have seen = "an organization [that] seeks to achieve the goal of a white supremacist revolution through the use of violence and intimidation against black citizens and others who disagree with

[its] racist aims." The White Student Union–Aryan Youth Movement = the "youth recruitment arm" of WAR. According to the narrative contained in Count 1, "intentional acts," in October 1988 the California defendants "established communications" with East Side White Pride "to recruit [it] into the WAR movement as a violent action agency of WAR." In addition to John Metzger's direct contact with Kenneth Mieske, "the California defendants [also] sent their agents Dave Mazzella, Mike Gagnon and Michael Barrett to Portland for the purpose of encouraging and rendering substantial assistance to East Side White Pride so that East Side White Pride would pursue white supremacist goals through violent means." This included the provision of "materials [that] indoctrinate[d ESWP] with white supremacist goals, incited violence [and] specifically encourag[ed] skinheads and the Oregon defendants in particular to use baseball bats and steel-toed boots as weapons against blacks and Jews." On November 12, 1988, Dave Mazzella and Mike Barrett attended a "regularly scheduled organizational meeting" of East Side White Pride, where "in accordance with the directions of the California defendants [they] encouraged members of ESWP to commit violent acts against blacks in order to promote white supremacy." Early the next morning, November 13, Ken Mieske and Kyle Brewster "spotted Mulugeta Seraw standing outside an automobile talking to two black companions. Encouraged and incited by the California defendants the Oregon defendants conspired to inflict serious bodily harm upon Seraw and his companions because of their race. In furtherance of their conspiracy . . . [they] intentionally and savagely struck and kicked Seraw and his companions, using their fists, a baseball bat, steel-toed boots, and other weapons. The actions of the Oregon defendants were taken against Seraw with racial animus, and with the encouragement and substantial assistance of the California defendants. As a direct result of the actions of the defendants . . . Seraw endured great mental and physical conscious pain and suffering and died." Count 2, "reckless acts," adds that, "in encouraging the Oregon defendants to commit acts of violence against black persons, when the California defendants knew or reasonably should have known

that the Oregon defendants were immature and prone to violence,"
and "in selecting agents" who they also "knew or should have known
were violence prone racists and white supremacists who had themselves committed crimes of violence and were likely to encourage the
Oregon defendants to commit such crimes," the California defendants were grossly negligent and reckless. Count 3, "negligence acts,"
is identical to Count II but claims negligence alone in the California
defendants' encouragement of East Side White Pride and their selection of agents, rather than recklessness and negligence both. The
fourth and final count is "racial intimidation."

More accessible than the legal claims are the over 150 pieces of
skillfully selected evidence. The letter from John Metzger to East
Side White Pride introducing Dave Mazzella and Mike Gagnon.
Phone records of numerous calls between Dave in Portland and Tom
and John in Fallbrook, including one immediately after Dave's arrival at Ken and Julie's apartment and another the day after the death
of Mulugeta Seraw. WAR newspapers and fliers with their merciless
racist contents. The AYM paper brought to Portland by Dave and
distributed downtown. Transcripts of WAR message lines indicating
that Tom had an interest in Portland both before and after the killing. Photographs and videos connecting Tom to violence. Inflammatory comments by John. The bats from the Portland skinheads'
apartments. An enlargement of Kyle's anti-immigrant poem, "Keep
Out." A drawing of a black man with a bullet entering his head
allegedly drawn at the final ESWP meeting minutes before Mulugeta
Seraw was killed. Photos of the Ethiopians' smashed car. Autopsy
photos. And more. But the evidence by itself is inconclusive. To do
its work of supporting the SPLC's case against Tom Metzger, it must
be shown to be part of a real chain of characters and events leading
to the death of Mulugeta Seraw, a story that can be told only
through the witnesses. *The Trial of Tom Metzger, by Morris Dees,"*
starring Dave Mazzella, is a moral drama in which the necessities of
law give rise to an understanding of history markedly different from

the one the reader has been following throughout this book. But it is a compelling narrative.

45

The leading role is played by the killer and Ken Mieske is well cast in the part:

M. D.: Mr. Mieske, do you have an alias that you go by?
K. M.: Yes, I do.
M. D.: Would you please tell the jury what that is?
K. M.: Ken Death.

In truth, he looks like a killer. With his bearlike walk and shoulder-length hair, his body thickened by prison workouts, Ken scares even the police, who fear he is about to explode. The Metzger people call him "Conan the Barbarian." Ken Mieske feels he is being screwed. The fight at Southeast Thirty-first and Pine has been misrepresented from the beginning. The twenty-year minimum sentence recommended by the DA, the Justice Department, and the judge in return for his "racial motivation" plea has been disregarded by the State Parole Board, which has upped it to thirty. The plea has become the basis for a sensational case against Tom Metzger in which he himself is only a pawn. Now he is trapped in a courtroom where he knows that nothing he says will be believed. Other than being deposed by Morris Dees at the Oregon State Correctional Institution six months earlier—a deposition at which his lawyer was Tom Metzger—Ken Mieske has had no preparation for this trial. He has little sense of the protocol of the courtroom, what is or is not in his interest, how the rules of a trial trump ordinary give and take. Nor can he always follow the proceedings. Asked concretely, "Did you do X?" he can answer clearly enough if he chooses, but asked abstractly, "On such and such a date did you tell me that on such and such a date you did X?" he gets confused, as if he is unable to hold two time frames in his mind at once. In a matter that requires different tenses it is hard to differentiate when he might be deliberately lying from when he is merely lost. He forgets the point. When Morris Dees shows him photos of the damage he did to the Ethiopians' car with the bat immediately before he killed Mulugeta Seraw and neglects to mention a dent on the rear bumper, Ken interrupts with a rude "Aren't you going to show this? I did that, too," as if an important item has been left off his C.V. He is his own worst adversary. Ken Mieske knows he is being used to get Tom Metzger, but he does not understand the nuances. His alternations of insolence and ingenuousness make him the perfect "hostile witness" for Morris Dees.

M. D.: I show you [the letter from John Metzger to East Side White Pride] and ask you if prior to my showing [it] to you at your deposition, had you seen this letter before?

K. M.: I vaguely remember seeing it from the past. I was getting a lot of mail between now and then. Actually this is a letter I told you my girlfriend set aside when I was on the road with the band.

M. D.: Did you tell me when I took your deposition that you had never read [it] before?

K. M.: Yes, I did.

M. D.: Is that the truth today or do you want to change your testimony?

K. M.: Well, now that I have thought about it, I did see it. You can't expect me to remember every letter I read.

M. D.: Yes.

K. M.: Between here and 1988—sir.

M. D.: I'm going to read you [another question from the deposition]: "When was the first time you talked to Tom Metzger?" What did you say?

K. M.: "Oh, when I got arrested for this incident here."

M. D.: That was, in other words, November the twentieth?

K. M.: I'd like that cleared up.

M. D.: Sir?

K. M.: I do recall talking to him that first day Mazzella got into town.

M. D.: Oh. I see. So your memory has cleared up? Is that what you are telling me?

K. M.: Basically, yeah. Sometimes stuff comes back to you. Things come and go. You can't remember every little sentence.

M. D.: Well, that was a pretty important telephone call that you got there. You were talking to the national director of the White Aryan Resistance, weren't you?

K. M.: So?

M. D.: Sir?

K. M.: Yeah. Big deal.

M. D.: And in fact he was in that deposition room with you at the time, wasn't he?

K. M.: In the what?

M. D.: Wasn't he sitting at the Correctional Institution in the deposition?

K. M.: Oh, yeah.

M. D.: He was sitting there.

K. M.: Yeah. You're right. I thought you were talking about this phone call.

M. D.: Did Dave Mazzella come to East Side White Pride meetings for the purpose of educating [its] members about WAR?

K. M.: I recall he only joined in one meeting.

M. D.: He only came to one meeting?

K. M.: Yeah. He stood outside all the other ones.

M. D.: Was this the meeting that took place on the day Seraw was killed?

K. M.: Yeah, I believe so.

M. D.: And you're telling this jury that he never came to any other East Side White Pride meeting or organized a meeting himself for East Side White Pride members to come to before that?

K. M.: No, he didn't, and he didn't organize nothing either, to make that clear for the record.

M. D.: I want to read you [another question from the deposition]. "How many times did you attend meetings of East Side White Pride when Mazzella and Barrett were present?" What was your answer then?

K. M.: Looks like I garbled up my words on my answer. I said, "Once before that, we—before we got together, and that afternoon on the twelfth."

M. D.: You said once before we got together, and then that afternoon on the twelfth, didn't you?

K. M.: Right. And I just got done saying he probably attended one or two meetings.

M. D.: Well, let me ask you this. During those two times that you acknowledge that he came to your meeting, did he ever talk to the group or discuss anything about WAR?

K. M.: He just told about a couple of marches he was in.

M. D.: What else did he tell you?

K. M.: I don't recall. It sure wasn't what you're trying to accuse.

M. D.: Look at ["Operation Warlords," a 1987 issue of the AYM newspaper.] You see a heading called "Clash and Bash"?

K. M.: Yeah, I see it.

M. D.: Would you read it to the jury please?

K. M.: I object. I don't feel I should have to read this. Why don't you read it, if you would? I'm not going to read it. [The court informs Mieske that he is required to read from the document, which is in evidence.] Yeah, but I deny to read it. Throw me in jail. I don't care. I'm not going to read it. I'm not that good a reader in the first place.

M. D.: [Morris reads instead.] "White students and youths who are fans of both heavy metal and punk rock music are experiencing a phenomena across the nation. It's called Bashing, a sport in which hunting parties of white youth seek out non-white individuals and break their bones, while others, white youths, go out and confront government officials in several ways."

Isn't it a fact that Dave Mazzella told your group [about]

"Clash and Bash" and passed those [papers] around and the members read them?

K. M.: I don't believe he did.

M. D.: You're not sure?

K. M.: Either that or I wasn't present.

M. D.: You wasn't present. But you just got through telling the jury how you don't think he did. Is that right?

K. M.: Like I said, if he did, I wasn't there.

M. D.: But when I took your deposition I asked you, "Well, he never said a word?" And what was your answer?

K. M.: "Oh, I'm sure he did, but I don't recall."

M. D.: All right. Now you're telling the jury you don't believe you read this?

K. M.: Yeah. I told you I had read [the cartoon in another issue] and that was all I read.

M. D.: My question was, now you're telling the jury you don't believe Mr. Mazzella ever taught ["Clash and Bash"] to East Side White Pride members?

K. M.: Like I told you, if he did, I wasn't there. I don't recall.

M. D.: But I thought for some reason you told the jury just now you didn't think he did?

K. M.: Well, I'll just say, before you twist the words up again, that if he did say it, I don't recall.

M. D.: You don't recall.

K. M.: And if he did say it, I wasn't there.

Since no matter how Ken responds either to the exhibits or to Morris's leading questions it is Morris's insinuations rather than Ken's disavowals that are going to be believed, he is in effect authenticating the chain of evidence even while denying it. The more he tries to explain, the more it seems that he is lying, even when he is telling the truth.

But the role assigned to Ken Mieske in this trial is more than to corroborate evidence: it is to personify evil. Seeing Ken's anger during his deposition, and wanting to make sure the jurors see it too, Morris has decided, as he will later write, to "push [Ken's] buttons." This is not very hard. As Morris pushes and Ken pushes back, an aura of evil indeed permeates the courtroom. But it is deliberately being exaggerated. Ken Mieske did not set out to kill Mulugeta Seraw and he did not kill Seraw because Tom Metzger sent Dave Mazzella to Portland to tell him to do so. The greater the gap between what Ken feels in his heart is true and what the jury is led to believe, the greater his rage— thus the better his performance. Ken Mieske is hardly repentant. He is still a white supremacist. After the killing, as we have seen, he embraced the mantle of "Hero to the White Race" that had been assigned to him and wrote many triumphant letters to other white supremacists, with which Morris confronts him now. But while he has not changed his views, he has told several people that he was "out of line" in using the bat during the fight and that he "majorly over-reacted" when Seraw was down, a phrase he now repeats on the stand. In fact, the memory of the killing is so uncomfortable for him he resists reliving it in the trial. "Do we have to go over this?" Ken questions Judge Haggerty when Morris begins recapitulating the events on the street. "I don't really feel like talking about the murder, if that's what he's trying to get at. I mean, it's done, and I don't feel like discussing the murder scene." The judge tells him he must testify.

> M. D.: Before you got [into the car], when you [were] out on the sidewalk, didn't you look up there and didn't Kyle Brewster say, "There's some black people up there?" In fact, he said, "Niggers," and he said, "Let's go F or mess over them"?
>
> K. M.: No, he didn't.
>
> M. D.: Well, you have read Heidi Martinson's statement to the police [where] she said he said that, didn't you?
>
> K. M.: Yeah, but she wasn't telling the truth.
>
> M. D.: Slow down. Slow down. She was lying. Is that right?
>
> K. M.: She was lying. Yeah.

M. D.: And Steve Strasser gave a statement to the police that said the same thing, didn't he?

K. M.: Yeah. Probably words [got] put in their mouths during the interviews. I would like to bring this to record. Each of those witnesses gave two or three statements and each statement was different. The first statements were almost correctly what happened. And then after the police told them they thought they were lying and [were] going to charge them with murder, they changed their story. That's what happened.

M. D.: Is that what you think?

K. M.: That's what I know.

"You pled guilty to the murder of Mr. Seraw, didn't you?" Morris asks, finally getting to his point. "Yeah," says Ken. "I did."

M. D.: And did you say to that judge, in open court, in this building, that you killed Mulugeta Seraw because of his race?

K. M.: Yeah. That was part of a plea bargain. They told me that if I didn't say that part that they wouldn't accept my plea.

M. D.: So, you're saying the judge was part of forcing you into an illegal plea?

K. M.: I'm not saying that. I'm just saying the whole situation, you know, all the pressure.

M. D.: Are you saying your lawyer sold you out?

K. M.: I'm not saying he sold me out. I'm just saying we're talking about the directions I was getting from federal prosecutors. I didn't want to say that I killed Seraw because of his race, but that was part of the plea.

M. D.: So, you're telling us that you was lying to the judge when you stood up and said you killed Seraw because of the racial reasons?

K. M.: Yeah.

M. D.: Well, how are we to believe what you're saying now?

K. M.: It's up to you whether to believe my statements or not.

M. D.: The reason you said you killed him for racial reasons was because when you looked up and saw him standing on the side of the street you all said, "There's a nigger. Let's go get him." That's the reason you made that plea, isn't it?

K. M.: I think you should take that back.

But in a trial there is no "back." The rampaging "Batman"—a name by which Dave Mazzella alone claims Ken has been known since the killing—has played his part. The climax of his testimony comes at its close when Morris produces the song, "Senseless Violence," that has been clinging to Ken since the killing and asks him to read it aloud. "No, I'm not going to read it! This has nothing to do with the case!" Ken responds. "May I read it to the jury?" Morris asks Judge Haggerty. "You may." Suddenly it is November 13, 1988, all over again and we are back at the darkened corner of Southeast Thirty-first and Pine.

Victims all around me
I feel nothing but hate
Bashing their brains in
Is my only trade.

Senseless violence is the only thing I know
Piles of corpses never ending watch them grow
Kill my victims for pleasure and for fun.
Beat them over the head. Shoot them with my gun.

"This song [was] written by a band after a horror movie called *The Hidden*," Ken protests. "[It] takes after a movie."

M. D.: It does?
K. M.: Yeah, it does.
M. D.: And that's in your handwriting?
K. M.: That's my handwriting.
M. D.: And that was found in your room?
K. M.: Huh?
M. D.: And that was found in your room?
K. M.: Are you trying to say I wrote this song?

M. D.: I don't know. This is in your handwriting?

K. M.: It's in my handwriting. I just copied it down.

M. D.: No further questions.

"Whoa! Whoa! Whoa! What are you trying to say here?" Ken cries out. But what the court reporter hears, and what she writes, is, "Woe! Woe! Woe!"

In case anyone has missed the point that Kenneth Mieske is a liar and a killer, the next two witnesses, whom the SPLC has subpoenaed, quickly underscore it—his girlfriend, Julie Belec, by contradicting him on points such as whether he had another address during the time he was sharing her basement apartment, whether he had read John Metzger's letter, and whether the posters on the walls were his, hers, or theirs, Steve Strasser's girlfriend, Heidi Martinson, by reiterating her statement to the Portland police that the skinheads had seen black people up the street before they drove up there and had deliberately confronted them, thus confirming a murderous intent.

Dave Mazzella is in an awkward position. Talking to the ADL is one thing. Testifying at a trial is something else. Things have happened much faster than he expected. One moment he is meeting Morris Dees, who at the time thinks it may take years to bring the case to trial. The next he is in a courtroom facing his old mentor and his new one simultaneously. What's more, his life lately has not been exactly exemplary. Morris knows about Dave's assaults in Medford but he does not know the extent of Dave's leadership of the Southern Oregon Skinheads. Together they have arrived at the common understanding that, lacking a real source of stability in his new life in Ashland, Dave has occasionally lapsed into his old skinhead ways, but the full story could well sabotage the trial if it becomes known. Behind the scenes, Dave's legal status and the

SPLC are intertwined. Thanks to an arrangement with Jackson County officials who admire the SPLC and respect Dave's willingness to testify, he has been held in the Medford jail for jaw number two without being charged, so he will not appear in the Portland court as a felon. A large bond okayed by the same officials has secured his temporary release. He is now being housed, along with his new girlfriend, Ruth Moran, in a suburban Portland motel where they are enjoying as-much-as-you-want sex, pizza, and videotapes under the genial protection of a young center intern who even occasionally takes them on outings. "It was a little fantasy. We were like Donald and Ivana Trump. Ya know, your own butler-type guy," Dave tells me later. Compared with their previous diet of jail visits and letters, it is especially blissful. "The best time we ever had," Ruth chimes in. The only downside is having to testify. Visiting Dave on the eve of his testimony, Morris finds him anxious and, anxious himself, revises his planned strategy of a slow drawing out of Dave's story in favor of a rapid opening that will establish the legal basics in case the witness falls apart, but Morris need not have worried. "I believe that where the body goes, the head follows," WSU-AYM founder Greg Withrow observes when I later ask whether he thinks there was any real change of conviction on Dave's part when he began cooperating with the SPLC. For the moment the body is in the courtroom.

M. D.: In November 1988, Dave, when Mr. Seraw was killed, were you the vice president of WAR's youth division?

D. M.: Yes, I was.

M. D.: In that capacity, did Tom and John Metzger instruct you to teach skinhead recruits to commit violent acts against blacks and Jews and other minorities?

D. M.: Yes, he did.

M. D.: Did these instructions include the commission of physical violence?

D. M.: Yes, they did.

M. D.: Were you sent to Portland by Tom and John Metzger in

October 1988 to organize East Side White Pride and to work with a group called POWAR?

D. M.: Yes, I was.

M. D.: Now, David, while you were in Portland, did you teach and direct East Side White Pride members to commit violent acts against blacks and other minorities in the Portland area?

D. M.: Yes, I did. Several times, as a matter of fact.

So much for the essentials of "agency" law. Dave was an officer of an organization with an official policy of violence officially carrying out his duties in Portland when the death of Mulugeta Seraw occurred. Now on to the central subject of Dave Mazzella's testimony, which is Dave Mazzella. It is a moving story. How as a young teenager "alienated from everything and anybody" he turned to Metzger and WAR as to a second family, entering a "dehumanizing" world where "people didn't matter," "nothing looked real," blacks and Asians looked "like bugs you could step on," and entering it so fully he was willing to die for his beliefs. How he sent his "second father" "report cards," news accounts of acts of racial intimidation and violence like the San Jose "nigger toll" incident, and was "patted on the back" by being moved up in the organization. How in his capacity as vice president of the WSU-AYM, a branch of WAR controlled by Tom, he was told in a phone conversation between Fallbrook and Salinas in September 1988 to go to Portland to recruit skinheads.

M. D.: When you found East Side White Pride, was it really a tight-knit group?

D. M.: When I first saw them I was really depressed. A lot of them were into drugs, a few of them was smoking crack, heavy drinking problems. A lot of them used dope. They were unorganized. They didn't have no direction.

In short order, he whips them into shape. The very night he arrives he takes a large group of skinheads to a park on the edge of town, where, demonstrating Tom Metzger's strategy of provoking people until they attack you so you can claim self-defense, he says, "Hey, there's a nigger, I'm going to get him!" and a fight starts, with Ken Mieske and others jumping in. "Still hyped up," the skinheads stop at another park, where Dave finds another example and "I'm all, 'Hey, you're not white!' He's all, 'Yeah I am.' And I'm all, 'Get in the light!' So I took this guy over to the trail and I'm all 'What's your name?' And he's all 'Ramiro' and I'm all 'Ramiro what?' And he said 'Ramiro Cruz.' And I'm all, 'Liar! Why don't you get down on your knees and kiss my boot?' So he got down on his hands and knees and I kicked him." When he was not teaching violence directly, Dave was preaching it indirectly, using the WAR news-papers and fliers he had brought up with him from California as his texts. The morning of the day Mulugeta Seraw died he had met with East Side White Pride, passing around the very issue of the WSU-AYM newspaper, "Operation Warlords," from which "Clash and Bash" as well as many other of the SPLC's trial exhibits are drawn. Later that night, back at Nick Heise's after the newspaper-distribution expedition downtown, he continued his instruction. Leaving the corner of Southeast Thirty-first and Pine minutes before the fight, he had returned to his apartment to sleep, only to be disturbed by Steve Strasser bursting in with his graphic accounting. Dave knew what he had to do next. With "the heat coming on" and "the articles in the *Oregonian* getting bigger and bigger," he called Tom Metzger, advised the members of ESWP how to handle them-selves, and tried to hold the line, but in the Portland police station he weakened, "caught between doing the right thing and still trying to belong to the organization." Afterward, too, he tried to retain his place, writing the letters that denied he had snitched and describing plans for the future. It was only later, after the close call with Marty Cox in California, that he realized "I didn't feel right about every-thing I have done in my life, I did a lot of bad things, a lot of evil things, and I wanted to come clean so I called the Anti-Defamation League," setting in motion the events that put him on the witness stand today. Except for an "occasional beer here, there" when prob-lems with his parents or being laid off work have led him to seek comfort in his old ways, he has had little contact with racist skin-heads in the Medford area because "I've had my full of organizations. I don't want to be part of anything anymore."

M. D.: Several months ago did you get arrested for an assault in Medford?

D. M.: It was just a little something over a girl. We just got in a little fist fight and that was that.

M. D.: Right now, you're serving a ninety-day sentence for that, are you not?

D. M.: Yes, I'm in jail.

M. D.: How much of that time have you served?

D. M.: I have about another week left.

M. D.: Now I believe you have also been indicted for another fist fight. Have you had any hearing on that?

D. M.: Yeah. There was someone who had a taped statement from someone who personally did the assault, and I wasn't even involved. We've already had someone confess to that.

M. D.: There's already a taped confession for that by somebody else who did it?

D. M.: Yeah.

M. D.: You're not guilty of that? You didn't assault the person? Is that what you're saying?

D. M.: Yeah. That's what I'm saying.

He has not been promised monetary or any other reward for his testimony at this trial. He has not been offered leniency by the authorities in Medford. Other than expenses, he has not been given money or anything else of value since he has been in Portland. He is doing what he is doing voluntarily. "I've grown fond of him. He's a good boy," Morris will tell the jury in closing.

And not only a "good boy": a good witness. It is an aspect of his helpful personality. I noticed this side of Dave myself when we talked at length three years after the trial. Once we had formed a relationship, he was a faithful resource, authorizing an FOIA request, sending me tapes and photographs, helping me locate Mike Barrett, generally keeping in touch. Sometimes he was ahead of me, calling my attention to the availability of a certain person or document before I even realized I might need it. That is also his style in the courtroom. He does more than what is required. Often he describes his acts in the very language of the lawsuit. When he refers to "Clash and Bash" he remembers to add, "which is a skinhead sport," a phrase straight from the "Operation Warlords" exhibit. He talks about "random incidents" of violence, ditto. Questioned by Tom about exactly how Tom and WAR had taught him to be violent, he replies that he "was spurred on" by Tom's material, making one of the precise legal points the SPLC must prove to win its case. His blends of fact and fiction are seamless. If anything, Dave is stronger on cross-examination than on direct, explaining to Tom, who professes not to understand it, how his propaganda method works. While Tom is missing the point with a *Clue*-like interrogation into where in his Fallbrook household Dave's indoctrination took place—"Did I teach you to kill people and hurt people in my living room?" the family room? the kitchen?—Dave responds with a patient "You didn't put up a poster and say, 'Shoot.' You're more subtle than that," a case he makes with considerable subtlety himself. An example of Dave's knack for knowing what is needed is the evolution of his testimony about the drawing of a black man with a bullet going through his head and the caption "Nigger Get OUT!!!" which is now in evidence. Introduced by Morris as representative of the violent material Dave solicited from skinheads to send to Tom for publication—Dave says it was drawn by Nick Heise—the drawing grows in importance under cross when Dave adds that it was drawn at the party at Nick's at Southeast Thirty-first and Pine minutes before Mulugeta Seraw was killed, and grows again on redirect when he adds further that it was drawn with himself, Nick, Steve Strasser, Kyle Brewster, and Ken Mieske all sitting around a coffee table. For the case that Dave Mazzella, acting as an agent of WAR, encouraged the violence that led to the death of Mulugeta Seraw, the drawing of the black man with the bullet through his head cannot be beat. Like the lynching cartoon in the Klan case, which it closely resembles, it played a significant role in Morris's summation and with the jury. The problem with this drawing is its uncertain provenance. It happens that I met Nick Heise in 1992 shortly after the drawing was featured in a Bill Moyers PBS special about the case called "Hate on Trial," and the first thing Nick said to me—indeed, the reason he wanted to talk—was, "I didn't do that lame drawing!" It is true that what was involved, among other things, was professional pride, but it is also true that his artwork, which we looked through together, bears no resemblance to the style of the drawing. When I asked Dave why Nick—an artist— would have drawn in his—Dave's—notebook, he said that because Nick did not have any paper he had run down the stairs to his van and brought it back. When I told Morris that Nick denied drawing the picture, he snapped, "Nick's a liar!" and when I told Dave the same thing, Dave claimed that if he ever saw Nick again he could persuade him that he had in fact done it and had merely forgotten, which may very well be true—he *is* persuasive. The convenient drawing is not the only deus ex machina in Dave's testimony about the end of that evening. From police reports and my own conversations, it is clear that Ken Mieske was not sitting around the table at Nick and Desiree's right before the fight with Mulugeta Seraw. Ken was driving around town with his longhaired friends looking for Julie and, reaching Nick's moments before Desiree had returned and thrown the skinheads out, he never got in the door. The representation of the skinheads as having a political meeting focused on the drawing with Ken present just before their encounter with the Ethiopians is Dave's and Dave's alone. This is not to say that Morris Dees or anyone associated with the SPLC may have misattributed a drawing, overcoached a witness, or even suborned perjury: it is to say that they wouldn't have had to. Dave Mazzella is smart. The usefulness of the drawing in a case whose parallels to the Donald case he understood very well would not have escaped him. If anything, he overdoes it. He is so smooth he almost embarrasses his keepers. During a break while Dave is on the stand I ask SPLC investigator Danny Welch what they expect people to make of him. Danny raises his eyebrows, shrugs, and replies, "This guy is good!" Other observers are more skeptical. A Portland police officer working security finds Dave's performance too "practiced." A prosecutor from another city attending the trial sees everything that follows from what he always refers to as Dave's "quote 'going to the ADL' unquote" as informant boilerplate. When the local newspaper *Willamette Week* headlines an article about his testimony "Can This Man Be Believed?" it captures the buzz of the courtroom. Dave Mazzella is not fundamentally wrong. Much of what he says Tom Metzger told him Tom Metzger undoubtedly said, and much of what he says Tom Metzger deliberately left unsaid Tom Metzger undoubtedly meant. But Dave knows exactly what he is doing in this trial. "If I had me a sales manager like Dave Mazzella I would give him a raise," Morris says in his closing. That is just what he has. At one point Dave uses the word *pitch* to describe his different approaches to different skinheads. At another, supporting his testimony that Tom speaks more violently in private than in public, Dave explains, "If you're like a salesman [and] you're selling a product, if it has a defect, you're not going to say, 'Well, you know, this has some problems with it.' You're going to give them a line to sell what you're selling." The wisdom of the shop also works in the courtroom. Dave Mazzella is still a salesman. He is just handling a different line.

John Metzger is hard to take seriously. In spite of his good looks, his calm manner, his earnest attempt to appear to be respectful to the court, with every answer he becomes a less, not more, believable figure. The principal reason is what he is actually saying, most of which makes no sense. It is John's lot to have contributed more than his share of material to this lawsuit. While nominally John and Tom are separate defendants, the evidence against them is the same.

Not only is John the author of plaintiff's Exhibit 1—the letter to East Side White Pride mailed to Ken Death—but in various interviews he has left a trail of loose statements the SPLC is using to track the death of Mulugeta Seraw back to WAR. A few months before the killing, John told a *New York Times* reporter that, having worked with skinheads for two years, "I pat myself on the back a little bit for organizing them. We have been able to influence them and fine-tune their perceptions." A few weeks afterward, he replied to an interviewer's question about skinheads' right to fight back if attacked with "Not only every right, every obligation. . . . We are like Viking beserkers. . . . If someone attacks you, go for it. Go for gusto. Destroy them. . . . Poke their eyeballs out. Beat the hell out of them. Who cares what you have to do. . . . I would rather be tried by twelve than carried by six." At the same time he told a *Seattle Times* reporter that "skinheads these days are deadlier than the skinheads of just two years ago. They're more disciplined." According to the reporter, who, following negotiations between the *Times*'s lawyers and the SPLC, had given a videotaped deposition that was shown to the jury, John had also said that if asked he would send another agent, like Dave Mazzella, to Seattle to repeat the success in Portland, words that did not appear in quotation in the article and that John now denies but that further weaken his case. Trying to explain himself on the witness stand, John says that by his reference to influencing skinheads he meant "keeping them out of trouble," by "deadlier" he meant "more effective in combatting a lot of the problems they were seeing in their community," by "Viking beserker" he meant "someone who's not going to take it anymore. They are just tired of being attacked." His definitions of key phrases from the AYM "Operation Warlords" issue are equally idiosyncratic. In the line "We feel the most important project in America today is to create a new wave of predatory leaders among youth," "predatory leaders" = "They should go out there and instead of taking other people's thoughts they should create their own. They should install telephone lines or their own newspapers. They shouldn't just sit there." In the sentence "We shall continue to encourage sporadic incidents to rebuild the hunter-killer instinct in our youth," "sporadic incidents" = "They should get organized and get things going on their own level," and "hunter-killer" = "White students have been pushed around so often that we were trying to get them to be a little gutsy and a lot of times you have to say stuff like that to get them encouraged." There is so much of this circumlocution that when Morris Dees says in his closing, "John Metzger gives new meaning to the word mealy-mouthed," you can practically see the jurors nod in agreement.

But John's problem is not so much legal as it is personal. In individual conversation he seems very much the proverbial boy next door, but in the courtroom he is disturbing. He is speaking out from inside such a self-contained system that his basic assumptions cannot be understood. That he is so "normal" he slips a reference to his two years as a baseball All-Star into a series of questions about skinheads and bats somehow only makes it worse. His dense answers to such factual questions as when he succeeded Greg Withrow as head of WSU-AYM and which of them was responsible for which issues of the AYM paper sound less like the qualifications of the scrupulous historian he is making himself out to be than the hallucinations of a certifiable nut. His frequent appeals to the Constitution suggest a reading of that document far from what our forefathers intended. From his opening statement that there is "nothing wrong" with his having joined the Klan Youth Corps at age eight or nine to his final statement, immediately following a powerful closing by Morris, that he "almost felt like laughing through the whole thing," he seems to be living on a different moral planet. John is not the only citizen of this planet to appear as a witness. Ken Mieske, asked by Morris Dees where he learned the term ZOG, replies, "I've known about ZOG since I was a little kid." Rick Cooper, a minor witness, also decries ZOG, how the reach of the "international Jewish bankers" extends even to Portland. "I'm very, very angry about it. Sometimes I wonder how long I can go without breaking," he tells Morris Dees. But it is John's strangeness, and no one else's, that really matters. Dull and flat in his direct examination by Morris Dees, John wakes up, comes alive, in his back-and-forth with his father on cross, which is unsettling in itself. The real Exhibit 1 in this trial is not the letter, it is John Metzger. Not only has this apple not fallen far from the tree: it has not even fallen. After the trial, when Tom's mother wrote him from Indiana criticizing him for what he had done to John's life, John reassured him. "I'm in it as much as you," John told me he told his father.

Tom Metzger, the next major witness, has a conflict of interest. As the lawyer in a major lawsuit he ought to have anticipated the evidence against his clients and prepared them to refute it, but as the defendant in the political trial he believes this to be Tom does not want to refute the evidence: he wants to claim it. Every time the SPLC puts in an exhibit that would bring an ordinary lawyer to his feet, Tom lets it in. The result is like a documentary history of WAR. From its vast files the SPLC staff has selected what seems to be every speech, phone message, editorial, photograph, or videotape from Tom's recent political history that has any suggestion of violence and pieced them together into a kind of Aryan *This Is Your Life* spectacular, with Tom as star. In Tom's view, there is nothing to be ashamed of. Reading from a yellow legal pad during a self-cross-examination conducted from the witness box, he asks, "Mr. Metzger, are your primary weapons ideas?" and replies, "Yes. That's all I have ever used. . . . changing people's minds and putting ideas in their heads through . . . television, newspapers, telephone machines, fax machines, any legal means," as if the form would protect him from the content. Somewhere in the mind of every American radical is the image of a heroic leader whose avowal of his convictions in the face of personal disadvantage will impress or even move the masses and who is willing to be martyred in the cause and Tom Metzger shares this ideal. Against this challenge not only to his own rights but to the rights of all Americans, he will stand fast.

The essence of the SPLC case against Tom Metzger is that he deliberately cultivates violence. Here he is intimating to members of a Tulsa skinhead band at the 1988 Aryan Fest that they should "kick ass." Here he is in the Arizona desert with an all-age passel of racists known as the Arizona White Battalion, shooting an AK-47. Here he is at his own trailer, Mathews Hall, holding a handgun and a copy of the Constitution, declaiming, "A piece of paper won't save you, but this [pistol] can." Here he is selling U.S. military manuals on explosives and demolition in his WAR classifieds. Here is an editorial evoking Hitler's Beer Hall Putsch. Here are inflammatory racist and anti-immigrant cartoons. Other accusations are designed to establish that the violence is part of a business operation. Here is Tom, for instance, as a petty capitalist, sneakily intermingling his "WAR" and "Fallbrook TV" checking accounts, using nickels and dimes donated to WAR by impoverished skinheads for personal expenditures such as—of all things—a hairpiece. As far as Tom is concerned, these items do not give a true picture. For years he has had the same vision of a movement of disenfranchised white workers across the left-right spectrum defending itself against the repressions of the sinister alliance of business and state he calls the Iron Heel, and if the latest disenfranchised whites happen to be a little younger and more violent than the ones he originally had in mind and have to be approached accordingly, who can blame them? Nor has he ever cared about money. It has never been the point. Feeling that he is not being fully described, Tom tries to remedy the problem by going through a huge pile of WAR newspapers that show WAR as having a radical political and economic agenda much broader than Morris Dees is trying to prove, but since he has gone through the same papers while cross-examining Dave, by now the jury is mainly bored. Missing, too, from Tom's response is the understanding that, although most of the words Morris is using against him are indeed constitutionally protected, as he believes, that protection will get him nowhere in this "agency" trial. Here, for instance, is a volley between Morris and Tom about the speech at the 1988 Oklahoma Aryan Fest, in which Tom had asked his audience, "Do you know why Jews are afraid of skinheads?" and answered his own question, "Because skinheads kick ass":

M. D.: Mr. Metzger, [in your deposition] I asked you "[if] in reading your speech, [you could] find the word *self-defense* in referring to the skinheads using physical brutality?" And what was your answer?

T. M.: I said no. And the reason for that is that I had spent hours with these young people before I ever made the speech, and they were all instructed on obeying the law and not getting your ass in a jam because it didn't help the movement. They know what my position is.

M. D.: So they know this already?

T. M.: If they don't, they had better.

M. D.: But when you made this speech you didn't say one word about self-defense?

T. M.: And I didn't call for imminent violence either, did I?

Since constitutional issues are never discussed in open court in this trial, this exchange can mean nothing at all to the jury. Whatever harm Morris can do this self-representing defendant-lawyer in his planned examination, however, is no worse than the harm Tom does himself. He seems to believe that offensiveness is part of the Bill of Rights. "Some [Jews] are even a little worse than 'mud,' " he says when asked if Jews are "mud people." "I can take you out here in Portland and find you some people that act just like that and look just like that," he says of one his nasty racist cartoons. There is no one to shut him up. Perhaps Tom's worst blunder is his filing of a countersuit against the city of Portland, claiming that Dave Mazzella is an agent provocateur of the Portland police.

M. D.: Are you saying to the jury that Mazzella is not your agent but the city of Portland's and as their agent he provoked Mieske and Brewster to kill this man?

T. M.: I said I believe that is possibly true.

M. D.: So you're not questioning whether Mazzella provoked [Mieske] to kill [Seraw]. You just said he did it as the agent of the ciy of Portland?

T. M.: That may be possible, and we're going to have to see about
it as time rolls on. Another civil trial, Mr. Dees.

The defendant whose lawyer's ideas open him up to the possibility
of testimony like that should consider suing the fellow for malprac-
tice.

Besides proving that Tom Metzger promotes violence in general, the
SPLC must link him to Portland in particular. Here the most important evidence after the testimony of Dave Mazzella is excerpts from
four "Aryan Update" hot-line messages "datelining" the city, one
before the death of Mulugeta Seraw, three afterward. The first,
October 24, 1988—three weeks after the arrival of Dave Mazzella—
is the taped conversation with Rick Cooper: "Unofficially, the fights
and attacks against the race-mixers and some of the race-traitors and
the racial scum has been picking up because of the new warriors
moving into the area, but I am sure there will be more on that later.
When it comes out, it will be all at once." The second is the message
from January 30, 1989: "Now that the initial BS is waning in the
skinhead-Ethiopian confrontation, we find that . . . many of these
beautiful Negroes had long arrest records. Sounds like the skinheads
did a civic duty and they didn't even realize it!" Third, June 12,
1989: "One young fighter, Ken Mieske, received life for winning a
fight with an Ethiopian recently. If your rotten government was not
letting in all this mud, young white men would not have to be doing
this time. . . . Tell them to get their Ethiopian ass out of this country." Fourth, October 23, 1989: "In Portland, Oregon, black Ethiopians confront white skinheads in a dark street. During the fight,
one Ethiopian died. Skinhead gets life for the alleged crime that
normally would be at most manslaughter." Together these excerpts
create an almost tangible presence, a rhetorical murder weapon
placing Tom morally if not physically at the scene of the crime.
Legally they support the SPLC's claim that he approved of—technically, "ratified"—the killing after it happened, an important com-

ponent of the "agency" case. The fact is that Tom Metzger's comments on Portland are an infinitesmal fraction of the words he has poured out on his telephone lines since the death of Mulugeta Seraw. Typed transcriptions of his 1989 messages alone measure about an inch—more than two hundred pages—while the four Portland messages above comprise a total of forty-three lines. Even in the "Portland messages" the Portland references are only parts of a whole. The "civic duty" message is one "Dateline" out of eight. "Young fighter" is one out of seven. A different selection would show him "ratifying" a host of other racist-related events and developments in the United States and abroad, which in a political sense he is. The "Aryan Updates" are a movement bulletin board in which diverse items from all over the world are unified through his own commentary and if the commentary amplifies the presence of WAR simply by its existence, that is exactly the effect that he intends. "WAR IS EVERYWHERE!" The hot line, however, is double-edged. Its exaggerations are shameless. The same propaganda that in the context of the movement has been an instrument of Tom's growth in the context of the trial is an instrument of his downfall. A favorite exaggeration of Tom's in the period before the trial has been a phantom cadre of covert WAR agents he calls "Special Operatives" or "Special Ops," with which Morris confronts him now. February 5, 1989: "Special Ops! In Section 5, you've done it again! Great!" February 17, 1989: "All twelve sectors are cooking!" June 19, 1989: "Special Ops . . . use the couriers, do not target yourselves." "Disinformation," insists Tom, as he did at his deposition. "A joke." But it is a joke only he gets. Such linguistic dodges are used by many of the witnesses in this trial. Charged by Tom with falsely testifying that he has been at Tom's house "thousands of times," Dave Mazzella explains on cross-examination that the phrase is "a figure of speech." The Metzgers have "millions" of videos? "Figure of speech." John uses the same escape hatch. The "nine million" Aryan groups he referred to in his testimony is a "figure of speech." "President" and "vice president" of the Aryan Youth Movement were "fictitious" titles. His description of the followers of AYM as "members" was speaking "generically." Tom, too, claims semantic license. His "kick ass" to the Oklahoma gathering was "speaking figuratively." The reference to skinheads as "white mean machines" in one of his most-cited editorials was a "generic term." "Civic duty" in the critical Portland tape was also "generic." There is one figure of speech not heard in this trial that aptly summarizes Tom's position in the witness box. In medieval times a soldier attempting to breach a wall was sometimes blown up by the very charge he was trying to emplace, an effect preserved in the language by Shakespeare in Hamlet's words: " 'Tis the sport to have the enginer hoist with his own petar." Tom Metzger is hoist with his own petard.

The final phase in the plaintiff's case is the damages: in many ways the heart of the proceeding, for it has always been the goal of the SPLC "not only to win the case but to win big" and it is by the bottom line that the verdict will always be known. The medical expert is the perfect witness for this purpose. Tall, slim, silver-haired, smooth, pathologist William Brady both by appearance and training is the incarnation of authority, an Oregonian whose national credentials include both Harvard and the New York City Medical Examiner's Office but who returned west to serve first as Multnomah County coroner and later as state medical examiner for Oregon. Now in private practice, he has cut up so many bodies and testified at so many trials he needs no instruction on how to communicate to a jury. His analysis of Mulugeta's injuries is unbearable, even for a stranger. His language is so physical he makes even lesser bruises seem to be being inflicted right before your eyes, and when it comes to the major ones you want to cringe back in your seat and protect your head. His voice is slow and loud. "The injury to the skin overlies a fracture of the skull which I could fairly describe as devastating." "His head was struck with so much force that these tightly knit bones [the lambdoid suture] separated, one from the other." "This is not only a blow from a baseball bat. It is a blow from a baseball bat inflicted with a great deal of force." And not only was the fatal blow vicious, but Mulugeta was anticipating it. Knocked to the ground by a previous blow to the side of his face, "he was crawling, trying to get away and do what he could to escape" when it struck. The picture of professional dispassion, when Brady holds up a plastic skull to dramatize his points he conveys something much more human. For an instant Mulugeta's flesh is back on his bones.

With Mulugeta's own final moments so vividly established, Elden Rosenthal turns to the losses to others. Two Avis workers testify that Mulugeta was friendly, intelligent, caring. An economist says that his lifetime contribution to his family would have been about $292,000 had he remained at Avis and $475,000 had he completed two years of college. Now it is time for the person whose dedication to avenging Mulugeta has made itself felt throughout the criminal process and has helped bring this civil trial into being, Engedaw Berhanu, who has had to leave the courtroom during the medical testimony. The story he tells is the one we know: that long ago and far away in the mountains of Ethiopia a son was born to his oldest sister and when the sister died that son became his dearest nephew, following Engedaw's dream of an education to schools in Debre Tabor and Addis Ababa and then to Portland, always with Engedaw's help. Once he reveals his true feeling about the relative merits of his native and his adopted homelands, correcting a question about the remoteness of the Ethiopian highlands from the amenities of Western "civilization" with "so-called civilization, yes." He weeps many times on the witness stand. But not only have the plaintiffs laid bare the sorrow of Mulugeta's uncle, they have also managed the dramatic feat of wafting Mulugeta's father, Seraw Tekuneh, from his Gondar farm to the Portland courtroom, and now it is he in the witness box, speaking through an interpreter, a study in integrity, as seemingly at ease with the nuances of the proceedings as if he had been attending American trials his entire life. Mulugeta's nine-year-old son, Henok, whom the grandfather—like Mulugeta—had never met prior to their long flight together from Addis, is also in the courtroom, perching at times on the lap of Morris Dees. Seraw Tekuneh is the last witness. Echoing Engedaw's words about Mulugeta's character, his drive for an education, and the help he hoped to give his own sisters and brothers in the future, the father closes with a retelling of his family saga all the more touching because he cannot have understood what has been said before: "What I want to convey is that all my hope was on my son because I was counting on him that he would come here, benefit from the educational system, become a professional, and come back home and pursue a professional career and help me and help my kids. That is what I was counting on." Unable to accept this simple story, Tom Metzger breaks the first rule of trial law—never ask a question to which you do not know the answer—and asks Mulugeta's father:

> T. M.: At any time during Seraw's stay in the United States did he send money to his father?
> S. T.: He has sent me once.
> T. M.: Does he remember how much?
> S. T.: Six hundred dollars.

and then:

> T. M.: Did Mr. Seraw send money to his child back home?
> S. T.: Yes, he used to send money to his son, but I cannot tell you how much.

Since it has been established that Mulugeta made $5.80 an hour at Avis, these facts only highlight his family ties. The attempted character assassination of Mulugeta Seraw by Tom Metzger makes a strangely perfect ending to the plaintiff's case: a verbal echo of the attack by Kenneth Mieske that brought it into being in the first place. The line from Tom Metzger to Mulugeta Seraw is now complete and the man has drawn it himself. So strong and satisfying is the SPLC case against WAR that, sitting in the courtroom then and sifting through the evidence box later, I almost believe it myself. It is only when I remember what is not in the box that I am troubled.

46

It is now time for Tom Metzger's defense: or, rather, it should be. Instead, Tom is falling apart. One moment he is arguing rationally from his seat, a reasonable officer of the court, the next he is muttering venomous asides like "This whole case is smelly!" which sound like street talk. Pretrial motions won by the SPLC have denied Tom the right to bring in issues central to his own understanding of the case, such as evidence of the fund-raising practices of the SPLC, and the same thing is happening now. The source of Tom's frustration is Dave Mazzella. Not only has Dave drawn a picture of his relationship with Tom that Tom finds unrecognizable, things have been happening during the trial that suggest that Dave is also drawing a false picture of himself. On Monday, October 15, the start of the second week of the trial, an *Oregonian* columnist reports the curious news that Dave Mazzella, or at least a man claiming to be Dave Mazzella, has spent the preceding Friday night at the same teen hangout where East Side White Pride passed out AYM newspapers nearly two years before, now called the Confetti Club, only this time recruiting for the Klan. What's more, Tom has been contacted over the weekend by Dave's skinhead friends in Medford, who feel betrayed by what they have seen and read of his testimony through the news. Dave is not a skinhead!? Not the leader of Southern Oregon Skins!? Not violent!? As if these lies were not enough, Dave is also "narking," ratting out a man he was boasting to them about knowing only a short time before. Not from a commitment to Tom Metzger, of whom they have heard only through Dave himself, but from their own sense of outrage, SOS members Laura Dailey, Leif Barge, and Shane Bukowski have voluntarily come to Portland, delivering to Tom photographs and letters that could display Dave's treachery to the entire world—but Tom can do very little with them at the trial. Like Aesop's bullfrog, he blows himself up bigger and bigger, intimating to all who will listen that at last he is going to expose this "show trial" for what it is, but he ends up spattered on the ground.

What Tom has missed is that the defendants as well as the plaintiffs needed to prove their case. "Most of my evidence is the lack of their evidence," John argues in his opening, but that is not how it works. To topple the cumulative logic of the SPLC Tom and John have to show that WAR is more a "movement" than an "organization," that Dave Mazzella was not their "agent," that they did not "send" Dave to Portland, that Dave did not "substantially" influence either East Side White Pride in general or Ken Mieske in particular, that the bat was a random discovery in a random car, and that the fatal fight between the skinheads and the Ethiopians was unplanned. None of this is insurmountable, but it requires investigation. Tom and John have not done the work. Between the inception of the lawsuit and the trial they have read up on law, filed some motions, traveled to depositions called by the plaintiffs, and attempted to protect themselves from an adverse judgment, but they have not grasped the essential concept of evidence. They have not located the "agents" named in the suit to discover what proof of "agency" would be offered by the other side in order to counter it. They have not interviewed members of East Side White Pride other than Ken and Kyle to establish a version of how Dave Mazzella was received in Portland different from the interpretation they should have assumed would be offered by Dave Mazzella. They have not deposed Tilahun Antneh and Wondwosen Tesfaye to put on record the Ethiopians' unsubstantiated recollections of the fight, which could readily be challenged at trial. Etc. What they have done is cry "Foul!" By grace of the Medford skinheads, a case has materialized that, by undermining the credibility of the leading witness, could accomplish much of what they have failed to do themselves in advance—but they have to know how to put it on.

The problem with "Dave Mazzella: The Sequel" is the setting. It takes place in Medford in 1990, not Portland in 1988. The SPLC case against Tom has to do with his relationship to Dave Mazzella and East Side White Pride in Portland in 1988, period. Anything Dave may have done in Medford in 1990 is irrelevant to the circumstances surrounding the death of Mulugeta Seraw. In legal terms, it is a "collateral" matter. Under certain conditions, collateral evidence can be used to impeach a witness on the central issues but Tom does not know what these conditions are. The lawyers do. The evidence about Dave that Tom is hoping to get in, the SPLC is determined to keep out. They have an answer for everything. The "Morris is so cool" letter from Dave to Laura Dailey stating his belief that a grateful Morris "is probably gonna have all the charges on me thrown out" for his cooperation, which Laura has given to Tom, is swiftly characterized by Elden Rosenthal as "hopeful thinking." While "it is true that from Mr. Mazzella's point of view, Mr. Dees is rich and it is true that from Mr. Mazzella's point of view, Mr. Dees is influential and has friends in the government and law enforcement agencies, . . . those statements are irrelevant unless there is any suggestion that Mr. Dees or anybody on the plaintiff's team made any promises to this witness. It was made very clear when he was on the witness stand that no promises whatsoever had been made," the Portland counsel argues. From the standpoint of a potential reversal, the admissibility or nonadmissibility of the Medford skinhead letters is the most vulnerable judicial ruling of the Metzger trial, and it is a moment of anxiety for the lawyers. They are fearful as the careful Judge Haggerty, whose consistent allowance for the defendants' lawyerlessness has endowed this uneven contest with whatever moments of fairness it has managed to achieve, makes what numerous professional observers think may be his one conceivable error—not letting the Medford letters in—but they relax when he negates the error by allowing Tom to question the SOS skinheads from them nonetheless, thus rendering the error harmless. For Tom the ruling is devastating. Not only will the Medford evidence not go into the jury room with the jurors but the line between what Tom may and may not ask his witnesses is so finely drawn that, to prevent him from either accidentally or intentionally slipping in an unacceptable point, the judge requires him to first show the court what he intends to show the jury, a cumbersome procedure known as an "offer of proof," which necessitates an almost comical number of comings and goings by the jury. Between the judge's ruling, the plaintiffs' finesse, and the jury's annoyance, the portrait of Dave in Medford that Tom wants to present is hopelessly diluted. The extent of Dave's duplicity does not come through. On top of the derailment of the SOS witnesses comes another exercise in futility—Tom's questioning of Dave's well-prepared girlfriend, Ruth Moran, whom Tom has subpoenaed and who has in fact spent the preceding day, along with Dave, on the telephone in their motel room trying to persuade the Medford skinheads not to come to Portland to testify.

T. M.: Is Dave Mazzella a racist?

R. M.: No.

T. M.: [Showing her a photograph of Dave and two others in SOS jackets] Do you have any explanation why he would be in uniform having pictures taken with a racist group?

R. M.: It was for the picture. He just—they wanted him to be in the picture.

T. M.: How can you explain a nonracist being in a racist group in uniform and alleged to be the leader?

R. M.: I can't.

When another witness, a Portland private investigator who worked with Ken Mieske's public defender on the criminal case and is one of only a few people in the city familiar with the details of the Ethiopian-skinhead confrontation, is challenged on the grounds that a proper foundation for what is intended to be his impeachment of Dave Mazzella has not been laid during Dave's own testimony, Tom decides to stop the "charade." "At this time because I do not believe there is any proper way I can do what I need to do I'm not going to ask this man any more questions. What he knows is not going to get out," Tom tells the judge. With a last-ditch effort to call Morris

Dees himself to the stand to "clear the air of the charges that we make of bribery, suborning perjury, and other illegal tactics" also blocked by the court, Tom is uncontainable. Thanks to rulings made prior to the trial, he has not been able to expose what he believes to be Morris Dees's and the SPLC's history of unethical legal and financial dealings, and now, thanks to rulings during the trial, he cannot even get in what he feels are the crucial facts. His "theory of the case" cannot be articulated. He cannot present reality as he sees it. Rising angrily at the defense table, pointing at Morris Dees, he booms out his objection for the record: "The objection I would have, Your Honor, is I have attempted to open up the doors to evidence during this trial, and at every point that door has been locked to us. We have been locked, using other reasons, to keep us out of that area that I think is totally germane to the case. It goes to the point of the entire witch-hunt on Tom Metzger by Morris Dees. And if we don't get him here, we are going to get him some-where else!" "Is that a threat, Mr. Metzger?" asks Elden Rosenthal. "I'm talking about in court, Mr. Rosenthal," Tom returns. Earlier Tom has said that he is facing a "boundless conspiracy." What he will never understand is that it is not a conspiracy. It is the law.

47

Lawyers are not under oath. When Morris Dees tells Judge Haggerty at the start of the trial, "We haven't made those decisions exactly yet as to who we will call," while Steve Strasser and Mike Barrett are nowhere in the vicinity and Dave Mazzella is in a nearby motel room practicing his testimony, he is not committing perjury: he is concealing his hand. The same is true of other tactics. When he plants the unfounded idea that the reason Ken Mieske said at his deposition that he had not read John Metzger's letter to East Side White Pride was that Rick Cooper had visited him in prison and told him that "the best thing for you to do was deny that you had ever seen it or read it": when he elicits from Dave the misleading testimony that his jaw number one conviction in Medford is "a little fist fight" or leads him practically by the hand to fill in the blanks in the chart of alleged telephone calls between Dave in Portland and Tom in Fallbrook—"Did you ever make any pay phone charges?" "Yes. Yes, that's what I'm talking about. Pay phones.": he is not violating ethical standards. He is doing what makes him a favorite speaker at law schools. While outside their professional lives lawyers are neither more nor less honest than anyone else, inside it they are residents of a gated ethical community to which the members of the larger society do not have the key. Take, for example, the repeated accusation of Tom Metzger that the SPLC was "hiding witnesses." While it is true, as the SPLC maintained, that finding and deposing Tom's alleged "agents" were not things the plaintiffs were required to do for the defense, it is also true that keeping Tom Metzger away from Dave Mazzella had been the SPLC lawyers' central pretrial preoccupation, as we have seen. It is why they attached the affidavit from Mike Barrett rather than a statement from Dave to their defense against Tom's motion for dismissal of the case at the beginning. Not only did they hesitate to depose Dave formally in spite of their need to preserve his testimony because to do so would hand him over to the Metzgers: when they did finally schedule depositions for both Dave and Mike Barrett—for L.A., "to further confuse Metzger about where Dave lived"—they unscheduled them two days before the appointed date. "[I was told by one of the attorneys] that the depositions were canceled because plaintiff did not know the whereabouts of either Barrett or Mazzella," Tom complained both in a written pretrial motion for postponement and in an oral motion at the trial itself to exclude their testimony on the grounds that he had not been able to cross-examine them. "The plaintiffs have been playing hide and seek" with the witnesses, he charges. "Your Honor, this is about the point where my blood starts boiling!" cries Elden Rosenthal, rising to his feet. "I'm real tired—Mr. Dees is real tired—of being accused of unethical conduct in this case! We have not hidden any witnesses!" But consider the words of Morris Dees. "The first time a reporter asked me about the importance of Dave Mazzella to our case, I played dumb," he later wrote in his book, *Hate on Trial*:

> "Who?" I asked. Sometimes when we attended hearings or deposi-
> tions . . . I would write Barrett's name in bold letters on my legal pad
> accompanied by a big star. Later, I'd make the notation FIND DAVE
> MAZZELLA. It's common for opponents to . . . look at unattended
> papers during breaks . . . and the Metzgers were no less curious than
> others we've faced. I'd find an excuse to leave the room, making sure
> my pad was in a place where the Metzgers would see the misleading
> message."

To the lawyers, this was evidently not "hide and seek."

What is understood by "fact" also differs inside and outside the gated community. For the literal-minded, which includes most journalists and nonfiction writers, the facts are the building block of the story. What *did* Ken Mieske and Rick Cooper talk about on that prison visit? What *do* the court records say about the Medford assault? If Dave called Tom on pay phones, why are there no "collect" charges on the records? What matters is "what really happened." For law- yers, a fact is what can be gotten into the record, ideally without objection, and its relation to events in the actual world is neither here nor there. "I always tell law students that to give the jury a passion for justice, you have to lift them above the very simple facts of the case. Because look at the facts of this case. The facts of this case would beat you," Morris remarked when we talked several years after the trial. But "the facts" are the justification for the lawsuit. From a historical point of view, if Tom Metzger did not "send" Dave Mazzella to Portland: if Dave Mazzella did not have the influence on East Side White Pride that he alone maintained: if Ken Mieske, Kyle Brewster, and Steve Strasser did not "spot" Mulugeta Seraw standing outside Tilahun Antneh's car and go up the street to attack him: if Ken Mieske was not even present at the party at Nick Heise's where the drawing of the black man with a bullet entering his head was allegedly drawn minutes before the assault on Mulugeta Seraw: then the "agency" argument is false; but from a legal point of view, the absence of a defense competent enough to challenge any or all of these premises renders it effectively "true."

Nor is it only the facts of this proceeding that go unchallenged: it is also the framework on which it is based. A "theory of the case" is not an absolute statement of the relationship of a particular offense to a particular body of law: it is whatever will withstand the objections of other lawyers. A complaint can be brought under several theories at once. Just as a kid who has crashed into a floor lamp with a scooter might be described as having done it either purposely, absentmindedly, or stupidly, so the SPLC claims that WAR is responsible for the death of Mulugeta Seraw by acting either intentionally, negligently, or recklessly, and any one of the theories is enough. This is called "alternative pleading." When the American Civil Liberties Union, which had declined to represent the Metzgers, nonetheless enters an amicus brief criticizing the charges of "negligence," "reckless speech," and "reckless selection" of an agent, on First Amendment grounds, the entire "negligence" count is simply dropped from the complaint and the "recklessness" count trimmed to omit "reckless speech," which partially undercuts the ACLU. This is known as "conforming the pleadings to the evidence"—after the nonconforming evidence has been heard. Nor can it ever be unheard. For an appeals brief, Tom obtains the services of Chicago libertarian lawyer Michael Null, who writes a strong critique of the trial, but it is too late. Since Tom is not a lawyer he did not know how to "preserve his objections," and since he has not been able to preserve his objections they are forever lost.

To this nonlawyer, the absence of all but the merest constitutional discussion during the Metzger trial, together with the unanimous agreement of the SPLC, the ACLU, the National Lawyers Guild, the presiding judge, the Oregon Court of Appeals, the Oregon

Supreme Court, and the U.S. Supreme Court, which refused to hear the case in 1993, that *Berhanu v. Metzger* in the form it went to the jury raised no constitutional issues, is the ultimate illustration of the hermetic logic of the gated community. From outside its venerable walls, I disagree. The line between legal and illegal speech is not, like the equator, a fixed boundary. It shifts. The subject of constant interpretation and argument, it is the heart of our political freedom. If a civil claim made against a political group out of step with its times in order to shut it down does not merit the most stringent examination of the facts of the case against constitutional principles, what does? The examination does not occur. "This is a slick move to [prevent] a really healthy and spirited debate by the ACLU and other people on the constitutional issues," Tom protests of the SPLC's midtrial tinkering with its original complaint to circumvent the ACLU's objections, but he is only—Tom Metzger. However much common sense supports his view that a trial in which witnesses have spent hours poring over WAR newspapers and fliers and listening to WAR message lines is at least in part a free speech trial, the SPLC successfully insists that it is not. The key is the tradition that general law supercedes the Constitution. According to the doctrine of "judicial economy," if a case can be decided on other than constitutional grounds, it must be. "This case does not ask the court to break new ground," Richard Cohen tells the judge during the brief discussion. Indeed, the SPLC is asking the court not to. The National Lawyers Guild, which has submitted an amicus brief countering the amicus brief of the ACLU, agrees with the SPLC that "the principles of agency law overlay First Amendment issues." In spite of further argument by the representative of the ACLU that the "reckless selection of agents" clause of the "recklessness" count is a threat to freedom of association—a claim it does not pursue on appeal—Judge Haggerty declines to dismiss it. "The court sees this as just a common law count based on agency," he says. In a trial lasting more than two weeks, this short debate, occurring between the plaintiff's and the defendant's cases and lasting less than an hour, is all we hear of the Constitution. "The Nazis must be free to speak because Jews must be free to speak and because I must be free to speak," wrote Aryeh Neier in *Defending My Enemy*, his account of the ACLU's controversial defense of the Nazis' right to march in Skokie, Illinois, in 1978. The implication of this "agency case" is otherwise.

48

The jury must now do its duty. Ordinary citizens who have lived through the civic turmoil from the death of Mulugeta Seraw to this unsettling and intimidating trial, they are the ones who must bring it to a close. "[Jurors] would have to have lived in a cave not to have heard about this case already," Tom observes at the beginning—Judge Haggerty agrees—and they would have to have stayed there not to have heard about it more during the trial. The courtroom has not been a sanctuary. With the mutual scorn of the parties erupting unpredictably into open anger, the jurors have seen many things the judge has ordered them to forget and have reason to suspect more. The police and the Metzgers' entourage have never been far apart. For any juror who might have misread such directives from the Portland civic establishment as the march the day before the trial, they are made clear during the trial by appearances for the plaintiffs by both the police chief and the district attorney. "The people in Oregon tolerate diversity, Mr. Metzger," the district attorney reminds the jurors as well as Tom. The lawyers also remind them. The responsibility of the jury to the community is their closing theme. "Ladies and gentlemen, we have spent two weeks here together trying to get at the truth," Morris Dees begins his final argument. "This case is important for this community. It's important for the state. And it's important for this nation. Because the verdict that you're going to render is going to have very far-reaching effects. We hope that verdict will tell Tom Metzger and his organization and all other people who peddle and preach hate and violence in this country that this jury says, 'No!' We are going to nip you in the bud." Elden Rosenthal is even more blunt: "You are about to participate in the most important exercise in your lives as public citizens. Because you're not going to be a vote out of a million. You're going to be a vote out of twelve. And the community is with you in the jury room." Tom and John, as usual, do not help themselves. Rising immediately after a tender coda in which Morris compares his request for a mere $10 million in punitive damages for the life of his client with the millions more paid for art ("I know his life is not a Van Gogh, but I promise you it's precious. It's precious to his uncle. It's precious to his family") John appears to be made of stone. "Well, a lot of talk there, Morris. This is a Twilight Zone trial. I expected Rod Serling to come walking in the door any minute." Tom is rude. "I don't think there's four people in this jury that have the guts to find with Tom and John Metzger and go home and tell your family, 'I decided that they were not liable.' Let's face it. 'They were not guilty.' Because it's called a civil trial but you might as well call it a criminal trial. I know what's cooking here. We need four people that's got the guts to stand and hold out and I don't think we'll get it." He is also threatening. He will do what he has always done, regardless. Whatever the jury's decision, "it will not make any difference to me," he warns.

Besides the speeches, the jurors also receive the jury instructions: that is, they try to. American jurors "are treated like children till the end of the trial, [when] the system suddenly treats them as if they were law professors," observes one legal scholar. For forty-five minutes after the closings, Judge Haggerty reads aloud a compendium of legal distinctions so complicated they are difficult to follow even in the transcript later, let alone in court at the time. Like all legal language, the instructions are intrinsically convoluted. They descend from the general to the specific by so many steps that by the time they get where they are going it is impossible to remember the starting point. Everything is qualified by something else. The phrase "preponderance of the evidence" requires several sentences of explanation. The "civil conspiracy" instruction has many subplots. To make matters worse, in the course of the trial the judge has caught a cold and he is forced to interrupt himself often to clear his throat, sip water, or sniffle. He looks miserable. Head down, intent on the paper before him, he lifts his eyes to the jury only once to acknowledge their common plight, saying, apologetically, "We will get through this." Barely. But the problem with the jury instructions is not only that they are unintelligible: they are one-sided. They echo the plaintiff's case. They do not register the constitutional issues implicit in the prosecution of Tom Metzger for the death of Mulugeta Seraw any more than the trial has registered them. The instructions come from agency law. The sole First Amendment instruction is drawn from a 1961 Supreme Court decision (*Noto v. U.S.*): "The right of free speech protects a person's right to express political or social ideas. It even protects a person's right to advocate the abstract need for violence sometime in the indefinite future. But the right of free speech is not absolute. It does not allow a person to prepare a group for violent action and spur it on to such action in the immediate or near future. I instruct you that if you find by a preponderance of the evidence that John Metzger, Tom Metzger or WAR through an agent prepared Kenneth Mieske or Kyle Brewster for violent action and spurred them on to such action in the immediate or near future, the free speech defense fails." This, too, presumes the "agency" relationship. "Tom should have objected to the instruction on the First Amendment," SPLC theoretician Richard Cohen, who proposed it, tells me later. But Tom passes. The instructions are the last chance for the jurors to see this play other than the way it has been staged for them by the lawyers, and this opportunity, too, passes. There is no other reading. Against the 150 pieces of evidence submitted by the SPLC, the Metzgers have produced 5. The ratio of witnesses is 8:1. "Thank God that there are lawyers like Mr. Dees who have been marshaling this evidence over the years so that he can bring it to Portland so that we can clean our own house. Because that's what this case is about—cleaning our own house," Elden Rosenthal tells the jury. The theme of the play is not civil liability. It is civic virtue.

The instrument of the cleansing is a crisp six-question verdict form—as short as the jury instructions are long—prepared by the SPLC and accepted without objection by Tom.

QUESTION NO. 1: Did one or more of the Oregon defendants wrongfully cause the death of Mulugeta Seraw?

ANSWER: Yes _____   No _____

IF YOU HAVE ANSWERED "NO" TO QUESTION 1, YOUR VERDICT IS FOR ALL THE DEFENDANTS. YOU SHOULD NOT ANSWER ANY FURTHER QUESTIONS.

IF YOU HAVE ANSWERED "YES," PLEASE INDICATE WHICH OREGON DEFENDANTS WRONGFULLY CAUSED THE DEATH OF MULUGETA SERAW, AND THEN ANSWER THE REMAINING QUESTIONS ABOUT THE CALIFORNIA DEFENDANTS:

Kenneth Mieske   Yes _____   No _____

Kyle Brewster   Yes _____   No _____

QUESTION NO. 2: Did one or more of the California defendants—through their agents—substantially assist in, or encourage, the conduct of the Oregon defendants that caused the death of Mulugeta Seraw?

ANSWER: Yes _____   No _____

IF YOU HAVE ANSWERED "YES" PLEASE INDICATE WHICH CALIFORNIA DEFEN- DANTS—THROUGH THEIR AGENTS—SUBSTANTIALLY ASSISTED IN, OR ENCOUR- AGED, THE CONDUCT OF THE OREGON DEFENDANTS THAT CAUSED THE DEATH OF MULUGETA SERAW:

Tom Metzger   Yes _____   No _____

John Metzger   Yes _____   No _____

White Aryan Resistance   Yes _____   No _____

QUESTION NO. 3: Were one or more of the California defendants—through their agents—involved in a conspiracy with the Oregon defendants that led to the death of Mulugeta Seraw?

ANSWER: Yes _____   No _____

IF YOU HAVE ANSWERED "YES," PLEASE INDICATE WHICH CALIFORNIA DEFENDANTS WERE INVOLVED IN A CONSPIRACY WITH THE OREGON DEFENDANTS:

Tom Metzger   Yes _____   No _____

John Metzger   Yes _____   No _____

White Aryan Resistance   Yes _____   No _____

QUESTION NO. 4: Did one or more of the California defendants cause the death of Mulugeta Seraw by recklessly selecting or retaining agents to orga- nize East Side White Pride?

ANSWER: Yes _____   No _____

IF YOU HAVE ANSWERED "YES," PLEASE INDICATE WHICH CALIFORNIA DEFENDANTS RECKLESSLY SELECTED OR RETAINED AGENTS TO ORGANIZE EAST SIDE WHITE PRIDE:

Tom Metzger   Yes _____   No _____

John Metzger   Yes _____   No _____

White Aryan Resistance   Yes _____   No _____

QUESTION NO. 5: What percentage of the total fault for the death of Mulugeta Seraw is attributable to each defendant you have found liable, and what percentage, if any, is attributable to Seraw himself?

ANSWER:	% of Fault
Tom Metzger	_____
John Metzger	_____
White Aryan Resistance	_____
Kenneth Mieske	_____
Kyle Brewster	_____
Mulugeta Seraw	_____

QUESTION NO. 6: What are plaintiff's monetary damages?

1. For economic damages: $ _____
2. For noneconomic damages: $ _____
3. For punitive damages $ _____
   (Total may not exceed $10 million)

Tom Metzger	$ _____
John Metzger	$ _____
White Aryan Resistance	$ _____
Kenneth Mieske	$ _____
Kyle Brewster	$ _____

The verdict form is the final statement of the plaintiff's case. Not only does it not ask, "Is the conduct of the California defendants protected by the Constitution of the United States?" it does not ask, "Is Dave Mazzella in fact Tom Metzger's agent?" Like the jury instructions, it takes the relationship for granted and asks only about the unlawful conduct allegedly associated with it, "substantial assistance and encouragement" (question 2), "conspiracy" (3), and "reckless selection" (4)—the three surviving legal theories. Lest the jury be daunted by the form, Morris has led them through it beforehand, telling them exactly what to write where, starting at the top ("The

Oregon defendants, Mieske, Brewster, both pled guilty. So you would almost have to check 'Yes' there"), moving down through the other claims ("The answer to that is obviously 'Yes' " "Check 'Yes,' 'Yes,' and 'Yes' "), and ending with the justification for the huge $12.5 million "economic," "noneconomic," and, especially, "punitive" damages requests, "because if a case ever, ever screamed out for punitive damages, this one does." But the verdict form is much more than a financial judgment. It is a moral judgment. "I know it is not easy when you are in a jury room to fill in the marks and decide a person's fate for a long time," Morris has already warned the jury. But it is morally and politically necessary. "When [Henok's] father and [Seraw Tekuneh's] son and [Engedaw Berhanu's] nephew was out on the street seven days before his twenty-seventh birthday, Tom Metzger and these defendants was his jury, they was his judge, and they was his executioner. They didn't give him a trial for two weeks, and they didn't give him a chance to say 'Please back off,' like I know he would have said. They did what Tom and John told them to do. There's so much hate. There's so much malice. It's almost inconceivable that in America something like that could take place, especially in your town because I don't believe that Portland is that kind of town." Beneath the practical questions are the theological questions Morris has been trying all along: Are Tom Metzger, John Metzger, and WAR evil? Are Morris Dees and the Southern Poverty Law Center good? Can Portland be saved? In effect, he is passing the collection plate.

Five hours after the jurors leave the courtroom, they return with the "X"s, "%"s and "$"s in all the right places. They have also taken a vow of silence, which they largely observe. The decision is 11-1, but with civil law requiring the agreement of only nine, the dissent is weightless. The $12.5 million verdict is headlined around the world. In both their closings Morris Dees and Elden Rosenthal argue that their case has been based wholly on evidence, but in their hearts they have to know otherwise. Without an opposing attorney, they could hardly lose. "Once I said to him, 'This isn't fair. We're beating him all over the place,' " Elden Rosenthal told me he told Morris Dees. "He wouldn't be fair to you in an alley," Elden said Morris replied. "Why should we be fair to him in court?"

49

The encores take place not in the courtroom but in a packed conference room elsewhere in the building where the parties are meeting the press. Tom is so calm he is almost sentimental. He is being a leader. He has his pride: "We have stood in the breach and done our best." He has his family: "My wife and I made a pact in 1971 when we went against the Vietnam War that if we had to leave our home with only the clothes on our back, so be it." And he has the movement. "Other men and women who have died—who have been murdered by the government—have given far more than I am giving here today," he says. John, too, shrugs off the verdict. "I take this as just another trophy in our showcase," he says. "The only thing I'm upset about is that they got me personally for only $1 million." Nor are the Metzgers worried about the future. Indeed, they are going to go out and celebrate. Celebrate what? asks a reporter. "The white racist—white supremacist—movement!" Tom declaims. "The movement will not be stopped in the puny town of Portland! We're too deep! We're embedded now! Don't you understand? We're in your colleges, we're in your armies, we're in your police forces, we're in your technical areas! Where do you think a lot of the skinheads disappeared to? They grew their hair out. Went to college. They've got the program. We planted the seeds. Stopping Tom Metzger is not going to change what's going to happen in this country now. I just got up there like your great Northwest salmon and laid my eggs and now, if I die—no problem!" And they do celebrate. During the press conference Tom has recited the Order token he always carries in his pocket: "If you should fall, my friend, another friend will emerge from the shadows to take your place." Before leaving Portland, Tom, John, and their followers spend a pious night in Room 42 of the Capri Motel on Northeast Eighty-second Avenue from which Robert Mathews made his last escape before fleeing to his fatal encounter with the FBI on Whidbey Island. Then they go home to Fallbrook.

Morris is fittingly sober. Sometimes an exuberant phrase will slip out spontaneously—"Back home we say it cleaned his plow!"—but for the most part his language is contained. "The jury has said there will be a new season for justice in the Northwest," he says, anticipating the title of his forthcoming autobiography. And—his favorite instant version of the Seraw case, one he has repeated many times— "In America, we have the right to hate, but we do not have the right to hurt." Soon enough will come the honors, the acclaim, the public lectures and television appearances, and the millions upon millions of dollars these in turn will bring for the continuing work of the Southern Poverty Law Center, but for now, sitting around a table, flanked by Elden Rosenthal, Mulugeta Seraw's son, Henok, his uncle, Engedaw Berhanu, and his father, Seraw Tekuneh, Morris Dees is only a lawyer representing a family. Before leaving Oregon, he, too, has some loose ends to attend to, and the loosest of these is Dave Mazzella. Delivering Dave and his girlfriend, Ruth, to Medford, where they are met by Dave's mother, Morris shares a festive lunch with Dave, Ruth, and Dave's mother before Dave returns to the Jackson County jail, from which he will emerge not in a week— as he has testified at the trial—but three months later, in January 1991, when he will enter an informal witness protection program arranged by the SPLC. Then Morris flies home to Alabama.

A few months after he leaves jail, Dave Mazzella is again on national television. The show is *Donahue*. The topic is "Reformed Racists." The show is built around Morris Dees's just-released *A Season for Justice*. Besides Morris and Dave, the cast includes Engedaw Berhanu and Henok Seraw, from the Metzger trial, Michael Donald's sister, from the Donald trial, and a former militant racist with a claw hand who blew himself up in an explosives accident, later testified for Morris Dees in a case in South Carolina, and has also been in the SPLC witness protection program. Dave alone is camouflaged, a false nose, a goatee, thick-rimmed glasses, and a baggy sweater, along with his naturally receding hairline, making him look much older than his twenty-two years. Whether it is the ill-fitting disguise or the ill-fitting politics, he seems to have lost some of his powers. After once again reciting all the violent actions through which he incited the members of East Side White Pride to kill Mulugeta Seraw, he is asked by a member of the audience how much time he served for his role, and for a moment he is actually wordless. Caught out, he hesitates. Then: "A few months." Unlike the Portland jury, the TV audience gasps.

EPILOGUE

50

In January 1995, James McElroy, the San Diego lawyer who had been closely involved in the case almost from its inception, arrived in Ethiopia as the diplomatic representative of the Southern Poverty Law Center. An open-minded, open-hearted Irishman as comfortable on the California beaches as in its courts, Jim McElroy had the unique mission of arranging for the transfer of the money collected from Tom Metzger, held in the United States during completion of the appeals, to the family of Mulugeta Seraw. There were a number of delicate issues. Confused by the absence of any money so many years after the much-touted multimillion-dollar American verdict, some of Mulugeta's relatives had blamed Engedaw Berhanu, who was deeply upset. After the trial, he had taken Mulugeta's son, Henok, back to Oakland to raise him in his own family, but since that very act contributed to the falsehood that Engedaw was absconding with Mulugeta's estate, he had sent him home. Henok was now back in Addis living in a one-room, one-lightbulb house with his mother. Besides explaining that the huge sum won in the famous trial did not really exist, the lawyer had the additional task of negotiating an agreement between Henok's mother's and Mulugeta's father's sides of the family on the division of such money as there would actually be. Jim McElroy was a natural ambassador. The best kind of guest, he wove his way zestfully among the relatives, appreciating everything from the traditional coffee ceremony at Henok's mother's to the traditional dinner at Mulugeta's father's brother's, drinking Ethiopian beer, dancing Ethiopian dances, eating *enjera* with his hands, and gleefully revenging himself on his hosts by inviting them to dinner at his Western hotel and watching them fumble with butter knives—and being appreciated back. Everyone accepted him. He was particularly welcomed by Henok, now thirteen, whom he had met at the trial and whose education was to be one of the chief beneficiaries of the Metzger money. He even got a somber Seraw Tekuneh, Mulugeta's father, who had had to make the long journey from the country to Addis Ababa twice because of a delay in Jim's arrival, to smile for his camera. As a result of his visit, the family not only understood the realities of the verdict for the first time but agreed to what the SPLC believed would be the best disposition of funds, a single payment to Mulugeta's father, who lived beyond reach of banks, and a larger, and ongoing, payment to Henok's mother for his future. Since Henok's mother earned the American equivalent of about $20 a month as a fare collector on an Addis bus even with overtime, no matter what fraction of the verdict was eventually collected, it would make an enormous difference. "An Ethiopian proverb I learned last night loosely translates into 'I have a cow in the sky but it gives me no milk.' It occurs to me that [Henok's mother] may feel this way about the

$12.5 million verdict," the ambassador wrote in a journal-memorandum to Morris Dees. Now she would have some.

The milking had not been gentle. The lawyer who was so adaptable in Addis Ababa was unshakable in Fallbrook. The details of the many moves and countermoves that followed the trial will not be exhumed here, for their outcome was almost always the same: at every stage in the collection process, when Tom attempted to gain a little more time or money, Jim McElroy opposed him, and the lawyer won. The dispossession of Tom Metzger from the family home he had bought more than thirty years before was a sordid business. On May 1, 1991, at 7:30 A.M., a posse of sheriff's marshals made its way unannounced past the chain-link fence at 308 Sunbeam Lane and took away all the property defined by a California court as "business-related," including a pickup truck used for Fallbrook TV, several televisions and VCRs, tools, a fax machine, a video camera, and carton after carton of audio- and videotapes that turned out to hold not only the racist material sold by WAR but personal items such as family pictures and the children's cartoons. The same day the marshals also attempted to seize Mathews Hall, the meeting trailer located in nearby Rainbow, a maneuver that, to the satisfaction of the WAR onlookers, took some doing, because the trailer got stuck in the mud. In August, they took over the crammed five-bedroom, one-bathroom combination household-workshop-political-command-post where the Metzgers had raised their six children, its peeling paint, battered tin shed, waterlogged ceilings, and pockmarked walls marking various alleged attacks on Tom preserved forever for the annals of WAR in a final video tour by Tom and John. Tom, Kathy, and their two youngest girls moved to a nearby apartment. Whether because of the condition of the Metzgers' property or because of its history, the auctions that accompanied the various seizures were essentially nonevents, with the largest item—the house—being bought by the sole bidder, Jim

McElroy, on behalf of the Southern Poverty Law Center, for the court-ordered minimum bid of $121,500. After several adjustments, including a $45,000 exemption required by California law to be paid to Tom, the net proceeds from Tom Metzger's estate—the initial "milk" for the Ethiopians—was at most $100,000. In the two years after the trial, when the Metzger case was at the heart of the Law Center's fund-raising, its income from contributions was about $20 million. The eventual total, based on the fact that the case continued to be featured prominently in the center's mailings even beyond the end of the decade, would be much higher.

Tom Metzger's entanglements with the law in the aftermath of the trial were not limited to the execution of the judgment. His right to appeal was threatened at the start both by a dispute over the deadline and by an attempt by the SPLC to garnish funds being paid to the court stenographer for a transcript. His hodgepodge counter-suit against Tilahun Antneh, Wondwosen Tesfaye, Mike Barrett, Mike Gagnon, and Dave Mazzella was dispatched by a Portland judge, after argument from two local attorneys enlisted by the SPLC. He was called to testify at a grand jury investigating the September 1990 San Diego courthouse bombing by an admirer of WAR who had also threatened Morris Dees, and for a time he seemed to be facing the alternatives of turning over WAR's subscription list or going to jail. And in August 1991, as his house was being emptied in Fallbrook, he went on trial in Los Angeles with three other men for the 1983 Kagel Canyon cross burning associated with the founding of the Order—a case that, since it had already been thrown out of court and reinstated twice, was one of the major embarrassments of the Los Angeles district attorney's office up till that point. After a long trial, he was found guilty of "misdemeanor unlawful assembly" and sentenced to six months in jail, to be followed by two hundred hours of community service and three years' probation. "I think, frankly, Mr. Metzger deserves much more time than that for the evil he has caused in the world," one of the prosecutors told the judge, but the jurors thought otherwise. On the remaining charges of misdemeanor "unlawful burning" and felony "conspiracy to commit unlawful burning," they deadlocked 10-2 for acquittal, and there was a mistrial. On December 4, 1991, shortly after his sentencing, Tom told a reporter more personal news: Kathy Metzger, at fifty, had lung cancer and had spent the past two weeks in the hospital. At that point he was hopeful that her life might be saved by radiation, but she was a chain smoker who had ignored a cough for a long time and it was a late diagnosis. On February 19, 1992, six months after she left the Sunbeam Lane house and five weeks after her husband went to jail, Kathy Metzger collapsed at home and was placed in intensive care at Fallbrook Hospital. Following the intervention of her doctor, Tom was released to be with her. For a few days she was still able to communicate slightly but she was under heavy sedation for pain and soon could no longer do so. Tom spent most of his time at her bedside—leaving only to brief reporters on the resumption of his white supremacist activities and to film another edition of *Race and Reason*. On March 3, with Tom, John, and Lynn beside her, she died. "Kathy made it quite clear in the weeks before she died that she expected her family to redouble its efforts for the race," Tom said on his next "Aryan Update." The question was how they would be able to do that.

Of all the assets of WAR the SPLC could claim as a result of the lawsuit, none was harder to seize than the money coming in through the mail. The house, the tools, the truck, the trailers all had problems associated with their collection, but at least they stood still. When the auctions were over, the money was in the bank. The mail was going everywhere and it never stopped. Thanks to a scheme by Tom to evade the judgment by receiving his orders and donations at a variety of movement addresses other than his usual P.O. Box 65, it was a collector's nightmare. Shortly after the trial Jim McElroy had privately offered to delay the mailbox seizures pending appeals if Tom would agree to stop his political activities for the same period, but when Tom embarrassed him by releasing his draft "gag order" to the press, the collections games continued at approximately the childish level of "Who has the cheese?" Even after the court-ordered appointment of a receiver to supervise the collections, the proportion of the money being sent to Tom Metzger that actually passed into the hands of the SPLC remained hard to establish. The standoff over the mail collection was a political and professional embarrassment to both parties. For Jim, it meant that he could never be sure how much money was going where. The SPLC looked foolish and ineffective. For Tom, it meant that when orders came in to the P.O. box in spite of his requests that they be sent elsewhere, they went to the receiver instead of him and could not be filled. A thing like that was bad for his reputation. Ever since the days of the California Klan, "P.O. Box 65" had been Tom Metzger's signature possession, and if anything could make it look as if the SPLC had indeed put him out of business, this was it. He wanted the box back. The resolution of the delicate issue of Tom Metzger's ongoing income from racism casts a bright practical afterlight on the SPLC's trial of Tom Metzger for the death of Mulugeta Seraw: they cut a deal. In May 1992, after more than a year and a half of mutual frustration, Tom Metzger and the SPLC signed a stipulation agreement that restored P.O. Box 65 to Tom in return for its uncontested supervision by the receiver. The agreement was later renewed. Every week, Tom or his proxy and the receiver meet at P.O. Box 65 and together sort through the envelopes, the correspondence going directly to Tom unread by the receiver, the money divided. Following the appeals, details of the arrangement began gradually being spoken of here and there by representatives of the SPLC, including both Jim McElroy and Morris Dees, but Tom has held his silence and neither side has ever explained it to its supporters. It is a two-thirds, one-third split. To this day, if you send thirty dollars to P.O. Box 65 for materials such as "German Marching Songs" or film footage of George Lincoln Rockwell, as I sometimes did myself during the course of my research, ten dollars will go to the Southern Poverty Law Center. Twenty dollars will go to WAR.

51

Eleven years after Morris Dees asked the jurors for a judgment "so big that on the south border of the state of Oregon there's going to be a wall [$12.5 million] high that's going to stop Tom Metzger from coming back into this state and . . . put him out of business," Tom Metzger returned to Portland as the lead speaker at a tribute to a neo-Nazi skinhead who, killed by an anti-neo-Nazi skinhead, had joined the list of Aryan martyrs topped by Robert Mathews, whose December 8, 1984, shootout with the FBI the December 8, 2001, occasion also saluted. Conceived by a Portland-based "Euro-American" "folkish" organization known as Volksfront whose slogans—"Race over All" or "Setting the Standard for White Activism"—better capture its lineage, the "Erik Banks Memorial" "surpassed [the] expectations" of its planners. More celebration than funeral, it took place at a suburban Grange, brought together about a hundred people from five states, featured three white-power bands, including Portland's Intimidation One, and, with its menu of "traditional Northern European food" reminding all of the gastronomic satisfactions of Aryan ethnicity, generally enhanced the likelihood of further such events to come. Tom, too, had reason to be pleased. Experiences honored, expenses paid, he was relaxed as usual, even stopping off at a local restaurant to entertain his admirers with a rendition of Frank Sinatra's "That's Life" crooned into a karaoke mike. Nor were those his only reasons to be in good spirits. "The hardest thing in this first period when often only six, seven, eight heads met together . . . was to arouse and preserve in this tiny circle faith in the mighty future of our movement," read the quote from Mein Kampf the Portland police found in the apartment of a member of East Side White Pride in 1988. Today the movement is more secure. One hundred people from five states in a Grange hall in suburban Portland is not a Nuremberg rally—but it is more than a dozen or so skinheads from around the city meeting at a friend's apartment at Southeast Thirty-first and Pine. The interconnection of hundreds of white supremacist Web sites originating throughout the world does not establish the existence of a corresponding political force—but it is not a handful of white kids with P.O. boxes in separate cities putting out zines. The flourishing of an international white-power music business that has American bands regularly performing in Europe and European bands performing here and makes millions of dollars every year for the neo-Nazi political organizations with which it is associated is not exactly a threat to EMI—but neither is it the lone home video of the scrawny teenagers known as the Tulsa Boot Boys at the 1988 Oklahoma Aryan Fest packaged by Tom as "one of the hottest White Power bands this side of Skrewdriver" and sold for twenty-five dollars in the WAR paper. Tom's place in the movement's pantheon is also secure. Even if he did no more, his promotion of both the technological infrastructure and the ideological positions on which much of the international neo-Nazi movement now rests would guarantee his lasting reputation, but in fact he is still chugging along. The losses of the early nineties are behind him. There is a new woman in his life; John, now a father himself, lives not far away; and, no more materialist than formerly, Tom is able, between his portion of the SPLC judgment—about $20,000 a year—and, more recently, Social Security, to do whatever he decides to do in or out of the movement, much as he did before. Tom Metzger's welcome to Portland by a new crop of white supremacists whose enterprises also include a benefit CD for "prisoner of war" Kenneth Mieske has come for me to stand for what I think of as the historical emptiness of the Southern Poverty Law Center's victorious civil trial, an emptiness no less real because it has gone largely unnoticed. Whether in books, articles, or other public sources, the death of Mulugeta Seraw is never seen other than the way it was represented in the courtroom. Indeed, the opposite is true: the trial has become the history. The reach of the Southern Poverty Law Center has given its own interpretation of the lawsuit enormous credence. The central flaw of "*The Trial of Tom Metzger* by Morris Dees" is that it substitutes a moral drama for a political analysis. In the play about the evil Tom Metzger receiving his comeuppance for the death of

Mulugeta Seraw at the hands of the good Southern Poverty Law Center, not only is there no room for the real story of how the death of Mulugeta Seraw actually occurred: there is no room for the larger story of the independent origins and incorporation of Nazism in the 1980s by the Portland skinhead movement, a development mirrored in cities and towns across both the United States and Europe in the same years. Misrepresenting the nature of the movement, the trial makes the present harder to understand. I know no more than any other follower of the day's news where the next manifestation of the neo-Nazi movement will come, how far the movement itself might one day reach, or what forces not under its own control may hinder or advance its fortune, but I do know this: in the eventual histories of the worldwide reappearance of the fateful weapons of racialism and antisemitism in our time, the rise of Tom Metzger and the White Aryan Resistance will be an important chapter—but not the trial of Tom Metzger for the death of Mulugeta Seraw.

52

Like Kenneth Mieske sitting in the Oregon penitentiary serving out his time, I end my years of immersion in the events surrounding the death of Mulugeta Seraw with my own set of "ifs." If the shifting relationships between whites and blacks in the city of Portland had not required immediate vengeance for the death of Mulugeta Seraw. If the Police Bureau had been more interested in finding out what happened than in producing a politically acceptable case for the district attorney. If the Justice Department had not elicited the "racial motivation" plea bargain, which was the platform for all that followed. If Tom Metzger were not the white supremacist of the hour. If Morris Dees had not had his "agency" theory ready and waiting for his next target. If Dave Mazzella had not been such a good salesman. If Ken Mieske, Kyle Brewster, and Steven Strasser had gone to trial in the first place and the people of Portland had

been forced to face the emergence of their youthful white supremacist movement with more candor and less panic. Then the gulf
between history and law: between the death of Mulugeta Seraw and
the trial of Tom Metzger: between the roots of the contemporary
neo-Nazi movement and the illusion that something is being done
about it: would not be as disturbing to me as it remains even as I
close these pages. But that would have been a different story.

NOTES

This book is based on the cooperation of many people who would not like to be—and are not likely to be—in the same room: racists and antiracists, victimizers and victims, law breakers and law enforcers, public officials and private citizens. Their contributions range from a single interview to conversations extending over many years, from a single letter to extensive files. Most of this material is not in the public domain. While everything included in the official files of both the criminal and the civil cases could in principle be revisited by anyone wishing to make an independent reading of the matters depicted in these pages, many other items could not. The inaccessibility of much of the evidence is matched by the elusiveness of those who provided it, many of whom, each for his or her own reasons, have asked not to be named. These notes are an attempt to describe for the interested reader the general sources on which the different sections of this book are based. For the most part, specific citations are given only for published material whose origins are not obvious from the text. I have used the following abbreviations: PPB:C, for Portland Police Bureau criminal files; PPB:I, for Portland Police Bureau intelligence files; FOIA, for material released under the Freedom of Information Act; and VT, for videotapes. People who have asked not to be identified are referred to as "A"s, for "Anonymous." Both the police and the legal files contain a wealth of social history from personal letters to political leaflets far beyond the uses for which they were assembled. The case numbers are: 88-116986, for the PPB criminal investigation; C88-11-37775, for the state's case against Mieske; C88-11-37776, for the state's case against Brewster; and C88-11-37777, for the state's case against Strasser. The SPLC civil suit, *Berhanu v. Metzger*, is A8911-07007. A final point that these days perhaps barely needs stating: recollections differ. The appearance of a name in the notes for one or another section means only that that person is among the over-lapping sources out of which I formed my own interpretation of the events in question. Little is based on the word of one person, or one document, alone. Many of the events recounted here have been recounted differently in other venues. I can only reiterate that, after years of painstaking consid-eration, this is what I think took place.

PROLOGUE

Ifs: Ken Mieske's reflections are drawn from my seven conversations with him in the Oregon State Correctional Institution in Salem, Oregon.

History and Law: My investigative article appeared as a special issue of the *Nation* entitled "The American Neo-Nazi Movement Today" (July 16–23, 1990).

PART I: HISTORY

I. THE DEATH OF MULUGETA SERAW

Skinhead scenes: The Saturday afternoon meeting of East Side White Pride, November 12, 1988, is described in the police interviews of several participants, PPB:C, passim, and I discussed it myself with a number of those who were present. The emphasis on violence is, of course, theirs. "Whether they're racist or not, the one thing that ties all skinheads together is that they like to fight," one commented—a view shared by the police. With the exception of the "Safeway incident," the previous violence of the ESWP skinheads had been white-on-white and usually internal. "When a new person was coming around, everyone wanted to know where their heart was at. . . . And the way to find that out is to [make them] face off with one person, saying, 'Fight back.' If the person didn't fight back they were pretty much outcast but if they did fight back and give it their best, they would be accepted into the group." At the same time, they all said that the group had agreed to try something different in its venture into downtown Portland that evening. The descriptions of the early part of the evening and the "Girls' Night Out" come primarily from police reports.

Ethiopian scenes: The account of Mulugeta Seraw's family history is largely based on conversations with his uncle, Engedaw Berhanu. Tekuneh Seraw's testimony in *Berhanu v. Metzger* is at 1248, Metzger trial transcript. "It was hard . . ." and following quotes are from *Hirut Abebe-Jiri and Others v. Kelbessa Negewo*, transcript, case #190-CV-2010-GET, U.S. District Court, Atlanta, May 17, 1993, passim. The description of Mulugeta Seraw as an "extraordinary human being" is from a letter to the *Oregonian* by Cygnette Cherry, December 1, 1988. The Ethiopian party and other details are from PPB:C.

The fight: This account of the fight is based on hundreds, perhaps thousands, of pages of PPB witness interviews together with my own conversations with Ken Mieske, Julie Belec, Nick Heise, defense lawyers Pat Birmingham and Randall Vogt, private investigator William Driver, Dana Anderson, and others, none of whom would agree with its every detail. It has also benefited from conversations with PPB detectives Tom Nelson and Mike Hefley and Deputy District Attorney Norm Frink, who, while disagreeing with its main thrust, would acknowledge many of its assumptions. Obviously I did not witness the fight.

II. UNDERGROUND

The underground youth scene: The Portland youth scene was not so far underground that it escaped the eyes of police intelligence officer Larry Siewert, and much of the specific evidence for these sections is drawn from PPB:I. Material from the searches of the ESWP skinheads' apartments, as well as other legal files in PPB:C, provided some of the rest. The best source for a general understanding of the emergence of skinheads from the punk scene is a 1987 master's thesis from the Washington State University Anthropology Department, "Skinheads: From Britain to San Francisco via Punk Rock," by Eric Andrew Anderson, which combines the theoretical framework developed by the British Centre for Contemporary Cultural Studies with Anderson's own field studies in San Francisco in 1985. For developments in Portland, I had many further guides, including some who took me by the hand and said 'X' or 'Y' happened here. Among those who shared their knowledge, experience, and in some cases files were Jim Cartland, Dave Clingan, Pat Gihring, Nick Heise, Larry Hurwitz, Patrick Mazza, Ken Mieske, Rick Mitchell, Chris Phelps, Jim Redden, Chris Steele, and numerous "A"s. For the period after the death of Mulugeta Seraw, as well as for ideas and information in general, I am particularly grateful to Jonathan Mozzochi of the Coalition for Human Dignity, one of the first people in the city outside the Police Bureau to understand the importance of the skinhead movement.

Kenneth Mieske: The visual re-creation of Ken and Julie's apartment is based on police photos, as well as conversations with the officers who conducted the searches. PPB:C also includes other personal material, such as the letters between Ken and Julie mentioned in the text, as well as official material such as the documentation of the development of Ken's "Nazi" identification while a prisoner at EOCI (case number C8511-34683), as do other court files. The most important sources for this portrait of Ken are Ken himself, Sharon Schaub, Julie Belec, and Jim Cartland. Conversations with other friends and acquaintances of Ken's, including Walt Curtis, Gus Van Sant, Chris Warner, and Jack Yost, in the aftermath of the killing, also contributed. The "Safeway incident," eventually folded into the Seraw case, has the case number 88-92674; it was discussed with me extensively by Larry Siewert. Chris Steele's music video of the September 10, 1988, Starry Night concert, *Metal Madness*, made possible the picture of Ken as he was that night, two months before the death of Mulugeta Seraw.

Kyle Brewster: This portrait of Kyle Brewster at Grant High School could not have been written without the help of a handful of amateur sociologists from among his schoolmates, who supplied both the high school materials and many of the insights on which it is based but who have asked not to be identified. Conversations with a number of his skinhead friends—also "A"s—and with Dana Anderson, and those pieces of Kyle's writing that found their way into PPB:C, are further sources.

About possums: according to biologist Steven N. Austad, in "The Adaptable Opossum" (*Scientific American*, February 1988), the creature "gets little respect," even among scientists. "Wildlife biologist Durward L. Allen, for example, derides the opossum as a 'sluggish, smelly, disreputable critter without a semblance of character or self-respect,' " Austad writes. "As a marsupial, moreover, it is regarded as being primitive and therefore inferior to eutherian, or placental, mammals. At a given body size marsupials have a lower body temperature, lower metabolic rate and a smaller brain than eutherians do." Austad also reports that, unknown on the West Coast before the late nineteenth century, "possums flourished in their new home" and by 1937 were "thriving from Baja California to the Canadian border," which may in part account for their seeming to appear around Portland about the time of the substantial black migration connected with World War II.

Steven Strasser: Steve Strasser generated a good deal of loyalty among his friends both within and outside ESWP, and though several were willing to talk with me, none wanted to be identified. Letters written on his behalf by various relatives prior to his sentencing suggest the same affection for him there. PPB:C, PPB:I, other court files, correspondence between Steve Strasser and Morris Dees, and a personal letter from Strasser to me are other sources for this portrait.

Rick Cooper: Rick Cooper is his own best biographer. From the first issue of the National Socialist Vanguard *Report*, January–March 1983, to the present he has thoroughly charted his own activities as well as the activities of many other figures in the racialist movement and, in doing so, has created an invaluable archive. He is also a willing talker and we met many times during the course of this work.

Attributions:
p. 48 "The only defense": *History of WAR*, vol. 1, VT.
p. 48 "Punk rock was a desperate scream": Tim Brooks, *PDXS*, June 1999, p. 10.
p. 52 "lunatic right": *Two Louies*, October 1986, p. 6.
p. 53 "the most prejudiced [city] in the west": Elizabeth McLagan, *A Peculiar Paradise*, The Georgian Press, 1980, p. 175. For further documentation of Portland's racial history, see notes to chapter V.

III.   ARYAN UPDATE

Tom Metzger's beginnings: Tom Metzger is a natural oral historian and the best single source for his life is a photocopied 246-page document somewhere between a manuscript and a book written by San Diego journalist Jack Carter on the basis of many interviews with Tom (hereafter referred to as "Carter"). Originally intended as an official biography, it was rejected by several publishers as being insufficiently critical—an idea Tom found hard to grasp. "What do they mean, not 'critical enough?' " he asked me on the telephone one day. "I say, 'Someone stole my bicycle.' Are they saying someone didn't steal my bicycle?" In 1996, after several years of frustration, Tom printed it himself, and it is no longer technically un-available, but it was in the period I was writing this section and I treated it as an unpublished manuscript and drew on it freely throughout. I also talked with Tom myself about his early years, and it was he who provided me the names of, and in some cases introductions to, a number of helpful former Warsaw classmates: Bill Chinworth, who generously shared his high school memorabilia, Frank and Babs Coppes, Don Hanft, Harry Gigous, and Don and Sally Nichols. A number of people at both the Warsaw *Times-Union* and the public library answered many questions by phone. Corrob-oration of the life and career of Tom's father, Thomas Linton, was provided by Gene Zirkel of the Dozenal Society of America. Corroboration of my sense that the origins of Tom Metzger's idea of himself as "bad" lie in his Warsaw years comes from Tom himself, albeit after the years treated in this book: sometime after the SPLC trial he began referring to himself in the "Letters to the Editor" section of the WAR paper and on his message line and Web site as "Terrible Tommy."

Political evolution: "Carter" aside, the best single source for Tom's political career is a three-volume videotaped *History of WAR* featuring television news footage of such events as the Camp Pendleton Klan episode and Tom's expulsion from the Democratic Central Committee meeting in Sacramento and edited by his son, John, into a coherent visual narrative. Between the archives of WAR and the archives of its watchers, there also exist all the WAR newspapers, all the *Race and Reason* cable TV shows, and (thanks to the Southern Poverty Law Center, which generously made them available to me) the complete transcripts of the WAR message lines from 1985 on—so much raw material, in fact, that it would probably be possible to re-create Tom's development almost minute by minute if one were inclined to do so. The government was also watching at some points, and thanks to FOIA and the efforts of Duane Bosworth of the Portland law firm Davis Wright Tre-maine, I received about ten thousand pages of FBI and other reports, some of which, particularly for the Crusader period, contained political ephemera not necessarily available elsewhere. For Pendleton, materials provided by Berkeley attorney David Weitzman were also helpful. For the more personal matters, an unpublished manuscript by undercover informant Doug Sey-mour, "The Doug Seymour Story," the transcript of an interview of Seymour by Leonard Zeskind in 1986 (provided by the Center for Democratic Renewal), and my own conversations with Seymour later were invaluable, as were my conversations with Rick Cooper, Robert Heick, Wyatt Kaldenberg, Dave Mazzella, Lynn Metzger, and particularly Tom and John Metzger. A video tour of the personal and political memorabilia flowing into one another on the walls of the Fallbrook house made for me by John was a good silent companion to the official *History of WAR*.

In addition to this primary material, from the time of Tom's first mention in the press (an August 21, 1962, article in the *Santa Monica Evening Outlook* about the anti–union shop activity at Douglas Aircraft excavated for me by Lorraine Colson of the National Right to Work Foundation) his political development intersected with major movements on the American right that have had some—though not extensive—scholarly or journalistic treatment by other writers. A number of these secondary works provided valuable background: for an earlier generation of far-right leaders such as Gerald L. K. Smith, *The Old Christian Right: The Protestant Far Right from the Great Depression to the Cold War*, by Leo Ribuffo, Temple University Press, 1983; for the reinvigoration of the far right after World War II, *Roads to Dominion: Right-Wing Movements and Political Power in the United States*, by Sara Diamond, Guilford Press, 1995; *Danger on the Right: The Attitudes, Personnel, and Influence of the Radical Right and Extreme Conservatives*, by Arnold Foster and Benjamin Epstein, Random House, 1966; and *The Odyssey of the American Right*, by Michael Miles, Oxford University Press, 1980; for the Pendleton Klan episode, *Defending My Enemy: American Nazis, the Skokie Case, and the Risks of Freedom*, by Aryeh Neier, Dutton, 1979, and an article by Roger Rapoport, "The Marine Corps Builds Klansmen," *New Times*, May 27, 1977; for the major personalities and organizations of the far right, *Extremism on the Right*, a handbook published by the Anti-Defamation League, 1988; for the Christian Identity movement and William Potter Gale, *The "Christian Identity" Movement: Analyzing Its Theological Rationalization for Racist and Anti-Semitic Violence*, by Leonard Zeskind, National Council of Churches of Christ, 1986; *Committee of the States: Committee of the States*, by Cheri Seymour, Camden Place Communications, 1991; and *Religion and the Racist Right*, by Michael Barkun, University of North Carolina Press, 1994; for George Lincoln Rockwell, *One More Victim: The Life and Death of an American-Jewish Nazi*, by A. M. Rosenthal and Arthur Gelb, Signet, 1967, and *American Fuehrer: George Lincoln Rockwell and the American Nazi Party*, by Frederick J. Simonelli, University of Illinois Press, 1999; for the Wallace campaign, *George*

Wallace, American Populist, by Stephan Lesher, Addison-Wesley, 1994; for David Duke, *The Rise of David Duke,* by Tyler Bridges, University Press of Mississippi, 1994; and for the Order, *Brotherhood of Murder,* by Thomas Martinez with John Guinther, McGraw-Hill, 1988; *The Silent Brotherhood: Inside America's Racist Underground,* by Kevin Flynn and Gary Gerhardt, the Free Press, 1989; and *Talked to Death: The Murder of Alan Berg and the Rise of the Neo-Nazis,* by Stephen Singular, Beech Tree Books, 1987. A host of occasional publications issued by the Anti-Defamation League, the Center for Democratic Renewal, the Southern Poverty Law Center, and regional organizations such as the Louisiana Coalition against Racism and Nazism, as well as their newsletters, magazines, and, more recently, Web sites, have also often been helpful. Somewhere between "primary" and "secondary" sources for much of my overall understanding are conversations with Daniel Levitas, whose work on William Potter Gale in *The Terrorist Next Door: The Militia Movement and the Radical Right,* St. Martin's Press, 2002, was not available until my own work was nearing completion, and, above all, with Leonard Zeskind, the unofficial dean of far-right studies in the United States, who has been breaking new ground in the treatment of all of the above aspects of the movement and more since 1982 and has freely shared information and ideas along the way but whose book on the history and future of the white nationalist movement, to be published by Farrar, Straus and Giroux, will not appear until after this book goes to press.

Attributions:

p. 100 "Aphrodite had many": Theodore Dreiser, *A Hoosier Holiday,* John Lane Co., 1916, p. 296.

p. 101 Winona Lake description: *Indiana,* America Guide Series, 1941, p. 307, and "Recollections of Mr. William A. Sunday," by Mrs. J. N. Rodheaver, in *Writers and Writings of Kosciusko County,* Bicentennial Project of the Warsaw Branch of the American Association of University Women, 1976.

p. 114 "always, and by all means": *The Blue Book of the John Birch Society,* 25th printing, Western Islands Publishers, 1995, p. 175 (for Welch's popularization of Christian Identity, see, e.g., "The Neutralizers," part 2, *Religious Neutralism,* a 1963 Birch Society pamphlet still in print).

p. 121 "the most . . . anti-Semitic belief system": Barkun, *Religion and the Racist Right,* p. viii.

p. 122 "John Wayne's son": Seymour, *Committee of the States*, p. 79.

p. 124 "the Swastika first flew": George Lincoln Rockwell, *This Time the World*, 3rd ed., White Power Publications, 1979, p. 145. (Melissa Fay Greene's *The Temple Bombing*, Fawcett Columbine, New York, 1996, places a neo-Nazi group called the Columbians on the streets of Atlanta in 1946, so Rockwell may not have been as original as he thought.)

p. 125 "Reading *Mein Kampf*": Rockwell, *This Time*, pp. 83–84.

p. 127 "ultimate smear of the Jews": Ibid., p. 142.

p. 128–34 "Most of the principal leaders" and the informant quotations that follow draw on FOIA, particularly FBI files SD 157-4557, sections 1 and 2, which include James Warner's letter about David Duke, and LA 157-10447, which includes a description of the February 16, 1975, Patriotic Leadership Conference in Los Angeles.

p. 131 "The greatest American": Bridges, *Rise of David Duke*, p. 13.

p. 132 "I'd always thought of the Klan": Ibid., p. 46.

p. 135 "Over 11,000 people": Ibid., p. 57.

p. 143 "He's against" and other man-in-the-street comments about Tom's electoral campaign: *History of WAR*, vol. 1, VT.

p. 152 "I am a Socialist": WAR newspaper, vol. 3, no. 5, 1984, p. 5.

p. 154 "I, as a free Aryan": Flynn and Gerhardt, *Silent Brotherhood*, p. 98.

p. 154 "We declare": Ibid., p. 357.

p. 155 "White men killing white men": Ibid., p. 376.

p. 158 "He does not attempt to conceal": FOIA, October 30, 1986, FBI file number n.a.

IV. A HUNDRED LITTLE HITLERS

Greg Withrow and the White Student Union–Aryan Youth Movement: The principal source of the Greg Withrow story is an unpublished six-hundred-page professionally ghostwritten autobiographical manuscript titled "Child of the Fourth Reich: My Quest for Love in a World of Hate," a manuscript generously handed on to me by Morris Dees. More than a little melodramatic, where the material of the book converges with public events confirmable by other means, the book appears to be reliable and accordingly I have used it extensively. News coverage of Withrow in the *Sacramento Bee* and elsewhere; a phone conversation with Withrow himself; conversations with Dave Mazzella and with John and Tom Metzger; and in particular the items ferreted out of WAR's archives by John Metzger and referred to in the text were very helpful.

John Metzger: This interpretation of John Metzger is based on my own observations of and conversations with him over the years, as well as conversations with Lynn Metzger, Tom Metzger, Dave Mazzella, Greg Withrow, Wyatt Kaldenberg, and others, and it was John who told me about *Kitty: Return to Auschwitz* (Yorkshire Television Productions, 1978, available through the Oregon Holocaust Resource Center). The more I learned both of John himself and of how Tom operated in the family, the less I could accept the conventional opinion that John was "brainwashed."

Dave Mazzella: On the life of Dave Mazzella no one is better than Dave Mazzella and we had hours of conversations. The reflections of his mother and stepfather, Linda and Bob Ford, on his youth, were invaluable. Other people who talked with me about Dave's California years include John Metzger, Robert Heick, Wyatt Kaldenberg, Clinton Sipes, and Greg Withrow. An unpublished as-told-to book about Sipes by Ardyce L. Masters and James S. Masters, "Children Escaping Racist Environments: The Story of Clinton Sipes," was useful as well, as was other primary material shared by the Masterses. Other California material, including Dave's photograph album, found its way into PPB:I. In addition to personal reminiscences, from the time of his appearance on the *AM/San Francisco* show in late 1986, when he was seventeen, Dave attracted a lot of attention in the Bay area and his accounts of his doings are readily substantiated by articles such as those in the San Jose *Mercury News* described in the text, as well as by the national publications of the Anti-Defamation League on the skinhead movement, beginning with the 1987 "Shaved for Battle." For better and/ or worse, the television talk shows are also the opposite of ephemeral, available in most instances not only as commercial and home videos and commercial transcripts but as integral parts of the *History of WAR* videotapes. For more on WAR and the WSU/AYM, see also the notes to chapter III, above. In Portland: Dave's relationship to East Side White Pride during the five weeks between his arrival and the death of Mulugeta Seraw was a source of irritation to some of its members and their friends well before the SPLC lawsuit, and I discussed the relationship with some of them— "A"s—in 1989. Others who talked with me about Dave then or later include Julie Belec, Rick Cooper, Nick Heise, Ken Mieske, Jim Redden, and additional "A"s. Dave's letters as well as other personal items mentioned throughout the text turn up in PPB:I, PPB:C, defense files, and the legal files from the civil suit, often in multiple copies.

Attributions:

p. 159 "We, the older": Flynn and Gerhardt, *Silent Brotherhood*, p. 11.

p. 184 "Newspaper writers": Kevin Phillips, *The Politics of Rich and Poor: Wealth and the American Electorate in the Reagan Aftermath*, Harper Perennial, 1990, p. 19.

p. 184 "away from the bottom 80 percent": Ibid, p. 16.

p. 184 "less affluent segments": Ibid, p. 16.

p. 184 "proliferating billionaires": Ibid, p. 23.

p. 184 "Newspaper writers": Ibid, p. 19.

p. 185 "Reduced earnings": *Dollars and Sense*, November 1987, reprinted in *Utne Reader*, May-June 1989, p. 84.

p. 185 "Under the superficial": Phillips, *Politics*, p. 23.

p. 202 "By the time the tapings": Geraldo Rivera with Daniel Paisner, *Exposing Myself*, Bantam, 1991, pp. 476ff.

PART II: LAW

V.   THE CASE AT LAW

Racial history: The discussion of Oregon's racial history in these pages would not have been possible without the help of Professor Darrell Millner of Portland State University, whose generosity with ideas, references, and documentation provided much of the basic education on which it is built. Unlike other sections of the book, it is based substantially on published sources, which are cited in the Attributions, below.

After the killing: The investigation and the legal developments are largely drawn from PPB:C, together with my own conversations with many of the principals, in some cases going back to 1989. Material made available to me by both Morris Dees and Norm Frink was also helpful. In addition, I was a participant-observer at nearly all the public events described and had the benefit of numerous informal conversations with people from many different segments of the community. Both my own interviews and the police interviews quoted in the text have been edited for brevity and continuity.

Attributions:

p. 208 "It is not that blacks": Darrell Millner, in John Schrag, "White Like Us," *Willamette Week*, June 8–14, 1994, which also contains racial population statistics, as do "Ethnic and Gender Discrimination in Portland: 1844–1980," vol. 1A, ch. 2, of Mason Tillman Associates, Ltd., *Oregon*

Regional Disparity Study, made available by the Metropolitan Human Rights Center, n.d.; Quintard Taylor, *In Search of the Racial Frontier: African Americans in the American West, 1528–1990*, Norton, 1998, p. 223 and passim; and, of course, the census.

p. 208 "Niggers . . . should never" and "His feet": Eugene H. Berwanger, *The Frontier against Slavery: Western Anti-Negro Prejudice and the Slavery Extension Controversy*, University of Illinois Press, 1967, p. 84.

p. 209 "human servitude": Ibid., quoting Walter C. Woodward, "The Rise and Early History of Political Parties in Oregon," *Oregon Historical Quarterly*, 12, June 1911, p. 46.

p. 209 "Making Oregon a free state" and "Negro slaves are": Millner class handouts.

p. 210 "selfish policy": Berwanger, *Frontier*, p. 93.

p. 211 "It is not a question": Craig Wollner, "Not Quite Apartheid: A History of Unfair Housing and Housing Discrimination in Oregon, 1829–1923," ms., p. 52.

p. 211 "White labor only": E. Kimbark MacColl, *The Growth of a City: Power and Politics in Portland, Oregon, 1915–1950*, Georgian Press, 1979, p. 268.

p. 211 "No people of": Ibid., p. 70.

p. 211 "Koons, Kikes, and Katholics": Ibid., p. 7.

p. 211n. Hells Canyon: "The Terrible Secret of Hells Canyon," *Oregonian*, August 15, 1995, p. A-l.

p. 212 "became a high pressure defense city": MacColl, *Growth of a City*, p. 575.

p. 213 "It is . . . a serious": "The Negro in Portland," July 20, 1945, City Club report, p. 58.

p. 213 "pull the place down": McLagan, *Peculiar Paradise*, p. 174.

p. 213 "No line of demarcation": *Straight Ahead: Essays on the Struggle of Blacks in America, 1934–1994*, ed. William H. McClendon, Black Scholar Press, 1995, p. 25.

p. 215 "Scientific men have proven": July 20, 1945, City Club report, p. 1.

p. 215 "[These] reports": "Study of Racial and Ethnic Relations in Portland: Description of Study," City Club of Portland, September 1991, p. 76.

p. 215 "the most prejudiced [city] in the west": McLagan, Ibid, p. 175.

p. 216 "In confining": "The Negro in Portland: A Progress Report, 1945–1947," *Portland City Club Bulletin*, vol. 37, no. 46, April 19, 1957, p. 358. A number of works in addition to those quoted also contributed ideas and information to the discussion on pp. 207–19, including *Cornerstones of Community: Buildings of Portland's African American History*, Bosco-Milligan Foundation, 1997; *Experiences in a Promised Land: Essays in Pacific Northwest History*, ed. G. Thomas Edwards and Carlos Schwantes, University of Washington Press, 1986, particularly "The Ku Klux Klan of Oregon," by Eckard Toy; "Putting Their Hearts and Hands into This Work: A Recent History of the Anti-Bigotry Movement in Portland, Oregon," by Meroe Elahi, senior thesis, University of California, Santa Cruz, 1991; *The Story of American Freedom*, by Eric Foner, Norton, 1998; *Fleeting Opportunities: Women Shipyard Workers in Portland and Vancouver during World War II and Reconversion*, by Amy Kesselman, State University of New York Press, 1990; *Vanport*, by Manly Maben, Oregon Historical Society Press, 1987; *On the Road to Equality: A Fifty Year Perspective*, a history of the Portland Urban League by Darrell Millner, Urban League, 1995; *The Invisible Empire in the West*, ed. Shawn Lay, University of Illinois Press, 1992; and *The History of Portland's African American Community (1805 to the Present)*, Portland Planning Bureau, February 1993.

p. 231 "I've been a crook": Norman Mailer, *The Executioner's Song*, Warner, 1979, p. 738.

p. 244 "Did [the district attorney] make": Jim Thompson, *The Criminal*, Vintage, 1993, p. 94.

p. 248 "moral panic": Stanley Cohen, *Folk Devils and Moral Panics: The Creation of the Mods and Rockers*, St. Martin's Press, 1980.

VI.   CAKES AND CAUSES

Morris Dees and the Southern Poverty Law Center: The story of the rise of Morris Dees from a backwater Alabama existence to the White House guest list in a period of a few years is such a classic piece of Americana that it will doubtless eventually be the subject of an important biography, but in the absence of such a source I have relied extensively on two first-person works—*A Season for Justice: The Life and Times of Civil Rights Lawyer Morris Dees*, Scribner's, 1991, and *Hate on Trial: The Case against America's Most Dangerous Neo-Nazi*, Villard, 1993, both coauthored with Chicago writer Steve Fiffer—and on a lucid and straightforward account of the SPLC from the founding of Klanwatch to the Donald trial by former Klanwatch director Bill Stanton, *Klanwatch: Bringing the Klan to Justice*, Grove Weidenfeld, 1991. Of the many other words written on the subject, by far the best discussion, one that is neither hostile nor sycophantic, is a thoughtful essay titled "Morris Dees and the Southern Poverty Law Center," in *Shades of Gray: Dispatches from the Modern South*, by John Egerton, Louisiana State University Press, 1991, a shortened version of which, however, published in the July 14, 1988, *Progressive* under the title "Poverty Palace: How the Southern Poverty Law Center Got Rich Fighting the Klan," falls into the "hostile" camp and is still circulated by the Law Center's enemies. An eight-part investigative report published in the *Montgomery Advertiser* in February 1994 under the overall title "Rising Fortunes: Morris Dees and the Southern Poverty Law Center" is another widely circulated "hostile" analysis. The Law Center withstood the critique very well, as it has withstood all others.

The plaintiff: Unlike in the Donald case, where the initiative for the civil suit came from the SPLC, the initiative in the Metzger case came from Engedaw Berhanu, or, more precisely, from Engedaw Berhanu and the SPLC more or less simultaneously. The account in Dees's *Hate on Trial* and what Engedaw told me in my own conversations with him are substantially the same.

The chief witness: The legal situation that allowed Dave Mazzella to return to Portland in the spring of 1989 and take up his movement life is curious. The charge on which he was extradited to Salinas in the aftermath of the killing was a relatively minor misdemeanor/battery on which California would not routinely extradite. Extradition costs may have been paid by Portland authorities in the hope that he would remain in jail, and thus be findable, when the skinheads came to trial. While the Portland police and prosecutors and the Salinas police and prosecutors seem to have been of one mind on this matter—which would explain Dave's second extradition—the Salinas judge who threw out the parole violation charge evidently had a different view.

Dave Mazzella's "Medford period" was described to me by Dave himself, his mother and stepfather, his girlfriend (and, later, wife), Ruth Moran, Laura Dailey, Henry Sullivan, and a few "A"s, and there is also a substantial paper trail, including legal records, newspaper articles, and letters, some of which were initially extricated from their various niches by *Willamette Week* investigative reporter Jim Redden. Several of the Medford skinheads also made written statements (e.g., Leif Barge's, p. 299) about their relationships with Dave that circulated in Portland after the trial. The correspondence between Dave and Morris Dees was generously made known and available to me by Morris Dees. The other letters are from PPB:I and legal files.

Before the trial: On a factual level, this discussion of the background of the Metzger trial owes much to conversations with several of the participants— including, in addition to the leading characters, Danny Welch, Richard Cohen, Elden Rosenthal, and Jim McElroy—as well as to such written sources as "Carter" and *Hate on Trial.* On an intellectual level, it owes at least as much to Portland attorney Michael J. O'Brien, without whose tutorials the assumptions underlying the legal preliminaries might well have remained impenetrable to me. The version of the origins of the trial emphasizing the role of the ADL's Irwin Suall is from a speech by Dees to the Bluestein Leadership Conference excerpted in the ADL's *Frontline* newsletter, April-May 1992.

Attributions:
p. 260 "Years later": Dees, *A Season for Justice*, p. 88.
p. 260 "I wish I'd been there": *Montgomery Advertiser*, February 1994, p. 10.
pp. 260-61 "I'm sure": Egerton, *Shades of Gray*, p. 233.
p. 261 "Raising money for": *Newsweek*, July 18, 1977, p. 95.
p. 261 "I can't remember": Dees, *Season for Justice*, p. 183.
p. 262 "I learned everything": Egerton, *Shades of Gray*, p. 215.
p. 262 "Millard gave all.": Ibid., p. 218.
p. 262 "wealthy poor": Dees, *Season for Justice*, p. 56.
p. 262 "There was nothing": Ibid., p. 58.
p. 264 "Why [not] write": Ibid., p. 78.
p. 264 "Thousands of postal": Ibid., p. 79.
p. 264 Should they "stay in Tuscaloosa": Ibid., p. 31.
p. 265 "Fuller recalls": Egerton, *Shades of Gray*, p. 216.
p. 265 Millard Fuller's story is told in his own writings, e.g., *The Theology of the Hammer*, Smyth & Helwys 1994.
p. 268 "heady stuff"; Dees, *Season for Justice*, p. 134. The other quotations in this paragraph are from pp. 135–37.
pp. 269-70 "You can't raise money": Egerton, *Shades of Gray*, p. 223.
p. 270 "good, sound business practice": Ibid., p. 235.
p. 272 "most important case": Dees, *Season for Justice*, p. 314.

p. 273 "Any lawyer could": Ibid., p. 218.

p. 273 "When the Klan connection": Ibid., p. 214. (Stanton, *Klanwatch*, presents the decision to sue in much the same way.)

p. 274 "It's terrible": Stanton, *Klanwatch*, photos.

pp. 274-75 "if a black man": Ibid., p. 207.

p. 275 "I know that people's tried" and "I do forgive you": Jesse Kornbluth, "The Woman Who Beat the Klan," *New York Times Magazine*, November 1, 1987, p. 38 (there is no transcript of the Donald trial).

p. 275 "There was not a dry": Dees speaking at, e.g., Reed College, October 24, 1991.

p. 276 "History would show": Dees, *Season for Justice*, p. 330.

p. 276 "One of the most openly": *The Ku Klux Klan: A History of Racism and Violence*, SPLC Special Report, 1988, p. 51.

p. 285 "Tom, I think you'd better": Jack Carter, "A Man in a Den," *San Diego Reader*, December 7, 1989.

p. 288 "When we filed": *National Law Journal*, February 11, 1991.

p. 293 "prince of darkness": Dees, *Hate on Trial*, p. 140.

For the role of Montgomery in the civil rights movement, the best source is Taylor Branch, *Parting the Waters: America in the King Years*, Simon & Schuster, 1989.

VII.   THE TRIAL OF TOM METZGER

Trial: The trial of Tom Metzger was televised in the Portland area on cable access, there is a complete video record, as well as a written transcript, ordered for the appeals, and I was there throughout, but the distance between the exchanges of words in a courtroom and the meaning of what is taking place is far greater than this layperson, at least, ever imagined, and without the guidance of attorney Michael J. O'Brien I could not have begun to understand what I was seeing. The candor of all the involved lawyers—Morris Dees, Richard Cohen, Elden Rosenthal, and Jim McElroy—was also invaluable, as were the recollections of several other of the principals. For the civil liberties implications, conversations with Michael Simon, Michael Null, and particularly, again, with Michael J. O'Brien were indispensable. The excerpts from the transcripts have been edited to minimize repetition but preserve the sense of the exchanges.

The Confetti Club mystery: The first account of the Confetti Club incident was "Check Your Flight Jackets at the Door," by *Oregonian* columnist Phil Stanford, which appeared on Monday, October 15, the opening of the second week of the trial. What happened has never been proved. The SPLC maintained that the would-be Klan recruiter could not possibly have been Dave Mazzella because (a) Dave Mazzella was under twenty-four-hour guard and (b) they would not have been stupid enough to have allowed him go to the club. They speculated that Metzger bodyguard Carl Straight had represented himself as Mazzella to strengthen Tom's case that Dave was an agent not of WAR but of the Klan. There are numerous problems with the SPLC response, not least that Morris Dees and Richard Cohen contradicted each other when questioned by the press, Morris claiming that he and Dave were playing cards at the time Dave was supposedly sighted at the club, Richard saying that they were not. As for the center's guard: he was flexible enough to allow Dave to go out with his East Side White Pride friend Pogo on at least one occasion, and he took Dave and Ruth on a number of other expeditions as well, as did other staffers. As an out-of-towner, he would not necessarily have realized that the Confetti Club would be a disastrous idea. As for the Straight theory, while it is true that he came to court the following Monday with dyed hair, as the SPLC staffers pointed out, his new hair color did not make this large, crinkly-faced Irishman look the least bit more like small, somewhat dour Dave Mazzella, who had been on television, via the witness stand, the whole day preceding the night the identification was made. If Tom did authorize such a "secret op," which he denies, or if his followers staged it on their own, he was playing an exceedingly dangerous game, particularly because he allowed his posttrial counsel, Michael Null, to cite the incident in his—unsuccessful—appeal. The second article, "Can This Man Be Believed?" by Jim Redden, appeared in the *Willamette Week* (October 18–24, 1990) midway in the second week of the trial, a few days later. Redden, whose work has an excellent record for standing up, reinterviewed the four people who had told the *Oregonian* columnist they had seen Dave Mazzella at the Confetti Club and they repeated their story. I do not know what happened.

Attributions:
p. 314 "push [Ken's] buttons": Dees, *Hate on Trial*, p. 179.
p. 332 "not only to win": Ibid., p. 164.
p. 340 "to further confuse": Ibid., p. 113.
pp. 340-41 "The first time": Ibid., p. 88.
pp. 343-44 "The Nazis must": Neier, *Defending My Enemy*, p. 7.
p. 345 "are treated like children": William T. Pizzi, *Trials without Truth*,

New York University Press, 1999. (Pizzi credits the observation to Chicago law professor Albert Alschuler.)

EPILOGUE

Collections: Jim McElroy's journey to Ethiopia is vividly described in a memo to Morris Dees, which McElroy generously provided to me, and I am grateful to him as well for a particularly stimulating discussion of the trial, which he sees as analogous to such classic lawsuits as the Pinto litigation in which a claim brought on behalf of an individually injured party accomplishes the greater social good of getting the dangerous product off the market. Like all of the other lawyers involved in the case, McElroy has "no question in [his] mind that Tom Metzger caused the [death of Mulugeta Seraw]" and is completely comfortable with his role. "If Metzger can't afford to pay the judgment and he has to go out of business, then that's a good result and I'm glad to be a part of it," he commented. Morris Dees also spoke freely with me about the P.O. Box 65 deal. The collections struggles received extensive coverage in the San Diego and other West Coast newspapers, and both WAR and the Southern Poverty Law Center issued frequent updates.

The growth of the movement: There are no good estimates of the numbers of people involved in the far-right racist movement at any given time, and none have been used in this book. Both the Anti-Defamation League and the Southern Poverty Law Center prefer not to count but to speak instead of influence, a preference I share, in part because what can or even should be counted is hard to define. If one were being a stickler, for instance, Tom Metzger's WAR might not show up, because it does not have any "members"; and how, on the other hand, would one track the unknown people who have listened to its message lines or watched *Race and Reason* and felt in their hearts that they "belong"? The same is true for other contemporary manifestations of similar or overlapping political impulses, from the militiamen of the West to the neo-Confederates of the South. In spite of their reluctance to do so, when pressed, representatives of these monitoring organizations will come up with an estimate, one that has changed from about 10,000 to 20,000 active white supremacists in 1990, when I began asking the question, to perhaps 100,000 to 200,000 now. Of the two estimates, the earlier is believed to be the more accurate because it rested on a systematic pooling of the combined knowledge of several different observers while the later reflects independent guesswork. The experts of 1990 also used a figure of about ten passive supporters to every active one, a multiplier similarly based on their best combined calculations and similarly not recently collectively updated, but one that, if it could be shown to hold, would obviously yield a very high figure today.

ACKNOWLEDGMENTS

The help that has made possible the completion of a work whose roots go back to the death of Mulugeta Seraw in 1988 can never be adequately acknowledged. There is intellectual support, there is practical support, and there is moral support, and their roles cannot be ranked. Then, too, the categories overlap. To all those whose names appear below: I know how much your relegation to one or another of these lists understates your contributions to this project. To the numerous people who have asked to be omitted: my silent gratitude. To anyone I may have inadvertently overlooked: my apologies.

My first group of debts is to the people who provided the principal materials on which the book is built: Tom Nelson, Mike Hefley, Larry Siewert, and Loren Christensen of the Portland Police Bureau, who made it possible to reconstruct the history both of the Portland skinhead movement and of the killing; attorney Duane Bosworth of Davis Wright Tremaine, whose recovery of the Metzger files under the Freedom of Information Act yielded so much historical evidence not only about Tom Metzger but about the evolution of the racist movement in general; Morris Dees and the staff of the Southern Poverty Law Center, who cooperated extensively and unconditionally with this project and encouraged a number of other people to do the same; Tom Metzger, who returned phone calls and was always willing to pursue whatever point was on my mind; John Metzger, whose archives turned up many items only he was in a position to have; and Dave Mazzella, whose reconstructions of all the phases of his political career he generously put at my disposal. Others whose personal cooperation played particularly important roles in my understanding of some of the central issues or events of this book include: Dana Anderson, Julie Belec, Engedaw Berhanu, Jim Cartland (pseudonym), Richard Cohen, Rick Cooper, William Driver, Linda Ford, Robert Ford, Norm Frink, Nick Heise, Daniel Levitas, James McElroy, Ken Mieske, Darrell Millner, Rick Mitchell, Ruth Moran, Jonathan Mozzochi, Michael J. O'Brien, Jim Redden, Elden Rosenthal, Sharon Schaub, Doug Seymour, Clinton Sipes, Chris Steele, Danny Welch, and Leonard Zeskind. Still further assistance was provided by people in the longer list below. In many cases there is a fuller discussion in the text or Notes.

Another group of debts is to the people and institutions who made it financially possible to do this work the way it needed to be done: the late Carol Ferry, Peter S. Bing, the American Council on Germany, the Hedgebrook writers' retreat, the John D. and Catherine T. MacArthur Foundation, and the Open Society Institute. To Gail Goodman, program officer of the OSI's Individual Fellowship Program during the period in which I was fortunate enough to be a fellow, a particular thank you for making that connection so much more than the funding.

Finally, there are the people who have played essential roles in the creation of the book itself: Georges Borchardt, my wise and patient literary agent; Sara Bershtel, my brilliant and demanding editor, and her unstinting colleagues at Metropolitan Books—insightful senior editor Riva Hocherman, indispensable assistant editor Shara Kay, and their talented and meticulous associate, copy editor Roslyn Schloss; Linda Wright, a generous and perceptive transcriptionist; Adam Berg, an indefatigable and resourceful researcher; my assorted critical readers, Penny Allen, Anne Borchardt, Tom Engelhardt, Martha Gies, Todd Gitlin, Daniel S. Greenberg, DeAnna Heindel, Adam Hochschild, Harriet Watson, and Rhea Wilson; and the friends in Portland and elsewhere, too many to be named, who over many years, many drinks, many walks, and many talks have sustained me more than they may know by their simple faith in me and in this project. No one has given more, or in so many ways, to the completion of this book than the two people who have lived through it with me: my husband, Martin Zwick, and my son, Michael Zwick. It is as a family that we all say at last the blessing we like to use on special occasions, meaning "Thank you for bringing us to this moment": Shehekianu.

Others, whose varied forms of help (in some cases offered in connection with my 1990 *Nation* essay "The American Neo-Nazi Movement Today") played a part in the completion of this book, include:

Philip T. Abraham
Judy Albert
Stew Albert
Andrew Allen
Eric Anderson
Aaron Asher
Sasha Baguskas
Christine Ball
Chip Berlet
Nick Bertrand
Pat Birmingham
Casey Blake
Petty Blake
Jim Blashfield
Randy Blazak
Julie Bourgeois
Christopher Browning
Judy Bruno
Devin Burghart
Jon Butler
Peg Caliendo
Jack Carter
Connie Casey
Paul Chevigny
Bill Chinworth
Dave Clingan
Lorraine Colson
Laurel Cook
Jenny Cooke
Babs Coppes
Frank Coppes
Nancy Cott
Walt Curtis
Robert Dahlberg
Laura Dailey
Sue Danielson

Richard Davies
Jerome DeGraf
John Demos
Ellen DuBois
Eugene DuBow
Ronnie Dugger
Meroe Elahi
Raphael Ezekiel
James Farrands
Eric Feldman
Steve Fiffer
Heather Florence
Chris Fox
Josh Gamson
Gail Gans
Harry Gigous
Pat Gihring
David Goldstein
Linda Gordon
Thomas Grumke
Mark Hamm
Don Hanft
George Haslett
Abdi Hassan
Mohammed Hassan
Kathi Hastings
Kenneth Hastings
Linda Hawkins
Robert Heick
Anita Helle
Lance Hill
Darlene Himmelspach
Paul Hoffman
Allen Hunter
Larry Hurwitz
Wayne Inman

Edward Jones
Wyatt Kaldenberg
Michael Kazin
Wendy Kloke
Lisa Lapin
Patricia McGuire
Julie Mancini
Judith Margles
Melissa Marsland
Ardyce L. Masters
James S. Masters
Margit Mayer
Patrick Mazza
Peter Meyer
Leon Miller
Multnomah County Library
    Reference Line
Frank Mungeam
Victor Navasky
Aryeh Neier
Don Nichols
Sally Nichols
Michael Null
Jill Otey
Useni Perkins
Chris Phelps
Sandy Polishuk
Roger Porter
Mark Potok
Sally Pyree
Darius Rejali
James Ridgeway
Troy Roberts
Edward B. Rosenthal
Lisa Roth
Joe Roy

Kathy Samuelson
Alexis Sanders
John Schrag
Michael Simon
Frederick Simonelli
John Snell
Bruce Spear
John Sterling
Paul Sleven
Steve Strasser
Linda Stringer
Irwin Suall
Henry Sullivan
Jennifer Tobin
Kelly Too
Paula Traver
Joe Uris
Elizabeth Van Osdol
Gus Van Sant
Katrina vanden Heuvel
Randall Vogt
Eric Ward
Chris Warner
Warsaw, Indiana, Public Library
    Reference Line
Steven M. Wasserstrom
David Webb
David Weitzman
Joella Werlin
Randall Williams
Greg Withrow
Craig Wollner
Mark Wooley
Jack Yost
Rachel Zimmerman
Gene Zirkel
Mark Zusman

My thanks to all.

INDEX

ABOUT THE AUTHOR

Elinor Langer is the author of the acclaimed biography *Josephine Herbst*, which was nominated for a National Book Critics Circle Award. A finalist for a J. Anthony Lukas Award for a work in progress for *A Hundred Little Hitlers*, she has also written for the *New York Review of Books*, the *New York Times Book Review*, and the *Nation*, among other publications. She lives in Portland, Oregon, with her family.